GIS,
Spatial Analysis,
and Modeling

David J. Maguire, Michael Batty, and Michael F. Goodchild, Editors

ESRI PRESS
REDLANDS, CALIFORNIA

ESRI Press, 380 New York Street, Redlands, California 92373-8100

Copyright © 2005 ESRI

All rights reserved. First edition 2005
10 09 08 07 06 05   1 2 3 4 5 6 7 8 9 10

Printed in the United States of America

Library of Congress Cataloging-in-Publication Data
GIS, spatial analysis, and modeling / David J. Maguire, Michael Batty,
and Michael F. Goodchild, editors.
    p. cm.
  Includes bibliographical references and index.
  ISBN 1-58948-130-5
  1. Geographic information systems. 2. Spatial analysis (Statistics)
 I. Maguire, David J. II. Batty, Michael. III. Goodchild, Michael F.
 G70.212G584 2005
 910'.285—dc22   2005018160

Ask for ESRI Press titles at your local bookstore or order by calling 1-800-447-9778. You can also shop online at www.esri.com/esripress. Outside the United States, contact your local ESRI distributor.

ESRI Press titles are distributed to the trade by the following:

In North America, South America, Asia, and Australia:
Independent Publishers Group (IPG)
Telephone (United States): 1-800-888-4741
Telephone (international): 312-337-0747
E-mail: frontdesk@ipgbook.com

In the United Kingdom, Europe, and the Middle East:
Transatlantic Publishers Group Ltd.
Telephone: 44 20 8849 8013
Fax: 44 20 8849 5556
E-mail: transatlantic.publishers@regusnet.com

Cover design by Sara Bobbitt
Book production by Steve Pablo
Copyediting by Kandy Lockard
Printing coordination by Cliff Crabbe

Contents

Preface

This book is concerned with modeling and spatial analysis within a GIS framework. As such, it takes a pragmatic, software-centric view of the tools, techniques, methods, and models currently available to geographic analysts, modelers, software engineers, and GIS professionals. In all the work described in this book, geography is the pivotal issue. How can we represent the geographic world effectively and efficiently in a digital environment? How can we describe and explain geographic variations in geographic systems? Are there local or structural geographic trends in sample data? What are the most useful approaches for simulating geographic processes? What software is available for modeling the dynamics of space and time? How have spatial analysis and modeling been applied to substantive, real-world problems? What are the outstanding issues that need to be addressed in spatial analysis and modeling? In this book, we set out to investigate all these and several other important questions.

We define the terms *modeling* and *spatial analysis* quite broadly. Modeling, as used here, includes both "data modeling" and "process modeling." Data modeling we can think of as the descriptive representation of real-world patterns in a geographic database schema. Process modeling involves creating computer programs that represent static or dynamic activities that help us understand the way the world works. Both types of modeling involve the use of GIS software in one or more ways, be it data collection, storage, management, analysis, query, visualization, or mapping.

This book owes its origins to a workshop on "Modeling and GIS" held at ESRI in Redlands, California, September 25 to 26, 2003. The purpose of the workshop was to assemble a small, expert group with hands-on experience of modeling within, and linking to, commercial GIS software. The topics covered included agent-based modeling; cellular automata modeling; dynamic feedback and simulation modeling; environmental, atmospheric, and hydrological modeling; finite element modeling; linking models and GIS software; spatial analysis; statistical modeling; and urban, social, health, and economic modeling. Almost all of the authors at the workshop have written chapters for this book, and the editors invited a number of other key workers in the field to round out the content.

The twenty-one chapters in the book are organized into four sections. The first section contains three introductory chapters by the editors that outline the key issues and examine the subject from both the perspectives of GIS and spatial analysis and modeling. In section two, four chapters focus on the tools and techniques of spatial analysis and modeling in a GIS context. Section three comprises seven chapters that describe a wide range of socioeconomic applications covering urban growth, retail and service location planning, transportation modeling, and the dispersion of infectious diseases. The six chapters in section four focus on environmental applications. Again, the range of applications covered is quite broad and extends from land cover and landscape change to hydrological modeling and the conservation of animals. A concluding chapter by the editors summarizes the main discussion points and looks forward to the future.

The editors and authors are indebted to many people who have contributed to making this book a success. We would especially like to thank Amy Garcia, Jack Dangermond, John Calkins, Judy Hawkins, Kandy Lockard, Doug Huibregtse, Steve Pablo, and Claudia Naber.

David J. Maguire
Michael Batty
Michael F. Goodchild
March 2005

Authors

Name	Job Title	Affiliation	E-Mail
Sean Ahearn	Director and Professor, Center for Advanced Research of Spatial Information (CARSI)	Hunter College, 695 Park Ave., New York, NY 10021	sca@geo.hunter.cuny.edu
Luc Anselin	Professor and Director, Spatial Analysis Laboratory	Spatial Analysis Laboratory, Department of Geography, University of Illinois, Urbana-Champaign, Urbana, IL 61801	anselin@uiuc.edu
Michael Batty	Director, Centre for Advanced Spatial Analysis (CASA) and Bartlett Professor of Planning	University College London, 1-19 Torrington Place, London, WC1E 6BT UK	mbatty@ucl.ac.uk
Ling Bian	Associate Professor	Department of Geography, State University of New York at Buffalo, 105 Wilkeson Quad, Amherst, NY 14261-0055	lbian@geog.buffalo.edu
Mark Birkin	Director of the Informatics Network	School of Geography, University of Leeds, Woodhouse Lane, Leeds, LS2 9JT, UK	m.h.birkin@leeds.ac.uk
Daniel Brown	Associate Professor	School of Natural Resources and Environment, University of Michigan, 440 E. Church St., Ann Arbor, MI 48109-1041	danbrown@umich.edu
Peter A. Burrough	Ëmeritas Professor of Physical Geology	Utrecht Centre for Environment and Landscape Dynamics, Faculty of Geosciences, Utrecht University, Post Box 80.115, 3508 TC Utrecht, the Netherlands	p.burrough@geog.uu.nl

Name	Job Title	Affiliation	E-Mail
Carol Gotway Crawford	Senior Mathematical Statistician	National Center for Environmental Health, Centers for Disease Control and Prevention, Mail Stop E70, 1600 Clifton Road NE, Atlanta, GA 30333	cdg7@cdc.gov
Jiunn-Der (Geoffrey) Duh	Assistant Professor	Department of Geography, Portland State University, 1721 SW Broadway, Portland, OR 97201	jduh@pdx.edu
J. Ronald Eastman	Professor of Geography and Director, Idrisi Project	Clark Labs, Clark University, 950 Main Street, Worcester, MA 01610	reastman@clarku.edu
Rasmus Dyhr Frederiksen	M. Sc., Partner	Rapidis, Jaegersborg Alle 4, DK-2920 Charlottenlund, Denmark	rdf@rapidis.com
Michael F. Goodchild	Professor of Geography	National Center for Geographic Information and Analysis, and Department of Geography, University of California, Santa Barbara, CA 93106-4060	good@geog.ucsb.edu
Lewis D. Hopkins	Professor and Associate Dean	College of Fine and Applied Arts, University of Illinois at Urbana-Champaign, Room 100 Architecture, 608 Taft Drive, Champaign, IL 61820	l-hopkins@UIUC.edu
Thomas Israelsen	Managing Director, Partner	Rapidis, Jaegersborg Alle 4, DK-2920 Charlottenlund, Denmark	ti@rapidis.com
Derek Karssenberg	Lecturer in Physical Geography	Utrecht Centre for Environment and Landscape Dynamics, Faculty of Geosciences, Utrecht University, Post Box 80.115, 3508 TC Utrecht, the Netherlands	d.karssenberg@geog.uu.nl

Name	Job Title	Affiliation	E-Mail
Nikhil Kaza	Doctoral Student	Department of Urban and Regional Planning, Temple Buell Hall, Room 111, 611 Taft Dr., Champaign, IL 61820	nkaza@uiuc.edu
Stefan Knopf	Principal/Chief Programmer	GoldSim Technology Group, 22516 SE 64th Place, Suite 110, Issaquah, WA 98027	sknopf@goldsim.com
Rick Kossik	Principal	GoldSim Technology Group, 22516 SE 64th Place, Suite 110, Issaquah, WA 98027	rkossik@goldsim.com
Konstantin Krivoruchko	Software Developer	ESRI, 380 New York St., Redlands, CA 92373	kkrivoruchko@esri.com
David Liebner	Medical Student	School of Medicine and Biomedical Sciences, State University of New York at Buffalo, Amherst, NY 14261-0055	dliebner@buffalo.edu
David J. Maguire	Director of Products and International	ESRI, 380 New York St., Redlands, CA 92373	dmaguire@esri.com
David R. Maidment	Director	Center for Research in Water Resources, 10100 Burnet Road, Building 119, University of Texas at Austin, Austin, TX 78758	maidment@mail.utexas.edu
Thomas Maxwell	Senior Scientist	GSTI, 6800 Backlick Rd., Suite 300, Springfield, VA 22150	tmaxwell@gsti3d.com
Venkatesh Merwade	Postdoctoral Fellow	Center for Research in Water Resources, 10100 Burnet Road, Building 119, University of Texas at Austin, Austin, TX 78758	vmmerwade@mail.utexas.edu
Ian Miller	Principal	GoldSim Technology Group, 22516 SE 64th Place, Suite 110, Issaquah, WA 98027	imiller@goldsim.com

Name	Job Title	Affiliation	E-Mail
Varkki G. Pallathucheril	Associate Professor and Director, Design+Digital Rehearsal Studio	Department of Urban and Regional Planning, Temple Buell Hall, Room 111, 611 Taft Dr., Champaign, IL 61820	varkki@uiuc.edu
Dawn C. Parker	Assistant Professor	Departments of Geography and Environmental Science and Policy, Center for Social Complexity, George Mason University, 4400 University Drive, MS1E2, Fairfax, VA 22030	dparker3@gmu.edu
Oscar Robayo		Center for Research in Water Resources, 10100 Burnet Road, Building 119, University of Texas at Austin, Austin, TX 78758	robayoo@hotmail.com
J. L. David Smith		Department of Fisheries, Wildlife and Conservation Biology, University of Minnesota	smith017@umn.edu
Luis Solórzano	Director, Monitoring & Modeling Unit - Andes CBC, Conservation International	The Andes Center for Biodiversity Conservation, Conservation International, Av. San Juan Bosco, Edif. San Juan. Ofc. 8-A, Altamira, Caracas, Venezuela	l.solorzano@conservation.org
Willem van Deursen	Co-founder and co-owner	PCRaster Environmental Software, van Swindenstraat 97, 3514 XP Utrecht, The Netherlands	wvandeursen@carthago.nl
Megan E. Van Fossen	Regional Coordinator for Analysis and Modeling, Andes Center for Biodiversity Conservation	Andes Center for Biodiversity Conservation, Conservation International, Av. San Juan Bosco, Edif. San Juan. Piso 8 Ofc. 8-A, Altamira, Caracas, Venezuela	mvanfossen@conservation.org

Name	Job Title	Affiliation	E-Mail
Alexey Voinov	Associate Research Professor	Gund Institute for Ecological Economics & Computer Science Department, University of Vermont, 590 Main Street, Burlington, VT 05405	avoinov@uvm.edu
Michael Wegener	Professor of Urban and Regional Research	Spiekermann & Wegener (S&W), Urban and Regional Research, Lindemannstrasse 10, 44137 Dortmund, Germany	mw@spiekermann-wegener.de
Yuchun Xie	Professor and Interim Head of Department of Geography and Geology, and Director of Institute for Geospatial Research and Education	Department of Geography and Geology, Eastern Michigan University, 205 Strong Hall, Ypsilanti, MI 48197	yxie@emich.edu
Anthony G.O. Yeh	Chair Professor in Urban Planning and GIS, Director of the GIS Research Centre and Institute of Transport Studies, and Dean of Graduate School of the University of Hong Kong	Centre of Urban Planning and Environmental Management, University of Hong Kong, Pokfulam Road, Hong Kong SAR China	hdxugoy@hkucc.hku.hk

Chapter 1

GIS, Spatial Analysis, and Modeling Overview

MICHAEL F. GOODCHILD

NATIONAL CENTER FOR GEOGRAPHIC INFORMATION AND ANALYSIS

UNIVERSITY OF CALIFORNIA, SANTA BARBARA

SANTA BARBARA, CALIFORNIA

ABSTRACT

MODELING CAN BE DEFINED in the context of geographic information systems (GIS) as occurring whenever operations of the GIS attempt to emulate geographic processes in the real world, at one point in time or over an extended period. Models are useful and used in a vast array of GIS applications, from simple evaluation to the prediction of future landscapes. In the past, it has often been necessary to couple GIS with special software designed for high performance in dynamic modeling. But with the increasing power of GIS hardware and software, it is now possible to reconsider this relationship. Modeling in GIS raises a number of important issues, including the question of validation, the roles of scale and accuracy, and the design of infrastructure to facilitate sharing of models.

INTRODUCTION

The term *modeling* is used in several different contexts in the world of GIS, so it would be wise to start with an effort to clarify its meaning, at least in the context of this book. There are two particularly important meanings. First, a *data model* is defined as a set of expectations about data—a *template* into which the data needed for a particular application can be fitted. For example, a table is a very simple example of a data model, and in the way in which tables are often used in GIS, the rows of the table correspond to a group or class of real-world features, such as counties, lakes, or trees, and the columns correspond to the various characteristics of the features, in other words, the attributes. This table template turns out to be very useful because it provides a good fit to the nature of data in many GIS applications. In essence, GIS data models allow the user to create a representation of how the world *looks*. A later section of the chapter provides a more extended discussion of data modeling in the particular context of dynamic models.

Second, a *model* (without the *data* qualification) is a representation of one or more processes that are believed to occur in the real world—in other words, of how the world *works*. A model is a computer program that takes a digital

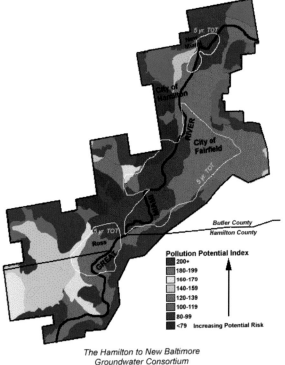

The Hamilton to New Baltimore
Groundwater Consortium
Drastic Ratings Map

Figure 1. The results of using the DRASTIC groundwater vulnerability model in an area of Ohio. The model combines GIS layers representing factors important in determining groundwater vulnerability and displays the results as a map of vulnerability ratings. (screen shot from www.gwconsortium.org/DRASTIC.gif)

representation of one or more aspects of the real world and transforms them to create a new representation. Models can be *static,* if the input and the output both correspond to the same point in time, or *dynamic,* if the output represents a later point in time than the input. The common element in all of these models is the operation of the GIS in multiple stages, whether they be used to create complex indicators from input layers or to represent time steps in the operation of a dynamic process.

Static models often take the form of indicators, combining various inputs to create a useful output. For example, the Universal Soil Loss Equation (USLE) combines layers of mapped information about slope, soil quality, agricultural practices, and other properties to estimate the amount of soil that will be lost to erosion from a unit area in a unit time (Wischmeier and Smith 1978). The DRASTIC model (fig. 1) estimates geographic variation in the vulnerability of groundwater to pollution, again based on a number of mapped properties (Aller et al. 1987). Dynamic models, on the other hand, represent a process that modifies or transforms some aspect of the Earth's surface through time. Contemporary weather forecasts are based on dynamic models of the atmosphere; dynamic models of stream flow are used to predict flooding from storms; and dynamic models of human behavior are used to predict traffic congestion.

This chapter provides an introductory overview of models and modeling, in the context of GIS. It begins with a discussion of the various types of models that have been implemented in GIS, then describes GIS from a modeling perspective, and finally identifies a series of major issues that confront modelers who use GIS. The chapter serves as an extended introduction to the book, providing a context for the chapters that follow.

All of the models discussed in this book are *spatial,* meaning that they describe the variation of one or more phenomena over the Earth's surface. The inputs to a spatial model must depict spatial variation, which is why a GIS is a particularly good platform for modeling (this subject is covered in detail in chapter 2). Moreover, a spatial model's results depend on the locations of the features or phenomena being modeled, such that if one or more of those locations change, the results of the model change.

Modeling can serve a number of purposes. Static models provide indexes or indicators that can provide useful predictors of impacts, sensitivities, or vulnerabilities. The USLE, for example, is widely used to predict soil erosion and to guide management strategies on the part of farmers or county, state, or federal governments to minimize erosion. DRASTIC is widely used as the basis for policies regarding groundwater and to make decisions about the environmental impacts of proposed developments. Dynamic models go further by attempting to quantify impacts into the future and are used to assess different management or development scenarios— *what if* scenarios. For example, urban-growth models can be used to predict the impact of land-use controls and future economic conditions on urban sprawl and to devise strategies to contain sprawl. Atmospheric models are used daily to predict weather conditions as much as seven days into the future.

This experimental aspect of modeling is perhaps its most compelling justification. Aircraft pilots are now routinely trained on simulators, which attempt to emulate the operation of an aircraft in a purely computational environment—as a result, pilots can be brought to a high level of training without the risks associated with the use of real aircraft. Whereas surgeons used to be trained on cadavers, much surgical training now occurs in virtual environments using precise digital representations of the human body. Dynamic modeling of the Earth's environment raises the possibility that we will eventually be able to evaluate the effects of such human activities as the burning of fossil fuels or the release of ozone-destroying chemicals long before such activities actually take place.

TYPES OF MODELS

This section explores the various types of models, placing them in a unifying framework. More detail on several of the contemporary modeling types, including cellular automata, agent-based models, and finite-element and finite-difference models is provided in chapter 3.

ANALOG AND DIGITAL

Although we rarely consider them in the context of GIS, analog models are even today perhaps the most common type. An analog model is defined as a *scale* model, a representation of a real-world system in which every part of the real system appears in miniature in the model. For example, architects designing skyscrapers routinely create scale models in order to investigate the effects of high winds on proposed structures, placing the models in wind tunnels to observe deformations under very high stress. Analog models play a key role in the design of aircraft wings, dams and canals, and a host of other engineering projects. Of course the success of analog models depends on the degree to which the system can be scaled—whether the operation of the system in a scaled model is identical to the operation of the real system. A key measure of an analog model is its scale or *representative fraction,* the ratio of distance between two points in the model to distance between corresponding points in the real world. In an analog model, all aspects of the system must be scaled by the same ratio for the model to be valid.

Ian McHarg, a landscape architect who made many contributions to GIS, originally developed his techniques of ecological planning using an analog version of GIS (McHarg 1969). Each factor important to a decision was represented as a transparent map, with darker areas representing areas of greater impact with respect to that factor. Maps were made for impact on groundwater, human populations, and any other relevant factors. The maps were stacked over a light source, and the areas appearing lightest corresponded to the areas of least impact and were, therefore, the areas most suitable for development. Today, the same basic principles are embodied in myriad site-suitability analyses conducted using GIS, but with the greater power of the digital computer to vary the weights assigned to each layer and with the mathematical approaches used to combine weighted layers (see chapter 16).

In a digital or *computational* model, all operations are conducted using a computer. Data is assembled in a data model and coded using a variety of coding schemes that reduce relevant aspects of the real world to patterns of 0s and 1s. The model itself is also coded in the same limited alphabet, as a computer program or software. Digital models do not have a representative fraction, since there is no distance in the model to compare to distance in the real world (Goodchild and Proctor 1997). Instead, the level of geographic detail is captured in the *spatial resolution,* or the size of the smallest feature represented in the database. For raster data, this is the size of the individual cell or pixel. When a GIS data set is created by digitizing a paper map, it is helpful to use a simple rule of thumb that the spatial resolution of the data set is approximately 0.5 mm at the scale of the map—in other words, a map at 1:24,000 has a spatial resolution of approximately 12 m. When such information on the lineage of vector data is unavailable, it is difficult to assign a value to spatial resolution since the size of the smallest polygon may be determined by the phenomenon being represented, rather than by the representation. For example, on a map of U.S. states, the smallest state will always be Rhode Island, however detailed the digitized state boundaries.

Besides spatial resolution, *temporal resolution* is also important in dynamic models since it defines the length of the model's time step. Any dynamic model proceeds in a discrete sequence of such steps, each representing a fixed interval of time, as the software attempts to predict the state of the system at the end of the time step based on inputs at the beginning of the time step. Both spatial and temporal resolution need to be appropriate to the real nature of the process being modeled. For example, in modeling the atmosphere for weather forecasts, there would be little point in using spatial resolutions as fine as 1 m or temporal resolutions as short as 1 sec because the processes affecting the atmosphere respond to variations that are much coarser than these. On the other hand, 1 m and 1 sec would be quite reasonable resolutions for a model of a small river or stream.

Spatial and temporal resolution determine the relationship between the real world and the model of the real world that is constructed in the computer. The two will never be identical, of course, and any digital representation will leave the user to some extent uncertain about the real world because of the detail that is present in the real world at finer resolutions than those of the model. A model of the atmosphere, for example, is not likely to represent the minute, local, and short-lived fluctuations in pressure caused by the flight of birds. It follows that the predictions of the model will be to some degree uncertain, in the sense that they leave the modeler in the dark about the precise nature of real-world outcomes.

DISCRETE AND CONTINUOUS

Dynamic modelers recognize two very different styles of models. Discrete models emulate processes that operate between discrete entities, such as the forces that operate between celestial bodies and govern their motion, or the behaviors that are exhibited by humans or animals as they interact over space (chapter 17). Continuous models, on the other hand, are cast in terms of variables that are continuous functions of location, such as atmospheric pressure or temperature, soil acidity or moisture content, or ground elevation. From a GIS perspective, these two possibilities mirror the widely accepted distinction between two conceptualizations of geographic space and geographic variation: the discrete-object view and the continuous-field view (Worboys and Duckham 2004). In the former, geographic space is empty except where it is occupied by point, line, or area objects, which may overlap, do not necessarily exhaust the available space, and are countable. From this viewpoint, the map of U.S. states is a jigsaw puzzle, with 50 pieces (51 including the District of Columbia) that can be moved around at will. The discrete-object view tends to work best in describing and representing biological organisms or human-made features such as buildings, vehicles, or fire hydrants.

In the continuous-field view, the geographic world is described by a series of continuous maps, each representing the variation of a different variable over the Earth's surface. There are no gaps in coverage, and there is exactly one value for each variable at each location. This view tends to work best in describing the variation of physical quantities. Models of the atmosphere are built using this view, though the results are often interpreted in weather forecasts in terms of the behaviors of discrete objects—highs, lows, and fronts. Continuous-field models typically express knowledge of the operation of the physical system in terms of partial differential equations (PDEs) which relate the values, rates of change through time, spatial gradients, and spatial curvatures of the continuously varying quantities. The Navier-Stokes equation, for example, describes the behavior of a viscous fluid, while the Darcy flow equation describes the flow of groundwater through a porous medium. PDEs must be solved through a process of numerical approximation, using either finite-difference methods that represent continuous variation as a raster of fixed spatial resolution or finite-element methods that use polynomial functions over irregular triangles and quadrilaterals (for a discussion of methods for constructing meshes for the solution of PDEs, see Carey 1995).

The so-called gravity or spatial interaction model (Fotheringham and O'Kelly 1989) is an excellent example of a discrete model since it can be used to predict the amount of interaction that will occur in the form of telephone calls, daily journeys to work, numbers of migrants, or numbers of shopping trips between a discrete origin and a discrete destination, arguing by analogy to the gravitational pull that exists between two celestial masses. The model is frequently and easily implemented in a GIS context, using vector representations of the origin and destination features. It is also possible to imagine hybrid models that combine aspects of both approaches, for instance, models in which discrete objects representing vehicles or organisms behave in response to local values of a continuous field. For example, the behavior of an individual in a crowd might be modeled as the response of a discrete object to a continuously varying field of perceived crowding, computed as some form of population density.

INDIVIDUAL AND AGGREGATE

In principle, it is possible to model any system using a set of rules about the mechanical behavior of the system's basic objects. The behavior of a crowd, for example, can be modeled through a series of rules about each individual's behavior, and the development of land-use patterns over an area can be modeled through a series of rules that describe the behavior of each decision maker. But for many systems, the number of basic objects is far too large for this approach to be practical. No coastal geomorphologist would think of modeling the behavior of beaches using rules about the behavior of each individual grain of sand because there would be far too many discrete objects to handle, and it would be far too costly to define the system at time zero—the position and movement of every sand grain at the outset of the simulation, or what are often termed the initial conditions. Similarly, no hydrologist would attempt to model a watershed with rules about the behavior of each molecule of water (chapter 14).

Continuous-field models address this problem by replacing individual objects with continuously varying estimates of such abstracted properties as density— the density of people in a crowd or the mean velocity and acceleration of water molecules considered as a continuous fluid. Another approach is to aggregate individual objects into larger wholes and to model the system through the behavior of these aggregates. Thus, much modeling of human systems occurs at the aggregate level of census blocks or tracts, and much modeling of hydrologic systems occurs with lumped systems that aggregate areas into entire watersheds or stream reaches. Lumped systems ignore within-lump variation as well as behaviors that modify the variation within lumps, in effect ignoring variation and processes that fall below the implied spatial resolution of the representation.

Over time, the increasing power and storage capacity of computers has made individual-level modeling more practical, and today it is possible to build models involving millions and even billions of objects. The problem of determining initial conditions remains, however, since it is often the result of real constraints on data gathering, which often requires the use of expensive human resources. Technologies such as remote sensing provide a partial solution, allowing the initial conditions over large areas to be characterized at fine spatial resolution, but optical remote sensing is limited in its ability to see through clouds and to differentiate areas based on properties relevant to an investigator's model.

CELLULAR AUTOMATA

In a cellular automaton, spatial variation is represented as a raster of fixed resolution, with each cell being assigned to one of a number of defined states. Such models have been used widely to study processes of urban growth (chapter 8), in which case the possible states will likely be limited to two: undeveloped and developed. At each time step, the next state of each cell is determined by a number of rules based on the properties of the cell and its neighbors and on the states of the cell and its neighbors. For example, the rules for a simple urban growth model might be as follows:

- If the cell is currently undeveloped, convert to developed with a probability that depends on the slope of the cell, its proximity to a major transportation link (chapter 10), the zoning of the cell, and the number of its neighbors that are already developed.
- If the cell is currently developed, make no change.

Clarke and his coworkers (e.g., Clarke and Gaydos 1998) have applied models of this type to a number of urban areas in the United States, typically using 30-m spatial resolution and 1-year temporal resolution and forecasting growth for up to 50 years.

The concepts of cellular automata were first explored by John Conway over artificial spaces that were typically uniform and undifferentiated. His interest lay in the sometimes stable properties that emerged after large numbers of time steps, based on particular sets of initial conditions. His Game of Life (Gardner 1970) generates some surprising and intriguing patterns (fig. 2) and was one of the key developments that led to today's strong interest in complex systems and the simple properties that sometimes emerge in such systems, largely independent of initial conditions. Many geographers and others have speculated that similarly surprising patterns might emerge on the Earth's surface through the operation of complex, dynamic processes.

AGENT-BASED MODELS

In an agent-based model, a system's dynamic behavior is represented through rules governing the actions of a number of autonomous agents. Such models can be regarded as generalizations of cellular automata in which agents are able to move around in space, rather than being confined to the cells of a raster—but in other cases the locations of the agents may be irrelevant to the model. Dibble (Dibble and Feldman 2004) has explored the operations of economic agents in simple nonraster worlds similar to the *small worlds* popularized by Watts and Strogatz (1998), in which agents occupy locations and can interact both with their spatial neighbors and with certain distant and randomly identified neighbors.

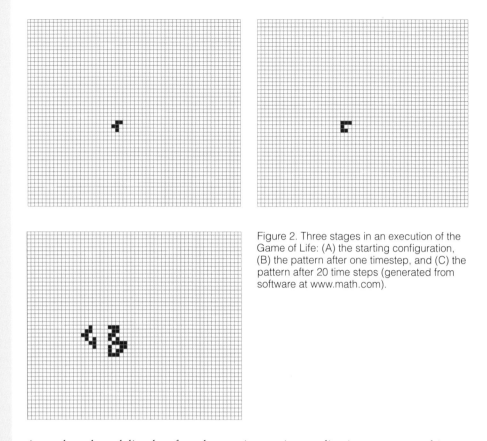

Figure 2. Three stages in an execution of the Game of Life: (A) the starting configuration, (B) the pattern after one timestep, and (C) the pattern after 20 time steps (generated from software at www.math.com).

Agent-based modeling has found many interesting applications to geographic phenomena. Benenson (2004) has explored the use of such models to represent the behavior of households in cities and the process by which segregation emerges through housing choices. Several efforts have been made to apply agent-based modeling to the emergence of land-use and land-cover patterns (chapters 6, 18, and 19), with particular emphasis on the processes that lead to greater fragmentation of land cover as a result of development and thus to problems for species that require specialized natural habitat (see, e.g., www.csiss.org/resources/maslucc).

One of the factors that has led to the recent explosion of interest in agent-based models is the emergence of the object-oriented paradigm in software development. Batty (1997) has described the concept of modeling the actions of individuals in a complex geographic landscape through the construction of a set of parallel, independent software modules, each representing the actions and decisions of one actor in the system. Object-oriented languages have made it much easier to conceptualize and build such simulation systems, which are very different in software architecture from the traditional serial approach to computing.

MODELING AND GIS   The traditions of GIS are firmly rooted in the map, and even today it is common for GIS to be introduced through the idea of representing the contents of maps in computers. Map-related ideas, such as layers, projections, generalization, and symbolization are still prevalent in GIS and account for a large proportion of the capabilities of a contemporary GIS. So it is by no means clear how a technology built essentially for handling maps can be adapted to the needs of dynamic simulation modeling, and indeed few would think of GIS in that light or suggest that GIS is in any sense the optimum platform for modeling. GIS has never handled time particularly well (Langran 1993, Peuquet 2002), and its representations of continuous variation do not include the irregular meshes of triangles and quadrilaterals that form the basic meshes of finite-element modeling.

On the other hand, there are many good reasons for urging that GIS evolve into an effective platform for spatial modeling, and the technical aspects of doing so are discussed further in chapter 2. First, GIS is an excellent environment for representing spatial variation, in the initial and boundary conditions of models and in their outputs. GIS also includes numerous tools for acquiring, preprocessing, and transforming data for use in modeling, including data management, format conversion, projection change, resampling, raster–vector conversion, etc.—in fact, all of the tools that would be needed to assemble the data for dynamic simulation. It also includes excellent tools for displaying, rendering, querying, and analyzing model results and for assessing the accuracies and uncertainties associated with inputs and outputs.

Second, much progress has been made recently in the handling of time in GIS. Object-oriented data models have moved the emphasis away from the representation of the contents of maps to a much more general and powerful modeling environment (Zeiler 1999), in which it is possible to represent events, transactions, flows, and other classes of information that would be difficult or impossible to render cartographically.

Third, and perhaps most important, many of the techniques used in GIS analysis would be much more powerful if they could be coupled with an extensive toolkit of methods of simulation. For example, it is widely accepted that the results of GIS analysis are often distorted or biased by the choice of spatial units used in its support. In a classic case study, Openshaw and Taylor (1979) showed that a strong and positive relationship existed between the percentage of people over 65 and the percentage registered as Republicans in each of the 99 counties of Iowa. But by reaggregating the data to units other than counties, in other words by changing the support, they were able to produce correlations ranging from almost perfectly negative (the greater the percentage over 65, the fewer registered Republicans) to almost perfectly positive (the greater the percentage over 65, the more registered Republicans). They coined the term *Modifiable Areal Unit Problem* (MAUP) for this dependence of analytic results on support and urged that researchers experiment with a range of zoning schemes to determine the specific sensitivity in any actual analysis.

More generally, many of the techniques commonly used for analyzing patterns of points, lines, or areas using GIS (Bailey and Gatrell 1995, Haining 2003, O'Sullivan and Unwin 2003) produce results that are similarly difficult to interpret. An extensive library of simulation methods would allow analysts to compare actual patterns with those expected under a wide range of suitable and interesting conditions. For example, instead of testing whether a map of incidence of cancer displayed a general tendency for clustering, one might test a specific hypothesis relating cancer incidence to data on some known cancer-causing atmospheric or groundwater pollutant.

GIS AND TIME

Over the years, researchers have devised a limited number of ways of handling time within the structures provided by a technology that, as noted earlier, has its roots in the representation of the essentially static contents of maps. The earliest GIS data models were topological, meaning that they included information on such topological properties as adjacency and connectivity. The *coverage* model—originally developed for the Canada Geographic Information System in the mid-1960s, then for the U.S. Bureau of the Census DIME project for the 1970 census, later for the ODYSSEY project of the Harvard Laboratory for Computer Graphics and Spatial Analysis in the late 1970s, and later still the basis for the original release of ArcInfo® in the early 1980s—was designed to represent a partitioning of two-dimensional space into nonoverlapping and space-exhausting polygons. Cartographers know this as the *choropleth* map, but it also provides an effective representation of any classification of soils, land cover, land use, or surficial geology and also of *cadastral* maps of land ownership. Many examples of such maps change through time—for example, the map of U.S. county boundaries has changed frequently since independence as new areas were divided into counties, as county boundaries moved, and as counties were split or merged.

One approach to handling such change is through the concept of a *region* as an aggregation of smaller areas. All of the county boundaries that ever existed are first mapped, creating a very large number of small *basic units*. In the coverage model, these are represented as a collection of *arcs,* each arc defining the boundary between two adjacent units. The counties at any point in time can then be re-created by selecting those arcs that separated counties at that time and assembling them into areas to form that time's regions (Maguire et al. 1992). The same concept of basic units has frequently surfaced in discussions of multiple land classifications, where an *integrated terrain unit* (ITU) is defined as an area of land that is homogeneous and contiguous with respect to all of the classifications—all of the original maps can be re-created from a map of ITUs by dissolving appropriate arcs. Regions are also useful for representing events through time that may overlap and do not exhaust space, such as forest fire footprints or land easements.

Another approach consists of tracking the locations of independently moving objects. For example, a collection of individuals might be tracked using GPS, their locations being recorded at every predetermined interval of time. Similar techniques are frequently used to track animals (chapter 18). In effect, this type of data yields a series of lines in a three-dimensional space formed by the two spatial dimensions (horizontally) and time (vertically), with the restrictions that each line intersects exactly once with any horizontal slice (fixed time) of the model. ESRI® ArcGIS® Tracking Analyst software has been developed to support simple forms of analysis, summary, and visualization of this type of space–time data. Agouris and Stefanidis (2003) have developed a representation of area objects whose orientation and shape change through time.

A third approach represents each time period as a simple snapshot, typically in raster, and change through time as an ordered sequence of such snapshots. This is the approach inherent in remote sensing. Moving objects are not part of the representation, though they might be detected by some form of image processing and represented using the tracking approach. The approach is used in many raster-based simulation packages, including the GIS PCRaster™ (chapter 16; pcraster.geog.uu.nl).

MODELING SOFTWARE

As noted earlier, traditional GIS was designed to support the representation and analysis of maps. Static modeling and the calculation of indicators are classic GIS applications and are well suited to this traditional architecture. Recently, the power of GIS for static modeling has been greatly enhanced by the availability of graphic interfaces that allow the user to interact with the various stages of the modeling process through a simple point-and-click environment. The first of these was perhaps the ERDAS® IMAGINE® software; more recently, ESRI ModelBuilder™ software is a powerful addition to the spatial analytic capabilities of ArcGIS. These technologies address a fundamental problem of GIS: the vast number of possible transformations and operations that can be performed on geographic data and the complexity in practice of many analysis sequences.

In principle, such software can be used for dynamic modeling through a process of iteration, in which standard GIS functions are used to transform the system at each time step, and the output of one time step becomes the input for the next. But two problems stand in the way of this. First, the command language of the GIS will not have been designed for iteration, requiring the user to reenter the transformation operations at each step, and second, the poor performance of the system is likely to be frustrating to the user. Scripting languages provide some help in the first regard by supporting the storage and execution of sequences of instructions and by allowing repeated execution of sequences (looping), and today's version of ArcGIS allows scripts to be written in standard languages such as Microsoft® Visual Basic®, Python®, and PERL.

PCRaster was perhaps the first GIS designed specifically for simulation, using the ordered-snapshot approach described above. As the name suggests, it is designed to operate on rasters and to implement a range of operations that includes the functions required by a cellular automaton approach to modeling. Tomlin (1990) was the first to systematize the functions that could be performed on raster representations, and his approach has been implemented in numerous raster GIS. Van Deursen (1995) developed the language used by PCRaster to operationalize simple raster functions, through commands that allow entire rasters to be addressed at once—for example, the instruction B = A*2 will take the values in all of the cells of A and double them to create a new raster B. PCRaster includes functions for visualizing its outputs as a movie and has been applied very successfully to the simulation of a range of environmental and social processes (see the examples in chapter 16 and at pcraster.geog.uu.nl).

Nevertheless, the one-size-fits-all approach that is inherent in GIS and in systems such as PCRaster is unlikely ever to address all possible needs, and instead much attention has been devoted to *coupling* GIS with packages that are more directly attuned to the needs of modeling (chapter 6). MATLAB® is a commonly used toolbox in this context because of its powerful mathematical routines. A prototype linkage between GoldSim® and ArcGIS is discussed in chapter 6. STELLA™ (www.iseesystems.com) was developed to support dynamic modeling and has the advantage of having a sophisticated visual interface that allows the researcher to express ideas about processes and causality through simple diagrams; STELLA has also been coupled with GIS (chapter 7). Coupling is also widely used to link stand-alone models to GIS (Goodchild, Parks, and Steyaert 1993), including models developed to simulate particular environmental processes in areas such as hydrology (chapter 15).

It is common to distinguish three types of coupling. First, a stand-alone package might be coupled with GIS by exchanging files—the GIS might be used to prepare the inputs, which are then passed to the modeling package, and after execution, the results of modeling would be returned to the GIS for display and analysis. This approach requires the existence of a format that is understood by both the GIS and the modeling packages or if no such format exists, of an additional piece of software designed to convert formats in both directions. Second, coupling may take the form of integrating the GIS with the modeling packages using standards such as Microsoft's COM and .NET that allow a single script to invoke commands from both packages. This type of integration is now common, based on the compliance to these standards of GIS programs such as ArcGIS and Idrisi®, and similar compliance by packages such as Microsoft Excel and MATLAB that have powerful capabilities needed by modelers. The integration occurs through a single script, written in a standard scripting language (Ungerer and Goodchild 2002). Finally, the entire model may be executed by calling functions of the GIS, using a single script (in this option the model is said to be *embedded* in the GIS). Coupling GIS and modeling systems is discussed at length in chapter 2.

CALIBRATION AND VERIFICATION

Any attempt to predict the future or to provide indicators of future impact is necessarily problematic, and various techniques are available to assess a model's validity and to build confidence in its results. In general, it seems better to regard a model as a basis for reducing uncertainty about the future from some prior state of complete ignorance to one of more limited uncertainty, rather than to think of a model as failing if its predictions are not perfectly accurate. In other words, and in the language of regression modeling, it would be better to think of a model as improving on $R^2=0$ than on failing to achieve $R^2=1$.

Many models require some form of *calibration,* a process of determining appropriate values for one or more parameters that are not specified by theory or past practice. Models are often calibrated and verified using past history, on the grounds that the future will repeat the past. For example, a model of urban growth might be calibrated and verified on the past decades of growth patterns before being applied to forecasting future decades. A common approach is to partition the data into a calibration set and a verification set, using the former to determine the best values of any unknown parameters (by adjusting them to give the best possible fit between the model and the data) and using the latter to verify the model's predictions. Of course, any process of calibration based on past history will only be as valid as its basic assumption that historic trends will continue into the future, at least over the period of the model's forecast.

Alternatively, a model's validity might be assessed based on the validity of each of its component parts. For example, a model that includes rules might be tested by comparing its rules to data on real behavior, rather than by comparing the results of the model as a whole to real data. In practice, this is often the primary basis of assessment, though it is dependent on the assumption that all relevant processes are incorporated in the model.

Sensitivity analysis is also commonly used to assess models. In this approach, the various parameters and inputs are systematically varied to observe their impacts on the model's results. The model might be rerun with the value of a given parameter increased by 10% and then reduced by 10% from its original value. If the impact on the results is substantially less than 10%, the modeler knows that the parameter is not of critical importance and its accuracy is not a major concern. On the other hand, the results may be extraordinarily sensitive to some parameters, and the modeler should therefore invest additional time in ensuring that their values are appropriate.

All geographic data leaves its users, to some extent, uncertain about the nature of the real world: because of measurement error, or because detail has been omitted, or because definitions of terms are not rigorous, or because error has crept into the compilation of the data in some way (Zhang and Goodchild 2002). Uncertainty *propagation* attempts to determine the effects on the results of modeling of known uncertainties in the input data (chapter 4; Heuvelink 1998). In principle, every prediction of any model should be accompanied by some form of confidence limits, expressing the researcher's uncertainty about the validity of the results.

THE VALUE OF MODELING

At this point, it makes sense to reexamine a question discussed earlier in the introduction to this chapter: why model? From a practical perspective, the answer is surely to reduce uncertainty about the future. But modeling is also conducted for several other reasons. Models may be simply formal representations of belief about process or of how various aspects of the real world work, rather than tools for prediction and forecasting. But formalization has value— in allowing people to communicate in terms that are mutually understood and in allowing knowledge to be expressed in the demanding environment of a digital computer. In court, a model may have great power as an expression of the modeler's willingness to think and operate clearly, to incorporate ideas explicitly, and to address known uncertainties.

Models may also be repositories, structures in which investigators can store knowledge in ways that can be readily executed in *what if* scenarios. In this sense, models are not tools for discovering knowledge, but places where discovered knowledge can be brought to bear on real policy questions—models are formal representations of what is known about a system.

But models also contribute to the creation of knowledge, as in the case of the emergent properties discussed in connection with the *Game of Life,* when the execution of a model reveals something about the real world that was not already known. Batty and Longley (1994) argue that their fractal model of cities led them to a clearer understanding of the processes by which cities develop, and similar arguments are often made about models in other contexts.

MODEL SHARING

Tested, operational models are among the most valuable forms of digital information since they encapsulate a wealth of practical and theoretical scientific knowledge in an easy-to-use form. Thus it is surprising that so much effort has gone into the creation of data repositories, digital libraries, data warehouses, and other sophisticated mechanisms for sharing digital data and so little into the equivalent infrastructure for sharing methods and models. There are no widely accepted methods for describing models in formal, structured terms equivalent to the metadata standards for datasets, and while some collections exist, there is no central clearinghouse for models. Crosier et al. (2003) have proposed such a standard and demonstrated its use in documenting several models. Model and method sharing, or more generally the sharing of process objects, is a core concept of the emerging Grid, the high-performance worldwide network of research computers, and of discussions over *cyberinfrastructure,* a general name for the use of information technology in the service of collaborative research. There is also increasing interest in providing basic GIS services, such as geocoding, as remotely invokable methods implemented on the Web. In the next few years, dramatic improvements are expected in the availability of techniques for sharing methods and models.

REFERENCES

Agouris P., and A. Stefanidis. 2003. Efficient summarization of spatiotemporal events. *Communications of the Association for Computing Machinery* 46: 65–66.

Aller L., T. Bennett, J. H. Lehr, R. J. Petty, and G. Hackett. 1987. DRASTIC: A standardized system for evaluating ground water pollution potential using hydrogeological settings. EPA/600/2-87/035. Washington, D.C.: Environmental Protection Agency.

Bailey, T. C., and A. C. Gatrell. 1995. *Interactive spatial data analysis.* Harlow, UK: Longman.

Batty, M. J. 1997. The computable city. *International Planning Studies* 2: 155–73.

Batty, M. J., and P. A. Longley. 1994. *Fractal cities: A geometry of form and function.* San Diego, Calif.: Academic Press.

Benenson, I. 2004. Agent-based modeling: From individual residential choice to urban residential dynamics. In *Spatially integrated social science,* ed. M. F. Goodchild and D. J. Janelle, 67–94. New York: Oxford University Press.

Carey, G. F., ed. 1995. *Finite element modeling of environmental problems: Surface and subsurface flow and transport.* New York: John Wiley and Sons.

Clarke, K. C., and L. Gaydos. 1998. Loose coupling a cellular automaton model and GIS: Long-term growth prediction for San Francisco and Washington/Baltimore. *International Journal of Geographical Information Science* 12: 699–714.

Crosier, S. J., M. F. Goodchild, L. L. Hill, and T. R. Smith. 2003. Developing an infrastructure for sharing environmental models. *Environment and Planning B: Planning and Design* 30: 487–501.

Dibble, C., and P. G. Feldman. 2004. The GeoGraph 3D Computational Laboratory: Network and terrain landscapes for RePast. *Journal of Artificial Societies and Social Simulation* 7(1). jasss.soc.surrey.ac.uk/7/1/7.html.

Fotheringham, A. S., and M. E. O'Kelly. 1989. *Spatial interaction models: Formulations and applications.* Boston: Kluwer.

Gardner, M. 1970. Mathematical games: The fantastic combinations of John Conway's new solitaire game "Life." *Scientific American* 223: 120–23.

Goodchild, M. F., B. O. Parks, and L. J. Steyaert. 1993. *Environmental modelling with GIS.* New York: Oxford University Press.

Goodchild, M. F., and J. Proctor. 1997. Scale in a digital geographic world. *Geographical and Environmental Modelling* 1: 5–23.

Haining, R. P. 2003. *Spatial data analysis: Theory and practice.* New York: Cambridge University Press.

Heuvelink, G. B. H. 1998. *Error propagation in environmental modelling with GIS.* London: Taylor & Francis.

Langran, G. 1993. *Time in geographic information systems*. London: Taylor & Francis.

McHarg, I. L. 1969. *Design with nature*. Garden City, N.Y.: Natural History Press.

Maguire, D. J., G. Stickler, and G. Browning. 1992. Handling complex objects in geo-relational GIS. In *Proceedings of the fifth international spatial data handling symposium,* 652–61.

O'Sullivan, D., and D. J. Unwin. 2003. *Geographic information analysis*. New York: John Wiley and Sons.

Openshaw, S., and P. J. Taylor. 1979. A million or so correlation coefficients: Three experiments on the modifiable areal unit problem. In *Statistical applications in the spatial sciences,* ed. R. J. Bennett, N. J. Thrift, and N. Wrigley, 127–44. London: Pion.

Peuquet, D. 2002. *Representations of space and time*. New York: Guilford.

Tomlin, C. D. 1990. *Geographic information systems and cartographic modeling*. Englewood Cliffs, N.J.: Prentice Hall.

Ungerer, M. J., and M. F. Goodchild. 2002. Integrating spatial data analysis and GIS: A new implementation using the Component Object Model (COM). *International Journal of Geographical Information Science* 16: 41–54.

van Deursen, W. P. A. 1995. *Geographical information systems and dynamic models: Development and application of a prototype spatial modelling language*. Utrecht: Koninklijk Nederlands Aardrijkskundig Genntschap/Faculteit Ruimtelijke Wetenschappen Universiteit Utrecht.

Watts, D. J., and S. H. Strogatz. 1998. Collective dynamics of 'small-world' networks. *Nature* 393(6684): 440–42.

Wischmeier, W. C., and D. D. Smith. 1978. Predicting rainfall erosion losses: A guide to conservation planning. *Agricultural Handbook* 537. Washington, D.C.: Department of Agriculture.

Worboys, M. F., and M. Duckham. 2004. *GIS: A computing perspective*. New York: Taylor & Francis.

Zeiler, M. 1999. *Modeling our world: The ESRI guide to geodatabase design*. Redlands, Calif.: ESRI Press.

Zhang, J. X., and M. F. Goodchild. 2002. *Uncertainty in geographical information*. New York: Taylor & Francis.

Chapter 2 · *Towards a GIS Platform for Spatial Analysis and Modeling*

DAVID J. MAGUIRE

DIRECTOR OF PRODUCTS

ESRI

REDLANDS, CALIFORNIA

ABSTRACT

THE LONG-STANDING VISION of an integrated platform for comprehensive spatial analysis and modeling that has the capabilities for geographic data management, analysis, and visualization of modern geographic information systems (GIS) is at last beginning to become a reality. Advances in computer hardware and software engineering, together with a growing interest in spatial analysis and modeling in the social and environmental sciences research communities, have stimulated the development of new capabilities within both GIS and modeling software systems, as well as the integration of existing GIS and modeling systems. Today, integrated spatial analysis and modeling systems have evolved from GIS-centric (e.g., ArcGIS, GRASS, Idrisi and PCRaster) and modeling-centric (e.g., GoldSim, RePast, SWARM®, and STELLA) software systems. Much progress has been made recently, especially in the areas of cartographic modeling, geostatistical estimation, network analysis, raster analysis, vector overlay, and visualization (2D and 3D). However, there are still neglected areas that warrant further investigation, including exploratory spatial data analysis (ESDA), dynamic system simulation, operations research optimization, spatial statistics, and visualization of multidimensional data.

Since the 1960s there has been a rising concern with building computer software for the purposes of spatial analysis and modeling. Enormous progress has been made in the past four decades due to massive advances in information technology (especially software engineering) as well as considerable improvements in the mathematics and science of spatial analysis and modeling. In the early years, all software for spatial analysis and modeling was custom built for a particular project data set. Gradually, GIS and spatial analysis and modeling software systems were developed that provided generic approaches to a range of problems. Initially, these were either GIS or spatial analysis and modeling systems, and a major task for workers in the field was to link systems of each type together. For example, in the area of environmental modeling alone, the book by Goodchild et al. (1996), which originated from the Second International Conference/Workshop on Integrated Geographic Information Systems and Environmental Modeling, has 33 chapters concerned with linking environmental models to GIS. More recently, as the foundation technologies of both GIS and spatial analysis and modeling systems have become more interoperable, there have been many more successful linkages. Useful reviews are provided on GIS and socioeconomic models in Fotheringham and Wegener (2000), planning systems in Brail and Klosterman (2001), environmental models in Clark et al. (2002), agent-based models in Gimblett (2002), and applied socioeconomic spatial analysis and models in Stillwell and Clark (2004). In the last few years both GIS and modeling systems have evolved so that models can now be developed within the framework of a GIS software system (e.g., Arc Hydro software described by Maidment 2002), and GIS capabilities can be embedded within the environment of a spatial analysis and modeling system (e.g., the GeoDa™ systems described by Anselin 2005, this volume).

This chapter explores the capabilities of GIS software systems for spatial analysis and modeling. It focuses on the architectural and software engineering patterns available today for spatial analysis and modeling work within a GIS software framework. The continuum of software options for spatial analysis and modeling are discussed, with some representative examples, starting with GIS-centric and concluding with modeling-centric systems. The capabilities of contemporary GIS software systems are reviewed, and the strengths and weaknesses of current systems are outlined.

From a software architecture perspective, we can define a GIS as an integrated software system for the collection, storage, query, analysis, and presentation of geographic information. GIS are a very interesting class of information system because, somewhat uniquely, they have a duality of purpose. They act as both transaction processing systems (e.g., government permit tracking, utility work order processing, and oil lease ownership) and analytical processing systems (e.g., business market analysis, pollution plume dispersal, and battlefield management).

Transaction processing systems must provide guaranteed reliability, security, and scalability. To fulfill a role as a transaction processing system, GIS have incorporated many industry-standard IT components, such as database management systems (DBMS) (e.g., IBM® DB2®, Microsoft SQL Server, and Oracle®), Web servers (e.g., Microsoft IIS and Apache), and application servers (e.g., BEA® Weblogic® and IBM Websphere®). To be successful as analytical processing systems, GIS have had to embrace the scientific computing paradigm (Chambers 1999, 2000; Gray et al. 2005). In this model, GIS are seen as a collection of functions that can be applied to data in an ad hoc and highly flexible way. Each task can be broken down into a series of atomic operations: data + function = data. A central plank of this mode of operation is a scripting or customization framework that allows users both to automate frequently performed tasks and workflows as well as extend the base system with new functions and data types (Maguire 1999).

To be successful in fulfilling its information system requirements, a GIS must have four key parts (fig. 1):

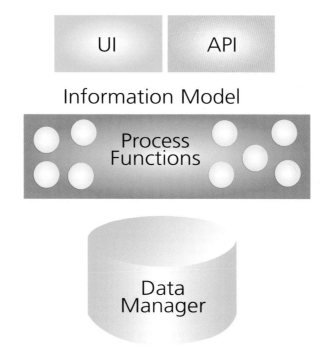

Figure 1. Four key information systems parts of a GIS: Information Model, Data Manager, Process Functions (tools), and Interfaces.

- Information Model. All information systems have a core information model that defines the classes of objects that can be represented from the domain of interest and how they behave and interact. The information model of a GIS defines the basic design pattern for describing the real world and how it is abstracted into a computer system. Modern GIS have a rich information model capable of representing a wide range of information types using a collection of submodels (Zeiler 1999, Arctur and Zeiler 2004, Longley et al. 2005). The most common geographic submodels are: simple vector, computer-aided design (CAD), image, raster/grid, vector topological, network, Triangular Irregular Network (TIN), and object. The information model of a GIS can also be extended programmatically using built-in customization frameworks (see below).

- Data Manager. Information is represented in contemporary GIS as a collection of objects which are instances of class templates. The information model is most commonly mapped onto a database schema with each object class implemented as a database management system (DBMS) table. Within the tables, rows are object instances, and object states (properties) are columns. In some systems, object behavior (methods) can also be stored in a DBMS, but for engineering development reasons, behavior is usually implemented as a collection of modular software component classes (dynamic link libraries—dlls—or shared object libraries). In this case, object state and behavior are bound together at execution time to present a completely functional package to processing software modules (e.g., visualization and analysis engines). In the modern era, GIS are large and very sophisticated information systems that must be able to deal with extremely large data volumes. They must also manage multiuser read and write access to large continuous geographic databases. There are several solutions to this challenging concurrency problem including feature- and area-level locking and versioning (Longley et al. 2005).

- Process Functions (Tools). Today, GIS have very extensive and rich collections of tools for processing geographic information. It is outside the scope of this chapter to provide details of the processing capabilities of GIS, but the key points can be summarized in terms of the life cycle of GIS data. This begins with data collection (digitizing/editing) and load or transfer, integration, storage and management, proceeds through data maintenance, and ends with data query, analysis, and visualization/mapping. Conceptually, the processing operations are usually presented to users as a suite of functions or tools that can be applied to collections of GIS objects organized as layers. As far as spatial analysis and modeling are concerned, all stages of the life cycle are relevant as we will see in later sections of this chapter, but it is query, analysis, and visualization/mapping that are of most interest.

- Interfaces. The information model, management, and processing capabilities of a GIS are exposed in two ways. End users interact with the systems via graphical or command line interfaces, and both have an important role to play in analysis and modeling. Developers interact with the underlying component building blocks via application programming interfaces. These interfaces can be accessed using lower level programming languages or higher level scripting languages, as described later. The Microsoft Windows® standard for desktop graphical user interfaces is well known to all computer users. This Windows, Icons, Mouse, Pointer (WIMP) system provides menus, dialogues, and many types of custom control in an event-driven, workflow-oriented paradigm. The browser interface of the World Wide Web (WWW) provides an alternative, but essentially similar, approach for interacting with Web resources that live in a distributed, networked computer environment. Many spatial analysis and modeling capabilities are exposed through the graphical user interfaces of GIS, and an example is shown in figure 2.

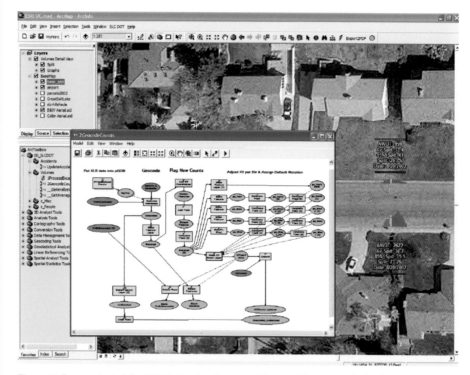

Figure 2. Screenshot of ArcGIS 9 showing transportation accident analysis for Salt Lake City, Utah. The foreground window is a model that shows data (ellipses) and operators (rectangles).

One of the most significant recent improvements in GIS, as far as spatial analysts and modelers are concerned, is the exposure to external developers of the underlying software components that GIS software vendor developers themselves use to build end-user versions of their system. The motivations of the GIS software vendor are simple; providing access to core functionality allows the GIS to be extended and customized for use in new applications areas and thus expands the market potential of systems.

Since the mid-1990s, the development of software systems has been dominated by the object-component paradigm, and this has found its way into the heart of GIS development (Maguire 1999b, Zeiler 2001, Longley et al. 2005). In the object-component paradigm, systems are assembled from self-contained atomic building blocks of code. Importantly, the capabilities of object-components are published as interfaces on the object-components. This isolates what an object-component does, from how it does it. Object-components communicate using messages that invoke processing operations and retrieve state information.

Figure 3 shows a small collection of object-components from the ArcGIS subsystem for geographic analysis (for more details, see edndoc.esri.com/arcgisdeveloper).

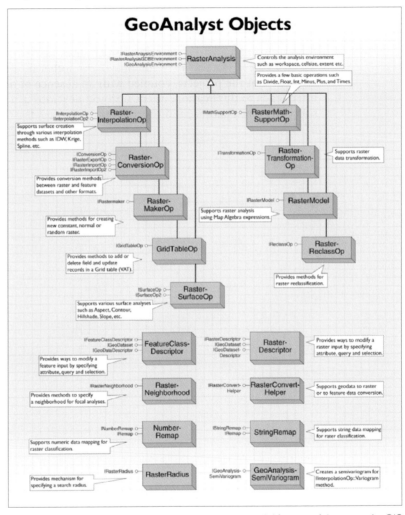

Figure 3. High-level, conceptual object-component model for one of the many ArcGIS subsystems. The boxes are object-component classes, the lines show relationships between the classes, and the "lollipops" are the object interfaces.

In the last few years, the object-component model has been extended to support distributed computing environments. Specifically, capabilities have been added for building Web services—self-contained applications that can be called over the Web. The Web services model has very important ramifications for linking GIS and spatial analysis and modeling systems because it offers a simple, well-defined, platform-neutral mechanism for loosely coupling systems together over a network connection.

**EVOLUTION OF
GIS SOFTWARE
ARCHITECTURES**

There are several IT architectural choices for implementing GIS (Coleman 1999, Longley et al. 2005). Usually, GIS is first introduced into an organization in the context of a single, fixed-term project. The technical components (network, hardware, software, and data) of an operational GIS are assembled for the duration of the project, which may be from several months to a few years. Data is collected specifically for the project, and typically little thought is given to reuse of software, data, and human knowledge. In larger organizations, multiple projects may run one after another or even in parallel. The *one off* nature of the projects, coupled with an absence of organizational vision, often leads to duplication, as each project develops using different hardware, software, data, people, and procedures. Sharing data and experience is usually a low priority.

As interest in GIS grows, to save money and encourage sharing and resource reuse, several projects in the same department may be amalgamated. This often leads to the creation of common standards, development of a focused GIS team, and procurement of new GIS capabilities. Yet it is also quite common for different departments to have different GIS software and data standards.

As GIS becomes more pervasive, organizations learn more about it and begin to become dependent on it. This leads to the realization that GIS is a useful way to structure many of the organization's assets, processes, and workflows. Through a process of natural growth, and possibly further major procurement (e.g., purchase of upgraded hardware, software, and data), GIS gradually becomes accepted as an important enterprise-wide information system. At this point, GIS standards are agreed upon across multiple departments, and resources to support and manage the GIS are often centrally funded and managed.

There are three key parts, or tiers, to any information system: the user interface, the tools, and the data management system (fig. 4). The three parts can be implemented on a single computer (single-tier architecture), two computers (two-tier architecture), or in the case of large systems, they are usually spread across three separate machines (three-tier architecture). In a single-tier architecture, the presentation (user interface), business logic (validation and processing functions), and data management functions all run on the same machine which is usually a desktop personal computer. At the other extreme, in a three-tier situation, the presentation tier runs as a client on a desktop PC, the business logic for data access, analysis, etc. runs on a middle-tier application server, and the data management software (RDBMS) runs on a data server. In this type of configuration, the client has sophisticated capabilities and in advanced systems, can comprise several hundreds of megabytes of code (a so-called thick client implementation). This configuration has served information system users well for the last decade and will continue so to do for advanced decision support tasks that require ad hoc analytical processing and scientific computing style information manipulation and analysis (for example, editing, cartographic compilation, 3D modeling, and spatial analysis). However, in recent years some organizations have become dissatisfied with this type of architecture for less demanding tasks for several reasons. In the case of large deployments, the cost of client machines and software is prohibitive; it is expensive for organizations to maintain and update widely distributed PCs—especially if users cannot do it themselves—and it is difficult to maintain corporate standards throughout a widely dispersed organization.

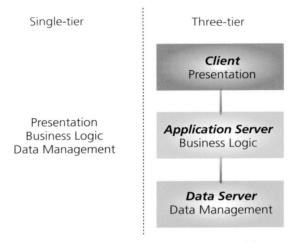

Figure 4. Single- and three-tier information system architectures.

An alternative, more centralized architecture is emerging that addresses these problems. At the heart of this new architecture approach is the idea that a middle-tier application server can be enhanced to encompass not only the data management GIS subsystem but also the mapping and spatial analysis subsystems. Running all the GIS components on a server means that only a very thin client is required to initiate processing requests and display the results of GIS tasks. Such centralized GIS implementations are now being referred to as Enterprise Geographic Information Servers (fig. 5). They allow both thin (browser) and thick (desktop GIS) distributed clients to access data and processing capabilities over a standard local or wide area network. The server itself has two parts. The server object manager is responsible for interfacing with the network via a Web server and for allocating requests to server worker containers that perform the actual work. Both parts can run on the same CPU, or more than likely for scalability reasons, they will be spread over multiple machines or CPUs on the same machine. The server worker containers obtain the data required to fulfill a task from a data server (a DBMS).

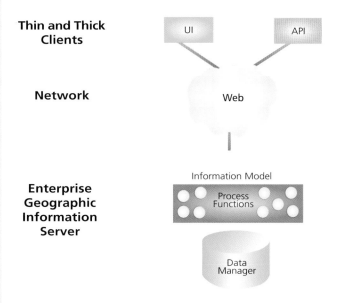

Thin and Thick Clients

Network

Enterprise Geographic Information Server

Figure 5. Conceptual view of an Enterprise Geographic Information System architecture.

These architectures form the basic design patterns for GIS-based spatial analysis and modeling systems. Presently, the project (desktop) pattern dominates the spatial analysis and modeling field, but as the demand for analysis and modeling solutions increases, as it surely will, the client–server, and especially the centralized/distributed architecture pattern, will become more important. This has important implications for spatial analysis and modeling software architects and implementers. For example, under the multitier pattern, models can be compiled on desktop computers which have strong interactive graphical capabilities and then executed on high-performance middle-tier servers optimized for complex, computation-intensive tasks. In this way, model access can be distributed throughout an organization, or indeed the public Internet, and accessed from thin-client systems. This also opens up the possibility of parallelizing models so that they can be executed in shorter time periods.

CURRENT CAPABILITIES OF GIS FOR SPATIAL ANALYSIS AND MODELING

There are many commercial and public-domain GIS software systems. All have visualization and data storage and transformation functions, but only a few have anything other than rudimentary spatial analysis and modeling capabilities (for useful compilations of Web links, see www.ai-geostats.org/software/index.htm and www.csiss.org/clearinghouse/links.php3). Much the dominant player in terms of install base and capabilities is ESRI ArcGIS which has extensive vector and raster tools (www.esri.com); Krivoruchko and Gotway Crawford (2005, this volume), and Maidment and Robayo (2005, this volume) both use it extensively. In the image/raster domain, Clark Labs Idrisi (www.clarklabs.org, Eastman et al. 2005, this volume), PCRaster Environmental Software (www.pcraster.nl, Burrough et al.

2005, this volume), GRASS (Neteler and Mitasova 2004), and Leica Geosystems' ERDAS IMAGINE (gis.leica-geosystems.com) have the strongest support for spatial analysis and modeling. As far as the social and economic sciences are concerned, the choices are more limited, but the public domain software GeoDa has some elegant tools for exploratory spatial data analysis (ESDA) (sal.agecon.uiuc.edu/geoda_main.php, Anselin 2005, this volume).

Before exploring the options for integrating GIS and spatial analysis and modeling systems, we need to understand the motivations for linking these two types of systems together. Although GIS are constantly evolving systems, we can evaluate the capabilities of the current generation of systems according to their suitability for spatial analysis and modeling. The main strengths of GIS for spatial analysis and modeling were discussed in Goodchild and Longley (2005). At the more generic and architectural level, they can be summarized as follows:

- Data management. GIS provide an environment in which to manage and model massive input and output data sets, as well as temporary data sets created during analyses. They can also manage metadata about model parameters. More than this, a GIS can be a source of data for analysis and modeling. The versioning capabilities of GIS can also be used to handle design alternatives or model scenarios.

- Data integration/transformation. Today's GIS usually offer an extensive collection of tools for loading, reformatting, transforming, and integrating data. This could be as simple as reprojecting several files to a common map projection or could involve many steps to transform data into a common database structure. GIS are also adept at bringing together disparate data and workers operating in different disciplines.

- Visualization/mapping. GIS have excellent mapping capabilities. They are especially strong at static 2D and 2.5D mapping and visualization. Some systems can display 2.5D scenes and moving objects in near real time, and some also offer basic ESDA facilities.

- Spatial analysis and modeling capabilities. In recent years, basic GIS software systems have been extended with an ever-more-sophisticated range of spatial analysis and modeling options. The main areas in which GIS software systems are strong include:

    - Vector processing (overlay, proximity, clip, etc.)
    - Raster map analysis including map algebra (Tomlin 1990) and surface interpolation/analysis
    - Image analysis, processing, and visualization
    - Surface visualization and analysis using TIN data structures and algorithms
    - Network analysis including pathfinding, service areas, territory design, and operations research optimization based on origin-destination matrices
    - Basic spatial interaction and location allocation modeling
    - Simple geostatistical analysis (e.g., kriging)

- Model specification and execution. Software such as ArcGIS ModelBuilder allows models to be authored and executed in a graphical environment. Not only is this a simple and productive way to author and revise models, but it also is a convenient way to document and share them.

- Customization/Scripting/Interfacing. Typically, all of the capabilities described above can be accessed via end-user graphical and command-line interfaces and are exposed via well-defined application programming interfaces (APIs). This allows for workflow automation, interface customization, and system extensibility and interfacing. Scripting is particularly important as a mechanism for implementing dynamic models that encompass state changes and feedback mechanisms. Recently in GIS there has been a move to use industry-standard low-level programming languages (e.g., Java™, C++, and Visual Basic®) and scripting languages (e.g., Python, VBScript, and JScript®), rather than proprietary, home-grown scripting languages. Today there is really no performance or development tool difference in programming within a GIS framework versus outside or in another system.

- Knowledge dissemination. A key advantage of using a GIS for spatial analysis and modeling is that it provides a connection to the business and policy formulation processes of organizations. GIS are already widely used in many enterprises, and they can be used as a medium to disseminate the results of analytical operations. Moreover, they are a persuasive tool in projects that involve public participation and decision making by senior managers (Craig et al. 2002).

Of course there is no such thing as perfect software for spatial analysis and modeling, and here we list some of the more fundamental and pressing issues. This is based in part on the University Consortium on GIS (UCGIS) research agenda (www.ucgis.org/priorities/research/2002researchagenda.htm). Many of these topics are addressed in the later chapters of this book:

- True 3D/4D modeling. Extending GIS from 2.5D to true 3D and 4D (x,y,z and t [time]) remains a challenge (Peuquet 2002). This is especially the case for those interested in modeling the lithosphere (e.g., mining geology), hydrosphere (e.g., ocean ecosystems), and atmosphere (e.g., global circulation). There are some promising areas of work that are extending the current frontiers, but much more remains to be done. For example, ArcGIS Tracking Analyst can handle temporal data, and Maidment and Robayo (2005, this volume) show how to work with hydrological time-series data in ArcGIS.

- Error and uncertainty. The subjects of error and uncertainty are fundamental to spatial analysis and modeling (Zhang and Goodchild 2002). UCGIS highlights the need to study and understand the mechanics of how uncertainty arises in geographic data and how it is propagated through GIS-based data analyses. It also advocates the development of techniques for reducing, quantifying, and visually representing uncertainty in geographic data and for analyzing and predicting the propagation of this uncertainty through GIS-based data analyses. The work of Krivoruchko and Gotway Crawford (2005, this volume) and Anselin (2005, this volume), among others, demonstrates that software solutions to this problem are tractable.

- Dynamic feedback/simulation modeling. Today's GIS are very much a product of their roots in static map-based analysis and their considerable success at managing natural and physical resources as assets (Batty 2005, this volume). The real world, however, is fuzzy, uncertain, and dynamic, and to be successful at characterizing and simulating real-world processes, GIS must be able to incorporate multidimensional space–time modeling. The absence of these capabilities is all the more surprising given the richness of implementations in nongeographic modeling and simulation software systems, for example, GoldSim (Miller et al. 2005, this volume) and STELLA (Maxwell and Voinov 2005, this volume). There are some encouraging signs that ArcGIS, Idrisi, and PCRaster now support some dynamic simulation capabilities through scripting.

- Spatial analysis and spatial statistics. It is now well understood that much of classical statistics is inappropriate for exploring, describing, and testing hypotheses on geographic data (Bailey and Gatrell 1995, O'Sullivan and Unwin 2003). There is a real need for GIS to support, directly or indirectly through an interface to external systems, advanced spatial analysis and statistical functions. At the most basic level, the requirement is for descriptive and exploratory spatial data analysis tools of the sort described by Anselin (2005, this volume). The need also extends to improved geostatistical estimation procedures as discussed by Krivoruchko and Gotway Crawford (2005, this volume) as well as confirmatory spatial statistical procedures. Significant progress has been made on adding spatial interaction, location–allocation, and operational research optimization techniques to GIS software (e.g., ArcGIS 9.1), but much more remains to be done before commercial GIS can be effective in these domains.

In summary, we can say that current GIS offer many important capabilities that are of great value to spatial analysts and modelers. In simple terms, GIS takes a lot of the hard (grunt) work out of day-to-day tasks such as data management, transformation, and visualization. This allows scientists to concentrate on the major activities of understanding data and the patterns and processes that they represent. Already, there are some important foundation spatial and modeling capabilities in existing systems. Also, GIS software is evolving very rapidly, and systems are nothing if not adaptable and extensible. There is every prospect that even some of the more challenging deficiencies of spatial analysis and modeling will be tackled in the not-too-distant future.

**CONTINUUM OF GIS
AND MODELING
SYSTEMS**

Faced with the task of analyzing or modeling the geographic elements of some aspects of the world, the modeler has a number of software architecture choices. These choices can be arranged along an axis from GIS-centric, via linked GIS and modeling, to modeling-centric software systems (table 1). Other external examples, as shown in table 1 and discussed below, help to show the breadth of work that has been undertaken in recent years and also the diversity of architectural patterns and linkages. These form a supplement to the examples discussed later in the other chapters in this book. In particular, the chapter by Parker (2005, this volume) discusses system integration.

Software Architecture	Characteristics	Examples from This Volume	Other Examples
GIS-centric Systems	• Extend GIS software system • GIS look and feel • Single GUI, information model, data management, etc. • Built using low- or high-level (scripting) programming • Geographic focus is explicit	• Krivoruchko and Gotway Crawford:4 (Geostatistical estimation, ArcGIS) • Birkin:11 (Retail and service planning, MapInfo) • Israelson and Frederiksen:13 (Urban transportation, ArcGIS) • Maidment et al:15 (Hydrological catchments, ArcGIS) • Burrough et al.:16 (Dynamic environmental spatial modeling, PCRaster) • Eastman et al.:17 (Land-cover change, IDRISI) • Ahearn and Smith:18 (Individual-based and Hidden Markov animal models) • Parker:19 (Agent-based models of land use)	• NatureServe Vista (Ecosystem management) • CATS (Emergency response) • MIKE BASIN (Hydrologic basins)
Linked GIS-Modeling Systems	• Loose- and close-coupled options • Two UIs, data models, data management, etc. • Custom file translation or software linkage	• Batty:3 (Pedestrians, MapInfo) • Batty and Xie:8 (Urban growth, ArcGIS) • Wegener:10 (Urban land-use transportation) • Yeh: 14 (Planning, ArcView)	• SLEUTH (Land-use estimation) • RAMAS GIS (Ecological population simulation) • TRANUS-ArcGIS (Transport Planning)
Modeling-centric Systems	• Extend public-domain and commercial modeling systems • Modeling system look and feel • Single GUI, information model, data management, etc. • Limited tools for visualization, data transformation, etc.	• Anselin:5 (ESDA with embedded GIS, MapObjects) • Miller et al.:6 (Ecological systems dynamics, GoldSim) • Maxwell and Voinov:7 (Ecological system dynamics, STELLA) • Bian and Liebner: 12 (Epidemiology, MATLAB) • Duh and Brown:20 (Landscape patterns)	• SWARM (Wildfire management) • RePast (Infectious diseases, civil violence, etc.)

Table 1. Software architecture choices for GIS, spatial analysis, and modeling with illustrative examples.

GIS-CENTRIC MODELING SYSTEMS

The core capabilities of GIS software systems for spatial analysis and modeling were outlined in the previous section. There are many examples of spatial analysis and modeling application solutions built on top of commercially available GIS. Three examples can be used to show the types of systems that have been created to date.

- NatureServe Vista is a GIS-based decision-support software system developed by NatureServe for land-use and conservation planners. It is implemented within the ArcGIS software framework using GIS scripting and interface builder capabilities (www.natureserve.org/library/factsheet_nature-serve_vista.pdf). The purpose of NatureServe Vista is to help planners understand local ecosystems, identify high-priority lands and waters, and evaluate competing land-use plans. It is an example of a model that exists entirely within and adopts the design pattern of the GIS software platform.

- One of the best-known, publicly available GIS-based modeling software systems for emergency response planning is CATS (Consequences Assessment Tool Set). CATS is a disaster analysis system for natural and technological hazards that runs inside ArcGIS (Greene 2002). It can be used before, during, and after a disaster strikes. CATS provides a package of hazard prediction models (natural hazards and technological hazards) and casualty and damage assessment tools. It also accepts real-time data from local meteorological stations. CATS is supplied with over 150 data and map layers. These include the location of resources to support response to specific hazards, infrastructure objects and facilities (communications, electric power, oil and gas, emergency services, government, transportation, water supply, etc.), a variety of population breakouts, and much more. It also offers the user the opportunity to add data for custom analysis. This is a relatively simple deterministic model which includes base data for cartographic analysis within the core system. It relies on the GIS framework for model access and interaction.

- For basin-scale hydrologic simulations, MIKE BASIN from the Danish Hydraulic Institute builds on a network model in which branches represent individual stream sections, and the nodes represent confluences, diversions, reservoirs, or water users (Jha and Das Gupta 2003). MIKE BASIN has been built within ArcGIS, and the user interface has been expanded accordingly so that the network elements can be edited by simply right-clicking on the screen to access context-sensitive tools. Technically, MIKE BASIN is a quasi-steady-state mass balance model that allows for routed river flows. It estimates water quality using purely advective transport; decay during transport can also be modeled. The groundwater description uses the linear reservoir equation. Typical areas of application are: water availability analysis such as optimization of conjunctive surface and groundwater use; infrastructure planning such as irrigation potential, reservoir performance, water supply capacity, and wastewater treatment requirements; analysis of multisectoral demands to find equitable trade-offs for domestic, industry, agriculture, hydropower, navigation, recreation, ecological uses; ecosystem studies such as water quality, minimum discharge requirements, sustainable yield, effects of global change; and regulation: such as water rights, priorities, and water quality compliance.

LINKED GIS AND MODELING SYSTEMS

In situations where GIS and modeling systems already exist (e.g., as commercial products) or the cost of rebuilding the capabilities of one type of system within another is too great, the GIS and modeling systems can be linked together. There are many different approaches for linking software systems together (Maguire 1995), and this is a subset of the much larger fields of enterprise application integration (EAI) (Linthicum 2000) and software interoperability (Sondheim et al. 1997). Westervelt (2002) compares different approaches to GIS and modeling software integration in terms of tightness of integration (table 2). Tight integration can be achieved by, for example, object-component interface calls, or function calls. Moderate integration uses techniques such as remote procedure calls and shared database access. Loose coupling employs common file structures, file translators, and more recently, Web services messaging.

	Loose	Moderate	Tight
Time to integrate	Fast	Medium	Slow
Programmer expertise	Low	High	Medium
Execution speed	Slow	Medium	Fast
Simultaneous execution capability	Low	Low	High
Debugging	Easy	Moderate	Hard

Table 2. Comparison of approaches to GIS and modeling system integration (after Westervelt 2002).

Currently the most popular approach to GIS, spatial analysis, and modeling is to link existing systems together, either loosely or closely. Three examples will help to illustrate the features of such linkages.

- SLEUTH is the evolutionary product of the Clarke Urban Growth Model that uses cellular automata, terrain mapping, and land-cover deltatron modeling to address urban growth (Clark and Gaydos 1998). It has been successfully implemented in San Francisco, Chicago, Washington-Baltimore, Sioux Falls, and the South Coast of California. The system generates multiple land-use layers that predict future development scenarios for a study region. These are used to guide local community planners in achieving desired smart and responsible urban growth throughout the region. The long-term goal of the project is to develop these tools to best predict urban growth on a regional, continental, and eventually global scale. The software is able to interface with a range of commercial GIS software systems via file exchange. GIS systems are simply used as a data source, and so a simple linkage is adequate.

- RAMAS GIS is designed to link GIS with a metapopulation model for population viability analysis and extinction risk assessment (Akçakaya et al. 2004). Habitats used by most species are becoming increasingly fragmented, requiring a metapopulation modeling approach to risk analysis. Recognizing habitat patchiness from an endangered species' point of view requires spatial information on habitat suitability. RAMAS GIS meets both these requirements by linking metapopulation modeling with landscape data and GIS technology. Spatial data, such as vegetation cover, land-use, or any other map that contains information on some aspect of the habitat that is important for the species (temperature, precipitation, slope, aspect, etc.), is imported as files from ArcGIS, GRASS, or Idrisi. A patch-recognition algorithm is used to identify areas of high suitability for subpopulation survival. If predictions are available about how habitat may change in the future (e.g., as a result of forest growth or logging), this type of time-series information can be used as input into the metapopulation model. The metapopulation model combines the spatial information on the metapopulation with user-input ecological parameters of the species to complete the metapopulation model and predict the risk of species extinction, time to extinction, expected occupancy rates, and metapopulation abundance. Multiple simulations allow sensitivity analysis of model performance. Here again, GIS software is used only as a source of base data for the models.

- Evans and Steadman (2003) describe how they linked TRANUS, a land-use transport model developed by Modelistica from Caracas, Venezuela, with ArcGIS using binary file transfer. ArcGIS software's underlying ArcObjects™ technology was used to create a custom loader. A major motivation for this work was enabling the outputs from a transportation model to be rapidly viewed in a consistent manner as a map. ArcGIS is also used to calculate specific indicators through cartographic modeling and as a switch yard to disseminate information to other software packages. This work has allowed the development of more policy-relevant environmental, social, and economic indicators rather than simple transport and land-use variables as has been the case in the past.

MODELING-CENTRIC SYSTEMS

There has been considerable interest in recent years in extending generic modeling software systems into the geographic domain. This is due in no small part to the development of software packages with scripting capabilities that do not require advanced computer programming skills and can be extended with spatial capabilities (Gilbert and Bankes 2002). Among the best-known and most widely used of these software systems are SWARM (SWARM Development Group 2005), RePast (Collier 2003), STELLA (Costanza and Gottlieb 1998, Maxwell and Voinov 2005, this volume), and GoldSim (Miller et al. 2005, this volume). Box (2002) reviews a range of agent-based and cellular automata spatial models in the areas of hydrologic processes, urban growth, wildfires, forest dynamics, lava flows, and groundwater flow; Grove et al. (2002) provide a similar review for urban systems, rural systems, health, epidemiology, pollution, and hydrology.

- Box (2002) describes a general-purpose Cellular Automata (CA) toolkit for conducting simulation-based experiments on landscape models built with GIS data layers. The GIS-CA toolkit was derived from the SWARM libraries which are licensed under GNU general protection. The primary purpose of the SWARM libraries according to Box (2002) is that they deal with many of the more difficult programming issues when implementing simulation models, especially simulation of truly independent agents that are acting in parallel but are processed by a sequential computer. This allows model developers to concentrate on higher-level issues, rather than on the detail of agent behavior. The GIS-CA toolkit is able to read raster data layers from ArcGIS and GRASS and has been used in several applications, including dynamic wildfire simulation modeling.

- The Recursive Porous Agent Simulation Toolkit (RePast), originally developed by Sallach, Collier, Howe, North, and others at the University of Chicago, is one of the leading agent-based modeling toolkits (Tobias and Hofmann 2004). The RePast system, including the source code, is available directly from the Web (repast.sourceforge.net/index.html). There are interfaces for the Java, .Net, and Python languages. According to the RePast Web site: "Our goal with RePast is to move beyond the representation of agents as discrete, self-contained entities in favor of a view of social actors as permeable, interleaved, and mutually defining, with cascading and recombinant motives. We intend to support the modeling of belief systems, agents, organizations, and institutions as recursive social constructions." RePast 3.0 has a variety of features including the following:

  - A fully concurrent discrete event scheduler that supports both sequential and parallel discrete event operations
  - Built-in simulation results, logging, and graphing tools
  - Automated Monte Carlo simulation framework
  - A range of two-dimensional agent environments and visualizations
  - The ability to dynamically access and modify agent properties, agent behavioral equations, and model properties at run time
  - Libraries for genetic algorithms, neural networks, random number generation, and specialized mathematics
  - Built-in systems dynamics modeling, social network, and modeling support tools
  - Integrated geographical information systems (GIS) support
  - Fully implemented in a variety of languages including Java and C++
  - Runs on virtually all modern computing platforms including Windows, Mac OS®, and Linux® (The platform support includes both personal computers and large-scale scientific computing clusters.)

- Dibble and Feldman (2004) describe a general suite of RePast-based tools for developing models of mobile heterogeneous agents on richly structured organizational and geographic landscapes. They have used these tools to build models of epidemics of infectious diseases, dynamics of civil violence, and social networks connecting geographically mobile team members.

CONCLUSION

It will be obvious from the foregoing discussion and also the other chapters in this book that there has been considerable progress in spatial analysis and modeling in a GIS context in recent years. Both GIS-centric and modeling-centric software systems have been extended so that social and environmental scientists with limited programming skills can now undertake quite sophisticated analytical and modeling work. There has also been great progress in linking GIS and modeling systems together using mainstream IT techniques such as file extract-transform-load (ETL), systems function calls, RPC, and Web services messaging. While much of the core modeling software originated in the open source community, the alternative commercial-off-the-shelf (COTS) software model is also well represented. In the GIS world, the reverse is true: the COTS software approach dominates, although there are some useful public-domain libraries.

The existing software systems are quite variable in terms of the maturity of their spatial analysis and modeling capabilities. Several areas of geographic analysis and modeling are now quite well developed including: cartographic modeling, geostatistical estimation, network analysis, raster analysis, vector overlay, and visualization (2D and 3D). Other areas that represent work in progress and would benefit from future attention include ESDA, dynamic system simulation, operations research optimization, spatial statistics, and visualization of multidimensional data.

REFERENCES

Akçakaya, H. R., M. Burgman, O. Kindvall, C. Wood, P. Sjögren-Gulve, J. Hatfield, and M. McCarthy, eds. 2004. *Species conservation and management: Case studies.* Oxford: Oxford University Press.

Arctur, D., and M. Zeiler. 2004. *Designing geodatabases: Case studies in GIS data modeling.* Redlands, Calif.: ESRI Press.

Bailey, T. C., and A. C. Gatrell. 1995. *Interactive spatial data analysis.* Harlow: Longman Scientific and Technical.

Box, P. 2002. Spatial units as agents: Making the landscape an equal player in agent-based simulations. In *Integrating geographic information systems and agent-based modeling techniques for simulating social and ecological processes,* ed. H. R. Gimblett, 59–82. Oxford: Oxford University Press.

Brail, R. K., and R. E. Klosterman, eds. 2001. *Planning support systems: Integrating geographic information systems, models and visualization tools.* Redlands, Calif.: ESRI Press.

Chambers, J. 1999. Computing with data: Concepts and challenges. *The American Statistician* 53: 73–84. cm.bell-labs.com/stat/doc/Neyman98.ps.

———. 2000. Users, programmers, and statistical software. *ASA Journal of Computational and Graphical Statistics.* cm.bell-labs.com/stat/doc/jmcJCGS2000.ps.

Clarke, K. C., and L. J. Gaydos. 1998. Loose-coupling a cellular automation model and GIS: Long-term urban growth prediction for San Francisco and Washington/Baltimore. *Geographical Information Science* 12: 699–714.

Clarke, K. C., B. O. Parks, and M. P. Crane, eds. 2001. *Geographic information systems and environmental modeling.* Upper Saddle River, N.J.: Prentice Hall.

Coleman, D. J. 1999. Geographical information systems in networked environments. In *Geographic information systems: Principles, techniques, application and management,* ed. P. A. Longley, M. F. Goodchild, D. J. Maguire, and D. W. Rhind, 317–29. New York: John Wiley and Sons.

Collier, N. 2003. RePast: An extensible framework for agent simulation. web.archive.org/web/20031115181952/repast.sourceforge.net/docs/repast_intro_final.doc.

Costanza, R., and S. Gottlieb. 1998. Modeling ecological and economic systems with STELLA: Part II. *Ecological Modeling* 112 (2-3): 81–4.

Craig, W. J., T. M. Harris, and D. Weiner. 2002. *Community participation and geographic information systems.* London: Taylor & Francis.

Dibble, C., and P. G. Feldman. 2004. The GeoGraph 3D Computational Laboratory: Network and terrain landscapes for RePast. *Journal of Artificial Societies and Social Simulation* 7(1): jasss.soc.surrey.ac.uk/7/1/7.html.

Evans, S., and J. P. Steadman. 2003. Interfacing land-use transportation models with GIS: The Inverness model. In *Advanced spatial analysis: The CASA book of GIS,* ed. P. A. Longley and M. Batty, 290–307. Redlands, Calif.: ESRI Press.

Fotheringham, A. S., and M. Wegener, eds. 2000. *Spatial models and GIS: New potential and new models.* London: Taylor & Francis.

Gilbert. N., and S. Bankes. 2002. Platforms and methods for agent-based modeling. *Proceedings of the National Academy of Sciences of the USA* 99: 7197–8. Washington, D.C.: National Academy of Sciences of the U.S.A.

Gimblett, H. R., ed. 2002. *Integrating geographic information systems and agent-based modeling techniques for simulating social and ecological processes.* Oxford: Oxford University Press.

Goodchild, M. F., L. T. Steyaert, B. O. Parks, C. Johnston, D. Maidment, M. P. Crane, and S. Glendinning, eds. 1996. *GIS and environmental modeling: Progress and research issues*. Fort Collins, Colo.: GIS World.

Goodchild, M. F., and P. A. Longley. 2005. The future of GIS and spatial analysis. In *Geographical information systems: Principles, techniques, management and applications*, ed. P. A. Longley, M. F. Goodchild, D. J. Maguire, and D. W. Rhind, 567–80. Hoboken, N.J.: John Wiley and Sons.

Gray, J., D. T. Liu, M. Nieto-Santisban, A. S. Szalay, D. DeWitt, and G. Herber. 2005. Scientific data management in the coming decade. *Technical Report MSR-TR-2005-10*. research.microsoft.com/research/pubs/view.aspx?tr_id=860.

Greene, R. W. 2002. *Confronting catastrophe: A GIS handbook*. Redlands, Calif.: ESRI Press.

Grove, M., C. Schweik, T. Evans, and G. Green. 2002. Modeling human-environmental systems. In *Geographic information systems and environmental modeling*, ed. K. C. Clarke, B. O. Parks, and M. P. Crane, 160–88. Upper Saddle River, N.J.: Prentice Hall.

Jha, M. K., and A. Das Gupta. 2003. Application of Mike Basin for water management strategies in a watershed. *Water International* 28: 27–35.

Linthicum, D. S. 2000. *Enterprise application integration*. Boston: Addison-Wesley.

Longley, P. A., M. F. Goodchild, D. J. Maguire, and D. W. Rhind. 2005. *Geographic information systems and science*. Hoboken, N.J.: John Wiley and Sons.

Maguire, D. J. 1995. Implementing spatial analysis and GIS applications for business and service planning. In *GIS for Business and Service Planning*, ed. P. A. Longley and G. Clarke, 171–91. Cambridge: GeoInformation International.

———. 1999. GIS customization. In *Geographical information systems: Principles, techniques, management and applications*, ed. P. A. Longley, M. F. Goodchild, D. J. Maguire, and D. W. Rhind, 359–69. Hoboken, N.J.: John Wiley and Sons.

Maidment, D. R. 2002. *Arc Hydro: GIS for water resources*. Redlands, Calif.: ESRI Press.

Netler, M., and H. Mitasova. 2004. *Open source GIS: A GRASS GIS approach*. 2nd ed. Boston: Kluwer.

O'Sullivan, D., and D. J. Unwin. 2003. *Geographic information analysis*. Hoboken, N.J.: John Wiley and Sons.

Peuquet, D., 2002. *Representations of space and time*. New York: Guilford.

Sondheim, M., K. Gardels, and K. Buehler. 1997. GIS interoperability. In *Geographical information systems: Principles, techniques, management and applications*, ed. P. A. Longley, M. F. Goodchild, D. J. Maguire, and D. W. Rhind, 347–58. Hoboken, N.J.: John Wiley and Sons.

Stillwell, J., and G. Clarke, eds. 2002. *Applied GIS and spatial analysis.* Chichester: John Wiley and Sons.

Swarm Development Group. 2005. Swarm 2.2. wiki.swarm.org.

Tobias, R., and C. Hofmann. 2004. Evaluation of free Java-libraries for social-scientific agent-based simulation. *Journal of Artificial Societies and Social Simulation* 7 (1): jasss.soc.surrey.ac.uk/7/1/6.html.

Tomlin, C. D. 1990. *Geographic information systems and cartographic modeling.* Englewood Cliffs, N.J.: Prentice Hall.

Westervelt, J. D. 2002. Geographic information systems and agent-based modeling. In *Integrating geographic information systems and agent-based modeling techniques for simulating social and ecological processes,* ed. H. R. Gimblett, 83–103. Oxford: Oxford University Press.

Zeiler, M. 1999. *Modeling our world: The ESRI guide to database design.* Redlands, Calif.: ESRI Press.

Zeiler, M., ed. 2001. *Exploring ArcObjects.* Redlands, Calif.: ESRI Press.

Zhang, J. X., and M. F. Goodchild. 2002. *Uncertainty in geographical information.* New York: Taylor & Francis.

Chapter 3

Approaches to Modeling in GIS: Spatial Representation and Temporal Dynamics

MICHAEL BATTY

CENTRE FOR ADVANCED SPATIAL ANALYSIS

UNIVERSITY COLLEGE LONDON

LONDON, UNITED KINGDOM

ABSTRACT

This chapter outlines a number of new approaches to spatial modeling which provide challenges for integration within geographic information systems (GIS). We begin by outlining a generic framework for thinking about how objects or agents and their aggregations interact and change in space and time, and we then illustrate how these ideas are being conceptualized in terms of cellular environments and agent-based behaviors. We identify different ways in which dynamics can be incorporated into models and suggest a series of processes that characterize the various models presented in the rest of this book. We illustrate a veritable cornucopia of model processes, all of which are difficult to represent within a single proprietary GIS, and we then define how some of these more challenging conceptions of dynamics involving spatial learning are generating quite different models which require their own software functions. Our example is an agent-based model in which pedestrians not only move within a local environment using obstacle avoidance but also seek to satisfy given higher-level goals based on quite sophisticated economic decision making. We conclude with a brief summary of the key challenges to integrating these new varieties of model within GIS.

Alan de Botton (2003), in his popular philosophy The *Art of Travel*, tells us that artistic accounts of people and places "involve severe abbreviations of what reality will force upon us" (p. 14) when we eventually come face-to-face with the situation in question. Art simplifies just as models collapse reality into a form that enables us to communicate the essence of a phenomenon to those who need to understand the world so that they might understand it, act upon it, or simply experience it for its own sake. As Morrison and Morgan (1999) say, modeling "is a tacit skill, and has to be learnt not taught" (p. 12). It acts as a bridge between the way we theorize about the world and the way the world looks to us in empirical terms. In chapter 1, Goodchild (2005, this volume) talks of models as being representations of spatial data and the processes that change them and there are many other definitions of models and modeling which readers will come across as they traverse the pages of this book. But all have in common the notion that models provide *abbreviations*: simplifications or abstractions that simplify in communicating ideas to a range of stakeholders, from scientists like those who are writing in this book to less scientifically informed publics who nonetheless have a central interest in what is being communicated.

The visual domain has become one of the most important ways of communicating spatial problems to a wide range of interests, particularly where the phenomena in question can be represented in digital form. Geographical systems are intrinsically visual because their clearest and most superficial form is in Euclidean space, whereby we can simplify their representation to two- and three-dimensional forms. GIS has thus become a powerful medium for communicating models of geographical/spatial systems in a wide variety of disciplines and from many different perspectives. Its software has rapidly developed to evolve ever more sophisticated visual representations and interfaces. Indeed, one of the cutting-edge developments is 3D GIS which is rapidly eclipsing and converging with computer aided design (CAD) systems, particularly in the building and architectural domains. However, new theories and applications, driven by new imperatives about how we must understand geographical systems on the one hand (science) and how we might change them on the other (design and policy), continue to tax the limits of GIS software. New representations of space and time and processes that link together different spaces and times are continually being invented. In fact, during the last twenty years as GIS has come of age, new conceptions of how we must deal with space and time in their geography have paralleled the development of GIS software, revealing a continuing but essential tension between GIS and modeling (Peuquet 2002).

In this chapter, we will focus on how new approaches to geographical theory in many different domains—from human to physical—are being represented as computer models which require GIS for everything from their storage of data to the operation of their processes. These are made available to the user through some visual medium, most obviously the map, the surface landscape, and the built form. But from these immediate visualizations, deeper patterns of interaction and association that GIS is focused on extracting and explaining remain the focus. We begin by sketching a generic model of spatial representation, interaction, and process which we use to illustrate the particular bias of many geographical models. This cannot embrace all the characteristics of every model, but it is sufficient to emphasize how space and time intersect and interact, and it enables us to illustrate the limits of conventional GIS software and the key challenges that need to be met. Many of these challenges are addressed specifically in the chapters that follow. We will then map this model onto a variety of new approaches to spatial modeling, noting particularly the way in which scales have become finer and how temporal change has become increasingly important. In particular, we will illustrate how cellular conceptions of space and mobile agents capture these requirements.

We will then illustrate how these new approaches can be embodied in particular applications. Cells and agents form the basis of very fine-scale modeling in which human agents search local space. We will present a model of pedestrian movement developed by Ward (2005) which identifies how physical form affects spatial interaction and vice versa and how within this representation, agents move to some purpose, learning from their environment and from each other. The example in question is only loosely coupled to GIS, but there are many avenues both within these kinds of model and within state-of-the-art GIS software which enable a much closer coupling. As software in general and GIS in particular breaks itself open on the desktop and the Web, a multitude of hooks and sinkers are forming that will enable much more integrated modeling in GIS than anything we have seen hitherto. This chapter presents ways in which new approaches to modeling might be supported by these new directions in GIS which are extensively discussed in the chapters that follow.

A GENERIC FRAMEWORK FOR GEOGRAPHICAL MODELS

Traditional geographies begin with describing how physical and human activities organize themselves in commonsense conceptions of space as depicted by the two-dimensional map. This spatial bias is deeply entrenched in theory and largely explains why geographic information systems essentially deal with spatial and physical structures at a cross section in time. However, from this starting point, most theorists agree that spatial processes are the real focus, and this inevitably involves the temporal dimension. In classifying models, space and time are thus central, and we will characterize them in discrete terms, notwithstanding the fact that we could easily transform our representations into the continuous realm as Goodchild (2005 this volume) notes in chapter 1. Our basic or atomic element is an entity, object, or agent k defined by an attribute or value p whose location is given by i and whose existence is predicated at time t, thus providing the composite variable p_{it}^{k}. This suffices to generate a multitude of possible changes in state which define a range of models that certainly cover all of those introduced in this book. A spatial process can thus be defined as a mapping through space and time whose transformation can be written as $p_{jt+1}^{\ell} \leftarrow f[p_{it}^{k}]$. This might be described as the position of object-agent ℓ in location j at time t+1 which is some function of the position i of object k at a previous time period t, from which a trajectory of change at this elemental level can be constructed. There are no restrictions in principle on how one object can influence or interact with another or on the locations of the respective objects, but there is a major constraint posed by time in that it is irreversible.

In fact, this kind of transformation can be generalized in that any object or set of objects at any location or set of locations at any previous time or set of times can influence the position of any object at the current time. That is $p^\ell_{jt+1} \leftarrow f[p^k_{it}, any\ k \in N\ and\ any\ \tau \in T, \tau = 0,1,...,t]$ where N is the total set of objects in the system and T is the total number of time periods, and where it is clear that time lags of any length can be present in the pattern of influence. If a model of a spatial process were to be specified in this kind of detail (and this is rare), then intermediate flow variables which explicitly track the changes in states are usually defined, as for example $m^{k\ell}_{ijtt+1}$. Correlations between all patterns which are generated within such a movement structure $\{m^{k\ell}_{ijtt+1}\}$ exist, and these form the essence of data analysis which is an important objective in the application of GIS.

It is now quite easy to see how restricted contemporary GIS is with respect to the multitude of interactions over space and time and between objects which this framework implies. Usually geographic information is recorded at one point in time, and the focus is on the spatial correlations within the distribution of objects $\{p^k_{it}\}$ with respect to the organization of locations $\{i\}$. Associations or implicit interactions across space comparing $\{p^k_{it}\}$ with $\{p^\ell_{jt}\}$ are sometimes the focus where the operators in question relate to the network of connections between $\{i\}$ and $\{j\}$ as implied in $\{m^{k\ell}_{ijt}\}$ and their concomitant processes such as diffusion. But such network representations, although existing within GIS software, tend to defer to point and area representations, hence the relatively poorly developed applications of GIS in transportation modeling as Israelsen and Frederiksen (2005, this volume) report in chapter 13. In fact, temporal analysis which involves tracing correlations in spatial patterns between different time periods and which is at the basis of all dynamic modeling is not undeveloped in GIS, but it is elementary in its characterization of spatial processes. As many readers already know, the data layer model is central to GIS where data is conceived of as layers and is operated upon using various forms of map algebra where different layers are factored and/or combined. So, for example, the same distribution at two points in time $\{p^k_{it}\}$ and $\{p^k_{it+1}\}$ implying movement or change $\{m^{kk}_{iitt+1}\}$ can be measured by simply assuming that changes through time are represented by additional layers and that map algebra can be invoked to generate transformations of these layers through time. Rarely, however, does GIS software extend to applications where changes through space and time, that is $\{m^{kk}_{ijtt+1}\}$ and/or $\{m^{k\ell}_{ijtt+1}\}$, are simulated.

We picture this framework in figure 1 where we show how objects at different locations in space relate to new locations at future time periods and to other objects in the same set of locations. Here we have five locations (as circles) with four objects in four of the initial locations (as solid circles) from which a series of trajectories can be generated as the figure implies. For example, if we pick object 1, which is in location 3 at time t, this moves to location 2 at time t+1 and then back to its original location at time t+2. This kind of recording is essential for agent-based models as implied in our example of pedestrian modeling below. However, within most proprietary GIS software, it is difficult, although never impossible, to record such intricate paths in space and time. In terms of figure 1, most GIS software is good at examining the patterns in the set of objects and their locations at a cross section in time and is sometimes used for examining changes in locations and objects between different cross sections. But detailed interactions in both space and time which are the focus of true dynamic modeling are hard to track.

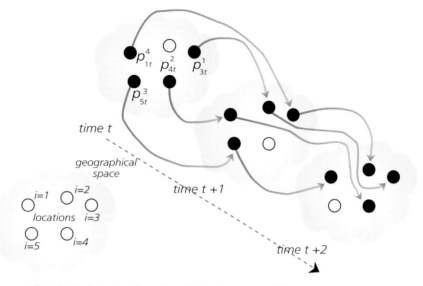

Figure 1. Detailed trajectories of moving objects in space and time.

There have been many classifications of models, and within GIS, spatial representation is used to encode data that reflects both iconic models in terms of their geometry—cityscapes, buildings, and landscapes—as well as symbolic models based on formal, usually mathematical processes. The focus of modeling in this book is on the latter. But at this point, a more appropriate distinction is between descriptive models and predictive (Lowry 1965). Descriptive analysis of cross-sectional geographic structures is the workhorse of GIS. Here the distribution of individuals or objects $\{p_{it}^k\}$ with respect to their spatial associations as well as aggregations of these objects into groups, such as $\{P_{it} = \sum_{k \in Z_i} p_{it}^k\}$ where Z_i is the set of individuals in location i, is central. But even using such direct analysis, simple predictive models can be built. If many different objects are associated with the range of locations, defined as $\{P_{it}\}$, $\{Q_{it}\}$, $\{R_{it}\}$, and so on, then these can form layers in a GIS. They can be combined in diverse ways to enable the construction of any composite variable ranging from spatial indicators to statistically dependent variables estimated using linear regression analysis, i.e., $Y_{it} = a + bP_{it} + cQ_{it} + dR_{it} + \ldots$. Many of the land-cover models discussed in later chapters, for example, are operationalized in GIS using such structures (Eastman, Van Fossen, and Solórzano 2005, this volume). Interaction patterns, usually at a cross section, can also be analyzed and predicted although in this case some data pertaining to the network of interaction as a physical artifact is usually required.

However, the key challenges in developing new and relevant geographical models involve temporal dynamics, but even here, conventional GIS software can do more than appears at first sight. For example, when similar variables are represented as layers at more than one point in time, for example as $\{P_{it}\}$, $\{P_{it+1}\}$, $\{P_{it+2}\}$ ....., it is easy to compute an obvious dynamic by differencing layers $\Delta P_{it+1} = P_{it+1} - P_{it}$. It is then possible to build predictive models which involve combinations of these temporal layers related through map algebras that enable complex functions to be implemented. If the dynamics follows standard econometric structures with dependent variables being lagged as independent and with M exogenous variables $\{X_{it}^{z}\}$ being introduced in each time period, we can build models of the form $P_{it+1} = f[P_{it}, g(P_{kt}, k \neq i), X_{it}^{z}, z = 1,...,M]$. Whether one would do so within GIS software depends on many issues other than the visual integrity of the map products associated with the software and the spatial organization of the data. It is quite likely that other software would be used and the visualization then accomplished through a loose coupling with a GIS. However, there are models building on the emerging tradition of transition potential in which land-cover and land-use change are the essential focus of interest, and these can be implemented within most GIS, with the Idrisi software one of the most closely shaped to this style of modeling (Eastman, Van Fossen, and Solórzano 2005, this volume).

The limits to conventional GIS in this framework can be demonstrated by reference to interaction modeling. Although rudimentary movement models do exist within some proprietary GIS, spatial demographic analysis which focuses on, say, the movements of populations over space and time as reflected in the aggregate migration variables M_{ijtt+1}, is rarely developed in this kind of software. Yet it is quite easy to develop population forecasting where the focus is on net change rather than the interactions which generate such change. For example, in a teaching context, Batty (2002) uses MapInfo® software to illustrate how simple demographic forecasts for Greater London can be constructed from layers of data—populations P_{it}, births B_{it}, deaths D_{it}, and net migration M_{it}—by setting up complex queries on these various data layers and producing a new composite layer as $P_{it+1} = P_{it} + B_{it} - D_{it} \pm M_{it}$. This in turn can also be set up in more conventional rate equations. However, where dynamic predictive models are embedded within GIS, then the software in question is usually customized to the specific processes in question. Idrisi with its focus on land-cover transitions has been noted, but PCRaster, which is illustrated later by Burrough, Karssenberg, and van Deursen (2005, this volume), is specifically adapted to simulate dynamic processes in which diffusion on a lattice is central. Software such as this, in fact, is conceived with physical rather than human processes in mind, and although with some ingenuity it can be massaged into other applications, most customized GIS software tends to be organized with specific models and applications in mind.

There is one last issue that makes our framework less than comprehensive. It is widely acknowledged that spatial models simply act as an interface to deeper system complexity. Many such models do not exclusively focus on geographic or spatial variation but link this to other kinds of system detail which cannot and need not be represented spatially. For example, there are many economic processes which relate to cities, such as the operation of financial markets and political constraints, which are not first and foremost spatial, while there are physical processes, such as climate change, which although ultimately impacting spatially can be simulated without recourse to geography. In fact, one of the most exciting areas of GIS in its science and software is the idea that this domain can have applications to nongeographical problems or at least to problems where the main focus need not be spatial. In a general sense, all human and physical endeavor can be characterized as geographic, but it is important to note that GIS as it currently stands will always be constructed in situations where the aspatial and the nonspatial are of equal import to the spatial.

NEW APPROACHES: CELLS, AGENTS, ACTIONS, INTERACTIONS

Defining the geography of any system is fundamental to spatial representation, affecting not only the way the data is stored but also the way the data is visualized through analytical and simulation processes embedded in or coupled to the software. Spatial variance and correlation depends upon how the space is resolved, at what scale it is measured, and how and where the objects that define the processes that drive its dynamics are located. All this is dictated by the way the system is conceived, by the theory that is explicit or implicit in the models that translate these conceptions into a form that can be manipulated mathematically and digitally. Spatial resolution also affects the number of subspaces into which the system is partitioned, the morphology or configuration of these units which is nontrivial, and its scale in terms of the way data is detected and measured. This is sometimes referred to as spatial aggregation, but it is not only an issue of resolution. The way the objects that characterize the system are defined determines their number and scale and in a different sense, their non-spatial morphology.

In the human sciences, the question of resolution is much more blurred than in the physical sciences. During the last twenty years, data collection has improved as computers have become more powerful at processing fine-scale data, and as our quest for realism at less abstract levels has assumed more importance, there has been a shift from aggregate to disaggregate in space, time, and in topic/object characterization. This is currently driving the notion that models should be constructed for each individual within a population. Agent-based models ascribe to this rhetoric. A more important driver for the move to finer scales is the fact that bottom–up processes appear to be much more effective explanations of geographic change than top–down; bottom–up capture the complexity of the system and enable phenomena to emerge at higher and more aggregate scales. Of course, both top–down and bottom–up, global and local, are required in any effective model, but this sea change to more decentralized bottom–up thinking is responsible for much of the effort currently being devoted to agent-based and cell-space models, for example. Many of the new ideas presented in the following chapters allude to this philosophy. In models of physical processes, there has been less change, for as one aggregates a physical process such as river flow, for example, the problem begins to change qualitatively: one measures run-off rather than river flow as the scale gets larger. In contrast for human systems, one can look at different aggregates of population at anything from the global to local-district scale without implying vastly different qualitative changes in how populations behave. It thus appears easier to abstract in the human than in the physical domain with respect to the geographic processes we are concerned with here, but only ever over a limited range of scales as in the models discussed in this book.

In terms of GIS, we need to distinguish between *locations* which are rooted in distinct coordinate representation and *networks,* links which occur between pairs of coordinates. Locations and networks are fixed but can change slowly in terms of the physical attributes, but usually the activities that are associated with them change more rapidly, involving actions at specific locations and interactions over networks between locations. There is a vast literature in GIS on location which is mainly focused on representations as points and areas. Both have mass, but mass at a point implies a density while mass over an area implies a volume which needs to be converted to a density. In this sense, areal representations may often be aggregations of individual point attributes. Both points and areas have morphologies which are either regular or irregular. Regular are often associated with tessellations of the plane, the most obvious being the grid which in turn leads to the raster. The irregular are more associated with vectors formed from arcs between points. In fact, the vector–raster distinction is not coincident with the irregular–regular but often raster–areal subdivision is more convenient because of the neutrality of each space. This is affected by the way data is collected and stored using sensors and is further reinforced by the fact that attributes of such spaces are densities. In contrast, vector subdivisions usually capture administrative geographies that reflect quite purposive spatial boundary definitions. There are a variety of other representations, but most originate from point–area/raster–vector distinctions.

Spatial representation is also central to the way objects and spaces relate to one another, for in one sense these are the measuring devices which pick up the level of interaction or relationship across space (and across space–time). The idea of cellular automata (CA) models, for example, is based on the notion that simple first-order diffusion processes which operate in the immediate neighborhood of any cell enable homogeneous processes of change to occur when the cells are regular. In contrast, the reason why administrative geographies are used for traffic zones and for urban land-use models is because interaction and traffic data are collected and managed according to the system for administering the territory. In fact, spatial representation is closely intertwined with model definition as the development of CA and agent-based models (ABM) illustrates. In CA modeling, for example, regular cells are usually the storage bins for aggregations of individuals. In our previous notation, p_{it}^{k} are aggregated with respect to the space or cell area around the point i to give a quantity associated with the cell P_{it}. This collection of agents acts as an attribute of the cell rather than being a collection of agents in their own right. When agents move in this kind of model, the population attribute of the cell—its state—changes as more or less population is associated with that cell. Thus diffusion, for example, is simulated by showing how cell states change rather than by showing how agents actually move to adjacent cells. In this sense, CA models might be seen as agent-based models where the agents are fixed or immobile in the simulation sense.

In contrast, agent-based models which work at the level of individuals often define their locational frame in terms of cells. The cellular landscape becomes the environment on which agents reside or locate, and it is the agents that move while the cells remain fixed. Cells states may in fact change too, for this measures the environment associated with the system which contains attributes which the agents can sense and even modify. In this way, there are multiple interactions in that agents can move from cell to cell, their moves can be influenced by other agents and/or by the environment which is encoded in the cells, while the agents can also change the environment as they move through space. The environment can also change itself; all these interactions can be conveniently summarized in the following transformation where E is the environment and A is the set of agents: $E \leftrightarrow E \leftrightarrow A \leftrightarrow A$ (Batty 2005). Figure 1 presents a reasonably faithful characterization of this process of movement and change.

Although this characterization of cells and agents is replete with suggestions about how interactions are handled, the notion of describing networks within GIS—in its science as well as its software—is curiously undeveloped. This is partly because, although there is substantial research in the spatial and transportation sciences on interactions ranging from trip-making to commodity flow and telephone calls, the science of networks and their morphology has only just begun to be researched in anything that might approach the sophistication of location science. This too is coming from a surprising quarter, largely from statistical physics (Barabasi 2002), and it will take some time yet before the same sorts of statistical science that characterize locational patterns will have emerged for network science. Accordingly, where networks have been represented as in transportation, the focus has not been on the morphology of the network and its sensitivity to representation at different scales but on the materials and interactions that use the network. This is clearly illustrated in chapter 10 by Wegener (2005, this volume) on urban land-use transportation models where interaction is the focus, and networks are implicit.

In the chapters that follow, there are several examples of these new styles of model and how they are beginning to present challenges to GIS. Cellular models are deeply entrenched in raster conceptions of GIS, largely because land-cover data of all kinds is now largely delivered to researchers and users alike using remote sensing technologies which record and store data in pixilated form. Batty and Xie (2005, this volume) show how cellular automata can be used to develop urban growth models where the focus is on limited action-at-a-distance in restricted neighborhoods, often at different scales. The exact analog of the diffusion processes used to control and spread urban growth exists for physical models of landscape evolution, river morphology, and erosion, and these are demonstrated by Burrough, Karssenberg, and van Deursen (2005, this volume) in the last section of this book. In fact, in both cases, because these notions of interaction and diffusion are quite explicit to these models and because the focus is upon the dynamics of interactions and change, customized software has been developed in both cases. This enables the logic of figure 1 to be adapted to these particular dynamics: DUEM™ and PCRaster are the two software systems in question with PCRaster being considerably more general, almost approaching "a GIS for geomorphic modeling."

In contrast, models which use irregular spatial units based on vector representations are best illustrated by statistical and mathematical urban models such as those presented by Anselin (2005, this volume) and by Wegener (2005, this volume). In fact these models treat such irregular spaces as being approximated by points—centroids—and although there may be considerable spatial averaging involved in getting such approximations, the models and analyses tend to sit above their spatial representation which is only ever invoked when inputs or outputs are visualized. In urban models, interactions are simulated between activities over a network which simply provides the infrastructure or environment on which movement takes place. When such models are iterated through time, the potential exists for changing this environment; when traffic is loaded on the network, capacity constraints are often breached, and this in turn produces a direct feedback on trip-making demand and sometimes on the capacity of the network itself. In this book, networks provide the fundamental infrastructure to the epidemiological models developed by Bian and Liebner (2005, this volume) where they show how their configuration actually determines the speed and extent of processes which spread on the network. The processes in question are those based on the standard SIR—susceptible, infective, recoverable—population model which they operationalize for a hypothetical urban situation using MATLAB. Although their model might be embedded as some kind of script within proprietary GIS, the need to develop very specific network graphics in this case tends to push model development towards specific, non-geographic but nonetheless mathematical graphics-based software packages.

Land-use change (LUC) models are to some extent much more basic to GIS than any of those we have noted so far. The layer model is well adapted to these kinds of model in which transitions between cells or zones, regular or irregular, can be implemented using map algebras of various kinds. In such models, networks and interactions do not explicitly appear although there is considerable focus, as in many of the urban models noted already, on ways in which such structures can be fitted to empirical data. GIS is not well adapted to embedding calibration routines within its structure although as developments of Idrisi show, this can be done quite effectively through various kinds of extension. The dynamics implicit in such models are quite well adapted to GIS, but there are urban and environmental models built around dynamic processes which are so convoluted that it would be foolhardy to develop these within contemporary GIS software. The systems dynamics models which originated in the 1960s in Forrester's (1969) work are being developed in diverse contexts at present, but these models are primarily nonspatial. Where they have been adapted to various spatial systems as in some variants of STELLA (see Maxwell 2005, this volume, and Miller, Knopf, and Kossik 2005, this volume), the coupling to proprietary GIS is extremely loose, or rather, specific GIS functions are embodied in the simulation-centric software which is developed explicitly for such modeling.

The last area of modeling that we must note involves the category referred to as *prescriptive*. This is where models are being used to optimize some set of goals or objectives, and this brings us directly to questions of planning, design, policy, and management. For a long time in human systems, the idea of developing and using explicit optimization models, other than in the most routine contexts, has been quite dormant. It is commonly regarded that planning and management processes are so complex and politically inspired that it is not possible to build a spatial model optimized in a fashion that meets the diversity and complexity of political aspirations that dominate even the simplest process. The nearest we get here is in the chapter by Duh and Brown (2005, this volume) where they show how heuristic search can be used to minimize the fragmentation of landscapes by various kinds of simulated annealing, TABU search, and genetic swapping algorithms. They argue that such an approach is for illustrative purpose only and indicate that embedding this kind of technique in a wider process is essential for considering any kind of optimization. These wider processes are developed in some detail by Hopkins, Kaza, and Pallathucheril (2005, this volume) where they present a formalized framework in which the spatial-geographical models in most of this book can be embedded. A similar kind of expert-system case-based reasoning framework is outlined by Yeh (2005, this volume). These metamodels show what is now becoming self-evident to all who work with GIS: that the models that we are illustrating and developing here always need to be set in their wider context for them to be politically relevant and useful.

SPACE–TIME DYNAMICS: MODELING CHANGE

Most spatial models do not deal with dynamic processes per se. Instead they measure, analyze, and simulate associations or relationships with variables at a cross section in time or at most between two or more points through time. These relationships sometimes mask truly dynamic processes that work themselves out in time by assuming that dynamic interactions are collapsed to a cross section or are abstracted to the point where actual movements (which must occur through time) are considered as static relationships across space. Associations can be of two kinds. First, there are static relations which might be within one spatial distribution or between distributions. For example, for the aggregated population variable P_{it}, associations between observations or predictions of the same variable—$P_{it} = f(P_{jt}, j = 1, 2, ..., N)$—and associations between different variables—$P_{it} = f(P_{it}, Q_{it}, R_{it}, ...)$—form the essence of spatial econometrics such as that discussed here by Anselin (2005, this volume). The second kind of association is also static but implicitly dynamic; relationships between variables across space, such as abstractions from interactions which vary with respect to distance as in gravitational models of the form $M_{ijt} \sim P_{it}P_{jt}d_{ij}^{-2}$, say, are proxies for diffusion which imply movements of some kind. In fact, these varieties of model lie at the heart of the land-use transport and locational models discussed here by Wegener (2005, this volume) and Birkin (2005, this volume).

Dynamic models are still rare within strict forms of GIS, especially where GIS software is used. Where they are being developed, they hardly mirror the sorts of processes that characterize truly space–time dynamics. For example, land-use change models mainly simulate first-order change which, for the first kinds of association, are implied by $\Delta P_{it} = P_{it+1} - P_{it}$; for the second, these are simulated by actual changes in movements $\Delta M_{ijt} \sim \{[P_{it+1}P_{jt+1}d_{ij}^{-2}] - [P_{it}P_{jt}d_{ij}^{-2}]\}$ where these might be changes associated with migration. In this book, the spatial epidemic models developed by Bian and Liebner (2005, this volume) can be loosely approximated by this style of model. In fact, truly dynamic models are those in which explicitly dynamic processes work themselves out over time. The simple first-order change models just noted are, in fact, elementary differencing of cross sections, and although dynamic processes might be implicit in such models, they are not formally represented. Truly dynamic processes involve effects such as aging and life-cycle effects in demographic populations, multiplier effects within economic activities where demand and supply drive growth or decline, various kinds of decision making that invoke chains or sequences of activities, and cognitive processes that involve trial and error, hence learning.

In any system, there may be many kinds of process involving different time scales which work themselves out at different rates. Wegener, Gnad, and Vannahme (1986) have classified these into slow, medium-speed, and fast in terms of urban systems, where the time scale ranges from epochal to generational to yearly to diurnal and thence down to minutes and seconds. Migration, for example, is more likely to be yearly or generational while the journey to work is clearly diurnal. Local movement, walking, is measured in terms of minutes while processes such as visibility calculations take place in seconds or even finer intervals. Epochal change involves very large phase transitions, such as the movement from agricultural to urban, from the classical to the modern, or from one major technology to another, such as the transition from an energy-based society to an informational one. We might also distinguish between fast and slow with respect to physical, economic, and cognitive in that in human systems, slow change takes place in the way physical infrastructure is built and renewed relative to faster changes that take place when individuals react to changed environments, such as moving job or house or changing consumption habits. Layered onto all this is the notion that change takes place with different frequencies: continuously, continually or infrequently, in ordered sequences, or at random time intervals. The range of possible models of temporal change is thus vast, and so far, very few spatial models have sought to categorize space–time dynamics in anything other than the simplest combinations of these features.

To elaborate these dynamics, we will identify three varieties and sketch how they might be incorporated into models. These are not all-inclusive but simply mark points along a spectrum of change. We distinguish between physical changes based on *diffusion*, socioeconomic change based on positive and negative feedbacks, *multipliers*, and cognitive changes based on learning. In terms of diffusion, a population variable P_{it+1} changes according to the spread or diffusion of similar population activity within its neighborhood Z_i, this being set at different sizes, from the most local based on adjacent cells as in strict CA modeling to the entire system as in gravitational modeling. We write the stock equation as $P_{it+1} = P_{it} + \phi \sum_{j \in Z_i} P_{jt}$ which at the next time period $t+2$ becomes $P_{it+2} = P_{it} + \phi \sum_{j \in Z_i} [P_{jt} + \phi \sum_{\ell \in Z_j} P_{\ell t}]$. If we continue the space–time recursion, we get an increasingly convoluted set of diffusions. Even if the diffusion is over the strict CA neighborhood, for systems of the size we might be dealing with, with something like 1 million cells (1000 × 1000), say, it would take something in the order of 1000 time periods for every cell to be affected by every other, the speed of diffusion relating to the linear dimension of the system itself. These kinds of processes are incorporated in the cellular models developed by Batty and Xie (2005, this volume) and by Burrough, Karssenberg, and van Deursen (2005, this volume) in the chapters that follow.

The second kind of dynamic is a multiplier effect that involves the generation of new or depletion of old activity from existing activity. These kinds of process take place in economic systems through the interplay of demand and supply, but they also mirror positive and negative feedback effects in systems dynamics models of the kind developed here by Miller, Knopf, and Kossik (2005, this volume). Imagine a process where successive increments of population $\Delta\rho_{it}$ are generated from a process in which this change is a function of the existing population activity which we can formalize as $\Delta\rho_{it} = \alpha P_{i0}$. This is not a first-order change as articulated above but one where simple increments are added to the population as $P_{it+1} = P_{it} + \Delta\rho_{it} = P_{it} + \alpha P_{i0}$ where at the point where the process starts, $P_{i0} = P_{it}$. As we iterate this equation, we generate successive increments (or decrements if the process is a negative one) from the initial population which we can write as $\Delta\rho_{it+n} = \alpha^n P_{i0}$. When added to the stock equation, $P_{it+n} = P_{it} + \sum_{\tau=t}^{t+n-1} \Delta\rho_{i\tau} = P_{it} + (\alpha + \alpha^2 + ... + \alpha^n P_{i0})$, this can be further simplified as $P_{it+n} = P_{it}(1 + \alpha + \alpha^2 + ... + \alpha^n) = P_{it}(1-\alpha)^{-1}$ where $(1-\alpha)^{-1}$ is the multiplier. This process is used extensively in land-use transport models (Wegener, 2005, this volume) where the dynamics is collapsed to a cross section of time on the assumption that these effects exist in determining the total of activity at the cross section. These are central to input–output and much macroeconomic modeling where there exist variants which are explicitly dynamic. This is a good illustration of a process which works itself out over many time intervals and which becomes highly convoluted if several such processes occur in every space and are initiated at every time period (Batty 1984).

The last set of processes is cognitive and cannot be formalized in quite the same way. As models are reduced to simulating the actions of individuals, much more purposive behavior is explicit, and various decision rules come to dominate the way spatial change takes place. Goal-directed behavior becomes the order of the day, and sequential processing of information which is acquired through learning comes onto the model agenda. A good example of this kind of process, as in the illustrative pedestrian model of the next section, involves the way individuals might learn about the environment through simply seeing the position of objects from a particular location. When pedestrians first enter the system, they look around and process the position where objects are located. As they walk through the environment, the information initially acquired is updated. The people being modeled do not need to rework the visibility by sweeping around the location whenever they move to another location but simply update what they have already seen. If this is the first time they are in space, then they will traverse it by accumulating about the same amount of new visual information each time they move. However, if they backtrack as they will eventually do or if they visit the same space at a different time, then they will already have the prior information stored and will not have to relearn all the positional information anew. In fact, this is essentially acquiring information which is stored in memory. The learning that is involved is based on the strategy for updating and knowing what strategy to use, depending upon prior experience and whether or not they have visited that location or a nearby one before. These kinds of processes are central to agent-based modeling at different scales as implied by Parker (2005, this volume) and for animal populations by Ahearn and Smith (2005, this volume).

To conclude this section, we will list a series of processes that are relevant to the various models in the chapters that follow. This is not an exhaustive but a generic set that illustrates the range of behaviors to be simulated in spatial systems of both a human and physical kind. Table 1 identifies ten processes and simply lists the authors of the various chapters in which these processes are most significant. Readers can thus judge the extent to which the GIS processes and platforms, illustrated by Goodchild (2005, this volume) in chapter 1 and Maguire (2005, this volume) in chapter 2, are beginning to respond to the new directions in modeling presented in this chapter. We have excluded those chapters which deal with metamodels of the planning process into which the models of this table are likely to be embedded.

Types of Process	Author (Chapter Number)
Simple Associations/Correlations	Anselin (5)
Spatial Relationships/Interactions	Wegener (10), Birkin (11)
Reprocessing/Averaging	Krivoruchko and Gotway Crawford (4)
Routine Movement/Flows	Israelsen and Frederiksen (13) Maidment, Robayo, and Merwade (15) Ahearn and Smith (18)
Aging and Epidemiologies	Bian and Liebner (12)
Simple First-Order Change	Eastman, Van Fossen, and Solórzano (17)
Multipliers and Feedbacks	Wegener (10), Miller, Knopf, and Kossik (6) Maxwell and Vionov (7)
Diffusion and Interaction	Batty and Xie (8), Burrough, Karssenberg, and van Deursen (16) Krivoruchko and Gotway Crawford (4) Ahearn and Smith (18)
Cognitive Processes	Parker (19), Batty (3)
Optimization	Duh and Brown (20)

Table 1. Dynamic processes in modeling in GIS.

MOBILE AGENTS IN LOCAL CELLULAR ENVIRONMENTS: WARD'S *JPED* MODEL

A key problem with the newer, finer-scale approaches to modeling which embody temporal dynamics revolves around the definition of agents. In some applications, particularly for land-cover and agricultural land-use modeling, agents are akin to institutions and definitional problems abound. In physical applications, care needs to be exercised over definition too so that the basic object or element is completely consistent with the physical processes involved. In this section, we will illustrate some of these new directions by defining the most obvious of agents for human systems, individuals, where the focus is on quite well-defined behavior—how agents walk within small spaces, interacting and avoiding other walkers, but also engaging in purposive tasks which involve making decisions once they reach specific destinations. These kinds of pedestrian model are being quite widely developed at the present time (Batty 2003) and provide good examples of how cellular automata is used to represent the environment within which agents act and interact with one another.

Our agents are individuals whose primary motivation is to walk so that they might reach some goal—a spatial location—and then carry out some task such as purchasing a good, interacting with another person, or engaging in some physical activity. In this context, agents are autonomous in that each one responds individually and therefore differently from any other. They have social ability in that they interact with other agents, are reactive in that they respond to other agents or objects in their environment who seek to constrain their behavior, and are proactive in that they make decisions which indicate initiative. In this sense, learning is central to the way they carry out these tasks. They live in cellular environments, which in turn contain information about the physical constraints they face and act as the locational frame in which all action and interaction takes place. Many different models have been developed hitherto, but two classes have emerged: first where the physical environment dominates movement and where the focus of interest is on how agents react to crowding, generating panic or avoiding disasters, and second where the main focus is on some social purpose which overrides local obstacles. The first kind of model tends to be applicable to very fine-scale spaces, such as movement in corridors and/or buildings, while the second, which is the style of model we present here, involves behavior which is social and economic in purpose.

In fact, in the generic model described here, these two types of behavior are present. Agents have to avoid obstacles as well as one another, or they have to meet one another and in doing so engage in scanning their local environment in physical terms. However, these lower-level tasks play second fiddle to the higher-levels goals which direct movement and navigation within the local space and which determine the overall spatial behaviors of the agents in question. Both the environment and the set of agents have physical and social attributes. The environment clearly encodes the geometry of the system while at the same time acting as a container for social and economic activities as well as the location of agents. Agents themselves have locational attributes, velocities of movement, apparatus which enables them to scan the environment and perform visibility calculations, assets such as time and money which both determine and restrict their tasks, and goals which reflect long-term higher-level targets reflect movement to specific locations. How all these features are tied together depends on the various learning functions embodied within the model.

We can also think of the model as having fixed and mobile components. The fixed tend to be the physical characteristics—the cellular environment—in which cells are used to encode buildings and other physical objects, locate agents at any point in time, and measure routing as encoded in visibility graphs, street segments, and related transportation structures. Mobile elements are the agents themselves, and although in principle it is possible for agents to change their environment, this is only possible in these kinds of model when they are embedded into the wider decision-making process reflected in the metamodels introduced later by Hopkins, Kaza, and Pallathucheril (2005, this volume) and Yeh (2005, this volume). These changes and interactions were developed in our Notting Hill Carnival model where stakeholders using the model were able to alter street patterns and the path of the Carnival parade according to the results of running the model (Batty, DeSyllas, and Duxbury 2003), but we will not deal with these any further in this example.

The model works in the following way. Pedestrians enter the space with specific higher-level goals that pertain to what they wish to purchase and where they wish to visit, even if they do not know that such places exist in the local space. They have fixed assets in terms of time and money which may run out as they move to try to fulfill their goals. They also need to continually scan their local environment to avoid colliding with objects or other pedestrians as well as engaging with certain locations and pedestrians if they consider that their goals are likely to be met on such contact. We always have at least two types of walker—those who have never been in the space before and those who already know something of the space. A sophisticated version of this distinction would enable the degree to which the space had already been comprehended to be continuously represented in the attributes of each walker. As walkers move in the space, their attributes are updated in terms of the added information acquired, and efficient strategies for processing such information are necessary for such functioning to take place.

A simple version of this model was developed for walkers visiting the Notting Hill Carnival where agents were visitors, paraders, and fixed sound systems (bands) but where the purposive behavior was simply based on moving to watch the parade and/or the bands. A much more general model has been built by John Ward, a researcher in CASA, who has embodied much of the machinery just sketched into a Java-based program called *JPed* (see www.casa.ucl. ac.uk/johnward.ppt). The model structure is illustrated in figure 2 where the environment is loosely coupled to a GIS, in this case MapInfo, which supplies detailed graphical raster and vector data to establish the cellular foundation on which agents move. As the model involves a separation of low-level and higher-level spatial processing tasks to establish obstacle avoidance through visibility calculations and to meet social targets through learning about what is available and whether an agent's budget is sufficient to enable some action or decision, it is difficult to see this kind of model as being scripted just within wider packages such as ArcGIS.

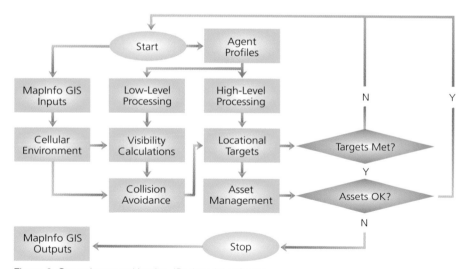

Figure 2. Operations used by the *JPed* model software.

In figure 3, we show Ward's interface which simply establishes how the user interacts with the model. Two varieties of spatial search—visibility analysis which is accomplished by ray tracing and establishing the presence of other agents within some neighborhood—are shown in figures 4 and 5 respectively. Detailed routines for obstacle avoidance are also shown in figure 5, while detailed strategies for establishing the existence of particular types of shops or other facilities are routinely implemented in the background using similar search techniques. As in the Notting Hill model (Batty, Desyllas, and Duxbury 2003), there are many parameters that need to be fixed ideally through some calibration. The main application to date has been to shopping in the central London market square of Covent Garden where 400 agents divided into two groups—50% "tourist" who need to learn anew about the scene and 50% "locals" who know the configuration of the square—interact over 2000 time periods and enter the square at four origin points or gateways. A steady-state picture of crowd density, following visualization techniques of the Notting Hill model, is illustrated in figure 6.

Figure 3. Graphical user interface for JPed displaying the cellular space and buttons for model computations (from Ward 2005).

Figure 4. Visibility using ray tracing in a 120° sweep around an agent (from Ward 2005).

We do not have space here to develop the detail of this model, but a key issue is the learning that takes place as agents explore the space. Models of this kind are still very much at the experimental stage, and there are many different ways in which spatial knowledge of the physical environment can be encoded and computed. For example, with fine-scale raster grids, in this case where the cell size is on the order of $1/2 \times 1/2$ meter, the choice of whether to represent visibility using some graph-theoretic structure where cells are nodes versus more continuous nonlink representation is still very much at issue. This is what makes the use of standard geoprocessing functions in proprietary GIS problematic, not only because of the overhead involved in terms of computation but also because of the need to store data and process many interactions in the most efficient way.

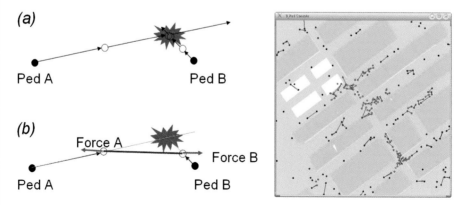

Figure 5. Computing collision trajectories for pairs of walkers (from Ward 2005). Left: (a) The trajectory. (b) Reaction forces avoiding collision. Right: Display of potential collision in a cellular space.

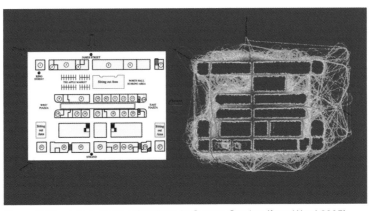

Figure 6. Simulated density of walkers in Covent Garden (from Ward 2005).
Left: The layout of the market shops with arrows indicating entry points.
Right: Display of the density of walkers in the steady state.

THE CHALLENGES FOR MODEL INTEGRATION WITH GIS

We will not prolong this chapter with a detailed catalog of research needs for modeling within GIS, but it is worth noting the key challenges. The age-old conundrum of knowing whether to embed models within GIS with strong coupling or to simply accept a weak coupling in which GIS is used only for visualization and preprocessing or postprocessing of input or output data is clearly changing. The crucial issue appears to be due to the nature of the model and for many cross-sectional static models, embedding within GIS is now much more likely that at any time hitherto. But until GIS software breaks up completely on the desktop or over the Internet and individual modules stand alone, then it is likely that GIS and modeling will continue to remain rather separate activities in terms of their software functionality. Moreover, new approaches to modeling as revealed in this chapter are posing new challenges not only to GIS but also to simulation software, particularly with respect to temporal dynamics and intricate dynamic processes that work themselves out at different rates over space and time. Yet there is much that is being accomplished in terms of integrations. For example, the Arc Hydro interface/extension presented later by Maidment, Robayo, and Merwade (2005, this volume) is a triumph of software engineering within proprietary GIS, and there are likely to be many more such extensions in the near future. Moreover, model-building kits within GIS are making GIS more open and transparent to different styles of modeling, thus enabling model builders to reflect on what is possible within GIS and to develop ingenious twists to the use of the software. Many of these challenges are addressed in the chapters that lie ahead, and we will return to these in the final chapter.

ACKNOWLEDGMENTS

The author wishes to thank John Ward of CASA, University College London (UCL), for allowing a description of his model to be included in this chapter and for the use of figures 3, 4, 5, and 6.

REFERENCES

Barabasi, A. 2002. *Linked: The new science of networks.* New York: Perseus Books.

Batty, M. 1984. Pseudo dynamic urban models. PhD Dissertation. University of Wales. Ann Arbor, Mich.: University Microfilms, NCB85 19527.

———. 2002. Using geographical information systems. In *Key methods in geography,* eds. N. J. Clifford and G. Valentine, 409–23. London: Sage.

———. 2003. Agent-based pedestrian models. In *Advanced spatial analysis: The CASA book of GIS,* eds. P. A. Longley and M. Batty, 81–106. Redlands, Calif.: ESRI Press.

———. 2005. *Cities and complexity: Understanding cities through cellular automata, agent-based models, and fractals.* Cambridge, Mass.: MIT Press.

Batty, M., J. Desyllas, and E. Duxbury. 2003. The discrete dynamics of small-scale spatial events: Agent-based models of mobility in carnivals and street parades. *International Journal of Geographic Information Science* 17: 673–97.

Botton, A. de. 2003. *The art of travel.* London: Penguin Books.

Forrester, J. W. 1969. *Urban dynamics.* Cambridge, Mass.: MIT Press.

Lowry, I. S. 1965. A short course in model design. *Journal of the American Institute of Planners* 31: 158–66.

Morrison, M. S., and M. Morgan. 1999. Models as mediating instruments. In *Models as mediators: Perspectives on natural and social science,* eds. M. Morgan, and M. S. Morrison, 10–37. Cambridge: Cambridge University Press.

Peuquet, D. 2002. *Representations of space and time.* New York: Guilford.

Ward, J. 2005. www.casa.ucl.ac.uk/johnward.ppt.

Wegener, M., F. Gnad, and M. Vannahme. 1986. The time scale of urban change. In *Advances in urban systems modelling,* eds. B. G. Hutchinson and M. Batty, 175–97. Amsterdam: North-Holland Publishers.

Introduction to Section 2: Tools and Techniques

DAVID J. MAGUIRE

ESRI

REDLANDS, CALIFORNIA

In this section, we review some of the spatial analysis and modeling tools and techniques that are available in GIS and modeling systems as a foundation for later chapters that take a more application-oriented view. The four chapters in this section are all different in the base platform that they use for spatial analysis and modeling. Krivoruchko and Gotway Crawford, chapter 4, use a GIS platform (ArcGIS) for their work on modeling uncertainty in GIS. Anselin, chapter 5, embeds a GIS component tool kit (MapObjects®) inside his spatial analysis system. In chapter 6, Miller, Knopf, and Kossik discuss their experience of extending their GoldSim modeling software into the spatial domain. Finally, in chapter 7, Maxwell and Voinov present their spatial extensions to the STELLA modeling software system. Chapter 2 and a number of later chapters in this book examine the SWARM and RePast agent-based modeling systems which have also become popular general-purpose modeling platforms for geographic applications.

The section begins with chapter 4 by Krivoruchko from ESRI and Gotway Crawford from the Centers for Disease Control and Prevention. They provide an introduction to quantifying and modeling uncertainty in GIS using probabilistic extensions to existing essentially deterministic geoprocessing frameworks. The term *geoprocessing* is used to describe the transformation functions such as raster and vector overlay, proximity analysis, and interpolation that are common in GIS today. They are often an important prerequisite for, as well as an intrinsic part of, much spatial analysis and modeling. In this chapter, the authors discuss a series of tools for modeling uncertainty including sensitivity analysis, Monte Carlo simulation, fuzzy set theory, error propagation, and Bayesian belief networks. Extending existing GIS software systems with basic spatial statistical estimation functions and a probabilistic framework for uncertainty analysis would significantly enhance the decision support role of GIS and extend the range of possible applications. It would, however, require users to acquire new analytical skills to interpret the superior, but more complex, results.

Anselin looks at three aspects of spatial statistics in chapter 5: exploratory spatial data analysis (ESDA), spatial autocorrelation statistics, and spatial regression analysis. He reviews the somewhat limited capabilities of existing software but notes the rapid rate of progress in recent years. He evaluates current software implementations of several important algorithms and suggests efficient and robust approaches based on his extensive experience. Anselin has worked on two main software systems, GeoDa and PySpace™. In his chapter, Anselin explains, "GeoDa is designed to provide nonspecialist users with an intuitive and interactive path through an empirical spatial data exercise, starting with mapping and geovisualization, proceeding through ESDA and spatial autocorrelation analysis, and ending up with basic spatial regression." Speaking about PySpace, he says, "PySpace is aimed at a more specialized audience of spatial econometricians. It consists of a collection of modules to carry out spatial regression analysis, without mapping or visualization. It currently contains maximum likelihood and moments estimation methods for linear models, as well as tools to estimate spatial panel regressions. The latter include pooled spatial error and spatial lag regression, as well as spatially seemingly unrelated regressions (spatial SUR)." Anselin's two systems, and indeed the others mentioned in this section, highlight a number of interesting design questions for software developers: commercial or public-domain development environment? Mapping and visualization or numerical output? Commercial or public-domain licensing? Embed, link, or build on a GIS platform?

In chapter 6 Miller, Knopf, and Kossik, from the GoldSim Technology Group, describe how to extend a dynamic simulation modeling system into the spatial domain. GoldSim is a general-purpose software system for visualizing and dynamically simulating nearly any kind of physical, financial, or organizational system. GoldSim is like a visual spreadsheet for creating and manipulating data and equations. The authors consider that a general-purpose dynamic modeling tool such as GoldSim is essentially a high-level programming language that allows users to define equations describing how systems evolve over time. In such systems, the ability to represent time either as a continuous function or a series of discrete events is of paramount importance. In their discussion of technical issues associated with this approach to spatial modeling, they highlight the need for handling stochastic uncertainty, model calibration, and 3D representations. The first of these is shared by Krivoruchko and Gotway Crawford in chapter 4, and the other two resurface in several later chapters.

Maxwell and Voinov look at dynamic landscape modeling and simulation in chapter 7. They have extended the STELLA systems dynamics modeling system into the spatial domain. Like GoldSim, STELLA has a graphic user interface that supports model authoring by specifying resources and resource links using a drag-and-drop interface. Maxwell and Voinov's Spatial Modeling Environment extends STELLA into the spatial domain by creating a cellular automata model that views landscape elements as cells. Complex ecosystem models can be associated with each cell, and cells are linked using fluxes of matter, entities, energy, and information. The authors discuss how the Internet provides a holistic environment for parallel model execution as well as interdisciplinary collaboration. In this way, models can move beyond the desktop, workgroup, or discipline to reach a much larger audience of modelers and information consumers.

Taken together, these four chapters illustrate that the state of the art in GIS, spatial analysis, and modeling software is evolving rapidly in both the commercial and public domain. The old world of static map analysis is being replaced by flexible, dynamic modeling systems that can estimate and model uncertainty, as well as support descriptive and confirmatory spatial statistical analysis. Today, there are strong foundations, and the major limitations of existing systems are well understood. This sets the scene for the next two sections that examine the applications of GIS, spatial analysis, and modeling in the economic, social, and environmental sciences.

Chapter 4

Assessing the Uncertainty Resulting from Geoprocessing Operations

KONSTANTIN KRIVORUCHKO

ESRI

REDLANDS, CALIFORNIA

CAROL A. GOTWAY CRAWFORD

CENTERS FOR DISEASE CONTROL AND PREVENTION

ATLANTA, GEORGIA

ABSTRACT

A GEOPROCESSING OPERATION consists of one or more algorithms that create new spatial data from specified input data. Many of these algorithms involve estimation or prediction of new data associated with new spatial features, and the resulting estimates and predictions are inherently uncertain. To be most useful for decision making, geoprocessing operations should also offer the GIS user a way to quantify this uncertainty so that its impact on the conclusions made from geoprocessed data can be assessed. In this chapter, we illustrate the utility of a probabilistic framework for model building with geoprocessing tools. We describe several different approaches to quantifying and modeling uncertainty in spatial data and discuss their utility in the geoprocessing environment.

Geoprocessing tools (e.g., buffering, overlay, union/intersection, interpolation) allow researchers to combine and interpret geographic data obtained from different sources. They form important components of an underlying model that takes input data (vector coverages and shapefiles, or raster grids) and assimilates them in a meaningful way to produce output information that facilitates an integrated interpretation of the original data that may be more suitable for a given application. The ease with which geoprocessing operations are used within a GIS makes it easy to forget that the geometric properties of the features of the input data are often altered to form new features and that functions of the input attribute values may be transferred to the new features. In many GIS applications, it is not necessary to focus on the modeling aspects inherent in geoprocessing operations; geoprocessing is simply a means to an end. In other applications, a more thorough understanding of the model may be desirable. The overall goal of modeling may be to understand how assumptions, parameters, and variations associated with the input data and the working model affect the resulting output data and the conclusions made from them. If data is not precise or the model is not exact, the uncertainty can only increase with each geoprocessing operation. In such cases, a probabilistic framework for model building with geoprocessing tools may be desirable.

"All models are wrong. We make tentative assumptions about the real world which we know are false but which we believe may be useful." (Box 1979.) This statement, although rather pessimistic, provides an interesting perspective on geoprocessing models. If there is more than a single data description, how do we choose the most useful one? Information about how far our predictions are from an assumed reality is crucial. If we had this information, our choice of model would be easy. Although we typically do not have such specific information, we often have much more information than we realize. For example, we might know that particular scenarios are more likely than others, and we can quantify whether or not our data is consistent with the model we have assumed. Even if we do not know the likelihood of different scenarios, for planning purposes, we might want to entertain several *what if* scenarios that reflect our uncertainty about the reality we are trying to model and then be able to assess the consequences of our assumptions. "Don't tell me how right you want to be, tell me how wrong you can be" (Lerche 2002) can be an important consideration in many practical applications. A poor assessment of how wrong we can be can have real and potentially severe consequences, costing time, resources, and money. However, our uncertainty about reality and the impact of our assumptions and estimates on conclusions and decisions can be integrated with the model using a probabilistic framework. We can use the probabilistic interpretation to provide information that can be extremely useful for decision making.

Consider the following geoprocessing scenarios:

- A buffer function is used to create a zone of a specified distance around the features in a layer. How do we know what distance to use? What happens to our results and conclusions if we change the distance slightly? Given a choice of distance, how wrong can our conclusions be? This latter question can have huge implications in environmental justice, for instance, where we are trying to decide if underprivileged people are more likely to live near toxic waste sites, landfills, or other environmental hazards.

- To find the most suitable location for a new park, we might overlay a map of population density and a map of travel distance to the potential new park, intending to locate the new park in an area that is easily accessible by a large number of people. While we can certainly define the concepts of "easily accessible" and "a large number of people," for example, as "within 5 miles" and for "5000 people," for planning purposes it may be more desirable to study the recommended location of the new park as a function of several choices for these values. We might also weight the importance of each component in determining the location of the new park; for example, perhaps it is more important to serve a large number of people, and their proximity to the park is of lesser concern. Thus, using a raster calculator, we can combine the two maps, setting the contribution of population density to 60% and the contribution of distance to 40%. However, neither the population density nor the travel distance is known with certainty. What effect does this uncertainty have on decisions regarding the placement of the new park? Also, how would our conclusions and recommendations change if we modified the 60/40 contribution ratio? What effect does our uncertainty about the real ratio have on our conclusions and recommendations? Is there a strategy that could minimize the risk of placing the new park in an undesirable location?

- Geoprocessing operations often result in output data that is obtained by aggregating or disaggregating given input data. For example, when the union and intersection geoprocessing operations are used, we may want to assign attribute data to the newly created features. Another common example occurs with the use of a digital elevation model (DEM). DEM data exists in just several resolutions and is often upscaled or downscaled to provide elevation estimates needed at a particular scale for a given geological or hydrological application. Spatial interpolation methods such as kriging and inverse distance interpolation are often used to provide maps of environmental variables whose values are then aggregated in order to link them to public health and disease information summarized for administrative (e.g., U.S. Census) regions. However, raster conversion, interpolation, and aggregation and disaggregation procedures provide only estimates for attributes associated with the newly created features, not the true values. Information on the accuracy of the resulting estimates is critical for decision making.

- In agriculture, agronomists often calculate loss functions that can be defined in monetary units based on the economic benefits that result from fertilizer application. The required amount of fertilization is the difference between that recommended for a particular crop and that which is available in the soil. The recommended rate of fertilizer depends on the desired crop yields, current crop prices, the cost of fertilizer, and the amount of various nutrients in the soil. Soil nutrient information is mapped (typically using kriging) from several soil samples regularly spaced throughout the field. Although kriging provides a measure of uncertainty associated with the predictions of soil nutrient content at any location in the field, it can be difficult to translate this uncertainty into the uncertainty about the recommended rate of fertilizer application and then to the economic impacts of this recommendation. If the amount of fertilizer required is underestimated, the crop will not grow optimally, and we can calculate the yield loss in dollars for every pound of fertilizer applied. Alternatively, if the amount of fertilizer required is overestimated, expensive chemicals have been applied unnecessarily, and we can calculate the cost of overfertilization. Thus, it is important to quantify, here in terms of dollars, the range of costs that might result from our (inherently) uncertain soil nutrient maps. An agronomist might also want to minimize the maximum possible loss, and this requires an estimate of the entire probability distribution of the amount of fertilizer in each field location, not just the prediction of an average quantity.

- The accuracy of spatial data has long been and continues to be a very important concern for GIS users. Locational (positional) errors occur when the geographical coordinates of a point feature are not known precisely. This can be due to measurement error, projection distortion, inherent data uncertainty such as representation of the areal/raster cells by points, or reporting errors. Locational errors always exist, and even small locational errors can have a substantial impact on spatial analysis. For example, spatial proximity is usually calculated using distances between pairs of data locations, and errors in location coordinates will translate into errors in the results of raster-based interpolation methods. When these raster layers are then used as input to other functions or geoprocessing operations, the errors propagate through the calculations, and small errors can quickly add up to large errors if many calculations are performed. If uncertain locations are buffered, attribute values from another layer may be misclassified. GIS users may want to make sure that locational errors do not greatly impact their results and conclusions, and if they do, users might want to be able to track them or adjust their results and conclusions accordingly.

- Consider the real-world example of the opening of the Waste Isolation Pilot Plant (WIPP) in southeastern New Mexico as a storage facility for transuranic waste (Gotway 1994, Zimmerman et al. 1998, www.wipp.ws). Scientists were evaluating salt deposits more than 2000 feet below the earth's surface as a potential storage facility for the waste. However, the deposits lie below an aquifer through which groundwater might potentially transport any waste that might leak from the site. In order to demonstrate that the WIPP is safe, scientists had to convince U.S. regulatory agencies that the travel time of the groundwater through the aquifer is very slow so that contamination of the accessible environment is extremely unlikely. Transmissivity values determine the rate of water flow through an aquifer, and several such values were obtained from the aquifer near the WIPP. To model the flow of groundwater, numerical methods are needed to solve hydrologic equations, and these require predicted transmissivity values on a regular grid obtained using rasterization methods. From this raster map, groundwater travel time through the aquifer can be computed. However, if traditional rasterization methods were used (e.g., kriging), the transmissivity map would be based on averages of neighboring transmissivity values, and the estimated groundwater travel time would also be an average through the region. Scientists had to consider the worst possible scenario and thus needed an entire probability distribution of travel time values so that they could use the lower tail (corresponding to extremely fast travel times) of this groundwater travel time distribution, not the average travel time, to evaluate the suitability of the WIPP (Helton and Davis 2003). The possibility that waste products might be transported by groundwater was only one of many different human risk scenarios considered in evaluating suitability of the WIPP. Complex risk analysis that incorporated many *what if* scenarios played a large part in assessing the suitability of the WIPP and convincing the public and government regulators of the stability of the site for nuclear waste disposal. After more than twenty years of scientific study, public input, and regulatory struggles, the WIPP began operations on March 26, 1999.

Many other examples of the uncertainty resulting from geoprocessing operations are discussed in Heuvelink (1998) and Zhang and Goodchild (2002). All of these examples demonstrate that sophisticated spatial analysis cannot be achieved using traditional, deterministic geoprocessing methods alone. They also indicate several key uses for probabilistic geoprocessing:

- Resource allocation: Evaluation of the *what if* scenarios.
- Quantitative risk analysis: The goal of risk analysis is to describe the probability of an event occurring and the likely consequences should it occur. Risk analysis is often a routine part of business management, policy decisions regarding environmental regulations, global climate change models, and water management.
- Error propagation: GIS users often have information on the range of data errors, the approximate error distribution of the model parameters, and/or the degree of belief that chosen weights, maps, or functional output describe the reality. This information can be incorporated statistically as part of the modeling process. Error propagation is inherent in geoprocessing, and decision makers must take the resulting uncertainties into account.
- Decision making: Input data and models are always imperfect, and geoprocessing functions produce estimates, not truth. Empowered decision

making needs to include cost–benefit and risk analyses that in turn may require an assessment of sensitivity to unknown or estimated parameters and the resulting uncertainty. Probabilistic geoprocessing can assist the user in making an informed decision.

THE EFFECT OF ERROR PROPOGATION

Consider averaging elevation values on a grid with a very fine resolution in order to obtain another grid with a much larger resolution. For example, figure 1 shows a raster map of elevation values using a grid of fine resolution overlaid with a target grid of larger resolution.

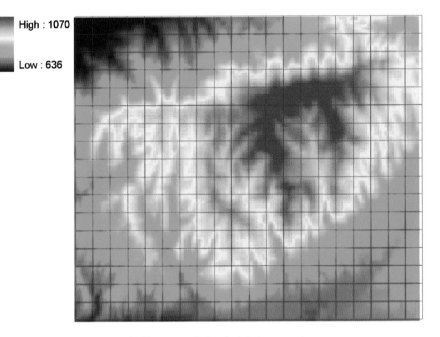

High : 1070

Low : 636

Figure 1. Two rasterized grids of differing resolution (height in meters).

Zonal statistics can be used to aggregate the elevation estimates falling into each cell of the target grid. The value assigned to a cell of the target grid is (typically) the arithmetic average of the original elevation values falling into that cell. Implicit in these calculations is the assumption that the data is independent. However, elevation data is very likely to be spatially correlated: elevation values closer together tend to be more similar than those farther apart. Thus, to aggregate the elevation estimates, a geostatistical method of averaging (block kriging) that accounts for the spatial correlation in the elevation values will provide more accurate values for the target grid. While the visual results of aggregation using zonal statistics and block kriging are not very different (fig. 2), the estimated uncertainty associated with the two approaches is dramatically different (fig. 3). The standard error of the mean elevation is $\sqrt{s^2/n}$, where s^2 is the sample variance of the original values in each cell of the target grid. This provides a commonly used measure of variability in the zonal averages (fig. 3, left). However, this measure of variability ignores the spatial correlation in the original elevation values, and it is much different than that depicted by the standard error of the block kriging predictions (fig. 3, right) that accounts for this correlation. This example illustrates one aspect of the Modifiable Areal Unit Problem (MAUP): aggregation typically reduces variability among units, but this decrease in variability is mitigated by spatial autocorrelation (Openshaw and Taylor 1979, Gotway and Young 2002). As heterogeneity among units is reduced through aggregation, the uniqueness of each unit and the dissimilarity among units are also reduced. However, this reduction in heterogeneity is moderated by the positive autocorrelation among the original observations. Thus, estimates of uncertainty from zonal statistics may give unrealistic, overly optimistic estimates of the averaging accuracy.

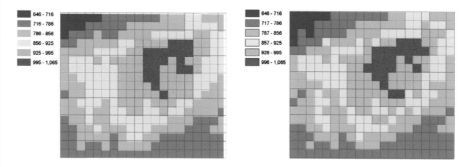

Figure 2. Estimates in meters from zonal averaging (left) and block kriging (right).

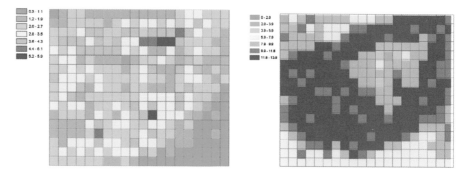

Figure 3. Estimated uncertainty in meters corresponding to zonal averaging (left) and block kriging (right).

The measure of uncertainty associated with the mapped values is very important as it affects the interpretation of the maps and the conclusions that can be drawn from them. For instance, the mean elevation can be predicted to be, say, 850 meters in two different places, but in one place the prediction is 850 ± 2.8 meters, while in another it is 850 ± 13.8 meters. While these predictions are similar, a telecommunications company looking for an optimal location for a new cell tower might make one decision if told that a hill along the route is predicted to be 850 ± 3 meters and might make another decision if told that the same hill has a predicted elevation of 850 ± 14 meters.

Errors such as these translate into uncertainty regarding the accuracy of the resulting map. Moreover, when these maps are used in subsequent calculations, the errors compound. GIS users need easily accessible tools for quantifying errors and assessing their impact on resulting maps derived from geographical layers.

TOOLS FOR UNCERTAINTY ANALYSIS IN THE GEOPROCESSING ENVIRONMENT

SENSITIVITY ANALYSIS

Sensitivity analysis investigates how a model (numerical, conceptual, or a complex integration of both) responds to changes in the information provided to it as input. Input information includes data used to calibrate the model, parameters assumed or estimated from the data used to drive the model, and the basic assumptions underlying the model. The main goal of sensitivity analysis is to identify the parts of the model that are critical and those that are not. For example, a small change in a key parameter may result in a substantial change in the results of the model and have a large impact on the conclusions drawn from the modeling exercise. Such analysis can be crucial for determining the reliability of the model output. Identifying components that are not so crucial can also be important. For example, the output of the model may be insensitive to uncertainties in the input information or may lead to the same conclusions even when very different inputs are provided. In general, sensitivity analysis can be an important analytical tool that can lead to more efficient allocation of resources (both data collection and computational effort), illuminate the need for model improvement, and provide an indication of the reliability of model outputs. Consequently, sensitivity analysis can be a very useful tool for model evaluation, planning, and decision making.

Since geoprocessing operations are important building blocks of complex models in a GIS, sensitivity analysis can help to answer important questions about components of models created by such operations. For example, biologists and ecologists often want to locate regions with favorable habitat conditions for a particular species, and conservationists want to protect such regions so that the species may thrive. As a particular example, suppose an ecologist wants to determine the regions that have the best habitats for the California gnatcatcher, a species of bird in the San Diego area (ESRI 2004). Suppose the California gnatcatcher prefers habitats that satisfy the following criteria:

- The impact of roads should be as low as possible. We assume that the impact of roads on gnatcatcher habitat increases proportionately with the road size and model this using a buffer of 1312 feet around interstate freeways and a buffer of 820 feet around other roads.
- The gnatcatcher prefers to live in areas where the primary vegetation is San Diego coastal sage scrub.
- Near the coast, vegetation patches should be greater than 25 acres, and in other areas, they should be greater than 50 acres.

- The elevation is less than 750 feet above sea level.
- The slope of the terrain is less than 40%.

Using a GIS and geoprocessing operations, these criteria can be used to formulate a model for estimation of the gnatcatcher habitat that is illustrated in figure 4.

Gnatcatcher Habitat Suitability

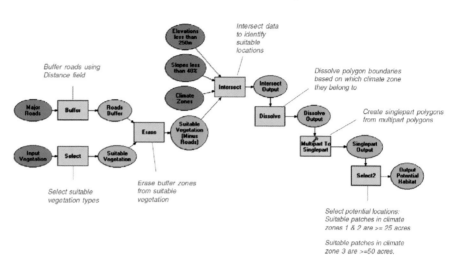

Figure 4. Model for estimation of the gnatcatcher habitat suitability.

Given input data layers delineating major roads, vegetation types, elevation, and the boundaries of the San Diego region, figure 5 shows the result of the analysis. Roads are colored in brown (freeways) and grey (others), suitable vegetation is shown by the green polygons, and polygons indicating regions of potential habitat are shown in red.

Figure 5. The result of the gnatcatcher habitat analysis.

To determine how sensitive this model is to changes in inputs, we can, for example, reduce the maximum permissible slope from 40 to 30, 25, and 20 percent, increase and decrease the size of the buffers around the roads, use a more detailed road layer, include information on population density (cats are a mortal enemy for these birds, and therefore, we may want to select areas that are at least 300–500 feet from homes), and so on. Figures 6 and 7 below show two examples of the resulting estimated habitat areas.

Figure 6. Original estimated gnatcatcher habitat in yellow and areas closer than 500 feet from the detailed streets layer that should be excluded from the estimated areas if cats are taken into account in red.

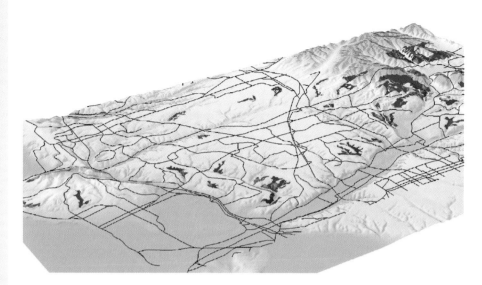

Figure 7. Original estimated gnatcatcher habitat (blue) and optimal habitat estimated using maximum permissible slope value of 20% (red).

Reasonable changes in the size of the buffer around roads and the maximum permissible slope lead to fairly different estimated habitat areas. To quantify this numerically, just changing the maximum permissible slope from 40 to 25 and 20 percent reduces the estimated area of optimal habitat in the study area by 24% and 40%, respectively.

The gnatcatcher habitat model is very sensitive to changes in the slope parameter. Thus, in order to reliably determine optimal gnatcatcher habitat areas, it is necessary to obtain more precise information about the slope of the terrain these birds prefer. Additional biological information, more precise data on the value of the slope parameter in preferred habitat areas, and statistical adjustments may be necessary to make this model reliable.

Effective use of complex biological and environmental models requires knowledge of the sensitivity of their outcomes to variations in parameters and inputs. Sensitivity analysis focuses attention on critical parts of a model. Systematic usage of sensitivity analysis is necessary even if parts of a model are well understood. This is because responses of the local parts of a large model may have little overall significance or be crucial and because complex behavior of the local parts of a model may aggregate into a model's overall behavior.

Even if the geoprocessing model is a fairly accurate description of reality, using sensitivity analysis will give better insight of possible data inconsistencies.

MONTE CARLO SIMULATION

Although sensitivity analysis is not aimed at explicitly quantifying uncertainty in the model, the results of sensitivity analysis can be used to quantify uncertainty. However, there are many other approaches to quantifying uncertainty. The very idea of an uncertain outcome suggests that the outcome is variable. This in turn makes a probabilistic interpretation of uncertainty very appealing. For each uncertain variable or parameter (one that has a range of possible values), the possible values and their likelihood are defined with a probability distribution. The type of distribution is based on the conditions surrounding each variable. For spatial analysis, however, we need more than just the probability distribution of the data. We also need the values to reflect the spatial properties of the variables. Depending on the type of data available, we may quantify these properties by, for example, a spatial intensity function for point pattern data that measures the number of points per unit area, a neighborhood structure that describes spatial relationships among geographical regions, or a spatial autocorrelation function for spatially-continuous (geostatistical) data.

Monte Carlo simulation tests are routinely used to test for spatial patterns (e.g., Besag and Diggle 1977). Monte Carlo simulation testing proceeds as follows. Given a null hypothesis about the value of a parameter of interest:

1. Generate simulated values from a specified probability distribution that statistically describes the input data under the null hypothesis.

2. Compute a statistic of interest, say U. For example, in spatial analysis this could be Moran's I or Geary's c.

3. Repeat M=1000+ times. This gives U_1, U_2, ...U_M.

4. Compare the observed statistic computed from the given data, say U_{obs}, to the distribution of the simulated U_j's and determine the proportion of simulated U_j values that are greater than U_{obs}.

If this proportion is small, this provides evidence against the null hypothesis in the direction of a particular alternative hypothesis being considered.

Sometimes, in spatial analysis, the statistic of interest is not a single variable, but a function of distance, $U(d_{ij})$ (e.g., Ripley's K function). In this case, Monte Carlo simulation testing proceeds as described above, but in step 2, an entire function, $U(d_{ij})$, is computed. At step 4, the observed function is compared to the functions computed from the simulated data. The spread of these simulated functions, often summarized graphically as 97.5 and 2.5% confidence envelopes, reflect the uncertainty in the observed spatial function.

A particular variant of Monte Carlo simulation called geostatistical simulation is often used in assessing uncertainty in functions of geostatistical data (Deutsch and Journel 1992, Lantuejoul 2002). In this approach, suppose the input is a set of data (e.g., measurements on a hydrogeologic parameter of interest in a particular region), and the output (e.g., an estimate of groundwater travel time) requires a detailed spatial map of the parameter on which the measurements were obtained. Such a map can be created through spatial prediction techniques such as kriging. The mapped values are used to obtain the output (e.g., a single value of groundwater travel time through an aquifer), but the uncertainty associated with the output, often as important as the estimated value itself, is typically much more difficult to infer.

Geostatistical simulation provides a way to quantify the uncertainty in the output of a complex model or system (called a transfer function) that is computed from spatial data. With geostatistical simulation, several plausible maps, each reflecting the same information on the parameter of interest, are generated, and the transfer function is then used to compute a system response for each. If the realizations characterize the spatial uncertainty in the parameters of interest, the resulting distribution of predicted system responses will reflect this uncertainty. Thus, in the groundwater example, the result is not a single prediction of groundwater travel time, but an entire distribution of groundwater travel times whose spread reflects the uncertainty in the input values (fig. 8). This allows us to analyze worst-case scenarios (usually defined by one tail of the system response distribution) and provides a better understanding of the data and the outcomes.

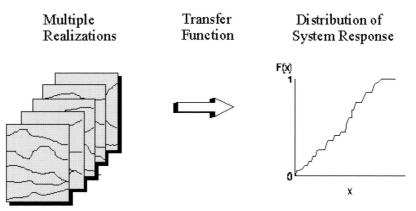

Figure 8. Illustration of geostatistical simulation. Adapted from Journel (1989).

The multiple realizations are each a plausible rendition of the input map of interest. They are a sample from the same probability distribution with the same autocorrelation properties as the available data, and they may also preserve more complicated spatial properties (Deutsch and Journel 1992, Gotway and Rutherford 1994). In some cases, the mapped surfaces may pass through the original data values, thus honoring the data. In the geostatistical literature, such simulations are called conditional. When multivariate simulation is needed, a technique called Latin Hypercube sampling can be used to preserve the correlation structure between the variables (see, e.g., Stein 1987, Pebesema and Heuvelink 1999, Helton and Davis 2003).

To see how geostatistical simulation might be useful in geoprocessing spatial data within a GIS, suppose an agronomist is working with two layers in a GIS. One layer corresponds to a map of soil temperature, and another corresponds to a map of soil moisture. The agronomist wants to objectively determine whether or not there is a relationship between these two maps (e.g., the agronomist expects that areas with high soil temperature should correspond to areas with low soil moisture). These two layers (based on data from Yates and Warrick 1987) are shown in figures 9 and 10, respectively.

Perhaps the simplest measure of the relationship between these two variables is the traditional Pearson correlation coefficient. For the soil temperature and soil moisture maps, r=−0.54, indicating a moderately strong negative association between the two variables. However, there are several problems with this approach. First, the agronomist has no idea about the error associated with this estimated correlation. Second, the maps were produced by co-kriging soil samples and so are a compilation of predicted values of soil temperature and soil moisture that have prediction errors associated with them. Finally, predictions from kriging are averages of local data, and average values are too smooth to accurately reflect the variability in soil moisture and soil temperature that form the basis for the correlation coefficient.

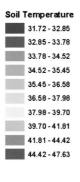

Soil Temperature
31.72 - 32.85
32.85 - 33.78
33.78 - 34.52
34.52 - 35.45
35.45 - 36.58
36.58 - 37.98
37.98 - 39.70
39.70 - 41.81
41.81 - 44.42
44.42 - 47.63

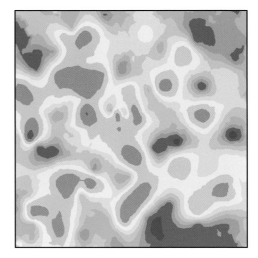

Figure 9. Map layer of soil temperature.

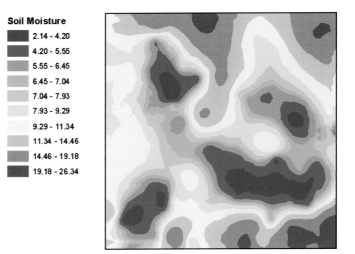

Figure 10. Map layer of soil moisture.

Geostatistical simulation was used to simulate 1000 plausible maps of soil temperature and soil moisture that are based on the probability distribution estimated for each variable, the spatial autocorrelation observed among the values for each variable, as well as the cross-correlation between soil moisture and soil temperature inferred from the original data on both variables. For each pair of maps generated, the correlation coefficient was computed and the distribution of the resulting 1000 correlation coefficients is shown in figure 11.

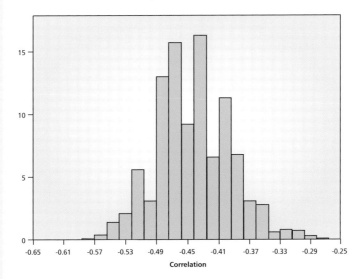

Figure 11. Distribution of correlations between soil temperature and soil moisture from geostatistical simulation.

The results in figure 11 indicate that the correlation between soil temperature and soil moisture could potentially range from –0.58 to –0.28, and a 95% uncertainty interval is (–0.53, –0.36). Thus, the estimated correlation coefficient computed from the smoothed maps (–0.54) is likely to be an overly optimistic estimate of the strength of the relationship between the two maps.

Instead of using the correlation coefficient to measure the association between the two maps, we could use the cross-correlation function that measures this correlation as a function of distance. In this case, rather than getting a histogram of values, we would obtain 1000 estimated cross-correlation functions, and each bound of the uncertainty interval would also be a function of distance. These 95% simulation envelopes can be used to measure the uncertainty in the estimated cross-correlation function.

One of the major advantages of geostatistical simulation, and of Monte Carlo simulation in general, is its flexibility. We can simulate data from different distributions, under different assumptions, with different choices for key parameters. Different variations can be used with different types of spatial data. It can be used to derive a measure of uncertainty associated with complex functions of spatial data whose analytical form may be difficult or impossible to derive. Given the complex nature of many of the geoprocessing operations and the tendency to combine many of them in complex modeling, Monte Carlo simulation can be a valuable method for assessing uncertainty resulting from geoprocessing operations in a GIS.

FUZZY SET THEORY

Fuzzy logic is a superset of Boolean logic that has been extended to handle uncertainty in data that arises due to vagueness or fuzziness rather than to randomness alone. In classical set theory, a subset U of a set S can be defined as a mapping from the elements of S to the elements of the set {0, 1}. This mapping may be represented as a set of ordered pairs, with exactly one ordered pair present for each element of S. The first element of the ordered pair is an element of the set S, and the second element is an element of the set {0, 1}. The value zero is used to represent nonmembership, and the value one is used to represent membership. The validity of the statement "x is in U" is determined by finding the ordered pair whose first element is x. The statement is true if the second element of the ordered pair is 1, and the statement is false if it is 0.

A fuzzy subset F of a set S can also be defined as a set of ordered pairs, each with the first element from S, but with the second element from the interval [0, 1]. The value zero is used to represent complete nonmembership, the value one is used to represent complete membership, and values in between are used to represent intermediate degrees of membership. The degree to which the statement "x is in F" is true is determined by finding the ordered pair whose first element is x, and the degree of truth of the statement is the second element of the ordered pair.

A fuzzy expert system is a system that uses a collection of fuzzy membership functions and rules, instead of Boolean logic, to reason about data. Each Boolean operation has a fuzzy counterpart:

Set Operation	Boolean	Fuzzy
Complement	What elements are not in the set?	How much do elements not belong to the set?
Containment	Are all of the elements in A also contained in B?	If x ∈ A to a high degree, to what degree does it also belong to B?
Intersection	Which element belongs to both sets?	How much of the element is in both sets?
Union	Which element belongs to either set?	How much of the element is in either set?

The rules in a fuzzy expert system are usually of a form similar to the following:

if x is low and y is high then z is medium

where x and y are input variables, z is an output variable, low is a membership function (fuzzy subset) defined on x, high is a membership function defined on y, and medium is a membership function defined on z. The antecedent (the rule's premise) describes to what degree the rule applies, while the conclusion (the rule's consequent) assigns a membership function to each of one or more output variables. Most tools for working with fuzzy expert systems allow more than one conclusion per rule. The set of rules in a fuzzy expert system is known as the rule base or knowledge base.

The key to working with a fuzzy set is delineation of a membership function that specifies, for every element x, the degree to which the statement "x is in F" is true. For example, consider the statement "the value of soil moisture is high." A Boolean classification for this statement might have membership function

$$\mu(x) = 0, \ x \leq 12$$
$$= 1, \ x > 12.$$

A membership function for a fuzzy classification can be any continuous function defined on the interval [0,1]. For example, for the statement "the value of soil moisture is high" we could use

$$\mu(x) = 0, \qquad if \ x \leq 10$$
$$= \frac{x-10}{3}, \ 10 \leq x \leq 13$$
$$= 1, \qquad x > 13.$$

Just as Boolean set theory forms a useful mathematical discipline with a variety of important applications, so too does fuzzy set theory. From the above example, we can see how the traditional geoprocessing operations such as intersection and union have fuzzy counterparts that reflect the uncertainty in attribute values or locations. A common spatial example arises with boundary problems related to classification, for example, soil and land-use classification, where the spatial boundaries between the different soil and land-use classes are not known exactly (see, e.g., Burrough 1989, Bonham-Carter 1994, Heuvelink 1998).

In addition to the brief and basic description here, there are fuzzy versions of many mathematical and statistical operations including fuzzy kriging and fuzzy mapping (Bardossy et al. 1988, 1990).

Consider again soil moisture and soil temperature and suppose we want to select all the raster cells for which

$$7 \leq \text{moisture} \leq 12 \text{ AND } 35 \leq \text{temperature} \leq 39.$$

The Boolean classification assigns a value of 1 to cells that meet this criterion and assigns a value of 0 to cell that do not. The corresponding selection is shown in figure 12 (left). If we want to avoid using the definitive boundaries that arise from this specification, we could instead use a fuzzy classification. For example, for the moisture criterion, we could use the membership function

$$\mu_M(x) = \frac{1}{1+(x-8)^2}, \quad \text{if } x < 8$$

$$= 1, \quad \text{if } 8 \leq x \leq 11$$

$$= \frac{1}{1+(x-11)^2} \quad \text{if } x > 11$$

and for temperature

$$\mu_T(x) = 0, \quad x < 35$$

$$= \frac{x-35}{4}, \quad 35 \leq x \leq 39$$

$$= 0, \quad x > 39.$$

The fuzzy intersection is defined as $\mu_{M \cap T}(x) = \min\{\mu_M(x), \mu_T(x)\}$. The resulting fuzzy classification is shown in figure 12 (right).

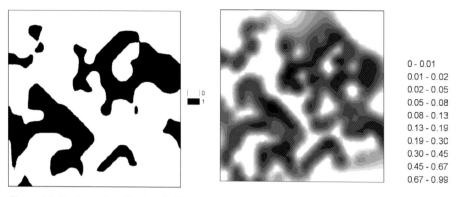

Figure 12. Boolean classification (left) and the corresponding fuzzy classification (right) showing cells where moisture is in the range 7–12 and temperature 35–39.

There are many other operators that can be used to combine fuzzy membership functions (see, e.g., Bonham-Carter 1994). For example, class intervals of any map can be associated with fuzzy membership functions, and fuzzy membership functions can be used to reflect the relative importance of a series of maps, resulting in a fuzzy version of a raster calculator. Thus, the use of fuzzy sets and continuous membership functions gives the GIS user much more flexibility in modeling with geoprocessing operations than the traditional Boolean logic formalism.

BAYESIAN BELIEF NETWORKS

The term *belief networks* encompasses a whole range of different, but related, techniques that deal with reasoning under uncertainty. Synonyms include graphical models, Bayesian networks, Markov networks, and chain graphs (see, e.g., Cowell et al. 1999). Graphical models are models for joint probability distributions that relate concepts of graphical independence (separation) to probabilistic independence (Edwards 2002).

Consider, as an example, relating the risk of asthma to one or more potential factors that might influence this risk, say mid-day ozone concentration, mid-day particulate matter concentration, and average daily temperature. Each of these can be displayed spatially as a rasterized map.

Creating a Bayesian belief network involves three basic stages. First, we specify a graphical model that indicates potential dependencies among the rasterized values. Second, we specify some information about the uncertainty in the system, giving probabilities for various situations.

Finally, to assess the uncertainty in the risk of asthma as a function of the three risk-factor maps, we need to combine the relationships described in the graph with their prior probabilities and obtain the joint distribution over all variables. For example, each raster cell of each of the risk-factor maps has some uncertainty associated with it, due to measurement error or interpolation. To assess the impact of these uncertainties on our predicted risk of asthma, we need the joint distribution over all variables. However, this is a complex task, even with just three maps.

Bayesian belief networks represent the full joint distribution more compactly with a smaller number of parameters by taking advantage of conditional and marginal independences among components in the distribution. They offer a means for computationally fast uncertainty assessment in complex, multidimensional systems and are thus ideally suited to GIS modeling.

The Bayesian approach to error propagation is particularly useful when there is insufficient information for scientific decision making because of data scarcity and complexity. Consider data on the occurrence of a particular type of bird in the past twenty years. This data may be imprecise due to such things as refinements in technology, locational errors, lack of access to property, and human errors. To quantify this locational uncertainty, an ornithologist assigned a credibility value to each observation (in the interval 0–1), and kriging was used to calculate a continuous credibility map of the bird sightings (fig. 13).

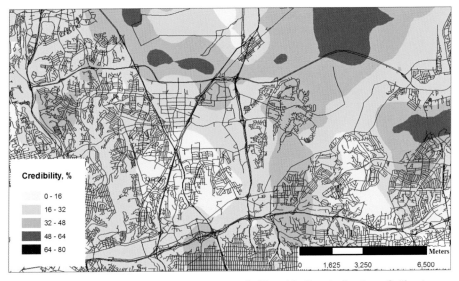

Figure 13. Predicted credibility of bird occurrences in Riverside County, Southern California.

In addition to this information, data on soil types, land use, slope, distance to roads, and human proximity to any location can also be used to define preferred habitats. Areas with a small distance to the preferred vegetation (obtained through buffering) can be constructed and considered as a possible preferred habitat for the bird (fig. 14).

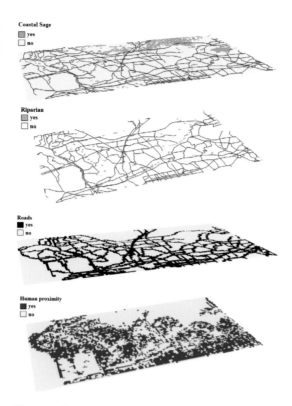

Figure 14. Data sources for preferred bird habitat locations.

Using GIS software, all of this information can be converted/predicted to raster grids with the same extent, and prior probabilities of relationships between bird occurrences and classes of each raster cell can be assigned. For instance, if a grid cell contains coastal sage shrub, we can assign the probability of finding a bird to be 0.9; if a grid cell does not contain coastal sage shrub, we assign this probability to be 0.1.

Then an adjusted habitat prior probability can be defined as in table 1, which gives this probability for all combinations of the variables desert shrub, coastal sage, riparian, roads, and previous sightings.

Adjusted habitat	Desert shrub	Coastal sage	Riparian	Roads	Previous sightings
0.25	yes	no	no	no	less than 0.5
0.30	no	yes	no	no	less than 0.5
0.40	yes	yes	no	no	greater than 0.75
...	...	...	...	...	...
...	...	...	...	...	...

Table 1. Example of the prior probabilities of adjusted bird habitat.

The prior probabilities for the predicted habitat are defined similarly.

Predicted habitat	Adjusted habitat	Human proximity	Slope
0.45	0.25	no	gentle
0.20	0.30	yes	flat
0.25	0.40	yes	flat
...	...	...	...
...	...	...	...

Table 2. Example of the prior probabilities of predicted bird habitat.

The joint probability distribution of the nine variables can be calculated using the chain rule for Bayesian networks

$$P(A_1,\dots,A_9) = \prod_{i=1}^{9} P(A_i \mid parents(A_i))$$

where parents are explanatory variables (if any), such as adjusted habitat, human proximity, and slope in the case of predicted habitat. In other words,

$$P(A_8 \mid parents(A_8)) = 0.4 \text{ if slope is gentle and } 0.6 \text{ otherwise}$$

$$P(A_9 \mid parents(A_9)) = P(A_9 \mid A_6, A_7, A_8).$$

Then the Bayesian belief network (fig. 15) calculates a predicted habitat probability for each raster cell, where probabilities are shown in percent.

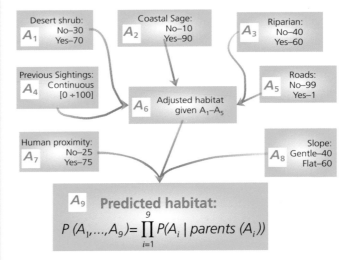

Figure 15. A Bayesian belief network for predicted bird habitat probability for Riverside County, Southern California.

The Bayesian belief network model is attractive because both qualitative and quantitative information can be used and because it works fast. It is also flexible. For example, different experts may provide different priors on relationships between birds and other available information and on the credibility of the data on birds' locations. Because there are many uncertainties in the model, each expert may suggest several variants of prior parameters that can be used as input to sensitivity analysis of the model. This can help to determine which parts of the model most influence the predicted habitat and which influence it the least. The geoprocessing environment can be extremely useful in comparing before-and-after probabilities at each network node.

The Bayesian belief network is a much richer model than the deterministic geoprocessing model discussed earlier because it has more parameters, and these parameters interact, either directly or indirectly. If the Bayesian belief network parameters are reliable, the result of the habitat modeling can be much more informative than that based on a deterministic geoprocessing scenario. However, because much of the information in the Bayesian belief network is subjective, interpretation of the prediction results can be challenging. We refer to Marcot et al. (2001) for further discussion on the advantages and disadvantages of this approach in ecological analysis.

CONCLUSIONS

Increasingly, scientists are recognizing the impact that uncertainties arising from various sources can have on the results and conclusions from spatial analysis. Indeed, Zhang and Goodchild (2002, p. 3) note: "Unfortunately, geographical data are often analyzed and communicated amid largely non-negligible uncertainty. Error-laden data, used without consideration of their intrinsic uncertainty, are highly likely to lead to information of dubious value." This is particularly true when data results from geoprocessing operations that form the backbone of much of the spatial analysis conducted within a GIS. In this paper, we have described several broad approaches for assessing the uncertainty resulting from geoprocessing operations. Our focus here has been on basic ideas, motivated by simple examples, in order to stress the powerful impact that modeling uncertainty can have on decision making. All of these approaches may be used in modeling complex, dynamic systems.

The ideas presented here can be easily integrated within current GIS frameworks:

- While methods for assessing uncertainty in geoprocessing operations seem complex, only three new components would need to be added: 1) input of prior distributions/alternative values/fuzzy membership functions; 2) user interface dialogues that allow for multiple outputs (sets of values or distributions); and 3) postprocessing options.

- GIS geoprocessing environments are typically flexible enough to encompass many complex tools, and uncertainty and sensitivity analyses can be considered as just parallel processes to the standard modeling capabilities currently available.

- The output/posterior distributions can be visualized and analyzed using graphs linked to maps and to other objects. The distribution can be approximated and compactly stored using a mixture of Gaussian distributions.
- Extensive sequential information can be stored in the form of time-series data, as it was prototyped in the ESRI hydrological model, Arc Hydro (Maidment 2002).

Implementing these techniques within a GIS also presents several challenges. First, at the present time, only a small percentage of GIS users are familiar with uncertainty analysis in the context of geoprocessing environments. Additional training with simple, yet realistic case studies is needed to educate GIS users and to help them learn the basics of scientific geoprocessing. Second, inputs into some methods for uncertainty analysis can be difficult or complex to specify (e.g., prior distributions and fuzzy membership functions). Thus, it will be necessary to balance comprehensiveness with a simple user interface. Finally, the results from uncertainty analysis can be extremely numerous, resulting in thousands of maps, charts, and tables. Summarizing this information in meaningful ways will require creativity. Nevertheless, the challenges are intriguing, and conquering them is important: assessing uncertainty resulting from geoprocessing can greatly increase the utility of spatial analysis within GIS.

REFERENCES

Bardossy, A., I. Bogardi, and W. E. Kelly. 1988. Imprecise (fuzzy) information in geostatistics. *Mathematical Geology* 20: 287–311.

———. 1990. Kriging with imprecise (fuzzy) variograms I, II. *Mathematical Geology* 22: 63–79, 81–94.

Besag, J., and P. J. Diggle. 1977. Simple Monte Carlo tests for spatial patterns. *Applied Statistics* 26: 327–33.

Bonham-Carter, G. F. 1994. *Geographic information systems for geoscientists: Modelling with GIS.* Tarrytown, N.Y.: Pergamon.

Box, G. E. P. 1979. Robustness in the strategy of scientific model building. In *Robustness in statistics,* ed. R. L. Launer and G. N. Wilkerson, 201–36. New York: Academic Press.

Burrough, P. 1989. Fuzzy mathematical methods for soil survey and land evaluation. *Journal of Soil Science* 40: 477–92.

Cowell, R. G., A. P. Dawid, S. L. Lauritzen, and D. J. Spiegelhalter. 1999. *Probabilistic networks and expert systems.* New York: Springer-Verlag.

Deutsch, C. V., and A. G. Journel. 1992. *GSLIB: Geostatistical software library and user's guide.* New York: Oxford University Press.

Edwards, D. 2002. *Introduction to graphical modelling.* 2nd ed. New York: Springer-Verlag.

ESRI. 2004. *Geoprocessing in ArcGIS*. Redlands, Calif.: ESRI Press.

Gotway, C. A. 1994. The use of conditional simulation in nuclear waste site performance assessment. *Technometrics* 36: 129–61.

Gotway, C. A., and B. M. Rutherford. 1994. Stochastic simulation for imaging spatial uncertainty: Comparison and evaluation of available algorithms. In *Geostatistical simulations,* ed. M. Armstrong and P. A. Dowd, 1–21. Dordrecht: Kluwer.

Gotway, C. A., and L. J. Young. 2002. Combining incompatible spatial data. *Journal of the American Statistical Association* 97: 632–48.

Helton, J. C., and F. J. Davis. 2003. Latin Hypercube sampling and the propagation of uncertainty in analyses of complex systems. *Reliability Engineering and System Safety* 81: 23–69.

Heuvelink, G. B. M. 1998. *Error propagation in environmental modeling with GIS*. London: Talyor & Francis.

Journel, A. G. 1989. *Fundamentals of geostatistics in five lessons*. Washington, D.C.: American Geophysical Union.

Lantuejoul, C. 2002. *Geostatistical simulation: Models and algorithms*. Berlin: Springer-Verlag.

Lerche, I. 2002. Don't tell me how right you want to be, tell me how wrong you could be. In *Proceedings from the annual conference of the international association for mathematical geology*. Berlin.

Li, J., S. Wu, and G. Huang. 2002. Handling temporal uncertainty in a GIS domain: A fuzzy approach. Symposium on geospatial theory, processing and applications. Ottawa.

Maidment, D. R., ed. 2002. *Arc Hydro: GIS for water resources*. Redlands, Calif.: ESRI Press.

Marcot, B. G., R. S. Holthausen, M. G. Raphael, M. Rowland, and M. Wisdom. 2001. Using Bayesian belief networks to evaluate fish and wildlife population viability under land management alternatives from an environmental impact statement. *Forest Ecology and Management* 153: 29–42.

Openshaw, S., and P. J. Taylor. 1979. A million or so correlation coefficients: Three experiments on the modifiable areal unit problem. In *Statistical applications in the spatial sciences,* ed. N. Wrigley, 127–44. London: Pion.

Pebesma, E. J., and G. B. M. Heuvelink. 1999. Latin Hypercube sampling of Gaussian random fields. *Technometrics* 41: 303–12.

Stein, M. 1987. Large sample properties of simulations using Latin Hypercube sampling. *Technometrics* 29: 143–51.

Yates, S. R., and Warrick, A. W. 1987. Estimating soil water content using co-kriging. *Soil Science Society of America Journal* 51: 23–30.

Zhang, J., and M. Goodchild. 2002. *Uncertainty in geographical information.* London: Taylor & Francis.

Zimmerman, D. A., G. de Marsily, C. A. Gotway, M. G. Marietta, and Members of Sandia's GXG. 1998. A comparison of seven geostatistically-based inverse approaches to estimate transmissivities for modeling advective transport by groundwater flow. *Water Resources Research* 34: 1373–1413.

Chapter 5 | Spatial Statistical Modeling in a GIS Environment

LUC ANSELIN

SPATIAL ANALYSIS LABORATORY

UNIVERSITY OF ILLINOIS AT URBANA-CHAMPAIGN

URBANA, ILLINOIS

ABSTRACT

THIS CHAPTER REVIEWS SOME generic methodological and computational issues pertaining to the implementation of spatial statistical analysis functionality within a GIS environment. Attention is paid to the types of research questions addressed in spatial statistics and how these affect computational implementation. A brief overview is given of techniques for spatial statistical analysis and how they are currently represented in commercial and open source software. Special attention is paid to the software development program that has been part of the U.S. Center for Spatially Integrated Social Science (CSISS) and its two main products, GeoDa and PySpace. The chapter concludes with some thoughts about future requirements and challenges.

Geographic information systems (GIS) provide an unrivaled software platform to support statistical analysis of spatial data. This has long been recognized in academic writings (e.g., Goodchild 1987, Haining 1989), and there is now a considerable body of literature devoted to the conceptual, methodological, and implementation issues related to the integration of spatial (data) analysis and GIS. In the early and mid-1990s, in particular, there were several discussions of how to link statistical methods with a GIS infrastructure and which methods to include in such a framework (e.g., Anselin and Getis 1992, Goodchild et al. 1992, Fischer and Nijkamp 1993, Fotheringham and Rogerson 1994). This was followed by an active development of different software implementations that attempted to augment GIS with analytical capabilities or presented self-contained solutions to specialized spatial statistical questions, such as the detection of clusters and the estimation of spatial regression.

Early forms of linked GIS and statistical software focused on straightforward data transfer between the two kinds of programs and the visualization of results of standard (nonspatial) statistical analysis in the GIS (e.g., the archeologist's workbench in Farley et al. 1990). Since then, a large number of more elaborate (mostly noncommercial) spatial statistical software tools have become available. Some of these are freestanding, but several are extensions of GIS that use a range of technologies, from scripts in macro languages to remote procedure calls and object-oriented component integration (for some recent overviews, see Anselin and Bao 1997, Anselin 2000, Symanzik et al. 2000, Zhang and Griffith 2000, Haining et al. 2000, Gahegan et al. 2002, Ungerer and Goodchild 2002, Anselin et al. 2004). In addition, there are active and ongoing spatial analysis software development efforts using open source environments, such as R (Bivand 2002) and Python (Rey and Janikas 2005). The range of available software solutions is also exemplified by the growing collection of tools contained in the clearinghouse maintained by the U.S.-based Center for Spatially Integrated Social Science (CSISS).[1]

In contrast to the activity in the academic sector, the implementation of spatial statistics–GIS integration in commercial software systems is still far from commonplace. In part, this may be due to an unclear division of labor between statistical software and GIS and which combination of tools is best supported by their respective markets (e.g., Anselin et al. 1993). Several commercial statistical packages now include mapping capability and even some (limited) GIS functionality, but apart from the somewhat dated S+SpatialStats™ extension to S-Plus® (Kaluzny et al. 1997), none includes a comprehensive set of spatial statistical methods. On the GIS end, statistical functionality has been included through specialized extension modules (e.g., the ArcGIS Geostatistical Analyst) and through direct links with statistical software (e.g., the now obsolete S-Plus ArcView® bridge and the SAS® Bridge for ESRI products). Arguably the most exciting development in this respect is the inclusion of a spatial statistics toolbox in the core of ESRI ArcGIS 9 software (ESRI 2004) although its functionality is (still) somewhat limited.

In this chapter, I review conceptual and practical issues pertaining to the implementation of spatial statistical analysis in a GIS software environment (broadly interpreted). The focus is primarily on the analysis of so-called lattice data, or discrete spatial objects, at the expense of ignoring point pattern analysis and geostatistical methods. First, a brief review is given of the relation between categories of spatial statistical analysis and the associated data structures required in a software implementation. The bulk of the chapter consists of a review of some illustrative computational issues, organized in terms of three types of investigations: exploratory spatial data analysis (ESDA), spatial autocorrelation statistics, and spatial regression analysis. This is followed by a short overview of existing software tools, with some special attention given to the development efforts carried out at the CSISS. Some comments on future directions and challenges conclude the chapter.

SPATIAL STATISTICS, GIS, AND DATA STRUCTURES

In his classic text, Cressie (1993) outlines three categories of spatial statistical analysis, based on the data type under consideration: geostatistical data, lattice data, and patterns (in particular, point patterns). From a statistical perspective, the distinction is fundamental: geostatistical analysis pertains to modeling random surfaces, lattice data to random values at discrete locations, and patterns to random spatial events. Each requires its own formal probabilistic framework for analysis. Also, typically, assumptions that work for one do not work for the others. For example, in spatial regression analysis, this is evident in the contrast between so-called expanding domain asymptotics (typically applied to lattice data) and infill asymptotics (used in geostatistical analysis). Statistical procedures that require one set of assumptions (regularity conditions) may become invalid under the other setting (for technical details, see, e.g., Lahiri 1996, Anselin 2002).

A GIS is agnostic to this distinction and handles spatial features without regard to the underlying statistical model. Without the proper caution, it is therefore possible for the unwary user to apply totally inappropriate techniques to spatial objects (point or polygon features) contained in a GIS. Points, in particular, require special attention, since a point could be a sample location from a random surface (geostatistical analysis), the location of a random event (point pattern analysis), or the representation of a discrete spatial object (lattice data). Ignoring this distinction can easily lead to problems. For example, it may be tempting to apply variogram analysis to data recorded at county centroids (point locations) although this is of doubtful statistical value. The distinction between the statistical model and the GIS data model is something that must be made explicit in any extension of standard GIS functionality with spatial statistical capability.

Spatial data can be considered as characterized by features (e.g., points, lines, polygons), supports (size, shape, orientation), and attributes (Waller and Gotway 2004, p. 38). The implementation of spatial statistical analysis in software systems, therefore, must be able to store and manipulate these characteristics. In all but the simplest situation, this requires data structures and functionality typically associated with a GIS, as opposed to standard statistical software. One exception is point data, where the x,y coordinates can be treated as attributes in the same manner as other variables associated with a given observation. This allows several elementary spatial statistical procedures to be carried out in standard statistical software. Examples are centrography (descriptive statistics of location) and trend surface regression (regression on a polynomial in the x,y coordinates). However, even in this simple setting, complications arise quickly, for example, when the interpoint distance needs to be computed. These distances pertain to pairs of observations and do not fit the standard data (flat) table format, where each row corresponds to a single observation. Hence, to carry out point pattern analysis or variography, which crucially depend on the computation and manipulation of distances, specialized data structures must be employed that can handle both individual observations as well as links between pairs of observations.

Unlike points, polygon spatial data objects cannot be readily encompassed in the data structures used in standard statistical software. A nonconstant number of vertices contained in the boundary files for irregular polygons does not fit the flat table format with a fixed number of columns (attributes) for each object. Instead, a more flexible database system is required, typically part of a GIS. In addition to the boundary vertex coordinates, however, most spatial statistical analyses also require information on the spatial arrangement or topology of the spatial objects. Formally, this is expressed in a spatial weights matrix, although the matrix is not an efficient data structure to store this information. Instead, the sparseness of the connectivity information should be exploited (Anselin and Smirnov 1996). Few GIS currently provide data structures with this information, and this almost always requires additional manipulation outside the GIS (Anselin 2000). Similar issues arise in the spatial statistical analysis of fields (as opposed to spatial objects), such as remotely sensed images in a raster GIS. While the regular structure of the pixels facilitates the definition of the notion of *neighbor* (e.g., north, south, east, west, using a rook criterion), the exploitation of this for the construction of spatial weights is typically not present in current systems.

So far, the discussion has been couched in terms of cross-sectional data analysis, for which the GIS data structures are well developed. In contrast, space–time analysis in commercial GIS is still in its infancy. Useful data structures are either collections of cross sections over time or of time series across space, largely precluding the analysis of true space–time dynamics (interaction effects between space and time). In practice, many types of statistical analysis, such as space–time correlations and panel data spatial econometrics (Anselin et al. 2005a), can still be carried out as long as the container (the spatial frame) remains constant over time (e.g., the same counties analyzed over time). However, when the locations vary over time, the associated change of support problem (COSP) is challenging, and no general and satisfactory solutions are yet available (Gotway and Young 2002). Finally, the definition of a meaningful metric for space–time distance remains a formidable problem, both conceptually as well as in practice (for the technical discussion, see Anselin et al. 2005a).

COMPUTATIONAL ISSUES

Several complex computational issues are encountered in the software implementation of spatial statistical procedures, either as part of a GIS or as an extension to a GIS. Some illustrative examples are briefly reviewed below, with particular attention to exploratory spatial data analysis, spatial autocorrelation statistics, and spatial regression. The discussion is focused on a lattice data context, where (discrete) spatial objects are represented as either points or polygons, and the spatial arrangement of these objects is an essential feature of the analysis. This is formalized in a spatial weights matrix, constructed either by using information on common boundaries (for polygons) or derived from a distance calculation (for points). Whether the spatial objects are represented as points or polygons is relatively immaterial, since centroids or central values can be readily computed for any set of polygons, and tessellations (such as Thiessen polygons) may be applied to points (for a more elaborate discussion, see Anselin 1998).

In contrast to lattice data, computational issues encountered in the implementation of point pattern analysis and geostatistical techniques do not require a spatial weights matrix. They depend primarily on the efficient calculation of distances and the identification of points within selected distance bands.

EXPLORATORY SPATIAL DATA ANALYSIS

Exploratory spatial data analysis (ESDA) can be defined as "a collection of techniques to describe and visualize spatial distributions, identify atypical locations or spatial outliers, discover patterns of spatial association, clusters or hot spots, and suggest spatial regimes or other forms of spatial heterogeneity" (Anselin 1999, p. 258). Its implementation in software requires the operationalization of different views of the data, such as traditional statistical graphs (e.g., histogram, box plot, and scatter plot) and maps (e.g., standard choropleth maps, outlier maps, cartograms, and conditional maps). While some of these graphs have been included in current GIS, most of them are absent. Most notably, very little functionality is available to construct alternatives to the familiar choropleth maps, such as cartograms or conditional maps.

An essential feature of effective ESDA software is the implementation of dynamic linking and brushing. *Linking* is a property whereby any observation selected in any of the views (typically through user interaction with a pointing device) is simultaneously selected in all views, usually by highlighting. *Brushing* is a dynamic version of linking, where a subset of observations is selected using a brush (circle or rectangle). Moving the brush over the view changes the selection dynamically, and this is again reflected in all the other views. Early implementations of these techniques in the form of brushing scatter plots and other dynamic graphics were outlined in Stuetzle (1987) and Cleveland and McGill (1988). Geographic brushing was introduced by Monmonier (1989) and first made operational in the Spider/Regard software of Haslett, Unwin, and associates (Haslett et al. 1990).

While a limited form of linking is implemented in many commercial GIS (e.g., linking between a location on a map view and a row in a data table), brushing is absent. The efficient implementing of brushing requires a software architecture that allows for instant updating of the (spatial) selection and a refreshing of all visible windows. This is not trivial, and even today very few systems contain true dynamic linking and brushing of multiple maps and graphs (for a technical discussion, see Anselin et al. 2002).

SPATIAL AUTOCORRELATION

Statistics to measure spatial autocorrelation are the basic tools in the analysis of spatial clustering and spatial clusters. *Clustering* is a global property of the spatial pattern in a dataset (values and/or locations are more closely together than they would be randomly), measured by a single statistic. This is not necessarily meaningful in a GIS setting, since it does not lend itself to mapping, but rather to a numerical display. In contrast, *clusters* are local (specific locations where the values are more similar than they would be randomly) and thus ideally suited for mapping and incorporation into a GIS.

Measures of spatial autocorrelation are constructed by combining an indicator of value (attribute) similarity and an indicator of spatial similarity. The latter is formalized in a spatial weights matrix, with elements w_{ij} that are nonzero for neighbors (with the definition of *neighbor* left to the specific context). Attribute similarity can be formalized in a number of ways, the most commonly used one being a cross product, such as x_i, x_j (with x_i, x_j as observations for locations i, j).

Arguably the most familiar global spatial autocorrelation statistic is Moran's *I* (for an extensive treatment, see Cliff and Ord 1981, Upton and Fingleton 1985, and more recently, Waller and Gotway 2004):

$$I = [\, \Sigma_i \, \Sigma_j \, z_i z_j \, w_{ij} \, / \, S_0 \,] \, / \, [\Sigma_i \, z_i^2 \, / \, N \,],$$

where z_i is the observation on a variable at i in deviations from the mean, N is the number of observations, and S_0 is a normalizing factor equal to the sum of all the weights, $S_0 = \Sigma_i \, \Sigma_j \, w_{ij}$.

The computation of this statistic is a straightforward application of basic algebraic operations, such as a sum of squares and cross products (again, requiring efficient loop structures in the software). It is facilitated by the use of a spatially lagged variable. For each location i, the spatial lag is defined as (following Anselin 1988):

$$[Wz]_i = \Sigma_j \, w_{ij} \, z_j,$$

for which the value at each location is obtained as a weighted average of the values at neighboring locations (with the neighbors defined by the nonzero elements in w_{ij}).

The Moran's *I* coefficient is also the slope of the regression line of the spatially lagged variable $[Wz]_i$ on the original variable (Anselin 1996). This is not only an easy way to compute the statistic (even in a standard statistics package), but it allows for the visualization of global spatial autocorrelation in a Moran scatter plot (Anselin 1996). A crucial step in this calculation is the spatially lagged variable, which can be implemented efficiently by exploiting the sparse structure of the spatial weights. More specifically, to compute the spatial lag for a given observation, a weighted average is needed (using the weights w_{ij}) of the values at the neighboring locations. As long as the latter are identified (e.g., in a sparse weights data structure), no explicit matrix manipulations are required. While this is arguably one of the most useful operations to facilitate spatial autocorrelation analysis (and spatial regression), a spatial lag constructor is not a standard feature of most commercial GIS.

A local version of Moran's *I* allows for the detection of spatial clusters and outliers (Anselin 1995). For each location, the statistic can be computed as $(1/m) z_i \Sigma_j w_{ij} z_j$ (where m is a constant scaling factor), and significant locations can be identified on a map. In addition to significance, the local Moran also indicates the type of local spatial autocorrelation, either clusters (of high or low values) or outliers (high–low or low–high).[2]

Inference for both global and local Moran's *I* can be obtained either analytically or by means of a permutation approach. Analytical approaches tend to be approximations of asymptotic (limiting) results. To obtain these results, the moments (mean and variance) of the statistic need to be computed, which requires considerable manipulation of the weights matrix (see Cliff and Ord 1981, and more recently, Tiefelsdorf 2002). For the local Moran statistic, the analytical approximations have been shown to be poor (Anselin 1995). In practice, the computation of the various weights matrix summaries (e.g., sum of all elements) depends on efficient loop structures. Many scripting languages are notoriously poor in this respect, and performance suffers accordingly, especially for larger datasets (N > 1000).

A preferred and more robust approach is to use random permutation. Here, inference is based on an empirical distribution of the statistic obtained by recomputing its value for a large number of resampled datasets. These datasets are obtained by randomly reshuffling the values to different locations. For local statistics, the permutation is conditional, holding the value fixed for the location under consideration. An efficient implementation of random permutation is essential in the practical calculation of local and global spatial autocorrelation statistics since analytical shortcuts are often of doubtful reliability. Again, to obtain reasonable computing performance, this requires efficient looping structures. It also is easily amenable to parallelization, allowing its application for even very large datasets.

SPATIAL REGRESSION

Spatial regression (spatial econometrics) deals with the incorporation of spatial effects (spatial autocorrelation and spatial heterogeneity) in regression models (Anselin 1988). It is the natural third step in the progression from spatial exploration/visualization to description and modeling. It can be envisaged to consist of four major components: model specification (formally specifying spatial effects in the regression), estimation, testing, and prediction.

The potential for greater analytical power resulting from a linkage between spatial regression and GIS is less clear than for exploration and description. The essential computational requirements for regression modeling involve linear algebra manipulations (determinants, inverses, and traces of possibly large and sparse matrices) and (nonlinear) optimization. This can be readily implemented outside a GIS, since there are no particular competitive advantages to incorporating these functions within the spatial data structures. One exception is spatial prediction, where the visualization power of the GIS is essential in presenting the results of computations.

Spatial prediction, also known as interpolation, or kriging, is a key part of a geostatistical modeling toolbox. It is therefore not surprising that one of the first analytical extensions added to desktop GIS implemented spatial interpolation. The main computational requirement of geostatistical analysis, however, relates to the calculation of distances and the sorting of pairs of points by distance. In contrast to the lattice data setting, this does not require information on spatial arrangement.

More importantly, the conceptual framework of continuous surfaces does not readily extend to discrete spatial objects. For the latter, spatial prediction does not imply interpolation (i.e., predicting values for locations where no values are observed), but instead the calculation of model output for the observed discrete locations. Clearly, predicted values and residuals from a spatial regression model lend themselves to visualization in a GIS. This is particularly useful in an interactive process of model refinement (specification, estimation, diagnostics, respecification). The visualization of predicted values is also important in the context of smoothed rate maps in public health and crime analysis (e.g., Lawson et al. 2003) and for maps depicting the spatial variability of model parameters (e.g., in geographically weighted regression, Fotheringham et al. 2002).

Of the other three components of spatial regression, only model specification can benefit from an effective interface with GIS. The essence of spatial regression models is the incorporation of spatially lagged variables in the regression specification (Anselin 2002). These spatial averages pertain to dependent variables, explanatory variables, or regression error terms, and their inclusion in the model leads to various specifications of spatial externalities and spatial multipliers (Anselin 2003a). Their computation must be based on effective data structures for the spatial weights, which should be (but are typically not) provided by the GIS.

The estimation and specification testing of spatial regression models requires a specialized methodology that explicitly takes into account the dependence structure among all observations (e.g., Anselin 1988, Haining 1990, Cressie 1993). Three main approaches have been suggested. The most familiar one is based on the maximum likelihood (ML) principle and requires the optimization of a nonlinear likelihood function. The latter is computationally very demanding due to the presence of the so-called Jacobian, the determinant of a matrix of dimension equal to the number of observations. In addition, the calculation of asymptotic variance estimates (needed for significance tests) is hampered by the need for a matrix inverse of the same dimension. Until recently, these computational issues precluded the reliable (in a numerical sense) estimation of spatial regression models for datasets with more than 1000 observations. Considerable advances have been obtained to tackle this problem, and currently several specialized algorithms exist that exploit the sparseness of the spatial weights in the calculation of the Jacobian and allow the estimation of models for very large datasets (e.g., Pace and Barry 1997, Barry and Pace 1999, Smirnov and Anselin 2001).

A second methodological framework for the estimation of spatial regression models is based on generalized methods of moments (e.g., Kelejian and Prucha 1998, 1999; Conley 1999). Compared to the ML approach, its computational requirements are minimal. Provided spatially lagged variables can be readily calculated, all other statistical inference can be implemented in standard (although advanced) econometric software.

A third approach to estimation of spatial regression models uses simulation estimators, primarily applied to models where the dependent variable is discrete, such as in a spatial probit model (Fleming 2004), or to hierarchical models for count data (Banerjee et al. 2004). These estimation methods require fast algorithms to implement the various samplers, such as the recursive importance sampler (RIS) and Markov Chain Monte Carlo (MCMC) methods (Gibbs sampler and the Metropolis-Hastings algorithms). While specialized software exists to implement these techniques (e.g., in the popular WinBUGS package), active methodological and computational development is ongoing. In spatial models, there are still considerable hurdles to applying the simulation estimators to medium and large datasets and to models that incorporate spatial simultaneity (as opposed to conditional spatial models).

SOFTWARE TOOLS

The availability of software to implement spatial statistical methods has increased tremendously since the early 1990s, when, apart from geostatistical software and some point pattern routines, only SpaceStat™ (Anselin 1992) existed as a self-contained package that implemented spatial autocorrelation and spatial regression. To date, mainstream commercial statistical and econometric packages still only have limited (if any) spatial functionality. This contrasts with a substantial number of freestanding niche software packages and applets, as well as various software toolboxes that implement the range of methods from ESDA to spatial correlation, cluster analysis, and spatial regression/spatial econometrics. With a few exceptions, most of these software implementations are noncommercial, developed in the academic world. In the United States, several were initially funded by major federal agencies such as the National Science Foundation (NSF), the National Institute of Justice (NIJ), the National Institutes of Health (NIH), and the Environmental Protection Agency (EPA), and a growing number are now open source.

While a comprehensive review is beyond the current scope, it is useful to list some examples to illustrate the tremendous advances made in recent years. Several modern toolkits for exploratory spatial data analysis include innovative geovisualization, as well as dynamic linking, and, to a lesser extent, brushing. Examples of self-contained packages (with varying degrees of functionality for spatial and space–time correlation analysis) are the cartographic data visualizer, cdv, implemented in tcl/tk (Dykes 1997), GeoVISTA Studio, developed using Java (Takatsuka and Gahegan 2002), and a system for space–time analysis of regional systems, STARS, built on a Python/Tkinter platform (Rey and Janikas 2005). These packages all contain their own internal mapping capability. In that sense, they can be seen as alternative designs to earlier efforts, where a commercial GIS was used for mapping and geovisualization (e.g., the XGobi™ and XploRe™ links to ArcView software of Symanzik et al. 2000, the SAGE™ toolbox, which interfaces with ArcInfo, Wise et al. 2001, and the DynESDA™ extension for ESDA with ArcView, Anselin 2000).

Common spatial autocorrelation and cluster statistics (both global and local) are included in niche software, such as CrimeStat (Levine 2005), geared to crime analysts, and SaTScan™ (Kulldorf 2002), aimed at the public health world. Commercial software is present in this arena as well, for example, ClusterSeer® (www.terraseer.com) and the spatial statistics toolbox in ArcGIS (ESRI 2004). Interestingly, while the former is proprietary (and even patented), the latter is open source, written in Python. Considerable functionality for cluster analysis is also contained in various packages of the R software environment, available from the Comprehensive R Archive Network (CRAN). Specifically, the spdep package (Bivand and Gebhardt 2000, Bivand 2002), and the recently released DCluster package (Gomez-Rubio et al. 2003) contain a wide range of local and global spatial autocorrelation and cluster (scan) statistics.

Spatial regression analysis, while largely absent in the commercial sector (a notable exception being the now somewhat dated S+SpatialStats extension for S-Plus, Kaluzny et al. 1997), is present in an increasing number of toolboxes developed in mathematical software environments, such as MATLAB and R, as well as in add-on macros for econometric software, such as Stata®. For example, the spatial statistical toolbox of Pace and Barry (1998) and the spatial econometrics toolbox of LeSage (www.spatialeconometrics.com) are implemented in MATLAB and contain maximum likelihood estimation routines for spatial regression models. LeSage's toolbox also includes a Gibbs sampler for Bayesian analysis of spatial regressions. These tools stand out in their use of specialized sparse matrix manipulation routines to allow the analysis of large data sets. Maximum likelihood estimation and regression diagnostics are also included in the Stata toolbox described in Pisati (2001). A very comprehensive toolset for spatial regression, still under active development, is contained in the R package spdep (Bivand 2002). Considerable activity has also focused on implementing Markov Chain Monte Carlo simulation estimators, with some limited application to spatial data analysis, as illustrated for WinBUGS and MLwiN in Lawson et al. (2003).

Finally, it is worth noting the spatial software tools development program that is carried out under the auspices of the Center for Spatially Integrated Social Science, CSISS (Goodchild et al. 2000). This effort has focused on two different approaches: one, embodied in the GeoDa package (Anselin et al. 2005b) is aimed at the nonspecialist user and is to provide an introduction to spatial data analysis; the other, PySpace, is geared toward advanced analysts and consists of a collection of modules for spatial econometric analysis written in the Python language.

GeoDa is designed to provide nonspecialist users with an intuitive and interactive path through an empirical spatial data exercise, starting with mapping and geovisualization, proceeding through ESDA and spatial autocorrelation analysis, and ending up with basic spatial regression. The distinctive characteristic of the software is the use of dynamically linked windows for all graphs, maps, and tables, resulting in a highly interactive environment for the exploration of spatial data. The core functionality of GeoDa is centered on mapping (choropleth maps, as well as outlier maps, smoothed rate maps, cartograms, map animation, and conditional maps), traditional EDA (common statistical graphics, including parallel coordinate plots and three-dimensional scatter plots), spatial autocorrelation analysis (global and local Moran's *I*, Moran scatter plot, and LISA cluster maps), and spatial regression (diagnostics for spatial autocorrelation and maximum likelihood estimation of the spatial lag and spatial error model). In addition, the software includes a range of tools to perform various spatial data manipulations, including conversion between points and polygons and spatial weights construction.

GeoDa's functionality is illustrated in figure 1, which shows a screen shot of an analysis of house prices in Seattle, Washington. The figure incorporates six views of the data, including a standard deviational map (upper left), a cartogram (middle center), and a LISA cluster map, which indicates the significant local clusters and spatial outliers, classified by type of association (lower left). Global spatial autocorrelation is visualized in the Moran scatter plot (upper center). Multivariate data exploration is illustrated by the parallel coordinate plot (bottom right) and the three-dimensional scatter plot (upper right). The selected observations are highlighted as yellow in all the graphs, demonstrating the linking process. Note also how the original house locations were converted from points to Thiessen polygons, using the GeoDa tools.

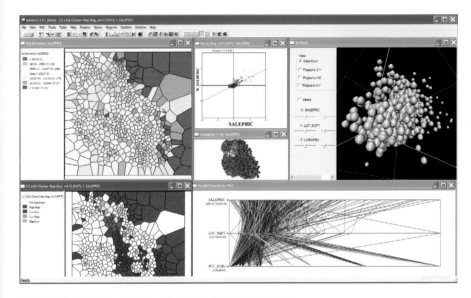

Figure 1. GeoDa screen shot exploring Seattle house prices.

A further illustration of the spatial regression capability in GeoDa is shown in figure 2, which includes a residual map from the classic ordinary least squares (OLS) regression in Anselin (1988), as well as for the maximum likelihood estimation of the spatial lag model. Two Moran scatter plots are featured as well, highlighting how the inclusion of the spatially lagged dependent variable has eliminated residual spatial autocorrelation.

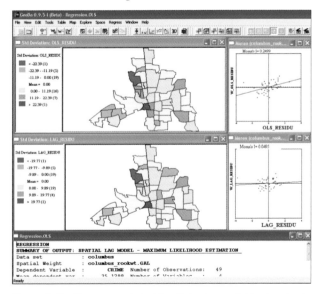

Figure 2. GeoDa screen shot of the Columbus neighborhood crime spatial regression.

GeoDa was first released by CSISS in January 2003 and has a fast-growing user base (counting over 4500 users in early 2005).[3] The software is written in C++ and is still under active development, with the latest efforts focused on making it cross-platform, using the wxWidget graphical library to create a uniform user interface. The cross-platform interface is illustrated in figure 3, with a linked box plot and box map for the Columbus crime data featured on Linux (Red Hat).

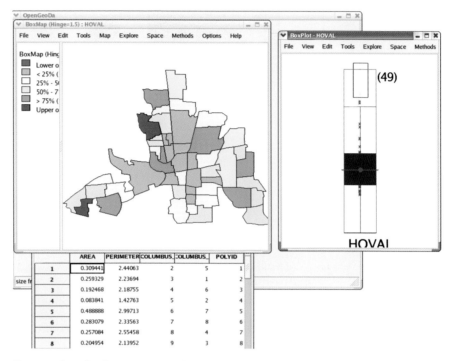

Figure 3. OpenGeoDa screen shot of linked windows on a Linux platform.

In contrast to the interactive and user-friendly design of GeoDa, PySpace is aimed at a more specialized audience of spatial econometricians. It consists of a collection of modules to carry out spatial regression analysis, without mapping or visualization. It currently contains maximum likelihood and moments estimation methods for linear models, as well as tools to estimate spatial panel regressions. The latter include pooled spatial error and spatial lag regression, as well as spatially seemingly unrelated regressions (spatial SUR). For example, in figure 4, the output illustrates a maximum likelihood estimation of the parameters of a SUR model with spatial autoregressive error terms applied to a growth convergence model for European regions. PySpace is still under active development and is intended to have its first public release sometime in 2005.

```
● ○ ○                     Terminal — bash — 83x37
SEEMINGLY UNRELATED REGRESSIONS (SUR)
MODELS WITH SPATIALLY DEPENDENT ERRORS
MAXIMUM LIKELIHOOD ESTIMATION

Observations = 290        Deg. of free. = 286        Variables = 4
R2 = 0.7625
LIK = 943.8481

EQUATION 1       DEPENDENT VARIABLE g80_89
Observations = 145     Variables = 2    Deg. of free. = 143    Var prop = 0.0735

VARIABLE     Coefficient   Std. Dev.    z-value     p-value
Const          0.166347     0.035969     4.6248      0.0000037
gdp80         -0.010207     0.004105    -2.4867      0.0128917
lambda         0.85336      0.049221    17.3375      0.0000000

EQUATION 2       DEPENDENT VARIABLE g89_99
Observations = 145     Variables = 2    Deg. of free. = 143    Var prop = 0.1275

VARIABLE     Coefficient   Std. Dev.    z-value     p-value
Const          0.152461     0.032798     4.6485      0.0000033
gdp80         -0.011636     0.003481    -3.3433      0.0008278
lambda         0.793301     0.063759    12.4421      0.0000000
```

Figure 4. Spatial seemingly unrelated regression output in PySpace.

CONCLUSIONS

Considerable progress has been made in terms of extending basic GIS function-ality with software to implement spatial statistical methods. A wide range of tools is readily available, but there is little standardization, and most packages implement their own data formats and conventions. The lack of commonly accepted program interfaces tends to result in a high degree of duplication. While some duplication is undoubtedly healthy, the replication of basic spa-tial data manipulation and mapping functions in specialized statistical software cannot be efficient. Progress would be aided by a greater degree of interoper-ability. In this respect, the growing move towards an open source approach is encouraging, since it promotes quality control, avoids duplication, encour-ages the use of well-documented API, and stimulates a modular approach. This should increasingly allow the user or tool developer to mix and match com-ponents in order to obtain an efficient combination of analytical methods best suited to each specific application.

Several formidable challenges remain, however, both on the methodological end as well as in terms of computational implementation. Increasingly, applied researchers do not hesitate to tackle data obtained at different scales and zonal aggregations, rather than avoiding such settings, as may have been the case in the past. This requires an appropriate solution to the change of support prob-lem (COSP), suggesting the need for efficient integration of spatial data struc-tures and statistical methods. In addition, new models are constantly being introduced to the spatial domain, such as specifications with spatially correlated latent variables and spatial panel data. These require methodological advances in estimation and diagnostic testing, matched by computational implementa-tion. Practical solutions to the latter are still unsatisfactory in dealing with the large data volumes generated in both social and natural sciences. The very size of these datasets presents a challenge to spatial statistical analysis, in terms of visualization, computation, and storage, and may require fundamental changes in the current paradigms. Much remains to be done.

ACKNOWLEDGMENTS

Earlier versions of this chapter were presented at an ESRI Seminar, May 28, 2003, and at the Workshop on Modeling and GIS, ESRI, Redlands, California, September 25–26, 2003. The stimulating environment provided by ESRI and comments by participants at these seminars are greatly appreciated. The research behind this work was supported in part by U.S. National Science Foundation Grant SBR-9978058 to the Center for Spatially Integrated Social Science.

NOTES

1. See www.csiss.org/clearinghouse.

2. A similar local statistic, Gi (Getis and Ord 1992), also distinguishes local clusters, but not local outliers.

3. An extensive description of GeoDa is given in Anselin (2003b, 2004) and Anselin et al. (2005b).

REFERENCES

Anselin, L. 1988. *Spatial econometrics: Methods and models.* Boston: Kluwer.

———. 1992. SpaceStat, A software program for the analysis of spatial data. National Center for Geographic Information and Analysis. Santa Barbara, Calif.: University of California.

———. 1995. Local indicators of spatial association–LISA. *Geographical Analysis* 27: 93–115.

———. 1996. The Moran scatterplot as an ESDA tool to assess local instability in spatial association. In *Spatial analytical perspectives on GIS in environmental and socioeconomic sciences,* ed. M. Fischer, H. Scholten, and D. Unwin, 111–25. London: Taylor & Francis.

———. 1998. Exploratory spatial data analysis in a geocomputational environment. In *Geocomputation: A primer,* ed. P. Longley, S. Brooks, B. Macmillan, and R. McDonell, 77–94. New York: John Wiley and Sons.

———. 1999. Interactive techniques and exploratory spatial data analysis. In *Geographic information systems: Principles, techniques, management and applications,* ed. P. A. Longley, M. F. Goodchild, D. J. Maguire, and D. W. Rhind, 251–64. New York: John Wiley and Sons.

———. 2000. Computing environments for spatial data analysis. *Journal of Geographical Systems* 2: 201–220.

———. 2002. Under the hood: Issues in the specification and interpretation of spatial regression models. *Agricultural Economics* 27: 247–67.

———. 2003a. Spatial externalities, spatial multipliers, and spatial econometrics. International Regional Science Review 26: 153–66.

———. 2003b. GeoDa 0.9 User's Guide. Spatial Analysis Laboratory (SAL), University of Illinois at Urbana-Champaign.

———. 2004. GeoDa 0.95i Release Notes. Spatial Analysis Laboratory (SAL), University of Illinois at Urbana-Champaign.

Anselin, L., and S. Bao. 1997. Exploratory spatial data analysis linking SpaceStat and ArcView. In *Recent developments in spatial analysis,* ed. M. Fischer and A. Getis, 35–59. Berlin: Springer-Verlag.

Anselin, L., and A. Getis. 1992. Spatial statistical analysis and geographic information systems. *The Annals of Regional Science* 26: 19–33.

Anselin, L., and O. Smirnov. 1996. Efficient algorithms for constructing proper higher order spatial lag operators. *Journal of Regional Science* 36: 67–89.

Anselin, L., R. Dodson, and S. Hudak. 1993. Linking GIS and spatial data analysis in practice. *Geographical Systems* 1: 3–23.

Anselin, L., Y-W Kim, and I. Syabri. 2004. Web-based analytical tools for the exploration of spatial data. *Journal of Geographical Systems* 6: 197–218.

Anselin, L., J. Le Gallo, and H. Jayet. 2005a. Spatial panel econometrics. In *The econometrics of panel data: Fundamentals and recent developments in theory and practice,* ed. L. Matyas and P. Sevestre. Dordrecht: Kluwer.

Anselin, L., I. Syabri, and Y. Kho. 2005b. GeoDa: An introduction to spatial data analysis. *Geographical Analysis.*

Anselin, L., I. Syabri, and O. Smirnov. 2002. Visualizing multivariate spatial autocorrelation with dynamically linked windows. In *New tools for spatial data analysis: Proceedings of a workshop,* ed. L. Anselin and S. Rey. Center for Spatially Integrated Social Science, University of California, Santa Barbara. CD-ROM.

Banerjee, S., B. Carlin, and A. Gelfand. 2004. *Hierarchical modeling and analysis for spatial data.* Boca Raton: Chapman & Hall/CRC.

Barry, R. P., and R. K. Pace. 1999. Monte Carlo estimation of the log determinant of large sparse matrices. *Linear Algebra and its Applications* 289: 41–54.

Bivand, R. 2002. Implementing spatial data analysis software tools in R. In *New tools for spatial data analysis: Proceedings of a workshop,* ed. L. Anselin and S. Rey. Center for Spatially Integrated Social Science, University of California, Santa Barbara. CD-ROM.

Bivand, R., and A. Gebhardt. 2000. Implementing functions for spatial statistical analysis using the R language. *Journal of Geographical Systems* 2: 307–17.

Cleveland, W., and M. McGill. 1988. *Dynamic graphics for statistics.* Pacific Grove, Calif.: Wadsworth.

Cliff, A., and J. K. Ord. 1981. *Spatial processes: Models and applications.* London: Pion.

Conley, T. 1999. GMM estimation with cross-sectional dependence. *Journal of Econometrics* 92: 1–45.

Dykes, J. A. 1997. Exploring spatial data representation with dynamic graphics. *Computers and Geosciences* 23: 345–70.

ESRI. 2004. An Overview of the Spatial Statistics Toolbox. ArcGIS Desktop 9 Online Help System. ESRI. Redlands, Calif.

Farley, J. A., W. F. Limp, and J. Lockhart. 1990. The archeologist's workbench: Integrating GIS, remote sensing, EDA, and database management. In *Interpreting space: GIS and archeology*, ed. K. Allen, F. Green, and E. Zubrow, 141–61. London: Taylor & Francis.

Fischer, M., and P. Nijkamp. 1993. *Geographic information systems, spatial modeling, and policy evaluation*. Berlin: Springer-Verlag.

Fleming, M. 2004. Techniques for estimating spatially dependent discrete choice models. In *Advances in spatial econometrics: Methodology, tools, and applications*, ed. L. Anselin, R. Florax, and S. Rey, 145–67. Berlin: Springer.

Fotheringham, A. S., and P. Rogerson. 1994. *Spatial analysis and GIS*. London: Taylor & Francis.

Fotheringham, A. S., C. Brunsdon, and M. Charlton. 2002. *Geographically weighted regression*. Chichester: John Wiley and Sons.

Gahegan, M., M. Takatsuka, M. Wheeler, and F. Hardisty. 2002. Introducing GeoVISTA Studio: An integrated suite of visualization and computational methods for exploration and knowledge construction in geography. *Computers, Environment and Urban Systems* 26: 267–92.

Getis, A., and J. K. Ord. 1992. The analysis of spatial association by use of distance statistics. *Geographical Analysis* 24: 189–206.

Gomez-Rubio, V., J. Ferrandiz, and A. Lopez. 2003. Detecting clusters of diseases with R. In *Proceedings of the 3rd international workshop on distributed statistical computing (DSC 2003)*, ed. K. Hornik, F. Leisch, and A. Zeileis. Vienna, Austria. www.ci.tuwien.ac.at/Conferences/DSC-2003.

Goodchild, M. F. 1987. A spatial analytical perspective on geographical information systems. *International Journal of Geographical Information Systems* 1: 327–34.

Goodchild, M. F., R. P. Haining, S. Wise, et al. 1992. Integrating GIS and spatial analysis—problems and possibilities. *International Journal of Geographical Information Systems* 6: 407–23.

Goodchild, M. F., L. Anselin, R. Appelbaum, and B. Harthorn. 2000. Toward spatially integrated social science. *International Regional Science Review* 23: 139–59.

Gotway, C., and L. Young. 2002. Combining incompatible spatial data. *Journal of the American Statistical Association* 97: 632–48.

Haining, R. 1989. Geography and spatial statistics: Current positions, future developments. In *Remodeling geography*, ed. B. Macmillan, 191–203. Oxford: Basil Blackwell.

———. 1990. *Spatial data analysis in the social and environmental sciences.* Cambridge: Cambridge University Press.

Haining, R., W. Wise, and J. Ma. 2000. Designing and implementing software for spatial statistical analysis in a GIS environment. *Journal of Geographical Systems* 2: 257–86.

Haslett, J., G. Wills, and A. Unwin. 1990. SPIDER – an interactive statistical tool for the analysis of spatially distributed data. *International Journal of Geographic Information Systems* 4: 285–96.

Kaluzny, S., S. Vega, T. Cardoso, and A. Shelly. 1997. *S+SpatialStats user's manual.* New York: Springer-Verlag.

Kelejian, H., and I. Prucha. 1998. A generalized spatial two stage least squares procedure for estimating a spatial autoregressive model with autoregressive disturbances. *Journal of Real Estate Finance and Economics* 17: 99–121.

———. 1999. A generalized moments estimator for the autoregressive parameter in a spatial model. *International Economic Review* 40: 509–33.

Kulldorff, M. 2002. *SaTScan 3.0: Software for the spatial and space–time scan statistics.* Bethesda, Md.: National Cancer Institute.

Lahiri, S. 1996. On the inconsistency of estimators under infill asymptotics for spatial data. *Sankhya A* 58: 403–17.

Lawson, A., W. Browne, and C. Vidal Rodeiro. 2003. *Disease mapping with WinBUGS and MLwiN.* Chichester: John Wiley and Sons.

Monmonier, M. 1989. Geographic brushing: Enhancing exploratory analysis of the scatterplot matrix. *Geographical Analysis* 21: 81–84.

Pace, R. K., and R. Barry. 1997. Quick computation of spatial autoregressive estimators. *Geographical Analysis* 29: 232–46.

———. 1998. Spatial Statistical Toolbox 1.0. Working paper, Louisiana State University at Baton Rouge.

Pisati, M. 2001. Tools for spatial data analysis. *Stata Technical Bulletin* 60: 21–37.

Rey, S., and M. Janikas. 2005. STARS: Space-time analysis of regional systems. *Geographical Analysis.*

Smirnov, O., and L. Anselin. 2001. Fast maximum likelihood estimation of very large spatial autoregressive models: A characteristic polynomial approach. *Computational Statistics and Data Analysis* 35: 301–19.

Stuetzle, W. 1987. Plot windows. *Journal of the American Statistical Association* 82: 466–75.

Symanzik, J., D. Cook, N. Lewin-Koh, J. J. Majure, and I. Megretskaia. 2000. Linking ArcView and Xgobi: Insight behind the front end. *Journal of Computational and Graphical Statistics* 9: 470–90.

Takatsuka, M., and M. Gahegan. 2002. GeoVISTA Studio: A codeless visual programming environment for geoscientific data analysis and visualization. *Computers and Geosciences* 28: 1131–41.

Ungerer, M. J., and M. F. Goodchild. 2002. Integrating spatial data analysis and GIS: A new implementation using the Component Object Model (COM). *International Journal of Geographical Information Science* 16: 41–53.

Upton, G., and B. Fingleton. 1985. *Spatial data analysis by example.* New York: John Wiley and Sons.

Waller, L., and C. Gotway. 2004. *Applied spatial statistics for public health data.* Hoboken, N.J.: John Wiley and Sons.

Wise, S., R. Haining, and J. Ma. 2001. Providing spatial statistical data analysis functionality for the GIS user: The SAGE project. *International Journal of Geographic Information Science* 15: 239–54.

Zhang, Z., and D. Griffith. 2000. Integrating GIS components and spatial statistical analysis in DBMSs. *International Journal of Geographical Information Science* 14: 543–66.

Chapter 6

Linking General-Purpose Dynamic Simulation Models with GIS

IAN MILLER, STEFAN KNOPF, AND RICK KOSSIK

GOLDSIM TECHNOLOGY GROUP

ISSAQUAH, WASHINGTON

ABSTRACT

A DYNAMIC SIMULATION MODEL is a computer-based model that simulates how a complex system will change over time. Dynamic simulation models are widely used in fields as diverse as biology, engineering, and business. However, most dynamic simulation models available today are not designed to simulate geographically-distributed systems, and applying a general-purpose simulation model to something as complex as a geographic system is very difficult.

While there are numerous special-purpose dynamic spatial models which have been designed for specific applications, there is a growing need for flexible general-purpose dynamic spatial models that are capable of representing the interactions between many different entities or subsystems. Such models can be used to develop improved understanding and to support better decisions about these complex systems.

This chapter describes different classes of dynamic GIS models and discusses two alternative conceptual approaches for linking general-purpose dynamic simulation models with GIS. The chapter closes by describing some of the technical issues involved in creating a robust system that would link general-purpose dynamic simulation models with GIS.

INTRODUCTION

A dynamic simulation model is a computer-based model that simulates how a complex system will change over time. Dynamic simulation models are widely used in fields as diverse as biology, engineering, and business. However, most simulation models available today are not designed to simulate geographically-distributed systems, and applying a general-purpose simulation model to something as complex as a geographic system is very difficult.

There are significant existing communities that are involved in spatially-based dynamic modeling, but these are by and large not composed of GIS specialists. Instead, they are the scientists and engineers who use finite element or other numerical models of spatially distributed processes such as groundwater flow and transport, atmospheric transport, river basin flow, ecosystems, etc. Their models may import base data from GIS systems, but they are generally not directly linked with GIS systems.

While numerous special-purpose dynamic spatial models have been designed for specific applications, there is a growing need for flexible general-purpose dynamic spatial models that are capable of representing the interactions between many different entities or subsystems.

A number of successful custom models that link specific spatial dynamic processes to GIS have been developed (e.g., Maidment 2002, Waddell and Alberti 2003, Sydelko et al. 2003, Bende-Michl et al. 2003). However, these tend to be of limited value as general-purpose models of dynamic geographic systems.

Some general-purpose modeling systems have been developed, such as the Spatial Modeling Environment (SME) originally developed at the University of Maryland (SME 2004, Maxwell and Voinov 2005, this volume), the PCRaster system from Utrecht University (Burrough et al. 2005, this volume), and the Idrisi system from Clark Labs (Clark Labs 2004; Eastman et al. 2005, this volume). Westervelt and Shapiro (2000) provide an excellent overview of alternative modeling concepts and systems that have been developed. These are primarily university-based model development and research initiatives, however, and for most applications, dynamic GIS modeling is currently more of a concept than a practical reality.

CLASSIFICATION OF DYNAMIC GIS MODELS

At a fundamental level, dynamic GIS models are used to project future properties of GIS objects such as features, grid cells, or values in attribute tables. Because most geographic systems are heterogeneous, with several different kinds of components, it is envisaged that a dynamic GIS model would frequently consist of a number of different interacting submodels, each modeling different processes, with the set of submodels defined so as to cover a map region. For example, a model might integrate and link submodels of terrestrial and aquatic ecosystems, rainfall/runoff, and erosion and transport processes. Note that several different submodels might be active within the same geographic location, for example, a rainfall/runoff and an ecosystem model which would coexist in the same GIS object.

The following list describes five levels of increasingly complex dynamic GIS models. The simple models at the top of the list are easier to create and would in general be more frequently used than the models further down the list. The more complex model types at the bottom of the list would be expensive to develop and require significant technical expertise by the modelers but would potentially be of great value.

SIMPLE EVOLUTION MODELS

These simple models use a rule to project the evolution of a particular type of attribute over time, with no interaction with other attributes or with neighbors. The projected value could be a floating-point attribute of a specific type of grid cell or feature (e.g., forest stand height) or an attribute value in a specific location in a table. An example of this type of model might be a simple growth model that predicts the average heights of stands of trees as a function of time based on a specified growth rate.

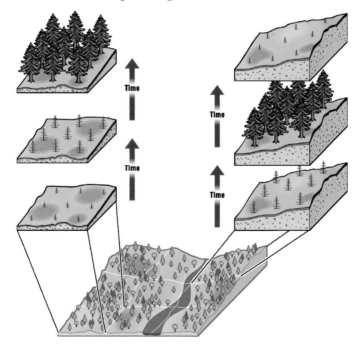

Figure 1. Schematic of simple evolution model that projects the tree stand growth at different locations, assuming no interactions between neighboring grid cells/features or between attributes of a single grid cell/feature.

LOCAL DYNAMICS MODELS

A local dynamics model specifies how multiple properties of a particular class of grid cell, feature, or table row interact with each other to evolve over time. However, there are no interactions with neighbors. Multiple types of model could be defined so as to cover a region so that every type of cell, feature, or unique table entry would have its own model (e.g., a model for lakes, another model for fields, and another for forests). An example of this type of model might be a tree growth model that explicitly considers the local soil nutrients levels, elevation, and solar orientation in order to predict growth rates.

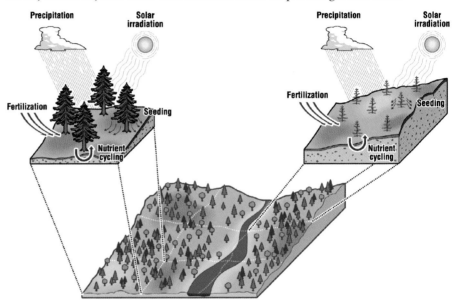

Figure 2. Schematic of local dynamics model that projects the tree stand growth at different locations based on the dynamic interactions of a number of local variables (e.g., nutrient levels) but assumes no interactions between neighboring grid cells/features.

COUPLED DYNAMICS, SINGLE-SYSTEM MODELS

In this class of model, members of a set of cells or features interact with neighbors of the same type to evolve over time. This allows one map region (grid cell or feature) to influence another, to represent propagation (e.g., seeds, fire, urbanization), or transport processes (e.g., erosion, contaminant transport, water flow). However, all of the local models are of the same type and have the same variables.

This approach requires the system to have topological knowledge of neighbors. The local systems defined on each map region need to automatically identify their neighbors (if any) and to define appropriate linkages to transfer information with them. Also, in addition to specifying how to interact with neighbors, the user may have to specify what boundary condition to apply in cases where there is no neighbor in a given direction.

An example of this type of model might be a tree growth model that not only explicitly considers the local soil nutrient levels, elevation, and solar orientation in order to predict growth rates but also allows for processes that transfer materials (e.g., soil, nutrients, water, seeds) between adjacent map regions.

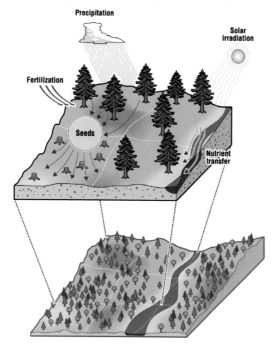

Figure 3. Schematic of a coupled dynamics, single-system model that projects the tree stand growth at different locations based on the dynamic interactions of a number of local variables (e.g., nutrient levels) and also allows interactions between neighboring grid cells/features.

COUPLED DYNAMICS, MULTIPLE SUBMODELS

This class of models has multiple types of submodels involved (e.g., models for lakes, fields, forests, rivers). In addition to the capabilities of the coupled single-system models, in these models each cell or feature has to determine if a different type of system is operating in its neighbors, and if so, it has to set up appropriate interactions with them. There could also be a possibility of several different submodels operating simultaneously within a single feature (e.g., biological and physical process models), with the user again having to specify the interactions between the models.

An example of this type of model might be a system that includes two very different models: a coupled dynamics tree growth model and a predator/prey model. The tree growth model would explicitly consider the local soil nutrient levels, elevation, and solar orientation in order to predict growth rates and would also allow for processes that transfer materials (e.g., soil, nutrients, water, seeds) between adjacent map regions. The predator/prey model would simulate the populations of predator and prey. The two models could be coupled if one of the populations impacts the trees (e.g., by feeding on young trees).

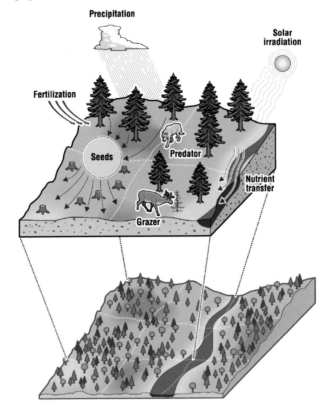

Figure 4. Schematic of a coupled dynamics, multiple-system model which projects the tree stand growth at different locations based on the dynamic interactions of a number of local variables (e.g., nutrient levels), allows interactions between neighboring grid cells/features, and simultaneously models a predator/prey system that interacts with the forest system.

Note that these types of models become even more complex if different types of GIS objects are involved in the different models. For example, if one sub-model is defined on a set of grid cells and another is defined on a river network that runs across the same domain as the grid, the topological relationships necessary to define the interactions between the two model domains may not be readily available in the GIS system.

DYNAMICALLY CHANGING MODEL STRUCTURE

In this most complex class of model, significant dynamic changes can occur, not just to the properties of model elements but also to the model structure itself. For example,

- Old features may be removed, or new features may come into existence. Automatically restructuring the model when this occurs will require disconnecting and disposing of old model elements or instantiating and initializing new elements and their coupling to neighbors.

- The type of system operating in a given cell or feature might change, for example, to represent conversion of land from one use to another. This is equivalent to removing the old local model and replacing it with a new one, though in this case it may be desired to inherit some properties of the old model in the new model.

- A feature's geometry might change with time, for example, to simulate transient flooding. This type of moving-boundary problem can be difficult if the boundaries are sharp, which can require adaptive local spatial discretization in order to compute the boundary location accurately over time.

The ability to represent these sorts of dynamic changes to a system will require sophistication both on the part of the user and on the part of the simulation system.

An example of this type of model might be a landscape evolution model that considers the gradual change of a forest to farmland and perhaps subsequently to an urban landscape.

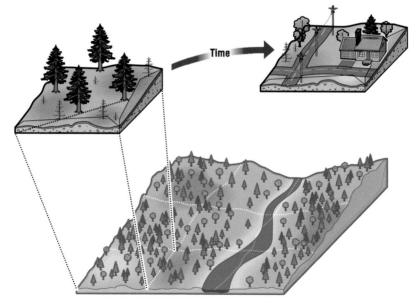

Figure 5. Schematic of a model with a dynamically-changing structure. In this case, the model structure of a particular geographic region can change (e.g., from a forest to farmland) during the course of the simulation, with different submodels being active for a region during different time periods.

GENERAL-PURPOSE DYNAMIC SIMULATION MODELS

Before discussing approaches for linking general-purpose modeling tools to GIS, it is useful to first clearly define what is meant when we speak of a general-purpose dynamic modeling tool.

A general-purpose dynamic modeling tool is essentially a high-level programming language that allows the user to define equations that describe how a particular system (e.g., a forest, an aquifer, a company) might evolve over time. Such a modeling system typically inherently has no specific built-in knowledge of the system being modeled; the user provides all the equations necessary to model the system. The most commonly used general-purpose modeling tool is spreadsheet software.

Although spreadsheet software is often used to model dynamically changing systems (e.g., by defining a new row or column for each time step in the model), over the last fifteen years a wide range of much more powerful general-purpose modeling software has emerged. These can generally be referred to as simulation programs, and they differ from spreadsheets in a number of important ways, the most significant being:

- They are typically graphical and object oriented, with different objects representing different parameters, processes, or physical objects in the model. For example, if one were simulating the spread of a disease through a population, there might be one object representing the susceptible population, another representing the infectious population, and a third representing the recovered population.

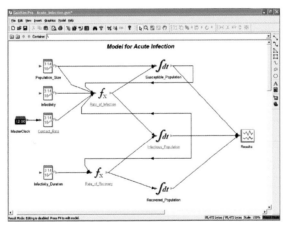

Figure 6. Screen shot from a simulation program (GoldSim) being used to simulate the spread of a disease through a population.

- They inherently understand time. Typically, the user simply specifies the duration of a simulation (e.g., 10 years, or perhaps from January 2004 through December 2007) and how often the program should compute and/ or save results (e.g., once per month). Results are typically presented in terms of time histories (time series of simulated outputs).

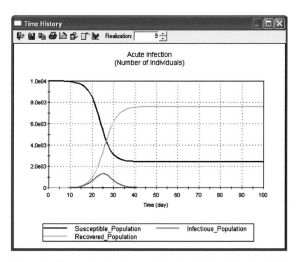

Figure 7. Output (in the form of simulated time histories) of a model that simulates the spread of a disease through a population.

General-purpose simulation programs can generally be broadly classified into two categories: discrete simulators and continuous simulators.

Discrete simulators simulate the movement and evolution of discrete entities through a system (e.g., calls through a call center, customers through a bank, parts through a factory). They generally rely on a transaction-flow approach to modeling systems. Models consist of entities (units of traffic such as parts moving within an assembly line), resources (elements that service entities such as stations on the assembly line), and control elements (elements that determine the states of the entities and resources). Discrete simulators are generally designed for simulating systems such as call centers, factory operations, and shipping facilities.

A special class of discrete simulators is *agent-based models.* In an agent-based model, the mobile entities are known as agents. Whereas in a traditional discrete event model the entities only have attributes (properties that may control how they interact with various resources), agents have both attributes and methods (e.g., rules for interacting with other agents). An agent-based model could, for example, be used to simulate the behavior of a small population of animals that are interacting with each other, with other animal populations, and with their local environment.

Continuous simulators essentially solve differential equations that describe the evolution of a system using continuous equations. These types of simulators are most appropriate if the material or information that is being simulated can be described as evolving or moving smoothly and continuously, rather than in infrequent discrete steps or packets. For example, simulation of the movement of water through a series of reservoirs or contaminants through soils can most appropriately be represented using a continuous simulator. Continuous simulators can also be used to simulate systems consisting of discrete entities. In particular, if the number of discrete entities is quite large, it is often appropriate to simulate such a system using a continuous simulator (such as the infectious disease example presented in figure 7).

Of course, these classifications represent the extremes of the spectrum of available tools. Some software packages (such as the one developed by the authors and used in the examples in this chapter) are actually hybrid packages that can represent both continuous and discrete dynamics.

The approaches for linking general-purpose dynamic simulators to GIS described below can be applied for any kind of simulation model, ranging from a purely discrete to a purely continuous or a hybrid of the two. Of course, the type of simulation model being used will determine the kinds of processes that can be simulated realistically.

ARCHITECTURAL ALTERNATIVES FOR LINKING GENERAL-PURPOSE DYNAMIC SIMULATION MODELS TO GIS

From the user's point of view, there are two fundamentally different ways in which a general-purpose simulation system could be integrated with a GIS. We refer to these approaches as the GIS-centric and the simulator-centric approaches.

In the *GIS-centric* approach, the GIS software provides the primary interface and data access tools. In effect, the user interacts primarily with the GIS software and accesses the simulation model through the GIS software. In the *simulator-centric* approach, the simulation software provides the interface and data access tools. In effect, the user interacts primarily with the simulation software and accesses the GIS data and tools through the simulation software.

Each of these two approaches is discussed briefly below.

GIS-CENTRIC APPROACH

In a GIS-centric design, we envision that the model would be described and built in an environment similar to that of ESRI ArcGIS ModelBuilder. ModelBuilder is a tool in ArcGIS Desktop that helps users build a model using a diagram that resembles a flowchart. ModelBuilder (or an equivalent application) would be responsible for providing a generic interface that allows simulation applications to be embedded.

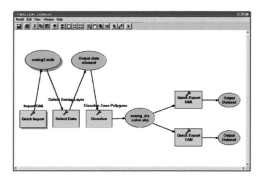

Figure 8. Simple ArcGIS ModelBuilder flowchart model for building a spatial model. Rectangles represent tools, green ellipses are input data layers, and blue ellipses are output data layers created when a model is run. In this particular model instance, data is imported from a GML file, processed, and then exported as GML and MapInfo TAB format files.

ModelBuilder uses the concept of linked data sets (variables) and process nodes. Processes represent function calls. Variables represent named values that are stored in a GIS database. Each process node references input and output data nodes, as well as a function that, when executed, uses the input data to produce the output data. Other ModelBuilder examples are presented by Krivoruchko and Gotway Crawford (2005, this volume) and by Maidment et al. (2005, this volume).

In ModelBuilder, the model is a set of spatial processes (such as buffer or overlay) that convert input data to an output layer. The model itself does not have an explicit temporal component (i.e., it is not dynamic), but this could be simulated by running the model multiple times as a script.

A dynamic simulation model could conceptually be embedded in ModelBuilder as a process node. The user would select data objects (linked to any type of GIS data) that define the input data to the simulation model process node. Indeed, in the examples shown in figure 8, this same architectural pattern was used to integrate Safe Software's Feature Manipulation Engine (FME®) (www.safe.com), an existing product used to convert geographic datasets between various file formats.

When a simulation model node was added to ModelBuilder's graphical diagram, a wizard would be shown that guided the user through the initial setup process for the simulation model. For instance, the user would define input and output data as well as simulation parameters (e.g., the length of each time step).

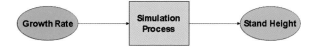

Figure 9. Schematic of GIS-centric approach using ModelBuilder.

Figure 9 shows a diagram of a fictitious ModelBuilder diagram with an input grid (Growth Rate) connected to a Simulation Process Node (an embedded simulation model) and an output grid (Simulated Stand Height) created or filled with data by the simulation model during the simulation.

After the simulation model process node has been created, the user would essentially work with two different models—the GIS model and the simulation model—in two separate applications (ModelBuilder and the simulation software package). For example, a double-click on the simulation model process node in ModelBuilder would open the simulation application interface and load the specified simulation model file.

After creating a simulation node in ModelBuilder, the user would define (GIS data) inputs to the simulation model. These inputs would also be shown as externally defined input data in the simulation model's own graphical interface.

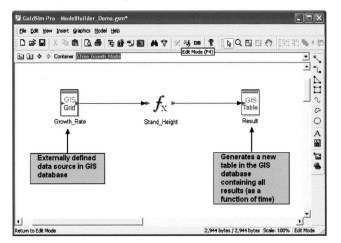

Figure 10. Schematic of simulation model user interface after it had been linked to a GIS via ModelBuilder.

In order to support such functionality, the simulation model would need to provide one or more standard interfaces which allow low-level communication between ModelBuilder and a process (a simulation node). A software interface would also need to be defined and implemented that would allow communication and (some) data exchange while both applications are in use (e.g., the simulation model must be informed if the ModelBuilder user changes the input data definition for the simulation process node).

SIMULATOR-CENTRIC APPROACH

In a simulator-centric approach, the simulation program would provide the interface and data access tools for creating and carrying out the entire model simulation. In contrast to the GIS-centric approach described above, the user would not have to deal with two separate applications. The user would build the model using functions, objects, and data provided in one user interface (that of the simulation program).

To represent a particular model (e.g., a tree growth model) that could be applied to different locations, the user of the simulation software would create a submodel that represents a generic template for a particular GIS object (e.g., a model that could be applied to a single grid cell). That is, template models would define the properties and dynamic behavior of a system or subsystem at a generic map region (e.g., grid cell).

This model template would then be replicated by the simulation software over a group of GIS entities (shapes or grid cells) for which the GIS model is specified. Screening criteria or masks would be required in order to specify which GIS entities would use each type of generic model (i.e., the masks or criteria would define where and how each model is replicated across the map region). For example, the tree growth model would only be replicated to forest grid cells, while a predator/prey model may be replicated to all grid cells (e.g., forests, fields, streams).

The figure below conceptually illustrates a coupled dynamics model where a template model is replicated for every grid cell matching a specific mask requirement (in this case, being forested).

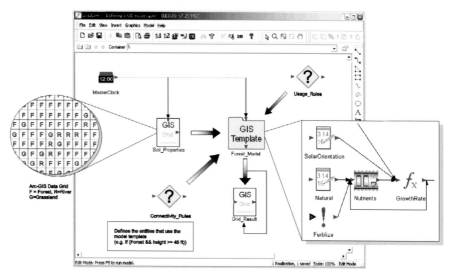

Figure 11. Schematic of simulator-centric approach using GoldSim.

The authors have developed a prototype of a general-purpose dynamic modeling system that can link to a GIS using a simulator-centric approach. This prototype has been developed as a module for the GoldSim software system, which is used for environmental and other modeling applications. While this prototype has been valuable for gaining insight into the issues involved in such systems, it is only a prototype and is not available for distribution.

TECHNICAL ISSUES

There are a number of technical issues that need to be addressed in order to create a functional GIS-linked general-purpose simulation model, including the following:

ACCURACY AND STABILITY REQUIREMENTS

In general, dynamic simulation models become inaccurate if they use a time step that is too long. Intelligent, adaptive model time steps that guarantee accurate results with no user intervention are required, and it may be necessary to use different time steps for different subsystems or locations.

RESULT CAPTURE REQUIREMENTS

The user must be able to identify what calculated results need to be stored, and what can be discarded. Dynamic models generate large quantities of intermediate results that do not need to be saved and in fact, may be too large to save.

TIME-BASED DATA REQUIREMENT

Dynamic models produce time sequences of results, which will typically be expressed in two ways: as longitudinal time histories of individual values (i.e., a history plot of the projected population density in a particular urban area) and as snapshots of the entire system at a number of specific points in time (i.e., movies illustrating the system response over time). The GIS data architectures involved need the ability to access time-based data in both of these ways.

CATEGORY MODELING REQUIREMENT

Dynamic models in general deal with quantities and with intensive properties of system components: temperatures, densities, fluxes, etc. However, GIS systems frequently assign geographic components to categories (e.g., urban, agricultural, forested), so an ability to model how components in a geographic system evolve from one category to another may be required. This implies that, in addition to the category assignment, additional properties of the system need to be simulated in order to ascertain when a given entity will change its category and what the new category will be. This sort of logic is not typically employed in dynamic models.

CALIBRATION REQUIREMENTS

Many dynamic models require adjustments of input parameters so as to provide a best fit to recorded, historical data before they are ready to use for predictive purposes. This process of model calibration (inverse modeling) can be extremely difficult for multivariate, nonlinear dynamic models. Single simulations of dynamic models can be demanding in terms of computer resources and run-times, and trial-and-error calibration involving numerous simulations of a large model can be challenging. Thus, there is a requirement for some level of support for model calibration. Ideally, the software would incorporate a search/optimization capability for automated model calibration.

UNCERTAINTY ANALYSIS REQUIREMENTS

Many systems are subject to stochastic uncertainty (e.g., due to weather or climate variations). Other common sources of uncertainty include parameter uncertainty (e.g., not being sure of a parameter, such as an erosion rate or a cost factor) and the chance of random events occurring. Random fields such as the spatial distribution of a hydrogeological parameter represent another type of uncertain component.

Models which can address these types of uncertainty, such as GoldSim, have to do repeated simulations, typically in the order of a hundred or more simulations of a given model. While this type of analysis is very valuable for decision-support calculations, at this time it is probably not realistic to expect to carry out uncertainty analyses in dynamic GIS models. The reason is the extreme amount of computer resources that might be required. There are also software design issues that would need to be addressed, such as how to display probability distributions of the modeled quantities on a map.

STATIC VS. MOBILE (AGENT-BASED) MODEL ENTITIES

Most GIS databases represent the properties of geographic entities in an essentially static map, and the most common form of dynamic GIS models will simulate the evolution of those entities over time. However, a completely different type of model exists where autonomous or semi-autonomous objects (agents) move through and interact with each other and with their landscape. These objects represent entities such as wildlife, vehicles, or military units.

Different modeling approaches could be used to simulate:
- dynamic agents moving through a fixed, static landscape with defined properties,
- a dynamic landscape subjected to and interacting with dynamic agents.

In either case, the software architecture required for agent-based modeling is significantly different from that required for just modeling the evolution of geographic entities in a static map.

THREE-DIMENSIONAL MODELS

A fraction of dynamic GIS models will need to represent systems with vertical spatial discretization and interaction, such as oceanic or atmospheric circulation models and models of vegetative cover, soil layers, and bedrock. These models will typically be an order of magnitude more demanding of computer resources than two-dimensional models.

CONCLUSIONS

Although some GIS-linked, general-purpose modeling systems have been developed, at the present time these are primarily university-based model-development and research initiatives such that for most applications, dynamic GIS modeling is currently more of a concept than a practical reality.

With the continuing evolution of computer hardware and software, however, it is becoming possible to model the behavior of complex coupled dynamic systems over geographical regions. At the heart of the approaches is the ability to separate the definitions of the different processes and how they are to be modeled from the topological, geometrical, and data attributes that can be stored in GIS systems. The simulation software then constructs the actual model system in real time, downloading GIS information in order to set up and model the overall system and uploading results to the GIS for storage and subsequent display.

One result of the current state of the art is that it is difficult to completely identify and quantify different users and their requirements with any accuracy. In fact, the real applications for dynamic GIS will probably not develop until suitable modeling systems are readily available.

REFERENCES

Bende-Michl, U., C. Busch, and D. Papendick. 2003. Development of a Web-based Integrative Water Quality Simulation Toolset (IWST) by coupling client–server oriented DBMS, GIS, and the process based solute model WASMOD. In *Proceedings of the 4th international conference on integrating geographic information systems and environmental modeling: Problems, prospectus, and needs for research*, ed. B. O. Parks and K. M. Clarke, M. P. Crane. CD-ROM. www.colorado.edu/Research/cires/banff/proceedings.html.

Clark Labs. 2004. Idrisi Web site: www.clarklabs.org.

Maidment, D., ed. 2002. *Arc Hydro: GIS for water resources.* Redlands, Calif.: ESRI Press.

Pullar, D. 2003. Embedding map algebra into a simulator for environmental modeling. In *Proceedings of the 4th international conference on integrating geographic information systems and environmental modeling: Problems, prospectus, and needs for research*, ed. B. O. Parks and K. M. Clarke, M. P. Crane. CD-ROM. www.colorado.edu/Research/cires/banff/proceedings.html.

Raghavendran, S. 2004. GIS interoperability: The 'Safe' way. Paper presented at GSDI 2004, Bangalore. www.safe.com/solutions/whitepapers/pdfs/GIS_INTEROPERABILITY_THE_SAFE_WAY.pdf.

Sydelko, P., J. Dolph, K. Majerus, and T. Taxon. 2003. An advanced object-based software framework for complex ecosystem modeling and simulation. In *Proceedings of the 4th international conference on integrating geographic information systems and environmental modeling: Problems, prospectus, and needs for research,* ed. B. O. Parks and K. M. Clarke, M. P. Crane. CD-ROM. www.colorado.edu/Research/cires/banff/proceedings.html.

University of Vermont. 2004. Spatial modeling environment Web site: www.uvm.edu/giee/SME3.

Utrecht University, 2004. PCRaster Web site: pcraster.geog.uu.nl/index.html.

Waddell, P., and M. Alberti. 2003. Integrated simulation of real estate development and land cover change. In *Proceedings of the 4th international conference on integrating geographic information systems and environmental modeling: Problems, prospectus, and needs for research,* ed. B. O. Parks and K. M. Clarke, M. P. Crane. CD-ROM. www.colorado.edu/Research/cires/banff/proceedings.html.

Westervelt, J., and M. Shapiro. 2003. Combining scientific models into management models. In *Proceedings of the 4th international conference on integrating geographic information systems and environmental modeling: Problems, prospectus, and needs for research,* ed. B. O. Parks and K. M. Clarke, M. P. Crane. CD-ROM. www.colorado.edu/Research/cires/banff/proceedings.html.

Chapter 7

Dynamic, Geospatial Landscape Modeling and Simulation

THOMAS MAXWELL

GSTI

SPRINGFIELD, VIRGINIA

ALEXEY VOINOV

UNIVERSITY OF VERMONT

BURLINGTON, VERMONT

ABSTRACT

THIS CHAPTER DESCRIBES the architecture and applications of the Spatial Modeling Environment (SME), an integrated tool suite for high-performance spatial modeling which bridges the gap between systems dynamics modeling and high-performance modular simulation, data processing, and visualization. This environment allows users to develop, share, and reuse models in a graphical, icon-based environment. Automatic code generators construct spatial simulations and enable distributed processing over a network of parallel and serial computers, allowing transparent access to state-of-the-art computing facilities. The modeling environment imposes the constraints of modularity and hierarchy in program design and supports the archiving of reusable modules in a Simulation Module Markup Language (SMML). The SME programming interface facilitates the incorporation of legacy simulation models and user-defined code into the environment. The SME Java portal provides a graphical interface for Web-based building, configuring, executing, controlling, and visualizing remote simulation models.

**COLLABORATIVE
MODELING OF
COMPLEX SYSTEMS**

Spatial (geographic) modeling of ecosystems is essential if one's modeling goals include developing a relatively realistic description of past behavior and predictions of the impacts of alternative management policies on future ecosystem behavior (Risser et al. 1984, Costanza et al. 1990, Sklar and Costanza 1991, Costanza and Voinov 2003). This chapter describes a form of spatial cellular automata modeling which views the landscape as compartmentalized into a large number of subareas (cells) and then associates a (typically quite complex) model of the local ecosystem and/or economy with each cell. Cells are linked by fluxes of matter (mostly water), entities (e.g., individual animals), energy, and information.

Development of large-scale models in general has been limited by the ability of any single team of researchers to deal with the conceptual complexity of formulating, building, calibrating, debugging, and understanding complex models. Realistic environmental models are becoming much too complex for any single group of researchers to implement single-handed, requiring collaboration between botanists, zoologists, hydrologists, chemists, land managers, economists, ecologists, and others. Communicating the structure of the model to others can become an insurmountable obstacle to collaboration and acceptance of the model. Policy makers are unlikely to trust a model they don't understand. There is a need for worldwide coupling of the modeling community within a collaboratory based on open standards and freely interchangeable data and models, bringing together experts in computational and environmental sciences with policy makers and stakeholders.

MODULAR MODELING

A well-recognized method for reducing conceptual and programming complexity involves structuring the model as a set of distinct modules with well-defined interfaces. Modular design facilitates collaborative model construction, since teams of specialists can work independently on different modules with minimal risk of interference. Modules can be archived in distributed libraries and serve as a set of templates to speed future development. A modeling environment that supports modularity could provide a universal modeling language to promote worldwide collaborative model development.

In order to achieve flexibility in knowledge representations, it is important to develop a formalism for coding archivable modules that allows maximal generality and applicability of the modules. This is best achieved by avoiding overspecification of modules, i.e., to achieve maximum generality by including only information essential to definition of a module. Every bit of spurious information included in a module definition becomes a constraint which can reduce the applicability of the module.

GRAPHICAL MODELING TOOLS

A second step toward reducing the complexity of the modeling process involves the utilization of graphical, icon-based module interfaces, wherein the structure of the module is represented diagrammatically, so that new users can recognize the major interactions at a glance (for further discussion and examples, see also Miller et al. 2005, this volume). Scientists with little or no programming experience can begin building and running models almost immediately. Inherent constraints make it much easier to generate bug-free models. Built-in tools for display and analysis facilitate understanding, debugging, calibration, and analysis of the module dynamics.

Graphical interfaces enable the modeling process to serve as a consensus building tool. The graphical representation of the model can serve as a blackboard for group brainstorming, allowing students, educators, policy makers, scientists, and stakeholders to all be involved in the modeling process. New ideas can be tested and scenarios investigated using the model within the context of group discussion as the model grows through a collaborative process of exploration. When applied in this manner, the process of creating a model may be more valuable than the finished product.

The modeling framework described in this chapter utilizes a commercial icon-based modeling tool called STELLA (Costanza 1987, HPS 1995). STELLA facilitates the creation of both simple and complex numerical system dynamics (Forrester 1992) models. Users construct models by connecting and linking icons representing stocks, flows, converters, graphs, etc. within the friendly graphical interface. STELLA will run the completed model and display the dynamics of selected variables via numerical readouts, tables, and graphs. It also provides the user with a toolbox of simulation utilities that facilitate documentation, analysis, and presentation of the model as a structured learning environment. An example of a STELLA graphical interface is displayed in figure 1.

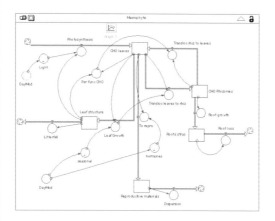

Figure 1. A STELLA model. In this diagram, boxes represent state variables, circles attached to pipes represent fluxes between state variables, and unattached circles represent auxiliary variables. Each of these icons is associated with an equation that is executed to generate the dynamics of the modeled system.

MULTIPLE SPATIO–TEMPORAL REPRESENTATIONS AND SCALES

Building realistic, spatially explicit ecological models generally requires the integration of multiple spatial data structures in a single model and the coupling of data and models designed to operate at different spatio–temporal scales. Entities such as vegetation cover, river/canal networks, and individual animals may coexist within a single model and require different classes of spatial representation, for example, raster, vector, or agent-based (for more discussion of these terms, see Goodchild 2005, this volume). The coupling of multiple scales requires methods for extrapolating data and models from one scale of observation and aggregation to other scales. Thus the implementation of the concept of space in the modeling environment must be general enough to allow the instantiation of a wide range of specific space–time representations, and the details of linking, transferring data between, and decomposing (over multiple processors) these spatial representations should be invisible to the modelers.

In addition, realistic ecological models require the integration of multiple temporal representations in a single model. For example, many processes are best represented using differential equations, others are best represented using event-based simulation, and still others, such as input–output economic models, use a black-box or look-up table implementation. Some processes, such as storm events, are best handled with a hybrid approach.

PARALLEL PROCESSING

Tremendous computational resources are required to integrate the equations of a large spatial model in a reasonable amount of computer time. This class of models can benefit from parallel processing since a typical model consists of a large number of cells that can be simulated semi-independently. Each processor can be assigned a different subset of cells, and most interprocessor communication is nearest-neighbor only. However powerful they may be, advanced computing resources must be transparent to the common user in order to be applicable in the collaborative modeling paradigm.

ENTITY-BASED MODELS

The need for supporting both mobile entities and landscape processes in management scale models is being increasingly realized by environmental modelers (Huston et al. 1988, DeAngelis and Gross 1992). Mobile entities, such as individual animals, move in the landscape while retaining their identities as unique individuals. Other chapters in this book describe how such mobile entities can be modeled as agents (e.g., Ahearn and Smith 2005, this volume). In contrast, landscape processes, such as erosion or plant growth, describe changing characteristics of the landscape in a fixed area. In modeling endangered species, for example, it is important to keep track of individuals over time and space, interactions among individuals, landscape processes over time and space, interactions among landscape processes, and interactions of individuals with landscape processes. Individual-based simulation modeling provides an essential complement to cell-based process models.

SPATIAL MODELING ENVIRONMENT

We have developed an integrated environment for high-performance spatial modeling called the Spatial Modeling Environment (SME 1995, Maxwell et al. 2003, Maxwell and Costanza 1995, 1997b). This environment, which transparently links icon-based modeling environments with advanced computing resources, allows students, educators, and scientists to develop, share, and reuse models in a graphical, icon-based environment. The SME software is available from SourceForge at sourceforge.net/projects/smodenv.

MODULAR MODELING USING A MODULE SPECIFICATION FORMALISM

At the core of this framework is an object-oriented module specification formalism (MSF) for implementing archivable modules in support of continuous spatial modeling (Maxwell and Costanza 1997a). Our basic premise is that the most common approach to model integration, which involves linking procedural models using distributed object formalisms, is greatly limited by the fact that the various submodels are, by their nature, overspecified as modules. In the process of implementing a submodel in a procedural programming language, the implementer generally hard-codes many choices such as programming language, spatio–temporal representation, model control and IO interfaces, computing paradigm (serial/parallel, message passing/parallel-shared memory), etc. When the submodel enters the collaborative domain as a reusable module, these fixed aspects are seen to be extremely limiting and irrelevant to the essential dynamics of the model.

We have utilized a more flexible approach which defines archivable modules using abstract model specifications that contain only enough information to specify the essential dynamics of the module and allow a wide range of customized procedural implementations to be generated automatically. This purely declarative formalism provides the high level of abstraction necessary for maximum generality, provides enough detail to allow a dynamic simulation to be generated automatically, and avoids the hard-coded implementation of space--time dynamics that makes procedural specifications of limited usefulness for specifying achievable modules. A set of these modules can be hierarchically linked within the MSF formalism to create a MSF model. We believe this approach has great potential for bringing the power of modular model development into the collaborative simulation arena.

SPATIAL MODELING INFRASTRUCTURE

The SME utilizes an XML-based MSF for specifying reusable, archivable modules, called the Simulation Module Markup Language (SMML) (Maxwell, 1999). Simulation modules can be archived in SMML module libraries and linked within the SME to produce full-scale models.

In order to separate the implementation of the model dynamics from the details of simulation code development, we have abstracted the module libraries from both the front-end module development tools and the back-end simulation drivers, resulting in a three-part View–Modelbase–Driver architecture (fig. 2). The View component is used to develop ecosystem unit modules, the Modelbase servers to archive and link unit modules into working models, and the Driver is the application that executes the simulation runs. These components will be described in more detail below.

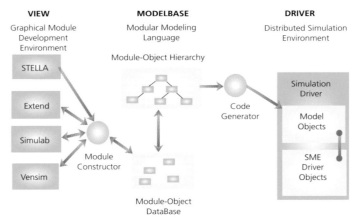

Figure 2. Overview of the View-Modelbase-Driver architecture.

The process of building and running a model using the SME involves the following steps:

1. *Unit Model development.* An ecosystem unit model is developed using a graphical modeling tool. The tool most typically used is STELLA (described above), which facilitates icon-based systems dynamics modeling. This unit model represents the ecosystem dynamics within a single cell of a spatial grid covering the landscape.

2. *Project creation.* A project is a directory tree that will contain all of the sources, executables, data, and simulation output associated with a simulation model.

3. *Module construction.* The SME Module Constructor application is used to translate the STELLA equation files into the Simulation Module Markup Language (SMML). Each STELLA sector is converted into an SMML Module entity. Each STELLA variable (i.e., State Variable, Flux, or Converter) is converted into an SMML Variable entity. Each STELLA equation is used to construct an update method on the corresponding

SMML Variable. The user can link modules from various sources at this step and create new SMML modules using a TEXT editor or a graphical SMML development tool.

4. *Data assembly.* The maps and time series data that will be input to the simulation must be assembled in the proper format. The SME includes tools for importing data from GRASS and ArcGIS and from a number of commonly used data file formats.

5. *Code generation and configuration.* The Code Generator (CG) application is used to convert the SMML objects into C++ objects which plug into our distributed simulation driver application. The user then provides configuration information, either by editing a set of configuration files that are generated by the CG application or by entering configuration information into the Java interface's configuration panel.

6. *Simulation run.* The user runs the simulation by executing the Driver application, using either the SME Java interface or the command-line interface.

7. *Output analysis.* The SME includes several built-in methods for displaying the nonspatial and spatial model output.

SME SIMULATION DRIVER

The simulation objects generated in step 5 (above) are linked into the SME Driver, a distributed object-oriented simulation environment which incorporates the set of code modules that actually perform the spatial simulation on the targeted platform. It enables distributed processing over a network of parallel and serial computers, allowing transparent access to state-of-the-art computing facilities. It is implemented as a set of distributed C++ objects linked by message passing, layered on top of a distributed grid library, and linked to the interfaces described in the following sections. A detailed description of the SME Driver can be found in Maxwell and Costanza (1995). The major driver components include:

- Application object. Handles general process of simulation execution and coordination and scheduling of the other SME objects.

- Imported objects and data. This is the set of objects and data that is created by the Code Generator and imported into the driver. The objects are C++ implementations of the SMML module entities. The imported object structure is described in more detail below.

- Geometry object. Maintains the catalog of Frames (see below) and handles all tasks relating to the spatial configuration of the simulation, such as translating/transferring data between Frames and the Network object.

- Network object. Handles communication between processors and the simulation host. It is implemented using the MPI message passing interface standard (MPI 1995).

- Interface object. Menu-driver interface facilitating user control of the simulation and real-time display of simulation output.

- File object. Handles archiving of simulation output in a variety of formats. Built-in converters allow users to easily import/export data to/from geographical information systems (GIS) and relational databases.

An associated library of module wrappers facilitates the incorporation of legacy simulation models into the environment. The SME programming interface allows users to add customized C++ code modules (building upon the SME object libraries) to a simulation in the SME Driver. This feature is typically used to add complex spatial dynamics (e.g., hydrodynamics) or spatial processing and analysis routines to the simulation. The UserCode is integrated into the simulation using the standard SME configuration interfaces and linked with the module objects that are imported from STELLA.

The constructed module objects (that are imported from STELLA), as well as the customized C++ code modules, are built upon the following classes:

- Module class. The CodeGenerator Application converts each module in the SMML model description into a Module object in the Driver. Each Module object contains a set of Variable objects and a Frame object. It also has a set of methods for responding to simulation events such as initialize and update.

- Frame class. A Frame is a driver object which specifies the topology of the spatial implementation of a Module object, including methods for interacting with and transferring data to other frames. A Frame contains a list of Point Objects (POs). Each PO corresponds to a cell in the Frame's map region. The map region includes a partition of the study area handled by the current processor plus a communication buffer zone. The driver maintains a catalog of available Frames, which include two-dimensional grids (e.g., for landscapes), graphs and networks (e.g., for river, canal, or neural networks), areas (e.g., for embedded lumped-parameter models), and point collections (e.g., for individual agents moving about in the landscape).

- Variable class. The CodeGenerator Application converts each variable declared in the SMML model description into a Variable object in the Driver. The Variable object encapsulates a mapping from the set of Point objects owned by the module's Frame object into the set of floating-point numbers.

SIMULATION CONFIGURATION

The Module Constructor, Code Generator, and Driver applications all read configuration information to customize their behavior. The required configuration information falls into several general categories:

1. Module Construction. This configuration can be used to automate the process of adding/deleting SMML code to/from the SMML module specifications. It is typically used to ignore some STELLA variables or integrate custom (C++) user-defined modules and utility functions.

2. Space–Time Implementation. This configuration associates each module with a Frame, which specifies its space–time implementation. The

frame specifies the topology of the spatial implementation of the module and includes methods for interacting with and transferring data to other frames, and temporal methods for handling the passing of time. The user specifies a frame type as well as a (set of) GIS map(s) that the frame will read at runtime to configure itself.

3. Input/Output Configuration. In this step, the user configures the data transfer between the simulation and the biological/ecological data-bases, runtime interfaces, and GIS. The SME Driver uses this information (together with the variable dependency graph) to determine variable types at runtime. This configuration data is supplied to the Driver, although default values can be specified in the Code Generator configuration files.

4. Driver simulation configuration. This configuration specifies dynamic driver characteristics, such as integration methods, time steps, debug and optimization levels, and other control parameters.

POINTGRID LIBRARY

The PointGrid library (PGL) is a set of C++ distributed objects designed to support computation on irregular, distributed networks and grids. It contains the core set of objects on which the SME Driver is constructed.

The PGL builds spatial representations from sets of Point objects (see below) with links. It transparently handles: 1) creation and decomposition (over processors) of Point Sets, 2) mapping of data over and between Point Sets, 3) iteration over Point Sets and Point Subsets, 4) data access and update at each Point, and 5) swapping of variable-sized PointSet boundary (ghost) regions. Some of the important PGL classes are:

• *Point:* Corresponds to a cell in a GIS layer.
• *Aggregated Point:* Corresponds to a cell in a coarser resolution GIS layer.
• *PointSet:* A set of Points with links (grid or network).
• *DistributedPointSet:* A PointSet distributed over processors with variable-sized boundary (ghost) layers.
• *Coverage:* Mapping from a DistributedPointSet to the set of floats.

SME PORTAL

A science portal is a human–computer interface which facilitates desktop access to remote resources including supercomputers, networks of work stations, smart instruments, data resources, and more. We have utilized the Java programming language to develop an environmental modeling portal built on the SME. The SME portal provides an environment to facilitate collaboration and discussion in model development and simulation. It provides the user with a single familiar environment in which to build, configure, and interactively run models on any one of a number of parallel or serial computers.

The SME portal allows the user to spawn, configure, control, and visualize a simulation running on a remote simulation server. The user is provided with a control panel to configure simulation data input and output, control simulation dynamics, and display simulation output. The display panel allows the user to browse through the objects in a paused simulation and view each object's internal data structures in a convenient format. The browser also provides a menu of each object's dependent objects, so users can quickly traverse the dependency tree while searching for anomalies in the simulation output. A palette of data viewers is provided, supporting many display formats, including 2D animations, 3D animations, 1D time series graphs, data and image spreadsheets, 3D isocontour viewers, and data browsers. Built-in converters allow built-in users to easily import/export data to/from GIS and relational databases.

During initialization, the portal's client application connects to a simulation server (in a manner analogous to telnet or FTP) which handles the spawning of a new spatial simulation on a host computer. The portal includes an interface to the Globus (www.globus.org) Grid Resource Allocation and Management (GRAM) utility, which is utilized to initiate execution of a model on a remote supercomputer. The SME GRAM control panel allows the user to select a Globus® gatekeeper, and then submit a run request. The user then interacts with the running simulation using the SME simulation control panel.

The simulation control panel allows the user to:

- Browse through all of the variables in a simulation and direct simulation output to the portal's visualization tools.
- Control the simulation dynamics through *run, step, restart,* and *stop* buttons, as well as fields to set the time step and end time of the simulation.
- Display the equations used to update the value of any variable in the simulation.
- Display a snapshot (visualization of the current state) of the data grid associated with any variable in the simulation.
- Browse through the variable dependency trees.
- See at a glance each variable's spatial mode (varying/constant), temporal mode (varying/constant), and input/output/intermodule connections via icons in the variable display tree table.

The SME Python shell provides an alternative interface for real-time control, evaluation, and debugging of simulation dynamics. It allows programming of simulation execution, visualization, and data processing using the Python object-based scripting language. This shell provides a single environment for controlling simulation configuration, execution, visualization, and output postprocessing.

The SME portal's visualization panel (ViewServer) is used to configure and control the real-time visualization of simulation dynamics. Data grids are piped to the ViewServer from a running simulation. This tool allows the user to view any of the available grids by choosing visualization modalities from a menu of available viewers. Data grids may be deleted or archived to disk and retrieved later.

The simulation data viewers currently available in the SME Portal include:

- **2D Animation Viewer.** This viewer allows the user to view 2D real-time or archived animations of simulation data. By default, all images in a simulation series are scaled uniformly, and the image is automatically updated when new data arrives from the simulation. A separate control panel allows the user to synchronously run or step (forward or backward) through all visible animation viewers. The user may rescale any image or animation sequence and save all data to disk.

- **3D Animation Viewer.** This viewer (fig. 3) allows the user to generate 3D surface plots of real-time or archived simulation data. The image can be zoomed, panned, rotated, or translated using simple mouse drag operations. The user can map different variables to the color and height components of the display, making this viewer particularly useful for generating comparisons between images. By default, all images in a simulation series are scaled uniformly, and the image is automatically updated when new data arrives from the simulation.

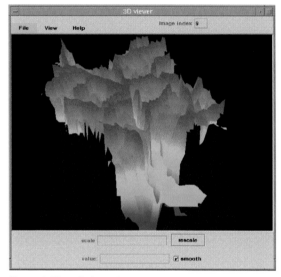

Figure 3. The 3D data viewer.

- **Data Sheet.** This tool is used to view the raw data being displayed in any of the other viewers. The user may select a rectangle of data in an Animation viewer which is displayed in a Data Sheet Viewer and automatically updated each time the animation image changes.

- **Image Table.** This tool (fig. 4) is used to view a number of image series in spreadsheet format. It is particularly useful for making comparisons between variables at various times in the simulation. By default, all image series are scaled uniformly and updated when new data arrives from the simulation. The user may easily rescale any image or image series, and change the magnification, time step, or time offset of the image sequences.

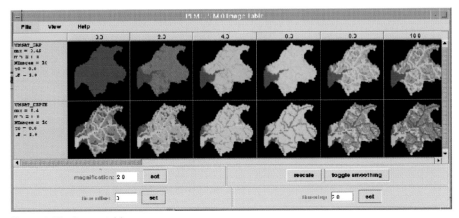

Figure 4. The image table.

- **TimeSeries Graphs.** This tool is used to visualize up to six overlapping timeseries graphs, each associated with a different variable in the simulation. By default each graph is scaled automatically and is updated when new data arrives from the simulation. The user can easily adjust the scaling, line color, and labels associated with any of the graphs in the Viewer.

APPLICATIONS

Various applications of the SME have modeled the interaction between socio-economic and environmental dynamics in support of sustainable management of water resources. These applications include the Patuxent Landscape Model (PLM 1995, Costanza et al. 2002, Voinov et al. 2003), the Everglades Landscape Model (ELM 1997), and the Land Use Evolution and Impact Assessment System (LEAM 1999). These decision support tools enable planners, students, policy makers, interest groups, and concerned citizens to visualize and test the impacts of policy decisions, enhancing our understanding of the connection between urban, environmental, social, and economic systems. They address the effects of both the magnitude and spatial patterns of human settlements and agricultural practices on hydrology, plant productivity, and nutrient cycling in the landscape. The collaborative modeling environment enables a consensus-based approach to modeling, enabling noncomputer scientists to participate in developing models and exploring the dynamics of complex systems through simulation in support of research, education, and policy making.

PATUXENT LANDSCAPE MODEL

The Patuxent Landscape Model is designed to serve as a tool in a systematic analysis of the interactions among physical, biological, and socioeconomic dynamics of the Patuxent River watershed. An example of PLM output is shown in figure 5.

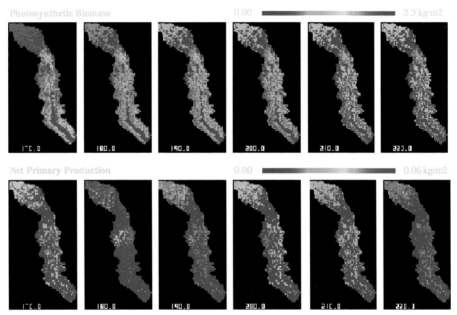

Figure 5. PLM model output.

In the ecological component of this spatially explicit model, the important processes that shape plant communities are simulated within the varying habitats distributed throughout the landscape. The principal dynamics within the model are: plant growth in response to available sunlight, temperature, nutrients, and water; flow of water plus dissolved nutrients in three dimensions; and succession in the plant community in response to the historical environment. The model includes sectors for hydrology, nutrient movement and cycling, terrestrial and estuarine primary productivity, and aggregated consumer dynamics. Using a mass balance approach to incorporate process-based data of a reasonably high resolution within the entire watershed, changing spatial patterns and processes can be analyzed within the context of altered management strategies such as the use of best management practices (BMPs).

The ecological model is linked to an economic model (Bockstael 1996) which predicts the probability of land-use change within the seven counties of the Patuxent watershed. The economic model allows human decisions to be modeled as a function of both economic and ecological spatial variables. Probabilities of land conversion are calculated from costs of conversion and predicted land value in residential land use. Land-value predictions are modeled as a function of local and regional characteristics such as distance to employment centers, percent open space in the neighborhood, and various other spatially explicit variables. The empirical model generates the relative likelihood of conversion of cells. Information about growth pressures allows final estimates of new residential development to be made. The linked model allows the effects of both direct land-use change through human actions and indirect effects through ecological change to be evaluated.

CONCLUSIONS

A global collaboratory, hosting models that cover the salient features of the world's climate, economy, and ecosystems—and the major interactions among them—will provide both an integrated conceptual framework and a practical tool allowing researchers from many disciplines to collaborate effectively in order to produce answers to the critical problems facing humanity. The development of this collaboratory should greatly facilitate the application of computer modeling to the study of earth systems in support of research, education, and policy.

REFERENCES

Bockstael, N. 1996. Modelling economics and ecology: The importance of a spatial perspective. *American Journal of Agricultural Economics* 78: 1168–80.

Costanza, R. 1987. Simulation modeling on the Macintosh using STELLA. *BioScience* 37: 129–32.

Costanza, R., F. H. Sklar, and M. L. White. 1990. Modeling coastal landscape dynamics. *BioScience* 40: 91–107.

Costanza, R., A. Voinov, R. Boumans, T. Maxwell, F. Villa, H. Voinov, and L. Wainger. 2002. Integrated ecological economic modeling of the Patuxent river watershed, Maryland. *Ecological Monographs* 72: 203–31.

Costanza, R., and A. Voinov, eds. 2003. *Spatially explicit landscape simulation modeling.* New York: Springer.

DeAngelis, D. L., and L. J. Gross. 1992. *Individual-based approaches in ecology: Concepts and models.* New York: Routledge, Chapman and Hall.

ELM. 1997. Everglades Landscape Model. www.sfwmd.gov/org/wrp/elm.

Forrester, J. W. 1992. *Industrial dynamics.* Cambridge, Mass.: Productivity Press.

LEAM. 1999. Land use Evolution and Impact Assessment Model. www.rehearsal.uiuc.edu/projects/leam.

Huston, M., D. DeAngelis, and W. Post. 1988. New computer models unify ecological theory. *Bioscience* 38: 682–91.

HPS. 1995. STELLA: High Performance Systems. www.hps-inc.com.

Maxwell, T., and R. Costanza. 1995. Distributed modular spatial ecosystem modeling. *International Journal of Computer Simulation: Special Issue on Advanced Simulation Methodologies* 5(3): 247–62.

———. 1997a. A language for modular spatio-temporal simulation. *Ecological Modeling* 103: 105–13.

———. 1997b. An open geographic modeling environment. *Simulation Journal* 68: 175–85.

Maxwell, T. 1999. A parsi-model approach to modular simulation. *Environmental Modeling and Software* 14: 511–17.

Maxwell, T., A. Voinov, and R. Costanza. 2003. Spatial simulation using the SME. In *Spatially explicit landscape modeling*, ed. R. Costanza and A. Voinov. New York: Springer-Verlag.

MPI. 1995. Message Passing Interface. www.mcs.anl.gov/mpi/index.html.

PLM. 1995. Integrated Ecological Economic Modeling. www.uvm.edu/giee/PLM.

Risser, P. G., J. R. Karr, and R. T. T. Forman. 1984. *Landscape ecology: Directions and approaches*. Champaign, Ill.: Illinois Natural History Survey.

Voinov, A., C. Fitz, R. Boumans, and R. Costanza. 2003. Modular ecosystem modeling. In *Spatially explicit landscape modeling*, ed. R. Costanza and A. Voinov. New York: Springer-Verlag.

Sklar, F. H., and R. Costanza. 1991. The development of dynamic spatial models for landscape ecology. In *Quantitative methods in landscape ecology*, ed. M. G. Turner and R. Gardner. New York: Springer-Verlag.

SME. 1995. Spatial Modeling Environment. www.uvm.edu/giee /SME3.

Introduction to Section 3: Socioeconomic Applications

MICHAEL BATTY

CENTRE FOR ADVANCED SPATIAL ANALYSIS

UNIVERSITY COLLEGE LONDON

LONDON, UNITED KINGDOM

The next seven chapters illustrate how spatial analysis and simulation modeling within the framework of GIS can be applied to problems in the socioeconomic domain where the emphasis is largely but not exclusively on urban activities, land uses, networks, and populations. In this area, human intervention in the systems of interest in the form of planning always dominates. Consequently, models and analyses are never solely descriptive or predictive but always contain some prescriptive or control element. In fact, over the last fifty years, as models in this domain have been slowly developed, a consensus has emerged that generally models should be predictive in structure but nested or embedded within a wider process of control or planning. These wider processes can be expressed as metamodels, within which predictive models are used to explore alternative futures, that is, to pose *what if* questions.

Many predictive models can also be interpreted as the outcome of some design or optimizing process. In the various models that follow—for example, those which deal with land use, transport, retailing, and the distribution of services—it is possible to formulate them as processes in which populations of various kinds attempt to optimize some utility or at least generate spatial behaviors as some form of trade-off between costs and benefits. In this sense, many of the models in this section can be interpreted as both predictive and prescriptive where each focus is a different side of the same coin. In fact, because of the complexities of representing human processes, the prescriptive element is usually implicit, and rather than operating such models by prescribing behavior within them, this function is assigned to the wider policy, design, and planning processes within which such models are nested.

The chapters that follow deal with most key aspects of the urban system: urban growth as land development, the location of different land-use activities, services and retail location, transportation systems, and the diffusion of diseases in urban populations. What cements these chapters together is the issue of spatial interaction between different locations and in some applications, as diffusion through time as well as space. Scale is important as well as networks. The models developed by Batty and Xie in chapter 8, for example, deal with very local diffusion of urban growth in restricted neighborhoods where urban form is developed from the bottom up as cellular automata. This is in contrast to the diffusion of disease in urban populations which is simulated by Bian and Liebner in chapter 12 and which takes place at different hierarchical levels but encompasses the entire urban system. Spatial interaction across the entire system is also central to the more traditional land-use, transportation, and retailing models developed by Wegener in chapter 10, Israelsen and Fredericksen in chapter 13, and by Birkin in chapter 11, where the decay of trip/interaction volumes according to travel time/distance is central to the way the gravitational-discrete choice models that simulate such interaction operate.

With respect to the way these models might be embedded in the wider processes of planning and control, two distinct approaches are developed. In fact, there are no chapters in this section on explicit optimization approaches to land use and transport location although in chapter 20, Duh and Brown do explicitly illustrate this line of thinking. In the following section, planning is represented in chapter 9 by Hopkins, Kaza, and Pallathucheril in terms of data where various data streams are brought together to resolve and solve various spatial planning problems. They set up a framework for integrating predictive models through their data in a form where they can be made consistent with model structures that operate across different hierarchical levels. In developing this approach, they exploit the unified modeling language (UML) as a means of illustrating how such structures can be built. This approach is quite unusual and rather new in comparison with the more traditional, looser approach advocated by Yeh in chapter 14, where he uses case-based reasoning as the central focus for the planning process that he advocates. This approach is even more flexible than the expert systems approaches to urban land-use planning which were developed a decade or more ago. Yeh thus argues that solutions are best generated using past cases which root alternatives and options in a feasible problem-solving context.

In terms of links to GIS, it is worth noting that, although many of the models in this section first originated some decades ago, their statement here is thoroughly informed by contemporary software and by concepts and techniques that are fast coming to represent the corpus of GIScience. Batty and Xie in chapter 8 develop various physical models of urban development, but to make these operational using their Dynamic Urban Evolutionary Model (DUEM) software, conventional GIS coverages are essential for organizing and inputting the data that drives these models. Hopkins, Kaza, and Pallathucheril in chapter 9 develop their geodatabase approach to planning support systems using the same sorts of tools that are now central to packages such as ArcGIS where UML is used to construct layers of data within models that are deeply embedded within GIS. In chapter 10, Wegener follows this by illustrating how traditional land-use models, which have a strong transportation component and are largely focused on simulating locational activity at a cross section in time, can be informed by GIS in the loosely coupled sense. However, as Maguire implies in chapter 2, Wegener argues that modular GIS, which is open in more obvious ways, represents the way forward for these relatively complex models. Wegener also notes the efforts that have been made in Europe to link such models to state-of-the-art GIS which in turn are embedded in planning support systems just as Hopkins, Kaza, and Pallathucheril imply in chapter 9.

Birkin, in chapter 11, charts the development of service and retail location models in theory and practice, showing how they have been adapted to practical problem-solving contexts which imply a variety of location problems associated with particular types of services associated with large firms and organizations. Birkin's approach is largely model- rather than GIS-driven in that he focuses on these models so that they better fit the spatial markets to which they are applied: in this, he shows how microsimulation and more individualistic agent-based approaches have come to play a more central role. Insofar as GIS enters the argument and it surely does, then his simulation models tend to pick up GIS technologies, almost magpie-like, adapting them to the problems in hand. In contrast to all the models so far, Bian and Liebner in chapter 12 introduce quite explicitly the idea of networks. Unlike Israelsen and Frederiksen's more conventional approach to transportation models which do of course use network infrastructures, in Bian and Liebner's models, the network and its topology are instrumental to the diffusion of spatial processes and the time taken for diseases to spread as infections through a population. Their focus does not explicitly involve GIS although, as their model is operationalized in MATLAB, it would be quite a straightforward matter to embed it within state-of-the-art GIS, as Maguire illustrates in chapter 2.

The most explicit use of GIS in any of the models in this section is in Israelsen and Frederiksen's demonstration in chapter 13 of how the conventional four-stage transportation model, based on trip generation, distribution, modal split, and assignment, can be implemented in ArcGIS. They show how the model can be deeply embedded in the software using UML to show how various layers can be morphed into structures that make the conventional, hitherto largely stand-alone, model structures quite consistent and compatible with GIS representations. This contrasts rather strongly with Yeh's chapter on case-based reasoning as a basis for planning support in which he shows how GIS provides the platform for representing case studies in the case data files that are central to the approach he advocates. All the chapters here illustrate cutting-edge developments, both in simulation modeling and spatial analysis and in GIS. Moreover, they illustrate the tensions and compromises that have to be made in fusing different traditions together, but they also show how, slowly but surely, GIS is being infused by both new and older forms of modeling that have hitherto remained quite separate.

Chapter 8

Urban Growth Using Cellular Automata Models

MICHAEL BATTY

CENTRE FOR ADVANCED SPATIAL ANALYSIS

UNIVERSITY COLLEGE LONDON

LONDON, UNITED KINGDOM

YICHUN XIE

INSTITUTE FOR GEOSPATIAL RESEARCH AND EDUCATION

EASTERN MICHIGAN UNIVERSITY

YPSILANTI, MICHIGAN

ABSTRACT

A NEW GENERATION OF URBAN GROWTH MODELS based on simulating temporal decisions concerning land development at a fine spatial scale has emerged during the last fifteen years. These models are established on notions about how cities grow and change dynamically from the bottom up through the development of adjacent cells which are activated according to different decision rules about the composition of development in their local neighborhoods. In their strictest form, they give rise to global patterns such as the dendritic forms that most cities display in terms of the morphology of their transport routes and related land uses. We begin by showing how these models can be consistently related to their cross-sectional static precursors and then illustrate how one such model, the Dynamic Urban Evolutionary Model (DUEM), can be used to simulate decisions about how cities sprawl under regimes of near-zero population growth. We present an example from the Detroit metropolitan region which serves to illustrate how we use the model and feed it with data from related geographic information systems (GIS). We then indicate the limitations of these models, stressing that the lesser levels of certainty in their predictions restrict their applicability in definitive decision making. But we also note that planning processes are becoming much more pluralistic and less definitive too and that multiple rather than single models or tools are now being used to inform policy.

A spatial system grows in two ways, through expansion and compaction. The first process leads to more space being occupied, which is reflected in its geometric extension, while the second leads to the mass increasing, as measured in terms of its density or intensity. In cities, these dual processes are often described as concentration–deconcentration or centralization–decentralization, sometimes with reference to centrifugal–centripetal forces (Bauer Wurster 1963). The way cities have grown, certainly in modern times, reflects a subtle balance between them. We speak of *growth*, of course, because this has been the predominant condition of cities during the last 200 years, but as overall population growth has slowed, the current focus is now more on *change*. Moreover, cities restructure themselves as their activities and populations age, mature, and die, thus changing the way concentration and dispersion interact. Sprawl, which represents the clearest focus of expanding cities in developed countries, for example, is no longer exclusively associated with a growing population but with a population that is more mobile, demanding greater space and lower densities of urban living.

Nivola (1999) makes this point very cogently when he says that cities "can only grow in four directions, in, up, down and out" with growth "likely to follow the last of these paths overwhelmingly, particularly in advanced countries endowed with abundant usable territory" (p. 2). In most western cities, this is the case, notwithstanding the fact that the balance of forces towards compaction or expansion varies substantially depending upon the history of urban growth and city development. The best icon of city growth was established more than half a century ago, when enough historical anecdote had been assembled to note that urban growth appeared to occur in waves: each revolution in transportation technology as well as rising personal wealth loosened the ties to the central city, with suburbanization the predominant form of new growth but with the invasion and succession of already developed neighborhoods by poorer groups occurring within the existing urban envelope. Blumenfeld's (1954) characterization of Philadelphia in these terms mirrored the archetypical growth pattern in North America although the same occurred in Europe in a more muted form of wave expansion where large towns tended to fuse with smaller ones in patterns that came to be known traditionally as conurbations or more recently, polycentric urban regions.

Mathematical models which mirrored the wavelike nature of urban growth were suggested as far back as the 1960s (Morrill 1968), but the focus was on how to simulate their equilibrium outcomes rather than on their dynamics. The tendency to centralization has long been viewed as reflecting urban agglomeration, economies of scale which reflect more than proportionate growth with size, while decentralization is regarded as quite the opposite force which seeks to avoid the diseconomies of concentration. The tension between them is poised in terms of the way activities and populations are connected to one another in cities: populations wish to be as central as possible to reap the benefits of scale but as far away from congested central locations as is feasible to achieve a better quality of life. This tension is complicated by the fact that, as the total population of a city expands, most new activity must locate on the edge where most empty space exists. In physical models, these processes of agglomeration and dispersion are encapsulated in a dynamic which consists of trading off action and reaction with diffusion, and it is no surprise that most urban growth models are based on this distinction in one form or another.

Models of urban growth developed in the 1960s were also based on the assumption that the dual processes leading to agglomeration and dispersion were well behaved, leading to spatial structures that could be clearly observed in the organization of land uses in cities. In short, although the models developed did simulate agglomeration and dispersion, they did so as if the city were in equilibrium. These kinds of model were aggregate and conceived from the top down; it was assumed that the pattern of interaction/movement/transport between land-use locations indicated stability where these processes were in balance. Such land-use transport models had many virtues, and their latter-day equivalents are still widely used as Wegener (2005, this volume) and Birkin (2005, this volume) both report in this book. But there has been a substantial shift in this perspective as we argued in chapter 3 (Batty 2005, this volume), as much due to the fact that we no longer consider urban processes to be well behaved; indeed, they can be as volatile as stock markets. Since the 1960s, growth and change in cities has been very rapid with massive restructuring, radical changes in transportation and income, the emergence of a global market place, almost zero population growth, and rising congestion in the central city, all manifesting themselves in the form and structure of the typical western city. A sea change from comparative static to dynamic modeling is occurring with models such as these considered to be part of complexity theory where systems are best understood from the bottom up (Batty 2005a). This approach admits considerably more uncertainty as to outcomes and predictions than any that has gone before, and this in turn is changing the nature of modeling. In the quest to understand cities and urban growth in this way, much more disaggregate objects and locations have become the focus, with agent-based modeling (ABM) and cellular automata (CA) underpinning the representations required to simulate land-use activities and their locations most effectively.

In this chapter, we will first introduce a generic model of urban growth which is applicable to both static and dynamic conceptions of urban form and structure. We then exploit the dynamic structure of this model and show how CA can be used to simulate urban growth processes. We will illustrate these ideas with a brief summary of the DUEM model (Xie 1994, Xie and Batty 2005), showing how CA approaches are built around the pixel-raster representation of urban space and how this fuses with contemporary GIS. We then sketch a wide array of applications of this model type to problems of urban growth, and we conclude by presenting the limitations and opportunities that this style of modeling provides. Although very few of these models have currently been integrated in a close coupling with GIS, there is considerable potential for such linkage using contemporary software.

Concentration or compaction implies that activities and populations are attracted to a core or center in contrast to dispersal or expansion which assumes that the same elements are deterred from such locations. Movement is thus key to location, and it is not surprising that most urban models attempt to simulate locational attraction and deterrence in a balanced structure. For well over half a century, these notions have been exploited under the banner of social physics, building on spatial interaction conceived in analogy to Newton's second law of motion which can be stated generically as

$$P_{ij} = G \frac{P_i P_j}{d_{ij}^{\alpha}}. \tag{1}$$

P_{ij} is the interaction between locations/zones i and j, P_i, P_j are measures of attraction at i and j respectively, usually population, d_{ij} is a measure of deterrence between i and j, often distance or travel time/cost, α is a parameter controlling the friction of distance, and G is a scaling constant. The attraction measures imply that movement reacts or acts proportionately to mass or size while deterrence controls the rate of diffusion between the two sources. Interaction is thus simulated as a trade-off between these quantities with a generation of land-use transportation models conceived in the 1950s and 1960s built on such assumptions. The amount of activity attracted to i (or j) is thus computed from (1) as

$$P_i = \sum_j P_{ij} = P_i \, G \sum_j \frac{P_j}{d_{ij}^{\alpha}}. \tag{2}$$

The term on the right-hand side of (2) is usually called potential, sometimes accessibility, which is the weighted trade-off of attraction and deterrence to all locations j around i. It is equivalent to the retail and service activity predicted by the models introduced here by Birkin (2005, this volume).

Equations (1) and (2) assume the spatial system is in equilibrium, and a perfect form of this balance exists if the distance matrix $[d_{ij}]$ is symmetric. Then $G \sum_k P_k d_{ik}^{-\alpha} = G \sum_\ell P_\ell d_{\ell j}^{-\alpha} = 1$, $i = j$ where G is simply a scaling constant that ensures that the units of attraction and deterrence are dimensionally correct, that is, populations are comparable to distances in value terms. In fact, it is unlikely that such a perfect balance can be simulated, and thus the usual form of equation (1) is weighted as

$$P_{ij} = G \frac{\gamma_i P_i \vartheta_j P_j}{d_{ij}^{\alpha}}, \tag{3}$$

where the weights γ_i and ϑ_j can be tuned to meet various constraints imposed on the system (Wilson 1970) or to simulate elasticities of demand and supply (Alonso 1978). These are the formal structures around which the land-use, the retail, and the transportation models presented by Wegener (2005, this volume), Birkin (2005, this volume), and Israelsen and Frederiksen (2005, this volume) are constructed. They describe urban structure as a snapshot in time and as such, encapsulate the entire history of urban growth (and decline) into the cross section. In fact, these kinds of equations are coupled into more comprehensive models dealing with two or more (disaggregated) sectors of the urban system—employment, population, and so on—the norm being the model first presented by Lowry (1964) which became the flagship for a generation of such models from the 1970s onwards (Batty 1976). In terms of simulating urban growth, these models were used in comparative static form; new inputs describing some future system are used to drive the model's predictions which assume an immediate reaction to a stable equilibrium within the forecast period implied.

In this chapter, we will develop a dynamic equivalent of this structure. We simply assume that the increment of change in movement over a given time period, called ΔP_{ij}, and change in activity/population at i, ΔP_i, can be simulated using the same forms of equation as

$$\Delta P_{ij} = K \frac{P_i(t)P_j(t)}{d_{ij}^{\alpha}} \quad , \quad \Delta P_i = \sum_j \Delta P_{ij} = P_i(t) K \sum_j \frac{P_j(t)}{d_{ij}^{\alpha}}. \tag{4}$$

We now write a dynamic relation between population $P_i(t+1)$ at time $t+1$ and population $P_i(t)$ at t as

$$P_i(t+1) = P_i(t) + \Delta P_i = P_i(t) + P_i(t) K \sum_j \frac{P_j(t)}{d_{ij}^{\alpha}}, \tag{5}$$

where K is the appropriate scaling constant. Equation (5) has the same structure as a reaction–diffusion equation used to simulate growth in many physical processes. The first term on the right-hand side is the reaction which makes sense as the population at the end of the time period is clearly derived from that at the beginning, and the second term is the change which is the product of diffusion from other locations in the system. If we change the weighting structure slightly by adding parameters ω and ϕ and add some noise $\varepsilon_i(t)$ to account for randomness and uncertainty, then the structure becomes much more general

$$P_i(t+1) = \omega P_i(t) + \phi P_i(t) K \sum_j \frac{P_j(t)}{d_{ij}^{\alpha}} + \varepsilon_i(t), \tag{6}$$

and it is equation (6) that forms the basis of our generic model of urban growth.

The biggest difference between the comparative static model in equations (1) to (3) and the dynamic in equations (4) to (6) is the way growth/change is treated. In the former, it is assumed that the total quantity of change is known—from other models or is assumed—and that the process of locational simulation is one of distributing this growth. In contrast, in dynamic urban growth models based on equations (4) to (6), growth is directly predictable from these equations; there is no overall constraint on the total that is generated, and it is assumed that each location reacts according to its position within the system. In a sense, these dynamic models are much more general than their comparative static precursors, and one of the reasons why they have been developed is to relax the limitations of the former. But this comes at a price, for predicting both growth and distribution within the same model is considerably more hazardous than building separate models for each. As we will see, this is the Achilles' heel of this generation of urban models. But before we elaborate this, we will show how the structure in equation (6) can be approximated by cellular automata models which have been used to translate this generic model into practical applications.

REPRESENTATION AND DYNAMICS USING CELLULAR AUTOMATA

Simulation from the bottom up implies that the system is composed of basic elements or objects, atoms if you like, rather than the kinds of aggregates which form the essence of the cross-sectional, top-down static models briefly noted above. In urban models, there are two obvious foci: the landscape and activities or populations which move and locate within the landscape. Landscapes are usually subdivided into zones or cells while activities and populations form agents which interact with each other and whose locations are fixed with respect to cells. In this context, our emphasis will be exclusively on modeling changes in cells which are uniquely identified with activities and populations. Agent-based models of urban systems have not been widely developed to date except for fine-scale movements in problems where transportation is the main focus (Batty 2005b), and thus our set of basic objects is the cells whose states represent the way the system reacts and diffuses with respect to growth and change.

We assume that cells are small enough, spacewise, to contain single activities—a single household or land use which is the cell state—with the cellular tessellation usually forming a grid associated with the pixel map used to visualize data input and model output. In terms of our notation, population in any cell i must be $P_i(t) = 1$ *or* 0, representing a cell which is occupied or empty with the change being $\Delta P_i(t) = -1$ *or* 0 *if* $P_i(t) = 1$ and $\Delta P_i(t) = 1$ *or* 0 *if* $P_i(t) = 0$. These switches of state are not computed by equation (6), for the way these cellular variants are operationalized is through a series of rules, constraints, and thresholds which, although consistent with the generic model equations, are applied in more ad hoc terms.

The next simplification which determines whether or not a CA follows a strict formalism, relates to the space over which the diffusion takes place. In strict CA, diffusion is over a local neighborhood of cells around i, Ω_i, where the cells are adjacent. For symmetric neighborhoods, the simplest is composed of cells which are north, south, east, and west of the cell in question—that is, $\Omega_i = n, s, e, w$ (the so-called von Neumann neighborhood)—while if the diagonal nearest neighbors are included, then the number of adjacent cells rises to 8 forming the so-called Moore neighborhood. The notion of these highly localized neighborhoods is essential to processes that grow from the bottom up but generate global patterns that show emergence. Rules for diffusion are based on switching a cell's state on or off, dependent upon what is happening in the neighborhood, with such rules being based on counts of cells, cell attributes, constraints on what can happen in a cell, and so on.

The simplest way of showing how diffusion in localized neighborhoods takes place can be demonstrated by simplifying the diffusion term in equation (6) as follows. Then $\phi\, K\, P_i(t)\sum_j P_j(t) = \phi\, K\, P_i(t)\sum_j P_j(t)d_{ij}^{-\alpha}$ as $d_{ij} = 1$ when $\Omega_i = n, s, e, w$. Thus the diffusion is a count of cells in the neighborhood i scaled by the size of the activity in i. In fact, this scaling is inappropriate in models that work by switching cells on and off, for it is only relevant when one is dealing with aggregates. This arises from the way the generic equation in (6) has been derived, and in CA models, it is assumed to be neutral. Thus equation (6) becomes

$$P_i(t+1) = \omega\, P_i(t) + \phi\, K \sum_j P_j(t) + \varepsilon_i(t), \tag{7}$$

where this can now be used to determine a threshold over which the cell state is switched. A typical rule might be

$$P_i(t+1) = \begin{cases} 1 & if \quad [\omega\, P_i(t) + \phi\, K \sum_j P_j(t) + \varepsilon_i(t)] > Z_{max} \\ 0, & otherwise \end{cases}. \tag{8}$$

It is entirely possible to separate the reaction from the diffusion and consider different combinations of these effects sparking off a state change. As we have implied, different combinations of attributes in cells and constraints within neighborhoods can be used to effect a switch, much depending on the precise specification of the model.

In many growth models based on CA, the strict limits posed by a local neighborhood are relaxed. In short, the diffusion field is no longer local but is an information or potential field consistent with its use in social physics where action-at-a-distance is assumed to be all-important. In the case of strict CA, it is assumed that there is no action-at-a-distance in that diffusion takes place to physically adjacent cells. Over time, activity can reach all parts of the system, but it cannot hop over the basic unit distance. In cities, this is clearly quite unrealistic as the feasibility of deciding what and where to locate does not depend on physical adjacency. In terms of applications, there are few if any urban growth models based on strict CA although this does rather beg the question as to why CA is being used in the first place. In fact it is more appropriate to call such models cell-space or CS models as Couclelis (1985) has suggested.

To illustrate a typical CA/CS model used to simulate urban growth, we will outline the DUEM[1] model originally developed by Xie (1994). The version of the model presented here is that developed by Batty, Xie, and Sun (1999) in which there are five distinct land uses: housing, manufacturing/primary industry, commerce and services, transport in the form of the street/road network, and vacant land. In principle, at each time period, each land use can generate quantities and locations of any other land use although in practice only industry, commerce and services, and housing can generate one other as well as generating streets. Streets do not generate land uses other than streets themselves. Vacant land is regarded as a residual available for development which can result from a state change (decline) in land use. The way the generation of land uses takes place is through a rule-based implementation of the generic equation (7) which enables a land use $P_i^k(t+1)$ to be generated from any other land use $P_j^l(t)$. Land uses are also organized across a life cycle from initiating through mature to declining. Only initiating land uses which reflect their relative newness can spawn new land use. Mature land uses do not generate new land uses although they still influence the locations of new uses. Declining land uses disappear, thus reflecting the usual life cycle of built form.

We are not able to present the fine details of the model here, but we can provide a broad sketch. The way initiating land uses spawn new ones is structured according to rule-based equations akin to the thresholding implied in equation (8). In fact, there are three spatial scales at which these thresholds are applied, ranging from the most local neighborhood through the district to the region itself. The *neighborhood* exercises a trigger for new growth or decline based on the existence or otherwise of the street network, the *district* uses the densities of related land uses and distance of the new land use from the initiating use to effect a change, while the *region* is used to implement hard and fast constraints on what cells are available or not for development. Typically, an initiating land use will spawn a new land use in a district only if the cells in question are vacant and if they are not affected by some regional constraint on development with these rules being implemented first. The probability of this land use occurring in a cell in this district is then fixed according to its distance from the initiating location. This probability is then modified according to the density of different land uses that exist around each of these potential locations, using compatibility constraints, and then in the local neighborhood, the density of the street network is examined. If this density is not sufficient to support a new use, the probability is set equal to zero, and the cell in question does not survive this process of allocation. At this point, the cell state is switched from empty or vacant to developed if the random number drawn is consistent with the development probability determined through this process.

Declines in land use which are simply switches from developed to vacant in terms of cell state are produced through the life cycling of activities. When a mature land use in a cell reaches a certain age, it moves into a one-period declining state and then disappears at the end of this time period with the cell becoming vacant. Cells remain vacant for one time period before entering the pool of eligible locations for new development. In the model as currently constituted, there is no internal migration of activities or indeed any mutation of uses, but these processes are intrinsic to the model structure and have simply not been invoked. The stages in a typical run of the model for one time period are illustrated in figure 1. The software for this model has been written from scratch in Visual C++® with the loosest coupling possible to GIS through the import of raster files in different proprietary formats. The interface we have developed, shown below, enables the user to plant various land-use seeds into a virgin landscape or an already developed system which is arranged on a suitably registered pixel grid which can be up to 3K × 3K or 9 million pixels in size. A map of this region forms the main window, but there are also three related windows which show the various trajectories of how different land uses change through time with the map and trajectories successively updated in each run. A feature which is largely due to the fact that the model can be run quickly through many time periods is that the system soon grows to its upper limits with exponential growth at first which then becomes logistic or capacitated. Lastly, the various rules which are implied in figure 1 are coded in various dialog boxes that can be accessed directly on the screen before or during a model run, thus enabling the user to change rules and parameters on-the-fly.

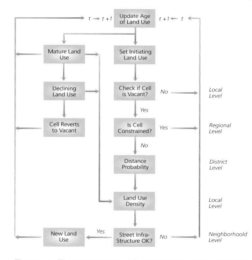

Figure 1. The sequence of operations in the DUEM model.

What we will briefly present here is a typical application of this CA model to urban growth using as an example the spread of Greater Detroit (Wayne County), where the key characteristic of change in this region during the last twenty years has been a decline in population but a massive spread in the extent of the urbanized area. This is typical of many cities in developed countries where there is jobless growth, near-zero population growth, but increased demand for lower densities where central cities and inner areas are being abandoned in preference for higher quality suburban environments. From 1980 to 2000, the population of this region fell by 4.8% and now stands at around 2.06 million, but from 1978 to 1995, parcels classed as residential increased by 3.8%, commercial by 4%, and industrial land even more by 11.1%. This is clear evidence of sprawl with every significant land use falling in density over the last twenty years. We have fitted the DUEM model with data from 1978 to 1990, tested its predictions from 1990 to 1995 using data independent of its calibration, and have then used the model to make various predictions from 1995 to 2030. The parameters of the model have been tuned to reflect the aggregate properties of this growth regime with independent predictions from the South East Michigan Council of Government suggesting that residential land will continue to grow at around 1% each decade, commercial by 0.6%, and industrial by 2.2% but set against a background of continuing population loss.

We have tested three alternative scenarios using the model, the first based on market forces which reflect development trends, the second on policies geared to the conservation lobby which squeezes growth of any kind from the system, and the third based on a more realistic planning-oriented scenario. We will not present these here but simply indicate how we used GIS in making predictions with this model. As we noted, DUEM is very loosely coupled to GIS in that much of its input is taken from GIS coverages which enable raster and vector layers to be converted to the pixel base that the model uses. We also use these layers to provide inputs which form the regional constraints on land-use development as well as coding the parcel maps and street/road network into a form that is convenient to the model. In figure 2, we simply show a typical screen shot of the model interface with the map and three trajectories of land-use change in their appropriate windows alongside a land suitability map based on buffering in GIS which illustrates the way in which conventional but large-scale databases are processed within GIS prior to their import into the model through a loose coupling. As this is central to the way most independently conceived models have been linked to GIS, we will now outline the key issues involved before summarizing several applications being developed using models similar to DUEM.

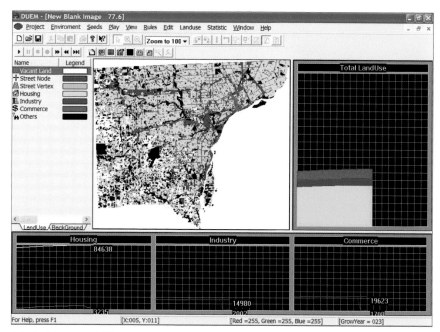

(a) The Duem model interface.

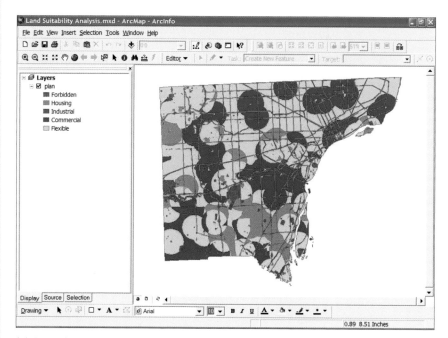

(b) The GIS interface showing land suitability buffers.

Figure 2. Graphical user interfaces to the model and its GIS.

A GIS is largely considered as a system for spatial representation with respect to two-dimensional spaces. Three-dimensional representation is in its infancy, and there has been little focus on representing space–time series, largely because both spatial data and its use have been largely confined to the 2D map. Insofar as processes exist within GIS, these have emphasized how map layers relate to one another, on how patterns can be extracted from map layers, and how map layers can be explained and generalized across spatial scales. Processes which reflect the causal structure of the systems represented and their dynamics are not usually part of traditional GIS although as both software and the science supporting it continue to develop, there is considerable interest in opening such software to these wider possibilities, as indeed the chapters in this book attest to.

To illustrate how these varieties of urban growth model have begun to be coupled with GIS, we will first look at different ways of spatial representation and the extent to which GIS is able to inform spatial modeling. There are four obvious ways of representing spatial phenomena which are consistently related within GIS. First, there is data which is collected at a point and whose location is sourced to an x,y coordinate. Second, there is data which is based on a neutral tessellation of space, a raster or grid, which is consistent with much physical data whose collection is either mapped to such a unit or is sensed automatically with the grid as collecting unit. Third, there is geometric data associated with built forms, man-made features which define parcels and boundaries which need to be represented as vectors but which are sufficiently fine scale to be directly associated with items of common recognition such as buildings and landscape features. Fourth, there is data which is made available using some administrative geography, a census tract or local municipality which is usually collected at individual level but aggregated to administrative units for purposes of analysis and delivery and the preservation of confidentiality. There is, in fact, a fifth method of representation which is network-based, and of course transport systems are organized in this way, but locational data can be so tagged to such networks (Israelsen and Frederiksen 2005, this volume). In fact, network data cuts across these five categories, notwithstanding the fact that there has not been much concern for such representations to date.

Transformations between these different representations are quite well worked out within GIS, thus providing a stable basis for data from the many different sources important to the comprehensive modeling and analysis of urban growth. Most urban growth models up until the early 1990s were based on geographic/administrative data units, and GIS has enabled this kind of data to be integrated with land suitability data, invariably raster in form. The new generation of urban models is much more spatially disaggregate than these original cross-sectional static models, and spatial interaction is no longer formally represented explicitly. Thus the coincidence of raster, pixel, and cell has wedded these models somewhat closer to GIS than their predecessors. In contrast, very few models have been developed which are rooted in land parcel representations of the urban system; in the very few cases where such models are being considered, zones or cells are represented as points, their tessellation being reflected in a network between these points and the vector representation of the parcels associated with each points being coded as attributes one step removed from the literal spatial representation associated with CA models (Bian and Liebner 2005, this volume; O'Sullivan 2000; Xie and Batty 2005).

Although the idea of the cell and that of the pixel/raster have tended to associate CA-based urban growth models with GIS and GI scientists rather than urban economists or transportation engineers (Wagner 1997), this coincidence has not really been exploited in the structure of these models or their software. Few if any of these models have been developed within GIS per se using the various scripting languages and interfaces to stand-alone programs that are now available to enable a close coupling of model and GIS. The focus on raster representation is, to an extent, a diversion because most urban data is still vector in source, based on administrative units such as block groups or census tracts or even land parcels rather than arbitrary cells. Moreover, the number of cells required to represent a single land use in models which are based on simple state switching is usually far greater than the number of land parcels available, and it has proved difficult to reflect the irregularity of the built-form geometry in terms of a pixelated base. Most CA models are thus more like caricatures of the system, for at the level at which they are represented, much simplification occurs when vector-based activities are translated into cell states. This is reflected in data for the Greater Detroit region in figure 3 where the vector layers need to be collapsed into the kinds of pixelated map base shown in figure 2. Coupling thus tends to remain loose. It is easier to manipulate data outside the model and then import it into the required form than to embed the models directly into the GIS. It is not possible to embed the range of functions in proprietary GIS into this model although more recent developments do now enable this (Maguire 2005, this volume).

Figure 3. Land parcel and road vector representations of data in Detroit.

It is quite possible to build these kinds of urban models within GIS either using the various scripting languages which have been adapted to enable new functions to be incorporated as extensions or plug-ins or to use the GUI functionality of the GIS to control a series of related programs accessible from within a common interface. GIS software is now so modular that virtually any other software function can be accessed across the range of loose to strong coupling, and it is easy to produce a variety of interfaces to GIS which are able to meet the flexibility required. As we noted in chapter 3 (Batty 2005, this volume), the way GIS is used formally within an urban model depends on the purpose in mind. The extent to which the overhead posed by GIS functionality needs to be sustained in any application and the extent to which a close coupling is needed in terms of visualization depends on the particular application. In most applications to date, detailed coupling has not been required. In terms of cross-sectional static models, this is largely because of the emphasis on spatial interaction (Wegener 2005, this volume). In the case of dynamic CA models, the processes of transition and the rule-based structures needed to implement these mean that it has been far easier to produce purpose-built software and special graphics and interface functions for the model than to embed these into GIS. Loose coupling to GIS inputs and outputs has been deemed sufficient.

This is not really very different from the situation when GIS first came to be associated with urban models some fifteen years or so ago. It then became clear that purpose-built software was far more efficient in terms of the process of model calibration, testing, and scenario production than trying to embed the same within GIS (Batty 1992). In fact, model functions based on thresholding and rule bases are hard to implement within current GIS software architectures while the temporal structure, around which software such as DUEM, for example, is written, is difficult to replicate within contemporary GIS. Although it is possible to represent linear and nonlinear equation structures in GIS through the addition and convolution of different variables represented as map layers, it is much easier to develop specific graphical user interfaces which control the model. In figure 4, we show an example of the interface to DUEM which enables rules to be fixed through parameter values essential to the calibration process. The same kinds of interface are relevant to setting up scenarios. In fact, it is more likely that urban models such as these will continue to be developed in special-purpose software or within standard CA, with GIS constituting the toolbox of functions for spatial analysis and cartographic display.

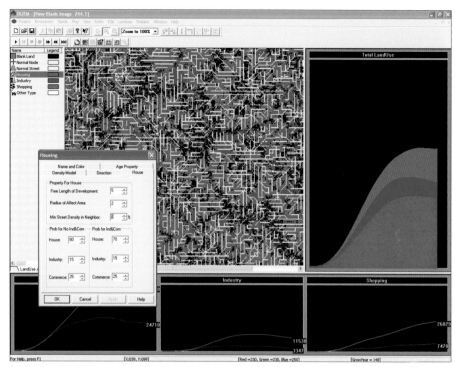

Figure 4. The GUI rule-based interface to DUEM.

The first bottom-up CA models applicable to urban structure and growth can be traced back to the 1960s. Chapin and Weiss (1968) used cell-space (CS) simulation whose locational attractivities were based on linear regression in their models of urban growth in Greensboro, North Carolina. Lathrop and Hamburg (1965) used gravitational models to effect the same in simulating growth in the Buffalo-Niagara region while from a rather different perspective, Tobler (1970) used CA-like simulation to generate a movie of growth in the Detroit region. All these applications were on the edge of the mainstream which thirty years ago was largely based not on formal dynamics but on cross-sectional static models. In the intervening years, CA, insofar as it was considered a simulation tool, was regarded as important mainly for its pedagogic and analytical value (Tobler 1979, Couclelis 1985). It was not until the early 1990s that models began to emerge which were considered to be close enough to actual real-world urban growth patterns to form the basis for simulation and prediction. In fact, there still exists a recurrent debate about whether or not CA models are most important for their pedagogic value rather than for their abilities to simulate real systems. These require gross simplifications of model processes and spatial units, rendering them somewhat further from reality than those cross-sectional models that came before.

The three earliest attempts at such modeling were geared to simulating rapid urban growth for metropolitan regions, medium-sized towns, and suburban areas. Batty and Xie (1994) developed simulations of suburban residential sprawl in Amherst, New York, where a detailed space–time series of development was used to tune the model. Clarke and Gaydos (1998) embarked on a series of simulations of large-scale metropolitan urban growth in the Bay Area and went on to model a series of cities in the U.S. in the Gigalopolis project. White and Engelen (1993) developed a CA model for Cincinnati from rather crude temporal land-use data, and in all these cases, the focus was on land development, suburbanization, and sprawl. Since then, several other groups have developed similar models focusing on suburbanization in Australian cities (Ward, Murray, and Phinn 2000), *desakota*—rapid urban growth in rural areas in China—specifically in the Pearl River Delta (Yeh and Li 2000), diffused urban growth in Northern Italy (Besussi, Cecchini, and Rinaldi 1998), and rapid urbanization in Latin American cities (Almeida et al. 2003). Other attempts at modeling and predicting sprawl have been made by Papini et al. (1998) for Rome and by Cheng (2003) for Wuhan, while Engelen's group at RIKS in the Netherlands has been responsible for many applications of their model system to various European cities (Barredo, et al. 2003). A list of these applications, the groups involved, and key references are given in table 1.

Active Research Group: Place	Research Focus	Early/Typical Publication
London (CASA)–Michigan	sprawl, urban morphology DUEM software	Batty, Xie, and Sun (1994)
UCSB–Santa Barbara	sprawl, metropolitan growth, CA theory SLEUTH software	Tobler (1979) Couclelis (1985) Clarke and Gaydos (1998)
RIKS Netherlands	comprehensive urban modeling The Dynamica software	White and Engelen (1993) Barredo, Kasanko, McCormick, and Lavalle (2003)
Venice (CASA/Sassari/LAMP)	sprawl and segregation AUGH, CAGE software	Besussi, Cecchini, and Rinaldi (1998)
Hong Kong University	rapid urban growth, rural-urban migration	Yeh and Li (2000)
Brisbane–Adelaide	sprawl	Ward, Murray, and Phinn (2000)
Cardiff–Southampton	spatial markets	Wu and Webster (1998)
Tel Aviv	segregation, residential filtering CITY software	Portugali and Benenson (1996)
INPE–Brazil	rural-urban migration SPRING-DINAMICA	Almeida et al. (2003)
Pisa–Milan	land development	Papini et al. (1998)
ITC–Netherlands	rapid urban growth, rural-urban migration	Cheng (2003)
Florence	scale and hierarchy	Semboloni (2000)
Santa Fe–Los Alamos Berlin–Gothenberg	physics of urban development	Andersson, Rasmussen, and White (2002) Schweitzer and Steinbrink (1997)

Table 1. Significant research groups in CA modeling of urban growth.

There are at least four significant groups working with CA models which do not focus on urban growth per se. Wu and Webster (1998) have been intent on adding spatial economic processes and market clearing to such models, while Portugali and Benenson (1996) in Tel Aviv have focused their efforts on intraurban change, particularly segregation and ghettoization. Semboloni (2000) has worked on adding more classical mechanisms to his CA models reflecting scale and hierarchy as well as extending his simulations to the third dimension, while there have been several attempts by physicists to evolve a more general CA framework for urban development which links to new ideas in complexity such as self-organized criticality and power law scaling (Andersson, Rasmussen, and White 2002; Schweitzer and Steinbrink 1997). There are many ad hoc applications, particularly in the Far East, and more recently there have been attempts at formal calibration of such model structures. However, many of these developments begin to expose the limits to these models, and in the next section, we will conclude by outlining these and indicating how such models are likely to develop in the near future, particularly with respect to GIS and GI science.

DIFFICULTIES, LIMITATIONS, AND NEXT STEPS

Although bottom-up approaches to modeling urban growth are consistent with the general notion that decision making in cities follows such processes, there are important consequences with respect to model calibration and use in forecasting. Essentially, comparative static models tend to be parsimonious in their organization in that usually an attempt is made to structure them so that they can be uniquely solved and calibrated. In terms of model equations, this means that the number of dependent and independent variables is balanced, that such models are not overidentified; in terms of model calibration, there needs to be as many goodness-of-fit measures as there are parameters, and that the response surface based on these measures is such that a unique fit exists. Considerable effort has been put into comparative static models to ensure that these conditions are met, but in contrast, the generation of models that has emerged based on cells and agents has not exercised anything like this discipline of parsimony. CA models, for example, invoke many rules specified *a priori* that cannot be tested. We rarely have independent data on the decision making that is implied, while often time series data is missing in that the minimum requirement for data at three points in time—two to enable calibration and a third for verification—is usually not met.

Calibration is also problematic because of the overabundance of processes and outcomes that the model should be strictly tested against. It is not good enough to simply replicate what has happened in terms of spatial outcomes because it is extremely well known in spatial systems that autocorrelated processes can lead to the same outcomes—equifinality—under very different parameterizations. Moreover, CA models are invariably operationalized using random number routines which enable choices to be made when transitions between states are framed probabilistically. Indeed, in applications where a cell is either on or off, full or empty, the only way to produce an outcome is to resolve the choice probabilistically. This means that models should be run to produce ranges of possible solutions. But computing an average is not feasible when the outcome is based on many cells being switched on or off although it might be possible to accumulate probabilities across different runs and produce an average run which would imply a typical outcome. In fact, there has been little discussion of how this uncertainty is to be resolved in the context of these models, and this implies that most applications to data have not been close to the policy process where definite outcomes are required. In fact, most applications have been research-orientated, notwithstanding the fact that some of these have been financed by government agencies with a mandate for spatial planning.

This lack of focus on the policy process is important. Although these models are predicated on the basis of informing our understanding of rapid growth which in developed countries is focused on urban sprawl, they lack explicit mechanisms for simulating spatial interaction which has long been regarded as crucial to the way cities grow at their edges. Indeed, one of the keys to controlling sprawl is transportation policy, and although such models do provide predictions of what locations might develop as cities expand, they are unable to associate this development with transportation movements. Even in the case where transport as a land use is simulated, as in DUEM, this is not movement; in fact, the focus on physical quantities, such as land use, rather than on levels and densities of activity, tends to exclude more substantive issues about how the urban economy works. Few if any of these urban growth models are rooted in the way the housing market works, which is also surprising given the importance of these markets in the land development process. In one sense, all of this is explicable given the heritage of these models. Unlike their predecessors developed in the 1960s where policy was a major driver of the activity, most of these applications have emerged from research groups involved with the physical morphology of the city sustained by the data and methods of GIS. Even where major agencies have been involved, such as the European Union for many of the projects that the RIKS group has developed and USGS for the Santa Barbara applications, the focus has been more on demonstrating what is possible, showing the state of the art, rather than on providing models which generate definitive policy advice.

Another limitation noted above relates to spatial resolution. Currently in most applications, the translation between the actual physical unit associated with the data—whether it be a land parcel, administrative geographic unit, or arbitrary pixel from automated sensing—and the cell has been tricky. Several applications do not give much attention to the way the actual data unit maps onto the cell, particularly where the cell used is much larger than the parcel or pixel from automatically sensed data or much smaller than the geographic unit in which the data is delivered. This means that in several cases, cell sizes are too big to contain a single land use, and often a decision is then made to simplify the cell state to its predominant use. In some such cases, the cell size is often not small enough to reproduce the irregularity of the parcel. There are clear ways beyond such difficulties, but they depend on better resolutions which in turn probably imply a rather different spatial representation using a network of points whose attributes reflect the local geometry.

We have not invoked the prospect of agent-based models of urban growth in this chapter, largely because there are none existing as yet from the CA point of view. Some agent-based thinking has been used in the disaggregation of models such as UrbanSim (Waddell 2002) which represents a more operational form of model with a stronger link to urban economic and cross-sectional transportation modeling than to the models of this chapter. At the regional level, Pumain's group is working with various agent-based structures (Sanders et al. 1997), but these models are even further away from explicit policy forecasting and use than the models presented here. What can now be said about this field, however, is that, far from any convergence of software and practice, there is a growing plurality of ideas both at the level of urban modeling theory, methodology, ideas about estimation, and ideas about representation. GIS plays a major part in all these ventures but not in a form that implies these models will all be merged in the future with GIS software. In fact, the plurality extends beyond models and representations to the planning process itself where more than one approach, more than one model, more than one GIS perhaps, appear to be in prospect as policy makers, researchers, and professionals all run to keep up with the burgeoning complexity posed by the problems of the contemporary urban world.

ACKNOWLEDGMENTS

The authors wish to thank Xinyue Ye of Eastern Michigan University for help with the DUEM simulations of Detroit reported here.

NOTES

1. DEM – Dynamic Urban Evolutionary Model, devised by Xie (1994) and developed by Batty, Xie and Sun (1999) and Xie and Batty (2004).

REFERENCES

Almeida, C. M. de, M. Batty, G. Câmaral, G. C. Cerqueira, A. M. V. Monteiro, C. P. Pennachin, and B. S. Soares-Filho. 2003. Stochastic cellular automata modeling of urban land use dynamics: Empirical development and estimation. *Computers, Environment, and Urban Systems* 27: 481–509.

Alonso, W. 1978. A theory of movements. In *Human settlement systems: International perspectives on structure, change, and public policy,* ed. N. M. Hansen, 197–211. Cambridge, Mass.: Ballinger.

Andersson, C., S. Rasmussen, and R. White. 2002. Urban settlements transition. *Environment and Planning B* 29: 841–65.

Barredo, J. I., M. Kasanko, N. McCormick, and C. Lavalle. 2003. Modeling dynamic spatial processes: Simulation of urban future scenarios through cellular automata. *Landscape and Urban Planning* 64: 145–60.

Batty, M. 1976. *Urban modelling: Algorithms, calibration, predictions.* Cambridge: Cambridge University Press.

———. 1992. Urban modeling in computer-graphic and geographic information system environments. *Environment and Planning B* 19: 663–85.

———. 2005a. *Cities and complexity.* Cambridge, Mass.: MIT Press.

———. 2005b. Agents, cells and cities: New representational models for simulating multi-scale urban dynamics. *Environment and Planning A.*

Batty, M., and Y. Xie. 1994. From cells to cities. *Environment and Planning B* 21: s31–s48.

Batty, M., Y. Xie, and Z. Sun. 1999. Modeling urban dynamics through GIS-based cellular automata. *Computers, Environments and Urban Systems* 23: 205–33.

Bauer Wurster, C. 1963. The form and structure of the future urban complex. In *Cities and space: The future use of urban land,* ed. L. Wingo Jr., 72–101. Baltimore, M.D.: Johns Hopkins Press.

Besussi, E., A. Cecchini, and E. Rinaldi. 1998. The diffused city of the Italian North-East: Identification of urban dynamics using cellular automata urban models. *Computers, Environments and Urban Systems* 22: 497–523.

Blumenfeld, H. 1954. The tidal wave of metropolitan expansion. *Journal of the American Institute of Planners* 20: 3–14.

Chapin, F. S., and S. F. Weiss. 1968. A probabilistic model for residential growth. *Transportation Research* 2: 375–90.

Cheng, J. 2003. Modelling spatial and temporal urban growth. PhD thesis. ITC Dissertation 99. Enschede, The Netherlands.

Clarke, K. C., and L. J. Gaydos. 1998. Loose coupling a cellular automaton model and GIS: Long-term growth prediction for San Francisco and Washington/Baltimore. *International Journal of Geographical Information Science* 12: 699–714.

Couclelis, H. 1985. Cellular worlds: A framework for modeling micro–macro dynamics. *Environment and Planning A* 17: 585–96.

Lathrop, G. T., and J. R. Hamburg. 1965. An opportunity-accessibility model for allocating regional growth. *Journal of the American Institute of Planners* 31: 95–103.

Lowry, I. S. 1964. Model of Metropolis. Memorandum RM-4035-RC, Rand Corporation, Santa Monica, Calif.

Morrill, R. L. 1968. Waves of spatial diffusion. *Journal of Regional Science* 8: 1–18.

Nivola, P. S. 1999. *Laws of the landscape: How policies shape cities in Europe and America.* Washington D.C.: Brookings Institution Press.

O'Sullivan, D. 2000. Graph-based cellular automaton models of urban spatial processes. PhD thesis, University College London.

Papini, L., G. A. Rabino, A. Colonna, V. Di Stefano, and S. Lombardo. 1998. Learning cellular automata in a real world: The case study of the Rome Metropolitan Area. In *Cellular automata: Research towards industry. Proceedings of the third conference* on Cellular Automata for Research and Industry, eds. S. Bandini, R. Serra, and F. Suggi Liverani, 165–83. London: Springer-Verlag.

Portugali, J., and I. Benenson. 1996. Human agents between local and global forces in a self-organizing city. In *Self-organization of complex structures: From individual to collective dynamics,* ed. F. Schweitzer, 537–45. London: Gordon and Breach.

Sanders, L., D. Pumain, H. Mathian, F. Guerin-Pace, and S. Bura. 1997. SIMPOP: A multiagent system for the study of urbanism. *Environment and Planning B* 24: 287–305.

Schweitzer, F., and J. Steinbrink. 1997. Urban cluster growth: Analysis and computer simulation of urban aggregations. In *Self-organization of complex structures: From individual to collective dynamics,* ed. F. Schweitzer, 501–18. London: Gordon and Breach.

Semboloni, F. 2000. The growth of an urban cluster into a dynamic self-modifying spatial pattern. *Environment and Planning B* 27: 549–64.

Tobler, W. R. 1970. A computer movie simulating population growth in the Detroit region. *Economic Geography* 42: 234–40.

———. 1979. Cellular geography. In *Philosophy in geography,* eds. S. Gale and G. Olsson, 279–386. Dordrecht: Reidel.

Waddell, P. 2002. UrbanSim: Modeling urban development for land use, transportation and environmental planning. *Journal of the American Planning Association* 68: 297–314.

Wagner, D. F. 1997. Cellular automata and geographic information systems. *Environment and Planning B* 24: 219–34.

Ward, D. P., A. T. Murray, and S. R. Phinn. 2000. A stochastically constrained cellular model of urban growth. *Computers, Environment and Urban Systems* 24: 539–58.

White, R. W., and G. Engelen. 1993. Cellular automata and fractal urban form: A cellular modelling approach to the evolution of urban land use patterns. *Environment and Planning A* 25: 1175–93.

Wilson, A. G. 1970. *Entropy in urban and regional modeling.* London: Pion Press.

Wu, F., and C. J. Webster. 1998. Simulation of land development through the integration of cellular automata and multicriteria evaluation. *Environment and Planning B* 25: 103–26.

Xie, Y. 1994. Analytical models and algorithms for cellular urban dynamics. PhD diss., State University of New York at Buffalo.

Xie, Y., and M. Batty. 2005. Integrated urban evolutionary modeling. In *Geodynamics*, eds. P. Atkinson, G. Foody, S. Darby, and F. Wu. Boca Raton: CRC Press.

Yeh, A. G-O., and X. Li. 2000. *A "grey-cell" constrained CA model for the simulation of urban forms and developments in the planning of sustainable cities using GIS.* Centre of Urban Planning and Environmental Management, Pokfulam, Hong Kong: University of Hong Kong.

Chapter 9

A Data Model to Represent Plans and Regulations in Urban Simulation Models

LEWIS D. HOPKINS, NIKHIL KAZA, AND VARKKI G. PALLATHUCHERIL

UNIVERSITY OF ILLINOIS AT URBANA-CHAMPAIGN

URBANA, ILLINOIS

ABSTRACT

If a data model were available for encoding the content of urban development plans in a database, then these plans could be more effectively made and used. This database must store both the logic of plans—how plans work—and the processes of urban development—what plans are about. Planning support systems that include such a database would encourage considering plans when modeling urban development and using plans when deciding what to do. A planning geodatabase that is derived from a planning data model is presented here, along with its use in supporting urban development modeling.

INTRODUCTION Urban development models are used to trace out the implications of particular ideas about how development works based on initial conditions, possible scenarios, and intentional actions. Plans are pertinent to these models in at least two ways. First, development processes being modeled respond in part to plans of the various municipalities, agencies, and other actors in a region. Plans of embedded actors are pertinent in predicting and forecasting because they provide information about the intentions of particular actors under various contingent and interdependent situations. Second, a frequent application of urban development models is to predict the effects of proposed plans and to compare these to the effects of other possible plans. That is, simulation models are used to test the effectiveness of plans: What differences will arise in development patterns with the plan compared to the situation without the plan or with one plan compared to another plan? Both of these uses of plans in urban development modeling require that plans be represented in a database so that they can be included in the model.

Geographic information systems (GIS) now provide only a portion of the required scope of an urban planning data model. The objective of this chapter is to use data modeling tools and the geodatabase approach (Zeiler 1999) to extend conventional GIS data models so as to implement as a geodatabase a planning data model (PDM). The logical structure of the PDM and its application to creating and accessing systems of plans in order to use plans when making decisions (Hopkins 2001) are described in Hopkins, Kaza, and Pallathucheril (forthcoming). The opportunity to extend the conventional data models is analogous to that undertaken in creating Arc Hydro (Maidment 2002, Maidment et al. 2005, this volume) to support various hydrology related analytical tasks.

First, we explain the application domain—modeling of plans and urban development processes—and the implied system requirements. Then, we set out the planning data model (PDM) in some detail, focusing in turn on the logic of plans, the processes of urban development, and the potential to use plans and their implied regulations and investments as inputs and elements of urban development models. Each of these aspects is then considered through more specific examples: the UrbanSim and LEAM models of urban development, plans for urban growth boundaries, and plans for capital improvements.

These efforts show that, by taking extensive advantage of nonspatial object classes, the required scope for a PDM can be implemented as a planning geodatabase. A planning geodatabase is one way to create information technology infrastructure that will support tasks of urban planning beyond those supported by conventional GIS data models.

Plans of an individual or an organization are statements about intentions and possible future actions. They address incomplete information about outcomes and situations in which decisions about actions are contingent on inherently uncertain future states. By identifying goals and objectives to be achieved, plans also set self-evaluation measures. Urban plans are different from land-use regulations. Regulations are enforceable by the police power of the state. Plans, on the other hand, provide information that may be the basis for enacting certain regulations or may influence action in other ways (Hopkins 2001).

Urban development modeling includes modeling of land use, transportation, population, housing, water quantity and quality, air quality, and ecosystem integrity and their systemic interactions. For any of these aspects, models may be used to forecast, build scenarios, identify needs, measure effects, or in some other way assist people in understanding what is happening and in deciding what to do. Such analyses depend on representations of actors and their activities as well as physical elements of development. Actions, including investments that change the state of development and regulations that constrain the scope of investments and activities, must be represented. Information gained by actors over time, for example, observing where development occurs and whether it succeeds in the market, may affect later actions. Urban simulation models should be able to represent these phenomena in order to provide useful predictions.

Current data models in GIS provide inadequate support for the tasks of modeling the land development processes. Urban planning concerns actions located in space and time. It comes as no surprise, therefore, that geographic information systems have long been associated with land development through the fields of landscape architecture and urban planning. The tasks of recording and analyzing attributes of land over space, and more recently over time, are well established. GIS data models do not, however, include investment and regulatory actions that change the state of development and plans about such actions. The actors who make these decisions and live, work, shop, and play in these places are not represented. Maps of particular patterns of development are commonplace, but they do not acknowledge the roles of organizations and actions in creating changes. There are maps of intended future land-use patterns and of zoned categories from regulations, but these maps simply show what attribute of land is intended where, not the logic behind these proposals, the contingencies to be considered when deciding to act, or the criteria involved in discretionary judgments about what to do.

Urban development models are intended to make predictions about actions that are taken at particular times and the effects of these actions. These actions may be predicted with explicit recognition of decisions that lead to them, or decision making may be only implicit. In either case, plans are pertinent to making these predictions. Incorporating the effects of plans into urban development modeling requires more than geographic features and their attributes. For example, a policy to focus commercial activity in mixed-use nodes can be stated without reference to a specific location, even if possible locations for such nodes are also identified. Mixed-use nodes might emerge in unexpected places if traffic patterns changed, major new employment attractors occurred, or new commercial agglomerations emerged. Only if the policy—that if commercial occurs, it should occur in mixed-use nodes—is included in the data encoding the plan, can an urban development model take into account the effects of the policy as other aspects of urban development patterns emerge. A planning data model that goes beyond GIS is required to represent the content of such plans so as to infer effects on decisions being predicted in an urban development model.

Regulations—enforceable constraints on the range of actions that can be taken—also affect modeled predictions of urban development. Regulations are not merely attributes of geographic features. For example, a regulation might require that adequate infrastructure facilities (roads, sewer systems) be available prior to development. This regulation, expressed as a relationship between the state of infrastructure and development actions, can be applied as a rule during the model run. Plans might also help predict when or whether, depending on time or relevant responses to changing states of the world, a regulation might change. As discussed further below, a plan might indicate where and when land is likely to be added to the supply within an urban growth boundary (UGB), depending on demand and supply at a given time step. The changes in the UGB further affect the pattern of development in future time steps.

Plans are also about investments. A road proposal that is expected to be finished in ten years' time, based on available budget estimates, is a simple example of a public investment. A school district proposal to locate a new school or expand the capacity of an existing school is another. These investments are identified in plans, and urban development patterns are affected by these statements because they shape expectations and stimulate speculative behavior. Urban development models should capture the effects of intentions in plans to help predict when and where such investments will occur in a particular model run and how the development pattern is affected by it.

A PDM provides three benefits for modeling. First, it enables users to specify scenarios involving combinations of more complex, dynamic, and endogenously triggered plans, investments, and regulations. Second, it enables users to work with more than one urban development model in order to consider the implications of potentially different results from partially substitutable models of the same phenomena (Hopkins 2003). Third, it enables users to link models of different phenomena such as transportation, land use, environmental effects, demographic change, and economic change (Westervelt 2001).

A PDM enables plans to be coded as inputs to urban development models and other impact assessment models. Models of urban development processes currently used to assess transportation, housing, land use, land cover, air pollution, and other environmental consequences can test only initial policy conditions, not dynamic interactions of plans, regulations, and capital improvements with the processes of urban development over time. If a capital improvements program is based on triggers of minimum available capacity, then capacity constraints in the model must change as development occurs.

If land parcels are rezoned in response to requests by developers as development spreads and land is annexed, then zoning should be represented dynamically, not as initially fixed constraints. Models of development processes should also be able to incorporate expectations about these changes. Landowners will expect future infrastructure projects and hold land vacant until expected infrastructure makes development at higher intensities possible.

Model triangulation is based on the procedure from navigation of finding an unknown point as a triangle from two known points and angles. We can learn more about an unknown situation by viewing it from two or more different perspectives. We can consider a larger scope by linking models of different phenomena than by trying to build a single, comprehensive model. To consider what the different models mean—whether they replicate and confirm, contradict and yield insight, complement and reinforce, or converge and enable action—requires some way to relate models to each other. A common data model is essential to enable translations of the inputs and outputs of different urban simulation models so that contrasts, comparisons, and links between these models are meaningful.

As the preceding discussion makes clear, the major task is to go beyond the representation of features in space, which is the primary focus of conventional GIS and the geodatabase approach, and to take full advantage of the possibilities to represent the many nonspatial objects required to support consideration of plans in urban modeling. An advantage of bringing these entities into a geodatabase is that many of them take on spatial attributes in some circumstances or are related in crucial ways to geographic features. Building on the geodatabase approach takes full advantage of the tremendous amount of database design work already accomplished for spatial entities.

A PLANNING GEODATABASE

This discussion and description of the planning data model follows the conventions established by ESRI authors for describing the geodatabase approach (Zeiler 1999, Maidment 2002), which builds on the Universal Modeling Language (UML) (Booch, Rumbaugh, and Jacobson 1999). The geodatabase approach focuses primarily on feature classes, entities that inherently have locations in space. A feature class is defined as a table that includes an attribute of geometric shape. Relationship classes describe relationships among other types of object classes, including features. Object classes that are not features or relationships are referred to as nonspatial objects or simply as object classes. In the rest of this chapter, object classes will mean nonspatial objects, even though this term could refer to all entities in a database.

An overall diagram of the planning geodatabase is shown in figure 1. The definitions and objects described here in geodatabase terms are based closely on the descriptions using UML for object class hierarchies and relationships in Hopkins, Kaza, and Pallathucheril (forthcoming). The major object classes are Actors, Activities, Assets, Investments, Capabilities, Regulations, and Plans. The relationships among these provide the connections necessary to specify scenarios and the content of plans as inputs to urban development models. These object classes can be used to describe a state of the world, which, if not yet realized, we label a future world. Actions, in particular Investments and Regulations, change the state of the world. Actors have Capabilities to perform Activities and make Plans, Investments, and Regulations. Activities occur on Assets. Investments change Assets. Capabilities can be changed by Regulations. Note that none of these major entities is inherently a feature with spatial attributes.

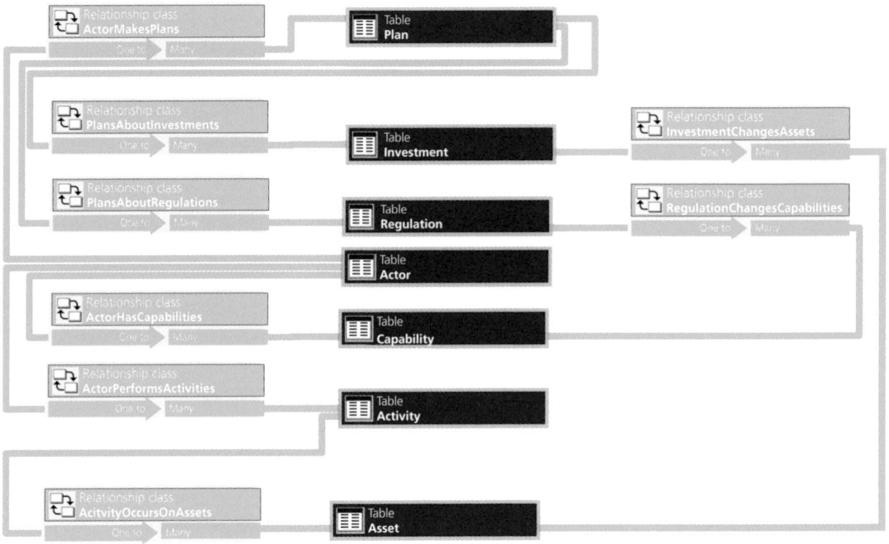

Figure 1. Overview of planning geodatabase.

PLANS: AGENDAS, POLICIES, DESIGNS, STRATEGIES, AND VISIONS

Plans are elaborated by encoding their content in five ways: Agenda, Policy, Vision, Design, and Strategy. These aspects are fully developed in Hopkins (2001) and summarized in table 1. Each defines a particular kind of relationship among Actions and among Actions and Consequences in a Plan. An Agenda is a list of Decisions or unrealized Actions. A Policy is a set of conditions in which an Action should be taken. A Vision is a state of the world expressed as an aspiration. A Design is an interdependent set of Actions with respect to Consequences. A Strategy is a set of contingent Actions and uncertain Consequences. Some elements of plans may be represented in more than one way. For example, particular Investments in roads might be represented as an Agenda in a capital improvements program, as a Design for a Network in a transportation plan, and as a Strategy to induce a land-use pattern in a comprehensive plan. Plans also frequently include statements of goals, important issues, and criteria for making decisions.

Aspect	Agenda	Policy	Vision	Design	Strategy
Definition	List of things to do; actions, not outcomes	If – then rules for actions	Image of what could be, an outcome	Target, describes fully worked out outcome	Contingent actions (path in decision tree)
Examples	List of capital improvement projects	If developer pays for roads, then permit development	Social equality, picture of beautiful city	Building plan or city master plan	Road projects built depend on how much land development occurs when and where
Works by	Reminding; if publicly shared, then commitment to act	Automating repeat decisions to save time; taking same action in same circumstances to be fair	Motivating people to take actions they believe will give the imagined result	Showing fully worked out results of interdependent actions	Determining which actions to take when and where depending on situation when actions are taken
Works if	Many actions to remember and need trust among people affected	Repeated decisions should be efficiently made, consistent, and predictable	Can raise aspirations or motivate effort	Highly interdependent actions, little uncertainty about actions, and few actors involved	Interdependent actions by many actors over long time in relation to uncertain events
Measures of Effective-ness	Are actions on list taken?	Is rule applied without constant reconsideration or is rule applied consistently?	Are beliefs changed as evidenced by beliefs elicited directly or revealed in actions?	Is design constructed or achieved?	Is contingent interdependence sustained in actions and is information used in timely fashion?

Table 1. Ways in which plans work (adapted with permission from Hopkins (2001).

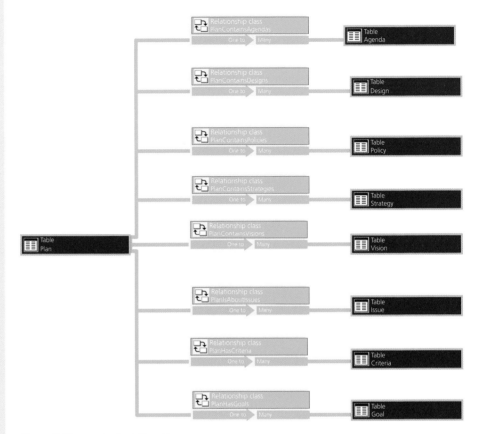

Figure 2. Plan content relationships.

A plan, in the sense of one document with a particular scope, can be represented as elaborated in figure 2. A plan may include statements that work in each of the five ways just described, and each of these requires a particular kind of data structure to encode its logic. Agenda, Policy, Design, and Strategy are elaborated in figures 3, 4, 5, and 6. Visions, goals, issues, and criteria are assumed to be graphic entities or text strings and are not elaborated here in data model terms.

181

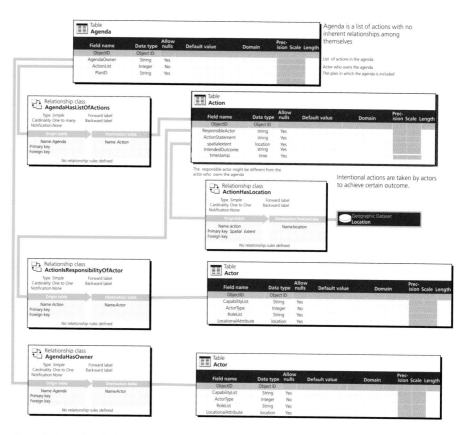

Figure 3. Agenda relationship diagram.

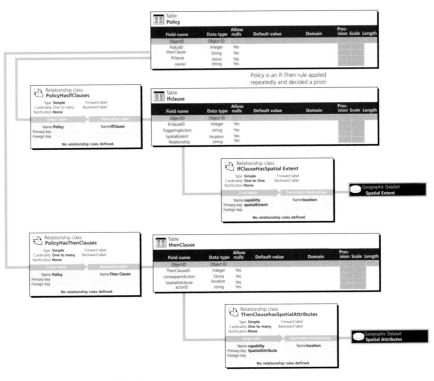

Figure 4. Policy relationship diagram.

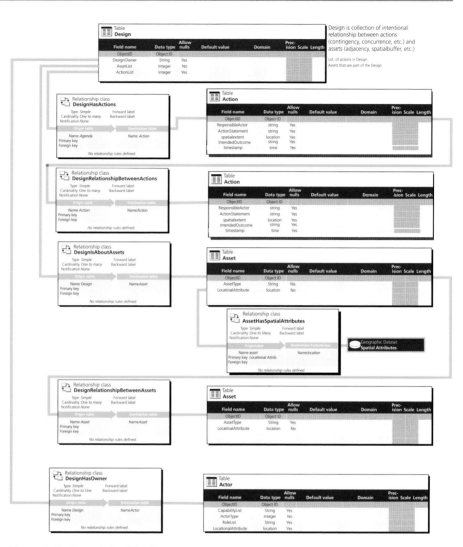

Figure 5. Design relationship diagram.

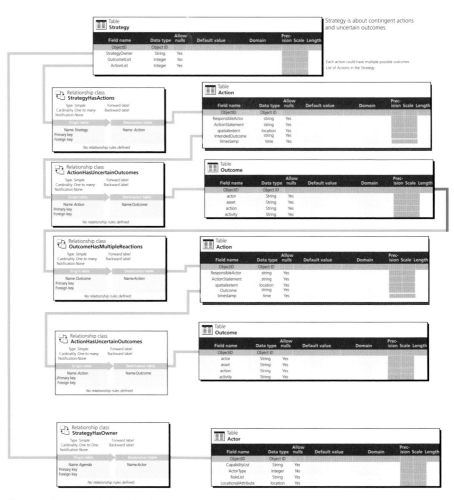

Figure 6. Strategy relationship diagram.

URBAN DEVELOPMENT: ACTORS, ACTIVITIES, ASSETS, AND ACTIONS

Urban development processes are represented in terms of Actors, Activities, Assets, and Actions. Actors are Persons, Organizations, or Populations of Persons or Organizations, as shown in figure 7. A group of Persons organized in Roles, Responsibilities, and Decision Rules is an Organization. Households, firms (in the economic sense), neighborhood groups, government agencies, and city councils are Organizations. Populations are collections of Actors without organizational structure, such as the Population of Persons in a census tract or the Population of Firms headquartered in a municipality.

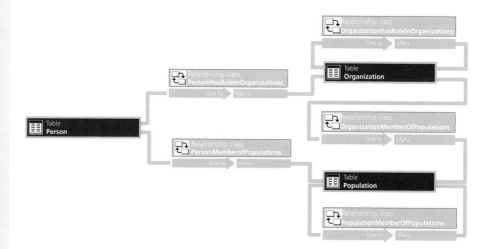

Figure 7. Actor, Organization, and Population relationships.

"Actors have Roles, and many of the Capabilities of Actors are associated with Roles rather than directly with Actors as shown in figure 8. For example, the Authority of a mayor goes with the Role, not the Person. Also Roles can exist without an Actor associated with them so that the Authority of a Mayor is defined regardless of the Person holding the office. Similarly an Actor can have multiple roles, the combination of which will determine the set of Capabilities the Actor possesses," (Hopkins, Kaza, and Pathucheril forthcoming). These Actors may have geographic location attributes such as home address, employment location, travel route to work, authority in particular areas, or an accessibility index to a set of destinations, but an Actor is not a geographic feature. An Actor is primarily a decision maker who has the capability to affect patterns of activity across locations.

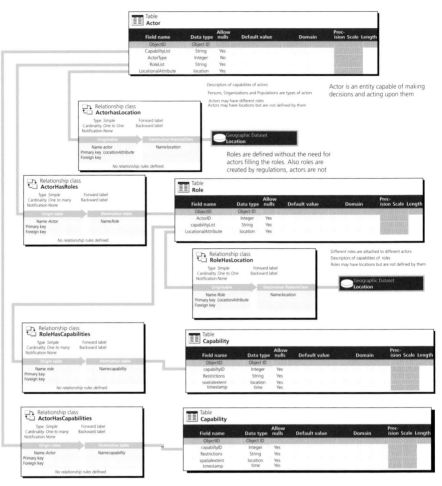

Figure 8. Actor, Role, Capabilities relationships.

Capabilities, as elaborated in figure 8, may have a spatial scope and location and thus be linked to a feature class, raster, or triangulated irregular network. The spatial representation is labeled a geographic dataset rather than a feature dataset because it could include all three types whereas a feature dataset is conventionally restricted to point, line, and polygon features.

Activities, as elaborated in figure 9, occur on Assets and are performed by Actors. Activities are aggregates of behavior occurring on Assets, performed typically by Populations of Actors. "Traffic on a street network (commuting), shopping by a Person, and retail services in a building are Activities. Activities are different from Actions in that Activities describe aggregates of behaviors that are not fundamental changes to the system of Assets and Capabilities and for which Decisions to act are not explicit. Activities are also constrained by Capabilities of Actors, but it may not always be possible to identify a one-to-one relationship between Activities and Actors," (Hopkins, Kaza, and Pallathucheril forthcoming). We can, for example, model traffic flow on a Network as the level of an Activity without specifically aggregating individual Actors' decisions to commute on that link. An Activity may have effects on Assets, for example, physical wear and tear degrading the facility. Activities are also subject to capacity constraints and congestion relative to Assets.

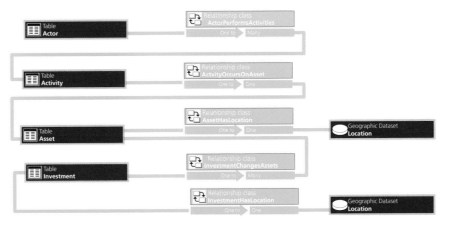

Figure 9. Actor, Activity, Asset relationships.

"Assets can be Facilities, Equipment, Consumables, or Intangibles. Facilities are Structures, such as buildings, or Networks, such as streets. They can also be Virtual Networks, such as microwave networks. Some Facilities are Designated Areas, such as land zoned for development or protected habitats. Assets are related to other Assets. For example, Equipment may be assigned to a particular Facility. Land or water in a river could be defined as an Asset from which resources are used. Buildings could be located on a site or a dam on a river at a location at a time or for a period of time. Actors in their Roles can own, lease, hold government jurisdiction over, have maintenance responsibility for, or have other use rights in Assets," (Hopkins, Kaza, and Pallathucheril forthcoming).

Assets, in their realized form, typically have physical location. A microwave tower, for example, is located at a particular place. A Regulation that restricts the height of such towers in specific swaths of land, such as airport approach corridors, will affect the way virtual networks are designed based on reach and capacity of each individual tower. These regulations are not associated with a particular tower at a particular location but with all existing and possible towers related to existing and future airports.

Actions and their relationships are elaborated in figure 10. "Actions change Assets, Capabilities, or their relationships to Activities or Actors. Actions are central to the planning domain and include Decisions and Realized Actions. Decisions are commitments to Actions that have not yet been realized. Thus a Decision by a city council to invest in a road project is distinct from the realization of that project on the ground. Decisions and Realized Actions include Regulations, Investments, and Transactions. Actions can also change Capabilities of Actors and include changing Rights and Responsibilities," (Hopkins, Kaza, and Pallathucheril forthcoming). It is useful to distinguish between Realized Actions and Decisions as commitment to Actions because responses to Actions by other Actors may be based on Decisions or expected actions before an Action is realized. Decisions occur at different times from their Realized Actions, which may never occur despite a Decision.

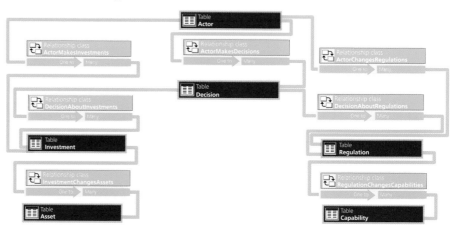

Figure 10. Action, Actor relationships.

This PDM, described as a geodatabase, incorporates plans and urban development processes in ways that are useful in working with urban development models. The next section shows how it could be used with two recent urban development models.

GEODATABASE FOR URBANSIM AND LEAM

PDM is intended to encompass the scope of data entities used in a wide range of urban development models (see, e.g., United States Environmental Protection Agency 2000). In this chapter, we focus on UrbanSim (Waddell 2002) and LEAM (Deal and George 2001) because they are quite different and thus illustrate the desirable scope of a shared data model. The general approach for using the geodatabase version of the PDM to support these models is diagrammed in figure 11. The system architecture consists of a planning geodatabase, a translator to and from the geodatabase, and a modeling environment. The modeling environment includes its own object store, a set of models that rely on that object store, and display and other associated capabilities.

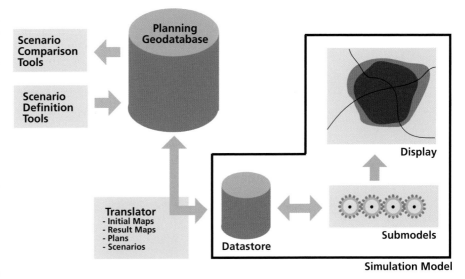

Figure 11. Planning geodatabase and urban modeling systems.

SUPPORT FOR URBANSIM

UrbanSim is an urban simulation model that includes land use, transportation, and environmental impacts (Waddell 2000; Waddell 2002; Noth, Borning, and Waddell 2003). It is object oriented in conceptual design with explicit recognition of actors, development of physical facilities, location of activities in facilities, and economic concepts of pricing. Its system architecture, as diagrammed in figure 12, relies on a data store of objects, a translation layer, and a set of models that draw on these data objects in a process of recursive simulation. This system architecture is consistent with the simulation model box in figure 11.

Table 2 shows how the geodatabase entities relate to objects or variables defined in UrbanSim and LEAM. It thus also shows how these two models differ in their representations of urban development processes. The planning geodatabase is sufficient to specify the major object classes for describing a scenario in UrbanSim. It is then possible to specify a run of UrbanSim in which the scenario dataset and plans are expressed first in terms of the planning geodatabase and then translated. In addition, it is possible to express more complex plans than can currently be expressed as input to UrbanSim, such as capacity expansion strategies contingent on states of the world or on future forecasts of states of the world. Such extensions may require that additional planning submodels be added to the UrbanSim system to simulate these phenomena.

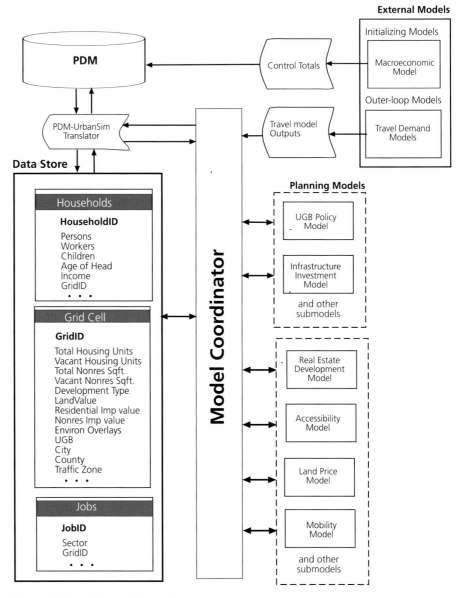

Figure 12. UrbanSim modeling system.

Scenario Inputs	Planning Data Model	UrbanSim Objects	LEAM variables
Urban Development			
Persons (e.g., population forecast)	Actor::Population	Population	Population
Households (e.g., direct forecast or derived from persons)	Actor::Population:: Organization::Household	Households	Households
Residence (e.g., residential demand for dwelling units)	Activity::Residence	Dwelling Units	Residential land area
Jobs (e.g., forecast)	Activity::Jobs	Jobs	Commercial/Industrial land area
Initial Land Use	Asset::Facility::Structure	Housing Stock	(No housing stock in the model)
	Asset::Facility::Structure	Nonresidential Sqft	(No building stock in the model)
	Asset::Facility::Network	Transportation Network	Transportation Network
Trip Generation	Actor-Activity Relationship: trips	Trips generated	Trips generated
Residential Density trend	Asset-Activity Relationship: Density:Time	(Computable but not used in the model)	Land use intensity trend
Plans			
UGB Policy	Plan::Policy	Policy Layer & Planning Submodel	Growth boundary driver
	Regulation	Policy Layer & Planning Submodel	Planning Submodel
Infrastructure Improvements	Plan::Agenda	Policy Layer & Planning Submodel	Direct Coding of time steps
	Plan::Design	Policy Layer & Planning Submodel	Planning Submodel
	Plan::Strategy	Policy Layer & Planning Submodel	Planning Submodel

Table 2. Comparison between UrbanSim and LEAM inputs in relation to geodatabase objects.

SUPPORT FOR LEAM

LEAM is a hybrid approach to modeling urban development and combines regional drivers of land-use change, such as the regional economy, with cell-based drivers, such as accessibility to jobs (Deal 2003). It combines use of STELLA for constructing the local rules that drive cellular change, and the Spatial Modeling Environment (SME) for spatializing the cellular models. SME is described in detail in Maxwell and Voinov (2005, this volume). STELLA is a graphically based dynamic simulation software package based on Jay Forrester's systems dynamics language that uses icons and symbols to communicate a model's structure (Forrester 1961). SME spatializes the single-cell STELLA models, applying them to a geographic area (represented as a grid of cells) and simulating the changes that take place to the state of each cell over multiple time steps. SME automatically converts the STELLA models into computer code that can be run on multiple processors (and multiple computers) in parallel.

Figure 13 describes the LEAM approach to simulating land-use dynamics. It includes model drivers, which are those forces that contribute to urban land-use transformation decisions. The model drivers individually produce land-use transformation probabilities for each cell that are then combined across drivers into development probabilities for each land-use type. Change from existing to new land uses is then predicted based on demand control totals from regional drivers and aggregate transformation probabilities for each potential land use. The resulting land-use pattern is then analyzed for environmental, social, and economic impacts. Impact models, which produce impact indexes that can be compared to sustainability benchmarks, may also feed back into the model drivers at the next time step of recursion, and thus act as drivers, or simply report indicators of the state of the system at a particular time.

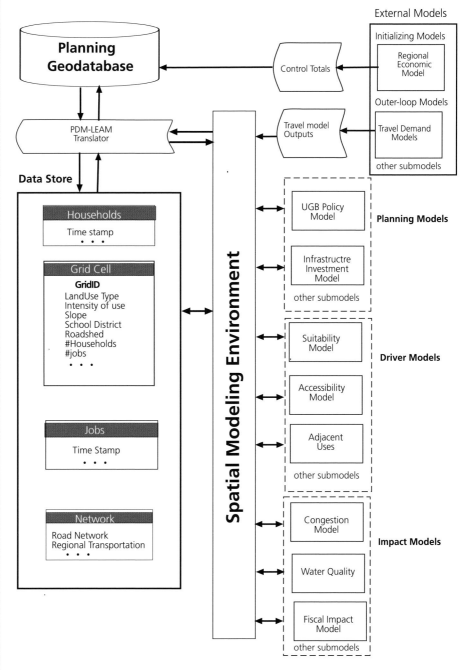

Figure 13. LEAM modeling system.

Table 2 shows the equivalence of geodatabase object classes and important variables for specifying a scenario in the LEAM modeling system. As illustrated by the example of a household size trend, some LEAM inputs are set for each time period for each cell. Thus household size varies over time and space. A translator from the planning geodatabase into LEAM input variables may require construction of additional STELLA models for recursion among time steps in order to incorporate more complex plans or regulations. For example, specification of contingent expansion of an urban growth boundary could only be expressed if an impact model/driver were available to aggregate cells as supply of land within the UGB and demand for land for a future time period. It would then be possible to compute information about how such a plan for regulation would affect land-use transformation probabilities.

LEARNING FROM MORE THAN ONE SIMULATION MODEL

Figures 12 and 13 and table 2 show UrbanSim and LEAM data types in similar form, suggesting that input data and output data could be translated through or from the geodatabase so that comparable simulation runs for the same scenario could be run on both simulation models. LEAM and UrbanSim model urban development processes in different ways. These differences will lead to different predictions. We should be able to make sense of these differences in terms of what we know about how the different models work and what is going on in the particular place being modeled and thus learn from these different perspectives.

For example, UrbanSim models development and redevelopment of Assets (such as dwelling units and commercial floor space), then allocates Actors (households) and Activities (such as shopping and jobs) to these Assets. LEAM directly allocates increments of population change to locations without distinguishing between the allocation of Assets and the allocation of Actors and Activities. LEAM could therefore not make a distinction between what attracts developers and what attracts households or consider vacancy patterns among Assets. In order to make comparable runs in the two modeling environments, external models of population and economic change would be used to generate population change, household size change, job growth by sectors, or similar external drivers of change. Expressing these phenomena in the geodatabase would then enable LEAM's translator to turn these into implicitly combined Dwelling Unit/ Household demand and UrbanSim's translator to generate separate Dwelling Unit and Household demands. The planning geodatabase in this way provides the means to create comparable runs across modeling environments.

Comparisons across modeling environments may also be useful when assessing particular proposed actions. An urban growth boundary policy in the complexity described below can be represented in the geodatabase so that both LEAM and UrbanSim can access the same UGB characteristics through their respective translators. Running both models might lead to discovery of interpretations from UrbanSim that are not evident in LEAM, such as decreasing rates of land consumption based on price increases, which are explicitly modeled in UrbanSim but not in LEAM. On the other hand, LEAM models habitat change, which might affect the direction of growth boundary expansion. These different insights can be used to think through complexities of the situation beyond the scope of either model alone.

The approach of specifying a planning geodatabase and translators enables both LEAM and UrbanSim to use their current modeling system architectures while enabling common specifications of plans, initial states, and scenarios of change as inputs. It is thus possible to support modeling about more complex plans, comparisons across models, and addition of submodels, such as models of the effect of plans on decisions over time.

MODELING PLANS IN URBAN DEVELOPMENT PROCESSES

Plans can be incorporated into urban simulation modeling in at least three ways. First, a plan can be fixed *a priori*. For example, certain locations can be identified before the model is run as places that will be more likely to develop in particular ways because the plan says they should, whether stated as goals, agendas, policies, designs, strategies, visions, or regulations. LEAM and UrbanSim implement such fixed plans through a policy layer, which, for example, identifies exogenously the plan designation of each cell or whether a cell is inside or outside an urban growth boundary. A fixed plan could also specify *a priori* time steps at which capital improvements would occur, but it could not make this timing contingent on any other action or modeled variable. For example, a fixed plan could specify that in year 10 of a simulation run, a new highway link would be added, but it could not specify that this link would be added only if another link was congested or a parcel had developed as commercial.

Second, a plan can be interactive, adjusted by a model user during a run of the simulation model. In this case, the user monitors indicators or spatial development patterns at each recursive time step of the model and decides whether and how to adjust the planned actions. For example, planned transportation improvements might be made only if and when, as observed by the model user based on reports each time step, congestion on certain links reached a certain threshold, or a transit link might be built only if air pollution standards were not met.

Finally, actions in a plan could be endogenous to the model run, responding to values of variables computed while the model is running. For example, a submodel added to the modeling system computes congestion on certain links and triggers expansion of these links when congestion reaches a certain level. Or a growth boundary is expanded by the model if the supply of available land falls below a twenty-year supply at current rates of development.

MODELING URBAN GROWTH BOUNDARY PLANS IN URBANSIM

An endogenous plan is illustrated by the following urban growth boundary example. In Oregon, a UGB must be reevaluated every five years and changed, if necessary, to accommodate the forecasted growth for the next twenty years (Knaap and Hopkins 2001). Figure 14 illustrates the idea of a changing urban growth boundary contingent on supply of land.

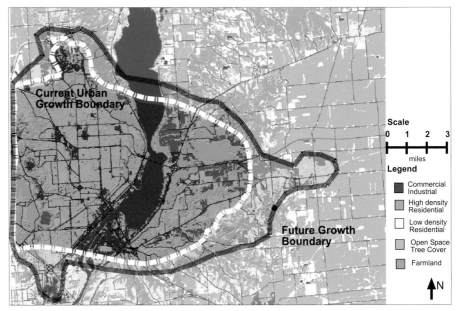

Figure 14. Urban growth boundary and supply of land.

A model should be able to represent planning behaviors in response to this requirement. Such a requirement could be represented in the planning geodatabase as a Capability, or indirectly by specifying a Regulation that would change the Capability, of Actors with Authority to set urban growth boundaries. This Capability could be represented as a Policy in a Plan of such an Actor, on the premise that expected behavior will be closer to an Actor intending to follow a Policy rather than an Actor meeting the strict rule of a Regulation. A Policy is not enforceable by some external authority and thus does not change Capabilities in the same way as a Regulation. Representation as a Policy rather than a Regulation is probably more consistent with observed behavior in Oregon. This representation as a Policy in a Plan is based on the elaboration of the structure of a Policy in figure 4. The Policy can be stated in the following pseudo code:

If

> area is designated as urban growth boundary,
>
> and 5 years since last revision,
>
> and capacity of remaining developable land within UGB < than forecast demand for 20 years,

then

> revise UGB to include developable land sufficient for 20 years' demand.

In the UrbanSim modeling environment, this Policy could be translated into a submodel that counts time steps to year 5, observes the state of development in year 5, calculates available land supply, forecasts 20-year demand based on past five years' land consumption rate, and expands the UGB in predefined directions to gain sufficient additional land if necessary. In other words, the geodatabase representation of a Policy requires construction by a programmer of a new submodel, not just translation of data values for cells in a feature database. A similar new calculation could be coded as a driver in LEAM. In both cases, however, the content required for this new submodel would be available in the planning geodatabase, and the endogenous operation of the new submodel would be supportable by the data store internal to the respective modeling system through translation of elements of the Policy. In other words, implementing this translation requires that the geodatabase not only define Plans but also define Actions in Plans in terms that make sense in the urban development model.

MODELING INFRASTRUCTURE INVESTMENTS PLANS IN LEAM

A plan for capital improvements can be represented as an Agenda, a Design, or a Strategy. These assumptions about the meaning of the Plan and the implied responses of modeled Actors will affect the patterns of urban development predicted by the models. Say that four new highway links are planned by a regional transportation agency as part of a long-range transportation plan. As shown in figure 15, two of these links contribute to a ring road, and two links increase radial capacity to and from the city center. The plan's intent is expressed as strengthening the core through increased access, then enabling peripheral interaction if and when the suburban area grows to sufficient size.

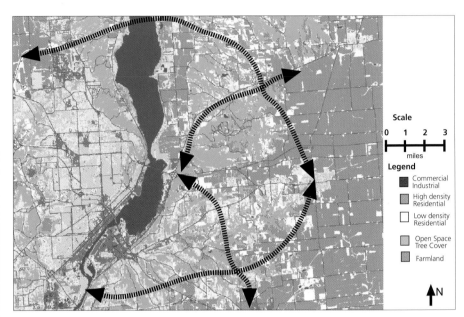

Figure 15. Infrastructure investments as design.

A simple approach is to model this plan as an Agenda with four Actions following the elaboration in figure 3. In order to account for budgets and financing effects, the attributes of these Actions would include costs, revenue sources, and expected times of construction for each project. The Actions would be linked to a geography dataset, which would be a feature class with each highway link defined as a line. The feature dataset should then use a transportation network data model (ESRI Support Center 2004) to enable computation of revised transportation models or revised accessibility measures as the links are added to the transportation system.

This approach could be implemented in LEAM by setting the links to be added at appropriate time steps. LEAM can recompute accessibility measures at each time step based on land-use changes in previous time steps and changes in the transportation network. In this case, the development patterns would be affected only after the links were actually built. Alternatively, the links could be set to exist from the first time step on the claim that developers would be responding as if the planned links existed and LEAM does not distinguish between developers and households. It would be better to model explicitly the expectation of these links based on anticipated dates of construction. In this case, development probabilities in LEAM might be recomputed by a planning submodel so that probabilities of development in areas likely to be attractive for higher intensity later would be reduced in the meantime. For example, the development probability of a cell might be less in time step 1 if an expected new road link would make the cell more valuable for a higher intensity use in time step 4. That is, a developer would refrain from lower density development in anticipation of later, higher intensity development as is rational and frequently observed (Ohls and Pines 1975).

This transportation improvement plan could also be modeled as a Design. In this case, the two radial links would be considered together because they would only be effective in strengthening the core if both links were built. And the two ring road links would be considered together because they would only be effective in improving peripheral access if both were built. The response or anticipation of developers would then consider the construction or anticipated completion of combinations of links rather than individual links. As shown in figure 5, these relationships among links are specified in the data model as design relationships. The translation of such a plan into a LEAM planning model would simply lump the links into the same time step to represent the effects, regardless of when the individual links are or are expected to be constructed. This is a very simple instance of design relationships.

Finally, this plan could be represented as a Strategy. In this case, the anticipated construction of the ring road links would depend on the prior construction of the radial links and the realization of the expected suburban growth because of the radial links. In this case, the timing of the construction of links and even the estimates of timing become endogenous to the urban development model. These contingency relationships are shown in figure 6. This approach could be implemented by specifying a time step in which the two radial links would be built. The model would then locate development in response to these links. If and when new development created congestion on peripheral road links, then the ring road links would be constructed in the next time step. Developers might begin holding land affected by the ring road for higher intensity development once the radials were completed, but not before. A planning submodel would be added to LEAM or UrbanSim to consider carefully how developers and infrastructure providers are expected to behave in anticipation of planned improvements (Schaeffer and Hopkins 1987; Knaap, Hopkins, and Donaghy 1998; Knaap, Ding, and Hopkins 2001).

This transportation improvement plan example illustrates three points. First, it illustrates that the same plan can be represented in different ways. Second, it illustrates that these different representations and the implied responses of developers and infrastructure providers should be explicitly considered in urban development models in order to understand the implications of such plans. Third, it illustrates that the geodatabase must represent the content of these plans and the content of the urban development models in order to support translation of not only data inputs but also the creation of plan submodels that are endogenous to the recursive steps of the simulation models themselves. Thus, this example demonstrates that the proposed planning geodatabase has the appropriate scope across the domain of plans and urban development processes.

CONCLUSIONS

Much work remains to create a planning geodatabase that will enable representation of plans as inputs and endogenous phenomena in a variety of simulation models of urban development. By showing that a planning geodatabase can be constructed, this chapter suggests that current urban development models that use GIS tools for managing input or output data can extend these tools to incorporate plans as inputs. The proposed planning geodatabase is sufficient to encode plans as more than just fixed inputs and thus to extend capabilities of models to consider plans endogenously. Comparisons among urban simulation models can begin by using the geodatabase to define common scenarios from which to translate inputs and outputs for partially substitutable models. The planning geodatabase clearly will be modified and extended based on the experience of such tests and should be imagined as an evolving common planning data model.

REFERENCES

Booch, G., J. Rumbaugh, and I. Jacobson. 1999. *The unified modeling language user guide*. Reading, Mass.: Addison Wesley.

Deal, B. 2003. Sustainable land-use planning: The integration of process and technology. *Regional Planning*. Urbana: University of Illinois at Urbana-Champaign.

Deal, B., and R. V. George. 2001. Ecological sustainability and urban dynamics: A disaggregated modeling approach to sustainable design. 7th International Conference on Computers in Urban Planning and Urban Management. Honolulu, Hawaii.

ESRI Support Center. 2004. Transportation data model. support.esri.com/index.cfm?fa=downloads.dataModels.filteredGateway&dmid=14.

Forrester, J. W. 1961. *Industrial dynamics*. Cambridge, Mass.: MIT Press.

Hopkins, L. D. 2001. *Urban development: The logic of making plans*. Washington, D.C.: Island Press.

———. (2003). Integrating knowledge about land use and the environment through use of multiple models. In *Integrated urban and environmental models: A survey of current research and applications*, ed. S. Guhathakurta, 45–52. New York: Springer-Verlag,

Hopkins, L. D., N. Kaza, and V. G. Pallathucheril. Forthcoming. A planning data model: Representing plans, regulations, and urban development. *Environment and Planning B: Planning and Design*.

Knaap, G. J., C. Ding, and L. D. Hopkins. 2001. The effect of light rail announcements on price gradients. *Journal of Planning Education and Research* 21: 32–39.

Knaap, G. J., and L. D. Hopkins. 2001. The inventory approach to growth management. *Journal of the American Planning Association* 67: 314–26.

Knaap, G. J., L. D. Hopkins, and K. P. Donaghy. 1998. Do plans matter? A framework for examining the logic and effects of land use planning. *Journal of Planning Education and Research* 18: 25–34.

Maidment, D., ed. 2002. *Arc Hydro: GIS for water resources*. Redlands, Calif.: ESRI Press.

Noth, M., A. Borning, and P. Waddell. 2003. An extensible, modular architecture for simulating urban development, transportation, and environmental impacts. *Computers, Environment and Urban Systems* 27: 181–203.

Ohls, J. C., and D. Pines. 1975. Discontinuous urban development and economic efficiency. *Land Economics* 51: 224–34.

Schaeffer, P. V., and L. D. Hopkins. 1987. Planning behavior: The economics of information and land development. *Environment and Planning A* 19: 1221–32.

U.S. Environmental Protection Agency. Office of Research and Development. 2000. *Projecting land-use change: A summary of models for assessing the effects of community growth and change on land-use patterns.* Cincinnati, Ohio: U.S. Environmental Protection Agency.

Waddell, P. 2000. A behavioral simulation model for metropolitan policy analysis and planning: Residential location and housing market components of UrbanSim. *Environment and Planning B: Planning and Design* 27: 247–63.

———. 2002. UrbanSim: Modeling urban development for land use, transportation and environmental planning. *Journal of the American Planning Association* 68: 297–314.

Westervelt, J. 2001. *Simulation modeling for watershed management*. New York: Springer-Verlag.

Zeiler, M. 1999. *Modeling our world*. Redlands, Calif.: ESRI Press.

Chapter 10 | *Urban Land-Use Transportation Models*

MICHAEL WEGENER

SPIEKERMANN & WEGENER (S&W)

URBAN AND REGIONAL RESEARCH

DORTMUND, GERMANY

ABSTRACT

URBAN LAND-USE TRANSPORTATION MODELS are computer simulation models designed to forecast the likely impacts of integrated land-use and transportation policies by explicitly modeling the interaction between land use and transportation. Today there is a new interest in these models because of the urgency of the environmental debate. However, the spatial resolution of most existing land-use transportation models is too coarse to model environmental impacts of urban land use and transportation. Linking these models to high-resolution GIS-based spatial data, therefore, presents an important challenge. GIS functions should be available as a library of analytical and mapping tools that can be called from the modeling software. Open, modular GIS could play an important role for disseminating the highest standards of analysis and mapping and improving the state of the art of urban land-use transportation modeling.

Cities in the most developed regions of the world are suffering from similar problems: with growing affluence, all human activities demand and can afford more space, while at the same time transportation has become more efficient and affordable. The combined effect is that more and more households and firms move to suburban locations, and cities continue to extend into the formerly rural countryside, even where the total population of the metropolitan area declines. The results of unconstrained urban sprawl are generally considered to be negative: nondescript faceless suburban neighborhoods, loss of open space, destruction of natural habitats, and a vast increase in traffic needed to connect the dispersed locations of activities. Moreover, the problem has aspects of global equity: people in the richest countries consume significantly more energy and resources per capita and produce more greenhouse gases, noxious emissions, and waste than people in the poorest regions.

This imbalance has a distinct spatial and urban dimension. It is the consequence of market-driven interaction between urban land use and transportation. The spatial separation of human activities requires travel and goods transport: as suburbanization of cities is connected with increasing spatial division of labor, inevitably mobility increases. Conversely, urban transportation affects land use: the development of the transport system and the accessibility it provides influences the location decisions of landlords, investors, firms, and households. In particular, the private automobile has made every corner of today's metropolitan areas almost equally suitable as a place to live or work.

Because of this two-way interaction of urban land use and transportation, only close integration and coordination of land use and transportation planning will lead to an environmentally and socially sustainable spatial urban development. It is therefore very important to forecast the likely impacts of urban land-use and transportation policies taking this interaction into account. This is the objective of the urban land-use transportation models presented in this chapter. This type of model differs from the urban growth models presented in chapter 8 (Batty and Xie 2005, this volume) and from the transportation models presented in chapter 13 (Israelsen and Frederiksen, 2005, this volume) in that it explicitly models the two-way interaction between urban land use and transportation.

However, besides this principal difference, there are other differences explained by the disciplinary background and genesis of land-use transportation models. As they originated in transportation engineering, early land-use transportation models were based on the social physics paradigm (gravity models) of early transportation models. However, the idea of modeling urban development was soon embraced by urban economists, social scientists, and geographers, and all left their mark on the state of the art. Therefore, the most advanced urban land-use transportation models of today typically encompass, sometimes eclectically, the best of theory from a wide range of urban sciences. The same is true for their scope. Originally focused on location and transport, they soon incorporated nonspatial aspects of urban development, such as demographic development, household formation, economic structural change, and firm life cycles. This naturally led to the abandonment of the comparative static approach of early land-use transportation models, which assumed a general equilibrium of the urban system, in favor of full-fledged dynamics with multiple feedback and delays. Finally, the spatial resolution of the models underwent significant change. Today most current land-use transportation models are still aggregate at the level of traffic analysis zones. However, with the growing need to forecast environmental impacts of land use and transportation policies, the most advanced models have become more spatially disaggregate with various resolutions from smaller zones to individual parcels or grid cells. The ultimate consequence of this is the fully-fledged microsimulation or agent-based urban land-use transportation model, and though to date there exists no operational model of this type, several are under development.

In summary, the models presented in this chapter differ from other models presented in this part of the book by their explicit modeling of the interaction between land use and transportation, but in most other aspects there seems to be a convergence between the various modeling traditions presented here in the urban domain. This chapter thus proceeds in four subsections. First, the theoretical principles of modeling land-use transportation interaction are discussed. Next, a brief overview of existing urban land-use transportation models is given. Then, it is shown how these models can be linked to environmental impact models. Finally, it is demonstrated how the models take advantage of geographical information systems and how future integrated urban models might benefit from GIS.

LAND-USE TRANSPORTATION INTERACTION

That urban land use and transportation are closely interlinked is a common wisdom between planners and the public. That the spatial separation of human activities creates the need for travel and goods transportation is the underlying principle of transportation analysis and forecasting. Following this principle, it is easily understood that the suburbanization of cities is connected with increasing spatial division of labor and hence with ever-increasing mobility. However, the reverse impact from transportation to land use is less well known. There is some vague understanding that the evolution from the dense urban fabric of medieval cities, where almost all daily mobility was on foot, to the vast expansion of modern metropolitan areas with their massive volumes of intraregional traffic would not have been possible without the development of first the railway and then, in particular, the private automobile, which has made every corner of the metropolitan area almost equally suitable as a place to live or work. However, exactly how the development of the transportation system influences the location decisions of landlords, investors, firms, and households is not clearly understood, even by many urban planners. It is therefore difficult for them to assess the impacts of transportation policies on land use and vice versa.

In the 1950s, the first efforts were made in the United States to study the interrelationship between transportation and the spatial development of cities systematically. Hansen (1959), in his seminal paper "How Accessibility Shapes

Land Use," demonstrated that locations with good accessibility had a higher chance of being developed, and at a higher density, than remote locations. The recognition that trip and location decisions codetermine each other and that, therefore, transportation and land-use planning needed to be coordinated quickly spread among American planners, and the "land-use transportation feedback cycle" became a commonplace in the American planning literature.

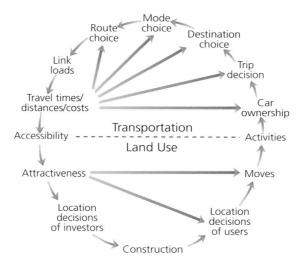

Figure 1. The land-use transportation feedback cycle.

The set of relationships implied by this term is illustrated in figure 1 and can be briefly summarized as follows:

- The distribution of *land uses,* such as residential, industrial, or commercial, over the urban area determines the locations of human *activities,* such as living, working, shopping, education, or leisure.

- The distribution of human *activities* in space requires spatial interactions or trips in the *transportation system* to overcome the distance between the locations of activities.

- The distribution of infrastructure in the *transportation system* creates opportunities for spatial interactions and can be measured as *accessibility.*

- The distribution of *accessibility* in space codetermines location decisions and so results in changes of the *land-use* system.

This simple pattern of explanation is used in many engineering-based urban development theories. In this paradigm, technical conditions determine the internal organization of cities; i.e., urban development is largely a function of transportation technology. The theories based on this paradigm start from observed regularities of certain parameters of human mobility, such as trip distance and travel time, and from these try to infer those trip origins and destinations that best reproduce the observed frequency distributions. It had long been observed that the frequency of human interactions, such as messages, trips, or migrations between two locations (cities or regions), is proportional to their size, but inversely proportional to their distance. The analogy to the law of gravitation in physics is obvious.

A second set of theories focuses on the *economic* forces of city growth, i.e., sees cities as systems of markets. According to these theories, firms look for the optimum constellation of size (economies of scale) and location (agglomeration economies), given their specific mix of products, production technology, and pattern of suppliers and customers, whereas households try to match their space needs and location preferences with their budget restrictions. A fundamental assumption is that locations with good accessibility are more attractive and have a higher market value than peripheral locations. According to the most influential theory of urban land markets proposed by Alonso (1964) in analogy to von Thünen's 1826 theory of agricultural rent, firms and households choose that location at which their bid rent (i.e., the land price they are willing to pay) equals the asking rent of the landlord, so the land market is in equilibrium. Alonso's theory explains why, with growing affluence, households choose more peripheral locations with larger lots and higher quality of life: because they can afford longer travel. It also explains the location of firms in today's urban regions: flexible production and distribution systems require extensive, low-density sites with good access to the regional and local road network. Therefore, new manufacturing firms prefer suburban locations. Retail facilities tend to follow their customers to the suburbs and similarly prefer large suburban sites with good road access. High-level services, however, continue to rely on face-to-face contacts and remain in the city center.

In *social* theories of urban development, the spatial development of cities is the result of individual or collective appropriation of space. Social geography theories refer to age-, gender- or social-group-specific activity patterns which lead to characteristic spatio–temporal behavior and hence, to permanent localizations. Action-space analyses (e.g., Chapin and Weiss 1968) identify the frequency of performance of activities reconstructed from daily space–time protocols as a function of distance to other activities. Hägerstrand (1970) made these ideas operational by the introduction of *time budgets,* in which individuals, according to their social role, income, and level of technology (e.g., car ownership), command *action spaces* of different size and duration. On the basis of Hägerstrand's action-space theory, Zahavi (1974) proposed the hypothesis that individuals in their daily mobility decisions do not, as the conventional theory of travel behavior assumes, *minimize* travel time or travel cost needed to perform a given set of activities but instead *maximize* activities or opportunities that can be reached within their travel time and money budgets and hence, travel more.

These technical, economic, and social theories are the raw material from which the urban land-use transportation models discussed in this chapter draw their conceptual foundations.

URBAN LAND-USE TRANSPORTATION MODELS

The first urban land-use transportation models originated in transportation engineering and so were based on the social physics paradigm (the gravity model) of early transportation models. Lowry's (1964) *Model of Metropolis* was the first attempt to implement the urban land-use transportation feedback cycle in an operational model. The Lowry model essentially consists of a residential location model and a service and retail employment location model nested into each other. The Lowry model stimulated a large number of increasingly complex modeling approaches and is still at the heart of several of the models discussed in this chapter.

However, the idea of modeling urban development was soon embraced by urban economists, social scientists, and geographers who introduced elements of their theories—referred to in the preceding subsection—into the models. Therefore, the most advanced urban land-use transportation models of today typically encompass, sometimes eclectically, the best of theory from a wide range of urban sciences. The same is true for the scope of the models. Originally focused on location and transport, they soon incorporated nonspatial aspects of urban development, such as demographic development, household formation, economic structural change, and firm life cycles. The land-use transportation feedback cycle of figure 1 shows only a small selection of the subsystems and interactions considered in the most advanced urban models. Figure 2 shows a more comprehensive view of the subsystems considered in a typical urban land-use transportation model of today.

The eight subsystems shown in figure 2 can be ordered by the speed by which they change, from slow to fast: *networks* and *land use* change are the most permanent elements of the physical structure of cities. Buildings for *work places* and *housing* have a life span of up to one hundred years and take years from planning to completion. The use of buildings by *employment* and *population* changes several times during the lifetime of buildings as firms and households have their life cycles. *Goods transportation* and *travel*, finally, are the most flexible phenomena of urban development; they can adjust to changed traffic conditions in a matter of hours or even minutes.

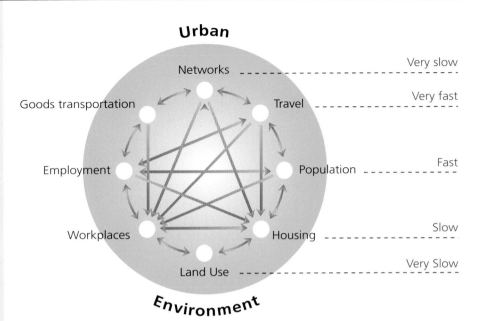

Figure 2. Urban subsystems in urban land-use transportation models.

The temporal behavior of the ninth subsystem, the *urban environment,* is more complex. The direct impacts of human activities, such as traffic noise and air pollution, are immediate; other effects, such as water or soil contamination, build up incrementally over time, and still others, such as long-term climate effects, are so slow that they are hardly observable. All other eight subsystems affect the environment by energy and space consumption, air pollution, and noise emission.

The framework presented in figure 2 is now used to review twelve currently operational urban land-use transportation models. The twelve models were selected as most representative from a larger review which contains more models and more details on the selected models (Wegener 2004). The twelve selected models are:

CUFM–the California Urban Futures Model developed at the University of California at Berkeley (Landis and Zhang 1998a, 1998b);

DELTA–the land-use/economic modeling package by Davids Simmonds Consultancy, Cambridge, UK (Simmonds 1999, 2001);

ILUTE–the Integrated Land Use, Transportation, Environment modeling system developed at several Canadian universities (Miller and Salvini 2001);

IRPUD–the model of the Dortmund region developed at the University of Dortmund (Wegener 1998);

ITLUP–the Integrated Transportation and Land Use Package by Putman (1983 1991) with residential model DRAM and employment model EMPAL;

MEPLAN–the integrated modeling package developed by Marcial Echenique & Partners (Williams 1994, Hunt and Simmonds 1993);

MUSSA–the 5-Stage Land-Use Transport Model developed for Santiago de Chile by Martinez (1997);

PECAS–the Production, Exchange and Consumption Allocation System developed at the University of Calgary (Hunt and Abraham 2003);

RURBAN–the Random-Utility URBAN model developed by Miyamoto (Miyamoto and Udomsri 1996);

TLUMIP–the land-use transportation model developed in the Oregon Transportation and Land Use Model Integration Program (ODOT 2002);

TRANUS–the transportation and land-use model developed by de la Barra (de la Barra et al. 1984, de la Barra 1989);

URBANSIM–the microeconomic model of location choice of households and firms by Waddell (1998, 2002).

Table 1 shows the subsystems of figure 2 which are considered in each model. It can be seen that the models indeed simulate more than just land use and travel. Ten of the twelve models forecast housing stock, and nine forecast also nonresidential buildings. However, only five of the twelve models forecast goods transportation.

Models	Speed of change							
	Very slow		Slow		Fast		Immediate	
	Networks	Land use	Workplaces	Housing	Employment	Population	Goods transportation	Travel
CUFM	(+)	+	+	+	+	+		(+)
DELTA	(+)	+	+	+	+	+		(+)
ILUTE	+	+	+	+	+	+	+	+
IRPUD	+	+	+	+	+	+		+
ITLUP	+	+			+	+		+
MEPLAN	+	+	+	+	+	+	+	+
MUSSA	(+)			+	+	+		(+)
PECAS	+	+	+	+	+	+	+	+
RURBAN	(+)	+			+	+		(+)
TLUMIP	+	+	+	+	+	+	+	+
TRANUS	+	+	+	+	+	+	+	+
URBANSIM	(+)	+	+	+	+	+		(+)

(+) provided by linked transportation model.

Table 1. Urban subsystems represented in land-use transportation models.

Table 2 shows characteristics of the twelve models which are important for the modeling techniques applied and the dynamic behavior of the models:

Models	Characteristics							
	Structure		Equilibrium		Prices		Agents	
	Unified	Composite	Trans-port-ation	Land use	Trans-port-ation	Land use	Trans-port-ation	Land use
CUFM		+	+		+			
DELTA		+	+	+	+	+		
ILUTE		+	+		+	+	+	+
IRPUD		+	+		+	+		+
ITLUP		+	+		+			
MEPLAN	+		+	+	+	+		
MUSSA	+		+	+	+	+		
PECAS	+		+	+	+	+		
RURBAN	+		+	+	+	+		
TLUMIP		+	+	+	+	+	+	+
TRANUS	+		+	+	+	+		
URBANSIM		+	+		+	+		+

Table 2. Characteristics of urban land-use transportation models.

- *Structure*. Five of the twelve models search for a unifying principle for modeling and linking all subsystems; the others see the city as a hierarchical system of interconnected but structurally autonomous subsystems. The resulting model structure is either tightly integrated, "all of one kind," or consists of loosely coupled submodels, each of which has its own independent internal structure. The former type of model is called *unified*, the latter *composite*.

- *Equilibrium*. All twelve models assume that the transportation system is always in equilibrium, i.e., that travel flows reflect travel times and costs on the network. However, only seven models assume that the land-use system is also in equilibrium, i.e., that the locations of activities at all times reflect their attractiveness. The other five models are dynamic (or quasi-dynamic as they work with discrete time periods) in that they explicitly model the adjustment processes over time discussed above. These models are based on the assumption that some adjustment processes are faster than others and that the differences in speed are so large that urban systems are normally in disequilibrium (Wegener 2004).

- *Prices*. All models consider both travel time and travel cost in their travel models, but only ten of them also model land prices and rents. Three models have endogenous prices but no land-use equilibrium; in these models, price adjustment is delayed.

- *Agents.* Two of the models are full microsimulation models modeling both transportation and land use at the agent level. Two models are hybrid combinations of individual microsimulation submodels with aggregate land-use and transportation submodels.

Today there is a new interest in urban land-use transportation models. In the United States, environmental legislation, such as the Clean Air Act amendments of 1990, the Intermodal Surface Transportation Efficiency Act (ISTEA) of 1991, and the Transportation Equity Act for the 21st Century (TEA-21) of 1998, gave a boost to the development and application of urban land-use transportation models. ISTEA and TEA-21 require cities to consider the likely effect of transportation policy decisions on land use and the environment. In Europe, the European Commission has funded a number of studies employing land-use transportation models. The SPARTACUS, PROSPECTS, and SCATTER projects applied several urban land-use transportation models, among them DELTA, MEPLAN, and TRANUS, and the PROPOLIS project connected MEPLAN, TRANUS, and IRPUD with environmental submodels and applied them to seven urban areas in Europe (Lautso et al. 2004).

Because the new interest in the models is largely stimulated by environmental concerns, the incorporation of environmental impact submodels into urban land-use transportation models becomes of critical importance. Moreover, environmental quality is becoming increasingly important as a factor influencing location decisions of households and firms and should therefore be considered in urban land-use transportation models. Figure 3 shows the most important impacts of urban land use and transportation and how they feed back into the land-use and transportation system.

The impacts of land use and transportation on the urban environment can be classified under the headings of resources, emissions, and immissions:

- *Resources.* Most human activities consume resources. For urban models, the most important resources are energy, water, and land: energy is a resource imported to the urban region in the form of fossil fuel or electricity. Water cannot be easily transported over great distances and is therefore consumed close to the source. Land is the ultimate resource of cities. With growing affluence, all human activities consume more land. Open space in and around cities is therefore continually declining.

- *Emissions.* Most human activities give rise to metabolisms producing obnoxious emissions. Emissions are produced locally but have local, remote, or global effects. For urban models, the most important emissions are gases, waste water, soil contamination, solid waste, and noise.

- *Immissions.* Air pollution, noise intrusion, and water contamination are environmental impacts of which emission and immission points differ. As their effect is felt at immission points, calculation of immissions from emissions is critical for these kinds of impacts and need to be included in urban models.

The relationship between the environment and urban land use and transportation is not symmetric. Land use and transportation affect almost all environmental indicators, but the reverse is not the case. Land-use changes, i.e., location decisions by households and firms, are strongly affected by land availability, soil contamination, air pollution, and noise; all other feedbacks from the environment are weak or potentially strong only in the case of a major change such as a substantial increase in energy cost. Transportation decisions are not affected by environmental indicators, except potentially by rising fuel costs. Nevertheless, as a minimum, feedback from environment to land use, i.e., the impact of environmental indicators on location decisions, should be included in urban land-use transportation models.

However, linking environmental impact models to urban land-use transportation models presents serious methodological challenges: the transportation submodels used by most existing land-use transportation models do not use state-of-the-art activity-based travel modeling techniques, and their spatial resolution is too coarse to model environmental impacts and environmental feedback. For instance, as Burrough, Karssenberg, and van Deursen (2005, this volume) and Eastman and von Fossen (2005, this volume) demonstrate, air distribution models modeling two- or three-dimensional distributions of pollutants from emission sources require raster data of emission sources, elevation, and surface characteristics, such as green space, built-up area, and high-rise buildings. Noise propagation models require raster data on emission sources, topography, land cover, and sound barriers such as dams, walls, or buildings. There are three ways to respond to this problem, which are illustrated in figure 3:

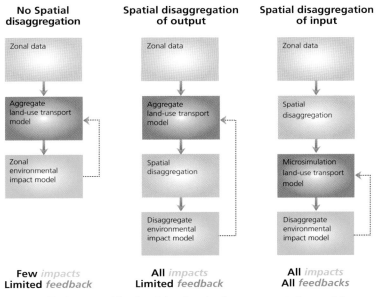

Figure 3. Environmental feedback in urban land-use transportation models.

- *No spatial disaggregation.* To ignore the problem of spatial resolution, as most current land-use transportation models do, implies that only few environmental indicators can be calculated and that only limited environmental feedback can be accounted for in the model. The left column in figure 3 illustrates this approach.

- *Spatial disaggregation of output.* The center column in figure 3 represents how disaggregate environmental indicators can be derived from zone-based land-use transportation models by spatial disaggregation of their output, i.e., by converting the zonal results to raster results using GIS-based land use information as ancillary information. In this way emissions, air distribution, and noise propagation can be calculated for raster cells. Also, as the population forecasts of the model are disaggregated to raster cells, environmental impacts on population and social equity issues can be studied (Spiekermann and Wegener 2000). This was the method applied in PROPOLIS for the comparison between policy scenarios. However, it is difficult to feed the environmental impacts back into the model at simulation time.

- *Spatial disaggregation of input.* The right-hand column in figure 3 represents the ultimate solution to this problem: a completely spatially disaggregate land-use transportation and environment model. The spatial disaggregation occurs already at model input. The results of the spatial disaggregation are synthetic populations of individual households and firms that live and work in raster cells connected by transportation networks stored both in vector form (for efficient travel and goods transportation modeling) and in raster form (for spatially disaggregate calculation of emissions). In this type of model, the disaggregate environmental model is fully integrated with the land-use transportation model as it works at the same spatial resolution. This makes full environmental feedback both possible and efficient. However, such a fully spatially disaggregate land-use transportation and environment model currently does not exist.

URBAN LAND-USE TRANSPORTATION MODELS AND GIS

It should have become clear from the discussion so far that urban land-use transportation models are prime candidates for being linked to powerful geographical information systems. Urban land-use transportation models require vast amounts of spatial data with growing requirements for spatial disaggregation. Urban land-use transportation models apply complex and computation-intensive methods of spatial analysis to this data and generate even larger amounts of spatial results which need to be communicated to a broad range of experts and nonexperts in appealing and understandable visual formats. Similar arguments are presented by Israelsen and Frederiksen for transportation models in chapter 13 (2005, this volume).

In light of the obvious affinity of such models to geographical information systems, it is strange that so far no real integration between these models and GIS seems to have taken place. None of the twelve representative urban land-use transportation models discussed above has been implemented within a geographical information system using the increasingly comfortable and flexible scripting tools made available by major GIS. To analyze the reasons for this abstinence of the developers of urban land-use transportation models, it is useful to compare the data organization of urban land-use transportation models with that of data geographical information systems (Wegener 2000). This is done in table 3.

	Urban land-use transportation models	Geographical information systems
Stock matrix	The study region is represented as a two-dimensional matrix where the rows indicate the zones and the columns contain the attributes. Some attributes are pointers to more complex information, i.e., distributions, for instance, of households or dwellings. There is one matrix for each point in time.	Zones are represented by polygons, and attributes are stored in polygon attribute tables. However, there are no facilities to store multiple sets of attributes with different time labels without duplicating the whole coverage.
Interaction matrix	The spatial dimension of the model is introduced by one or more interaction matrices and through networks (see below). The interaction matrices are usually square matrices where both rows and columns represent zones. The cells are indicators of the spatial impedance between the zones or spatial interaction flows. There is the same set of interaction matrices for each point in time.	There is no data structure in current GIS which corresponds to explicit interaction matrices between pairs of polygons.
Networks	Networks are coded by from-node, to-node, and link attributes. Node coordinates are not needed for the network calculations. Zones are linked to networks by pseudo links connecting zone centroids to one or more network nodes. Changes of links are stored as add/change/delete codes.	Networks can be represented as line coverages with link attributes stored in arc attribute tables and node attributes stored in point attribute tables. However, it is difficult to represent the evolution of networks over time.
Lists	Microsimulation models avoid the disadvantages of the stock matrix representation by using a list representation of individual persons or objects. Attributes can contain spatial information (such as address) or temporal information (such as year of retirement). Changes of list items are stored as add/change/delete codes.	Micro data can be stored as point data in point attribute tables. However, it is difficult to specify multiple events with different time labels for one point at one location or to specify the movement of one point from one location to another.
Raster	In raster organization, the topology is implicit in the data model, and operations such as buffering and density calculations are greatly simplified. Changes of cell data are stored as add/change/delete codes.	The organization of raster-based models corresponds to that of raster-based GIS, except for the difficulty of introducing time into the model.

Table 3. Data organizations of urban land-use transportation models and GIS.

It becomes apparent that urban land-use transportation models use quite specific data organizations, many of which cannot or only with difficulty be provided by current GIS. In particular, the implementation of the temporal dimension, which is becoming more and more crucial for urban land-use transportation models as these are getting more dynamic, is far from straightforward in current GIS, if not impossible—not much has changed since Langran (1992). However, the lack of suitable data formats for storing spatial interaction matrices in GIS is also a serious obstacle for a closer integration between GIS and urban land-use transportation models. Again this echoes arguments of Israelsen and Frederiksen in chapter 13.

Another issue is the quality and comprehensiveness of analytical methods provided by the GIS. Because the majority of GIS users perform rather basic analytical operations on static data, the analytical toolboxes provided by GIS are hardly sufficient for the highly specialized tasks required for urban models. Or turning the argument around, as urban modelers tend to be experienced programmers, it is generally more convenient for them to write their own analytical routines using resource books, such as Worboys and Duckham (2004), than to rely on procedures that someone else has written and that they are not familiar with.

A final point is computational efficiency. With growing spatial disaggregation, urban land-use transportation models are becoming very computation intensive, and code optimization tends to be an important issue. Therefore, the choice of computing language and optimizing compiler is already an important part of the implementation of a large urban land-use transportation model. It is not surprising that many modelers have chosen to write their own unified and optimized code rather than depending on general-purpose software where flexibility and user-friendliness have been guiding design principles and where complex applications have to be composed from multiple script-operated executables and require the presence of a complex and license-protected host software.

These considerations suggest that full integration between urban land-use transportation models and GIS may not be a goal to be pursued at all. However, GIS can provide valuable services in the preprocessing and postprocessing phase of model applications. To take advantage of these services, some sort of loose coupling, as suggested by Nyerges (1992), may be followed. With loose coupling, the linkage between model and GIS is performed by ASCII or binary files. One important advantage of loose coupling is that the preparation of input files can be performed offline or even on another computer than the one on which the model is running, which facilitates division of labor between members of large modeling teams.

In fact, all twelve urban land-use transportation models examined in this chapter use loose coupling with a GIS. All twelve models use the GIS for preprocessing of input, in particular, the generation and maintenance of their network database. Typically, interactive network editors and scenario generators are written in a scripting language and are fully integrated into the GIS. Figure 4 shows, as an example, the network editor used with the IRPUD model (Talaat and Schwarze 2003).

All but one of the twelve models use GIS for displaying the results of model simulations in maps. This requires the generation of interface files with model results by zone or by link which can be imported into the GIS. A different strategy was followed in the design of the IRPUD model, for which specific output graphics in the form of time-series diagrams, maps, and three-dimensional surfaces were written using standard Windows API facilities. The rationale behind this was that these graphics modules can be used not only for visualizing the model results to others but also for online monitoring of the model simulations, which is extremely valuable for understanding and validating the model where calibration and validation data are scarce. This integration of model execution and visualization could not have been implemented within a GIS.

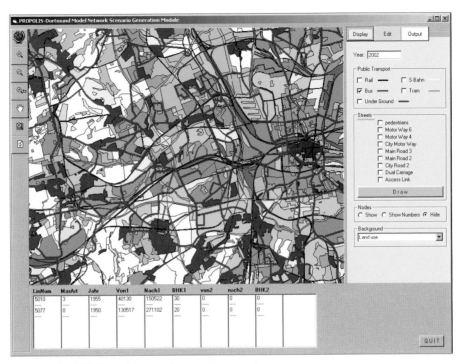

Figure 4. The IRPUD model network scenario generator.

CONCLUSIONS

Because urban land-use transportation models use vast amounts of spatial data as input and generate even larger amounts of spatial data as output, this type of model at first sight seems to be an ideal candidate for full integration with a geographical information system. However, on closer inspection, limitations in the data models provided by GIS, in particular the still insufficient provisions for storing spatial interaction data and data that changes over time, have so far prevented the full utilization of GIS by urban land-use transportation models. Also, because of the great variety of theoretical and technical approaches to modeling urban land use and transportation, it is unlikely that urban land-use transportation and environment models will ever be a part of a general-purpose GIS. In addition, considerations of computational efficiency, which is becoming more and more essential, make it unlikely that urban land-use transportation models will be fully integrated with GIS in the near future.

From the urban modeler's point of view, GIS are most useful as preprocessors of model input and postprocessors of model output for visualization and communication. However, loose coupling, as it is practiced today, is only a second choice. To be really useful, GIS functions should be available as a library of analytical and mapping tools that can be called from the modeling software in parallel with the simulation and without the complete GIS running. Such open, modular GIS could play an important role for disseminating highest standards of analysis and mapping and so improving the state of the art of urban land-use and transportation modeling.

REFERENCES

Alonso, W. 1964. *Location and land use.* Cambridge, Mass.: Harvard University Press.

de la Barra, T. 1989. *Integrated land use and transport modeling.* Cambridge: Cambridge University Press.

de la Barra, T., B. Pérez, and N. Vera. 1984. TRANUS-J: Putting large models into small computers. *Environment and Planning B: Planning and Design* 11: 87–101.

Chapin, F. S., and S. F. Weiss. 1968. A probabilistic model for residential growth. *Transportation Research* 2: 375–90.

Hägerstrand, T. 1970. What about people in regional science? *Papers of the Regional Science Association* 24: 7–21.

Hansen, W. G. 1959. How accessibility shapes land use. *Journal of the American Institute of Planners* 25: 73–6.

Hunt, J. D., and J. E. Abraham. 2003. Design and application of the PECAS land use modelling system. Paper presented at the 8th International Conference on Computers in Urban Planning and Urban Management. Sendai, Japan.

Hunt, J. D., and D. C. Simmonds. 1993. Theory and application of an integrated land-use and transport modelling framework. *Environment and Planning B: Planning and Design* 20: 221–44.

Langran, G. 1992. *Time in geographical information systems.* London: Taylor & Francis.

Landis, J. D., and M. Zhang. 1998a. The second generation of the California urban futures model, Part 1: Model logic and theory. *Environment and Planning B: Planning and Design* 25: 657–66.

———. 1998b. The second generation of the California urban futures model, Part 2: Specification and calibration results of the land-use change submodel. *Environment and Planning B: Planning and Design* 25: 795–824.

Lautso, K., K. Spiekermann, M. Wegener, I. Sheppard, P. Steadman, A. Martino, R. Domingo, and S. Gayda. 2004. PROPOLIS: Planning and research of policies for land use and transport for increasing urban sustainability. Final report. Helsinki LT Consultants. www.wsgroup.fi/lt/propolis.

Lowry, I. S. 1964. *A model of metropolis.* RM-4035-RC. Santa Monica, Calif.: Rand Corporation.

Miller, E. J., and P. A. Salvini. 2001. The integrated land use, transportation, environment (ILUTE) microsimulation modelling system: Description and current status. In *The leading edge in travel behaviour research*, ed. D. A. Henscher. Selected Papers from the 9th International Association for Travel Behaviour Research Conference, Gold Coast, Queensland, Australia.

Martinez, F. J. 1997. MUSSA: A land-use model for Santiago City. Department of Civil Engineering. Santiago: University of Chile.

Miyamoto, K., and R. Udomsri. 1996. An analysis system for integrated policy measures regarding land use, transport, and the environment in a metropolis. In *Transport, land use and the environment*, ed. Y. Hayashi and J. Roy, 259–80. Dordrecht: Kluwer.

Nyerges, T. L. 1992. Coupling GIS and spatial analytic models. In *Proceedings of the fifth international symposium on spatial data handling*, ed. P. Bresnahan, E. Corwin, and D. J. Cowan, 534–42. Columbia, S.C.: University of South Carolina.

Oregon Department of Transportation–ODOT. 2002. www.egov.oregon.gov/ODOT/TD/TP/TMR.shtml.

Putman, S. H. 1983. *Integrated urban models: Policy analysis of transportation and land use*. London: Pion.

———. 1991. *Integrated urban models 2: New research and applications of optimization and dynamics*. London: Pion.

Simmonds, D. C. 1999. The design of the DELTA land-use modelling package. *Environment and Planning B: Planning and Design* 26: 665–84.

———. (2001) The objectives and design of a new land-use modelling package: DELTA. In *Regional science in business*, ed. G. P. Clarke and M. Madden, 159–88. Berlin/Heidelberg: Springer.

Spiekermann, K., and M. Wegener. 2000. Freedom from the tyranny of zones: Towards new GIS-based spatial models. In *Spatial models and GIS*, ed. A. S. Fotheringham and M. Wegener, 45–61. GISDATA 7. London: Taylor & Francis.

Talaat, A., and B. Schwarze. 2003. The Dortmund region networks scenario generation module. Working Paper 179, Institute of Spatial Planning, Dortmund.

Waddell, P. 1998. UrbanSim Overview. urbansim.org.

———. (2002) UrbanSim: Modeling urban development for land use, transportation and environmental planning. *Journal of the American Planning Association* 68: 297–314.

Wegener, M. 1998. The IRPUD model: overview. www.irpud.raumplanung.uni-dortmund.de/irpud/pro/mod/mod_e.htm.

———. 2000. Spatial models and GIS. In *Spatial Models and GIS,* ed. A. S. Fotheringham and M. Wegener, 3-20. GISDATA7. London: Taylor & Francis.

Wegener, M. 2004. Overview of land-use transport models. In *Transport geography and spatial systems,* ed. D. A. Henscher and K. Button. Handbook in Transport 5. Kidlington: Pergamon/Elsevier Science.

Williams, I. W. 1994. A model of London and the South East. *Environment and Planning B: Planning and Design* 21: 535–53.

Worboys, M. F., and M. Duckham. 2004. *GIS: A computing perspective* 2nd ed. Boca Raton: CRC Press.

Zahavi, Y. 1974. Traveltime budgets and mobility in urban areas. Report FHW PL-8183. Washington, D.C.: U.S. Department of Transportation.

Chapter 11   *Retail and Service Location Planning*

MARK BIRKIN

SCHOOL OF GEOGRAPHY

UNIVERSITY OF LEEDS

LEEDS, UNITED KINGDOM

▶ ABSTRACT

IN THIS CHAPTER, WE WILL CONSIDER the development over the last twenty years of a research stream in spatial interaction modeling, microsimulation, and location planning. The research builds on the foundations laid by Alan Wilson (1974) over thirty years ago. The work which will be described in this chapter has a strongly applied flavor in relation to the provision of both commercial and public services. Many of the commercial applications have been pursued through a corporate entity—GMAP Limited—while many of the public-service applications have been developed through collaborations involving the School of Geography at the University of Leeds. However, there is considerable crossover between these organizations and activities.

The chapter begins with a brief review of the origins of our approach and considers some examples. Then we look at the elements of technical progression which have supported these activities. Next, we will discuss the computational and software architectures which are needed to support decision making for location planning. The chapter discusses the relationship between microsimulation and spatial interaction modeling and will argue that, while these techniques have independent merit, their integration will provide exciting new opportunities for understanding city regions and their functional subsystems. Finally, we will review some of the difficulties which have restricted the achievements from this research program and may continue to do so in the future.

The intellectual antecedents to the work described below lie in the work of Huff (1964) and Lakshmanan and Hansen (1965). These authors presented an applied tool, in the shape of a retail trade model, which could predict the flow of customers and associated expenditure to retail centers and outlets. The contribution of Alan Wilson, through a number of monographs and research papers (notably Wilson 1967, 1970, 1974), was both to embed such models in a rigorous theoretical and analytical framework and to absorb the specific class of retail models as part of a larger "family" of service and activity models, thus bridging to other applied streams in transportation and land-use planning within both the United Kingdom and North America (for a review, see, e.g., Foot 1981). In the early 1980s, Wilson and Martin Clarke formed GMAP Limited as a means to exploit the value of applied location modeling research. In commercial terms, GMAP was conspicuously successful, employing more than 100 full-time staff by 1995. For more details on the history of GMAP, see Clarke and Clarke (2001).

The work which we will describe in this chapter is representative of a whole domain of "market analysis" applications in which GIS are used to support locational decision making for retail and service businesses. Such market analysis applications have been most widespread in the United Kingdom, United States, and Canada, but some of the key organizations like CACI, Urban Science, and MPSI are also active in Europe, Asia, and elsewhere. Indeed, although the examples cited below are primarily UK-focused, GMAP itself has an active global client base and has operated in markets as diverse as Japan, Australia, Slovenia, India, Puerto Rico, and Brazil. We shall also argue further below that the combination of spatial analysis methods with GIS to support location decisions for retail and service businesses shares research themes with other application domains for spatial decision support systems, such as environmental management and city planning.

A typical early GMAP client is WH Smith (Birkin 1994). WHS is one of Britain's best-known and well-established retailers, having been initially established in 1792 as a seller of newspapers and books on the emergent railway network (WH Smith 2004). In the mid-1980s, the WHS business problem could be stated quite simply: how to increase turnover and profitability in a mature national network of 350 stores.

The core capability on which the GMAP approach was constructed is the means to generate model-based sales estimates for any geographical location given the size and configuration of retail activities in that location. The basic idea of Huff's gravity model is that retail expenditure can be identified for local geographical areas and then allocated between surrounding retail centers in proportion to their size, or attractiveness, and in proportion to their accessibility. For more technical detail on the models and their implementation, see Birkin and Clarke (1991) or Birkin et al. (1996, chapter 5).

For new sites, this kind of capability provides a powerful basis for investment appraisal: for a given location and store layout, higher sales means better margins and greater returns. Through systematic assessment of the variations between store layout and sales potential, it is also possible to identify the best format for a new retail outlet. In the case of existing outlets, a comparison of model-based performance estimates against observed sales performance provides an equally powerful basis for benchmarking and performance appraisal. Those outlets whose performance exceeds expectations would present themselves as exemplars, from which best practice may be inferred—for example, in terms of management, product offer, or local advertising and marketing. Conversely, those which underperform should be those with the most to learn from their more highly rated counterparts. Importantly, model-based estimates may be used as a rational basis for branch sales targeting, in contrast to the traditional approach of simply demanding an increase of x% in year-to-year performance across the board. And again, for an existing store of a fixed size, it is possible to run various alternative space planning scenarios to find the best layout and product mix for an existing store and, if appropriate, to experiment with various possibilities for expansion.

In addition to the process of revenue estimation and the associated investment appraisal and benchmarking activities described above, spatial models can also play an important role in impact analysis and local advertising and marketing. Regarding impact analysis, then, the great strength of spatial interaction models is that they provide not only an accurate assessment of sales potential but also an expectation of the cannibalization of sales from neighboring branches. Hence, WHS can answer the vital question of whether sales are being advanced at the expense of competitor outlets or simply through deflection of revenues from its own surrounding outlets. Since the model-based sales estimate for any store is also made up from a series of individual flows from local neighborhoods to retail outlets, this information can also be analyzed in order to direct promotional activity for new outlets such as poster advertising, leaflet drops, or inserts within local newspapers.

A typical example of the model estimation process is shown at figure 1. To facilitate the development of the first generation of sales estimation models, the United Kingdom was broken down into a series of 31 regions. For each of these regions, a separate model was calibrated. Each of the regions comprised approximately 100 postal districts, for which expenditure by product group was estimated based from census populations disaggregated by life stage and affluence. The flows were estimated to a slightly smaller number of centers, typically around 80 per region. The retail composition of each center was assessed using a combination of sources, including in-house surveys, Goad maps (Experian 2004), and retail directories. The pattern of customer flows was calibrated using a variety of Omnibus (residence-based) and in-store customer surveys. The attractiveness of WHS outlets was calibrated in relation to attributes such as floor space, layout, pitch, and adjacent retail opportunities.

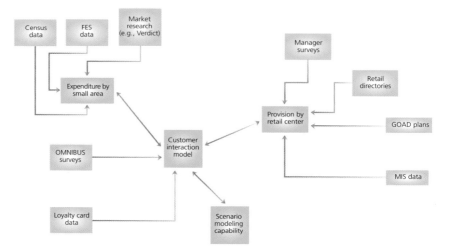

Figure 1. Structure of the model estimation process.

The initial development of the models on a region-by-region basis took an expended time of around two years. For each region, known sales data for around 10% of stores was withheld at the level of either products or whole outlets. The model was able to produce separate estimates for each of six different product groups, which provided enough detail to differentiate between the different group fascias of the time, i.e., Our Price (music), Sherratt & Hughes and Waterstones (booksellers), and Paperchase (greeting cards and stationery). As each region was calibrated, the model estimates were exchanged with the client as a model performance check. Only once was the model rejected outright. Fortunately, it transpired that the initial data had been corrupted due to a misallocation of store codes! Unfortunately, detailed records of the performance of the model at this time were never maintained. We return to a discussion of this point in the *Key trends and issues* section below.

At the completion of each region, GMAP delivered an executable model and associated data files and a report summarizing the findings for that region. The primary purpose of the model at this stage was to facilitate *what if* scenarios and impact analysis at new retail locations. The model was installed on a single desktop computer at WHS Head Office in Swindon. The function of the reports was slightly more strategic. In addition to an assessment of branch performance for each of the stores, market penetration maps for each product gave an indication of strengths and gaps in the store network, while catchment populations by product and retail center indicated the major centers without representation. The nature of the models, reports, and the information system containers is a subject of further discussion in the *Architectures* section below.

As we noted above, the first round of installations of this model was restricted to a single desktop machine. However, following the completion of a national system, the models became extensively used across both different departments and brands within the group. At its peak in the early 1990s, we believe that there were more than twenty separate installations of the same system across the WHS group, in areas such as marketing, property, corporate planning, logistics, and finance, and in Our Price, Waterstones, Sherratt & Hughes, Paperchase, WHS Limited, and WHS Group. This level of popularity continued for some time, although later, following changes in personnel and management, the model fell into less frequent use and was eventually displaced by a more geodemographically focused competitor. WHS ceased to be a client of GMAP in about 1999.

Although the experience with WHS is typical, it is by no means definitive or comprehensive in terms of commercial applications through the 1980s and 1990s. At one time, GMAP saw itself as positioned across six different service sectors: retail, financial services, petrol, automotive, pharmaceuticals, and telecommunications, with blue chip clients in each of these areas (e.g., Asda-Walmart, Halifax, Exxon, Ford, SmithKline Beecham, and Energis). The kinds of applications and benefits which spatial interaction modeling technologies brought to these clients is summarized in matrix form in figure 2.

	REVENUE ESTIMATION	NETWORK CONFIGURATION	TERRITORY PLANNING	BENCHMARKING	ADVERTISING	IMPACT ANALYSIS	PRICE MODELLING
TELECOMMS	*	**		*			**
AUTOMOTIVE	**	**	**	**	**	**	*
PHARMACEUTICALS		**	**	**	n/a		
FINANCIAL SERVICES	**	**		**	*	**	
PETROL	**	**		*	*	*	**
RETAIL	**	**	**	*	**	**	*

Figure 2. Benefits to commercial clients.

As we have seen above, the most obvious business benefit of this technology to retailers like WHS was the ability to estimate sales for new stores with confidence. The mid-1980s was a buoyant time for retail growth, and the company was constantly barraged with offers of new floor space by retail developers, with no satisfactory means for their assessment. It was also possible to set off these gains not only against the rental or acquisition costs but also to consider impacts on the existing stores. Local marketing could be targeted to the right places, and it was also possible to consider store closures, changes in format or layout, and even to consider rebranding from one fascia into another. Thus benchmarking, revenue estimation, advertising, and impact analysis are core activities for retailers.

We began to see in the discussion of regional reports that broader questions of network strength and configuration are also of importance to retailers. In later work, this concept was turned into a *representation planning* capability in which the objective was not so much to produce *what if* models for individual locations, but rather to generate blueprint solutions for an entire retail network. A good example of this was a project for the Great British Lottery Company in 1994 to identify an ideal network of retail outlets for the distribution of lottery tickets. Unfortunately, GBLC was ultimately frustrated by Camelot in its bid for distribution rights. This kind of capability has been most highly valued in the automotive and financial services industries, where overcapacity has tended to fuel a more urgent desire for rationalization and reconfiguration.

Also of particular importance to franchised retailers is the idea of territory planning. If a retailer is to be given responsibility for a specific geographical area as part of a franchise arrangement, then it is clearly useful if customers are actually inclined to utilize the retail center at which that retailer is cased. Again, this is the kind of question which the models are well-suited to address. This kind of application is even more important to organizations such as pharmaceutical companies, which are highly dependent on a sales network of representatives, each with responsibility for discrete territories.

Certain retailers may also use price discounting as a weapon for building sales performance locally. This practice is most widespread in the petrol sector, where frequent changes in petrol pump prices is a commonplace response to changes at a variety of scales, whether international (e.g., response to a change in the price of crude oil), national (e.g., Shell initiates a price war), or locally (e.g., Asda in Pudsey announces a new promotion). Modeling approaches can be used to support such strategies, for example, by providing an objective assessment of which competitors need to be monitored and therefore, whether any local price change demands an active response.

While GMAP has generally been commercially focused, it has not been exclusively so. Major work was also undertaken for organizations like the West Yorkshire Local Authorities, Yorkshire Water, the Training and Enterprise Council, Department of Transport, and various health authorities. Nevertheless, in looking towards more public service applications of spatial interaction modeling technologies, the thrust has tended to be rather more academically focused. Interesting and important examples can be cited in relation to food deserts, education, and health care delivery.

One interesting set of applications which maintains a retail flavor has recently studied the existence and distribution of *food deserts*. The origins of this work lie in the study of retail saturation (Langston et al. 1997) where the question is whether it is possible to identify geographical areas which have excessive provision of retail floorspace and thus are unattractive to new entrants. Food deserts research asks whether there are, in contrast, areas of poor retail provision and furthermore, how this might map onto geographies of social deprivation at a subregional scale (Guy et al. 2004). Similar research at the University of Bristol has looked at the impact of bank branch closures on access to financial services, particularly within rural areas (Leyshon and Thrift 1995).

Extensions of this style of research into other domains are also of interest. For example, Clarke and Langley (1996) have focused on the composition of local school catchment areas and their relationship to school performance. The relationship between access to services, social deprivation, need, and the availability of health care resources is of long-standing interest to social scientists but is particularly important given increasingly localized financial control through new structures such as Primary Care Trusts (Majeed et al. 2000, Secta 2002).

In figure 3, we present another matrix which now considers the application of spatial modeling technologies in a variety of service application contexts. While we have seen illustrations of some of this potential in the preceding discussion, it might be argued that much of figure 3 remains aspirational rather than having been actually realized. For example, we can argue that just as models have been used to evaluate actual retail sales against benchmark potentials, then just the same might be true of schools or hospitals. In the *Microsimulation approaches* section of the chapter we will consider some of the reasons that it may have proved harder to realize the value of such applications in a public-service rather than a commercial context.

	ANALYSIS OF PROVISION	BENCHMARKING	IMPACT ANALYSIS	FORECASTING	NETWORK CONFIGURATION	PRICE MODELLING	SERVICE EFFECTIVENESS
POLICE/ CRIME	**	**	**	**			**
SCHOOLS	**	**	**	**	**		**
HIGHER EDUCATION	**	**	**	**	**	**	
LABOUR MARKET/ EC DEV	**	**	**	**			
TRANSPORT		**	**	**	**	**	
HOUSING		**	**	**		**	
RETAIL	**	**	**	**			
HEALTH	**	**	**	**	**	**	**

Figure 3. Potential benefits to service providers.

Before moving on, we should also note two other features which are relevant to figure 3. One is that there is much work in these areas from both an applied and academic perspective which originates outside Leeds, but we will not review it here as it is reflected in other chapters within this book. This is most obvious in the case of transport and land-use modeling, a good example of which is seen in the work of Simmonds (2001), and this style of modeling is reviewed here in chapter 10 by Wegener (2005, this volume). It also applies to work on crime and policing (e.g., Ashby 2003), higher education (Tonks and Clarkson 1997), and retailing (Clarke and Wrigley 2004). The second, related, point is that spatial interaction modeling techniques may be of greater or lesser importance within these various domain applications. Thus in the case of land-use modeling, spatial interaction models are still quite central and can even be regarded as consistent with physical growth modeling using diffusion-based aggregation in cellular automata as shown by Batty and Xie (2005, this volume); for crime and policing, and related services, geodemographic techniques are increasingly of interest.

TECHNICAL DEVELOPMENT

In this section, we describe a number of issues which require that models be substantially extended if they are to prove commercially useful. Not all of these enhancements are necessarily required for every application although each is likely to be needed across the full range of applications described in the first section of this chapter. At the end of this section, we will provide an overview of the relationship between market characteristics and model functionality.

CLASSIC MODEL

The classic retail spatial interaction model has the following structure:

$$S_{ij} = A_i O_i W_j f(c_{ij})$$ (1)

where

S_{ij} is the flow of people or money from residential area i to shopping center j, O_i is a measure of demand in area i, W_j is a measure of the attractiveness of center j, c_{ij} is a measure of the cost of travel or distance between i and j, and A_i is a balancing factor which takes account of the competition and ensures that all demand is allocated to centers in the region. Formally it is written as:

$$A_i = \frac{1}{\sum_j W_j f(c_{ij})} \cdot$$ (2)

In summary, the model assumes that in order to forecast the flow of expenditure from an origin zone *(i)* to a destination (retail outlet - j), then one begins with a fixed demand pool at i. This demand is shared between retailers in proportion to their relative size, and in proportion to their geographical proximity, and is reflected in one of the key predictions from the model, D_j, the number of people attracted to center j or the sales at center j, defined as:

$$D_j = \sum_i S_{ij} \cdot$$ (3)

ELASTIC DEMAND

In practice, the assumption of a fixed demand pool is not always a good one. This is particularly the case when the levels of demand and supply for a product or service are interrelated. In the case of groceries, for example, it is safe to assume that customers have a reasonably fixed requirement for fruit and vegetables, meat, dairy products, and so forth. These requirements are unlikely to be altered by the decision of Safeway to build a new supermarket on the doorstep. On the other hand, providers of leisure services such as cinemas, sports clubs, or restaurants would do well to recognize that these facilities will, to some extent, generate their own demand. People lacking access to a cinema, for example, will tend to simply substitute other activities and will have a lower demand for cinema tickets than similar people who have easy access to cinemas. Other examples of this type include financial services (e.g., fig. 4) and (perhaps surprisingly) hospitals.

Modeling frameworks for the treatment of elastic demand have been proposed by Ottens (1989) and Rietveld (1991). The principle of these applications is that the level of demand in an area is not fixed but is related to some measure of service provision in that area. The relationship may be regulated through the introduction of a new parameter, which can adopt some very low or zero value for activities such as the sale of retail groceries to much larger values for a restaurant or cashpoint machine (ATM).

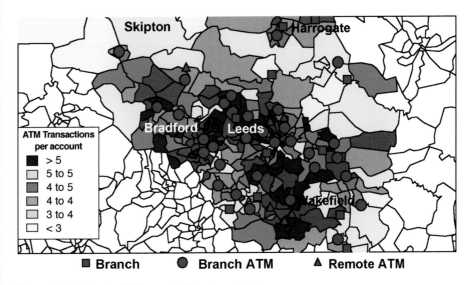

Figure 4. Variations in ATM usage by Leeds residents.

COMPLEX CONSUMER FLOWS

Even if it is safe to assume that the demand for products and services is relatively fixed, the assumption of a simple flow from the point of consumption (residence) to the point of sale (outlet or retail center) is an increasingly unsophisticated representation of the consumption process. To an increasing extent, retail consumption is satisfied through a complex web of multipurpose trips, including trips to or from places of work, education, or leisure.

One implication is that the demand pool needs to be segmented, at least into a portion which may be satisfied from the home and another portion which is satisfied from the workplace. Thus the buoyancy of retail sales within a typical city center owes as much to the proximity of workers as to its attractiveness to suburban neighborhoods. However, such work-based trips are also highly constrained in the geographical sense, so there will not be many trips of four or five miles undertaken within the lunch hour. There may also be an element of elasticity here between the demand components, so that householders employed within city centers may tend to spend heavily through the working week; others may be restricted to the usual evenings and weekends. This is the main reason why modeling petrol stations is such a difficult challenge. Rather than drawing from a captive local market, customers will typically be intercepted at the midpoint on trips which might connect the home, workplace, shop, cinema, nightclub, holiday resort, or any other of a myriad of possible locations.

RETAIL ATTRACTIVENESS

The model attractiveness measure (W_j) has conventionally been represented as size or floorspace. In practice, however, retail attraction might be related to any or all of the following:

i) **Brand preference.** The "name above the door" can affect retail attractiveness in at least three kinds of ways. In the first place, one retail fascia may generate a higher level of footfall and throughput than another, purely by virtue of the quality of its merchandise and the strength of its brand name: for example, Boots will typically attract more customers per square foot than Poundstretcher. Secondly, some brands will exhibit marked regional variations between outlets of a similar type: for example, Halifax branches are much more magnetic in the north than in the south. Thirdly, many brands will have a stronger pull among specific demographic segments. For example, Sainsburys and Tesco will appeal more strongly to customers of a higher social grade, whereas the reverse may be true for customers of Netto or Aldi.

ii) **Store maturity.** Many stores will take some time to reach peak trading levels. This is likely to be particularly true of large stores in out-of-town locations such as retail parks, which might easily take three or four years to achieve maximum potential. At the other end of the scale, stores which have become old-fashioned, or simply tatty, will also tend to perform less well. Thus a typical store may experience a life cycle of attractiveness, in which peak trading performance gradually builds up and then recedes.

iii) **Store agglomeration.** Whenever outlets are grouped together within city centers or retail parks, then there are potential scale economies to be obtained. In effect, these benefits may be closely related to multipurpose trip making so that customers can see benefits in visiting more than one destination within a center or cluster. Alternatively, this may be viewed as a hierarchical choice process in which customers first choose a center in which to shop and only then select an outlet within that center. This structure has been exploited and developed in the creation of the *competing destinations* model (Fotheringham 1986), in which a third parameter complements the traditional spatial interaction model parameters (α on distance/travel cots impedance and β on attractiveness). This structure is reproduced within GMAP's generic model, which is explicitly hierarchical in character so that individual customer flows are modeled to groups of retail outlets (but the attractiveness of the group is related to the attractiveness of its component parts). Individual outlets within each group then compete for market share within the cluster. In a sense, there is also a special case of the model, in which the clusters are constituted from single outlets. This is then the traditional model, which might still be most appropriate for single-purpose trip patterns, say to car dealers or hypermarkets.

iv) **Store performance.** An imponderable component to the modeling process is often provided by performance variations between outlets which may be difficult to explain. In some cases, these variations may arise because of the effectiveness of the local store manager. This is particularly true in markets such as automotive retailing, where entrepreneurial instincts and the ability to sell are important factors. Or performance might be related to historical factors— for example, serious roadworks outside the store may have led to an erosion of regular customer base in the past. Finally, performance variations might be related to other factors which are difficult to measure, such as visibility or store quality. It is important to include performance elements within the modeling, especially for scenario building. For example, if a new store is being evaluated in the vicinity of an overperforming store, then it will be harder to capture new business than from an underperforming store, and this must be reflected within the models, even though the underlying factors may be imperfectly measured and understood.

v) **Size.** Finally, the conventional representation of size is not redundant, even though it must be complemented by other factors. It is important in this context to combine different perspectives on size, however. For example, it may be possible to complement the footage of the store with measures of its frontage or interior shelf space and width of the aisles or the number of parking spaces outside the store and so on.

PRICES

The influence of geographical variations in the pricing of commodities is not commonly reflected within conventional spatial interaction and location models. The reason for this is perhaps that the models are usually concerned with performance at the level of retail centers, and it is only when we drill down to the level of individual outlets that pricing questions start to assume fundamental importance. Our everyday experience tells us both that substantial variations exist in retail prices between places (compare the price of an identical tin of beans between a supermarket and convenience store) and in customer response (we all know individuals who will go to considerable lengths to save a penny on a liter of fuel). Some early explorations into the macrogeographic effect of retail price variations was undertaken by Birkin and Wilson (1989). In the commercial environment, the Manchester-based business KSS (Knowledge Support Systems) has developed a price optimization model which allows retailers to find the ideal prices within locals markets (KSS 2005). Historically, the majority of KSS customers have been oil companies (with an interest in retail forecourts as much as fuel), but the company has also had major contracts in the telecommunications sector. In other recent research, we have begun to build in prices as an explicit component of the costs associated with spatial interaction, i.e., the c_{ij} term in equations (1) and (2). The application of such models to the petrol market has been explored in tandem with the representation of behavior for individual agents by Heppenstall et al. (2004), which we discuss further in the *Microsimulation approaches* section below. A very different class of applications which focuses on local house price variations is introduced by Stillwell et al. (2004).

ARCHITECTURES   In the first section of the chapter we described in some detail the origins of the spatial interaction modeling approach for one GMAP client. We saw that the model was originally implemented for 31 distinct regions in parallel and individual model applications and then made available on a single personal computer. Summaries of the model outputs were then made available in separate reports. At this stage in the development of the system, the major activities of data assembly and integration, modeling, mapping, and reporting are essentially all separable activities. While this approach makes sense while the analytical activities are still relatively exploratory and developmental, as the application began to mature, benefits from a higher level of integration were perceived. Thus the next phase saw the development of a National Information and Modeling System (NIMS), in which the underlying data, model scenarios and *what if* analyses, maps, and reports could all be accessed within an integrated decision support system.

The early structure of NIMS is illustrated in figure 5. In the early releases of the late 1980s, the databases were stored as dBASE files, and the models implemented as executable programs in FORTRAN-77. The maps and reports were generated using a homemade mapping capability with simple GIS functionality known as WinMap and written in C. The components were integrated within a Windows interface, again held together with various scripts in C. Over the course of the next ten years, the structure of these individual components changed from time to time. Eventually WinMap was displaced by MapInfo, the models were reimplemented in C++ and later in Visual Basic, while the databases migrated into SQL and later Microsoft Access. Nevertheless, the character of the systems developed for customers such as Asda and Exxon in the late 1990s is fundamentally similar to the NIMS from ten years earlier.

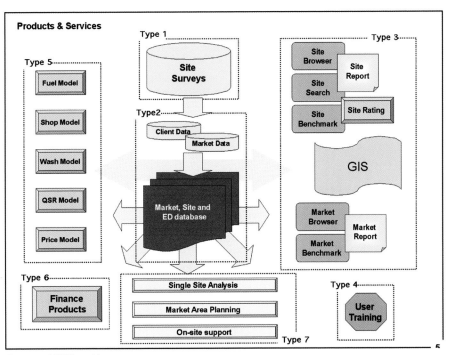

Figure 5. NIMS architecture.

Throughout the 1990s, there was a tendency for different flavors of system to emerge for different clients, with each customer having the luxury of a unique systems requirements specification. For many years, GMAP retained a decision support systems capability across both Windows and Unix® operating systems, only standardising to Windows in the mid-1990s. This process reached its logical conclusion in the current version of the NIMS product, which is now branded as MicroVision™, and is positioned as a generic package of decision support technologies which can be customized to the needs of any given client. (More information about MicroVision can be obtained from the EuroDirect Web site [Skipton Information Group 2004]). The same space is occupied by CACI's InSite™ product, while Urban Science and MPSI have similar offerings directed specifically towards the automotive and petrol markets respectively.

It is important to note, however, that both GMAP and CACI (as well as MPSI, Urban Science, and others) are fundamentally market analysis rather than systems businesses. In GMAP's case, one of the corollaries is that a lot of business has been undertaken without recourse to MicroVision or its antecedents. Of particular importance are the National Representation Plans. In this case, the market analysis objective is not to provide a *what if* capability of limitless flexibility but to produce a single network plan for future development (for more detailed discussion of examples in the financial services sector, see Birkin, Clarke, and Douglas 2002). In this case, the clock is turned back almost full circle in the sense that the country is usually broken down into individual regions for analytical purposes (often referred to as Customer Marketing Areas, or CMAs; see Birkin et al. 2002), and the data assembled, models run, and maps and reports then produced for those individual regions. Such integration as may be necessary will be undertaken in relation to the outputs, i.e., maps and reports and not the models or databases. So this activity is not dissimilar to the earliest WHS model implementation which we described above.

The same tendency towards an increasingly loose coupling of GIS with other technologies, including modeling and analytical applications, has been noted by a number of authors in relation to various application domains. For example, researchers at the University of Auckland have combined the ESRI Spatial Database Engine with three-dimensional computer-aided design (CAD) models and a virtual reality interface (van Maren 2002, Verbree et al. 1999). The system is used to perform visual impact analysis and traffic flow analysis in the context of the built environment. In the United Kingdom, government economic and housing policy has been informed by an approach in which both a sophisticated migration modeling capability and a more limited set of mapping and tabulation routines can be accessed through a common Java interface (Rees et al. 2003). Snyder (2002, table 6.1) describes the combination of the CommunityViz tool within ArcView together with more than twenty other software modules for community-based decision support. We are therefore sympathetic to the views of Geertman and Stillwell (2002, p. 7) who posit an increasing tendency for planning support systems to be realized through a loosely connected package of contributory technologies rather than through highly integrated and engineered software systems.

In terms of the future, the demand for market analysis support seems secure. Regardless of changing retail delivery and customer activity patterns induced by the Internet revolution, major service organizations will continue to depend on physical distribution channels and will require specialist advice and guidance if they are to configure such networks effectively. Whether they will require integrated decision support tools is perhaps more open to question. Increasingly, the customers for such analysis are sophisticated, not just as spreadsheet users (who are therefore able to access and manipulate data with relative ease), but they also have, or can readily acquire, skills to manipulate spatial data through easy-to-use GIS packages. We return to this theme in the *Key trends and issues* section below.

MICROSIMULATION APPROACHES

A related but distinct approach to urban and regional problems, with particular relevance to questions of policy and planning, *microsimulation* has also been championed at Leeds over a long period of time. The basic idea of microsimulation is simply to represent the population (of a city or region) as a set of individuals with unique characteristics rather than using an array to maintain counts of the number of people who share common characteristics. The individuals are usually generated synthetically so that they represent imaginary rather than real people although there are also examples in which samples of anonymized records from the United Kingdom census have been reweighted across small areas to provide populations which are not actually named individuals but do have look-alikes somewhere in the population (e.g., Williamson et al. 1998).

A big advantage of the microsimulation approach is that it provides the basis for a rich disaggregation of the population. A useful example is provided by the recent SimYork project (Ballas et al. 2003), in which demographic characteristics drawn from the census of population and households is linked with more detailed economic attributes from the British Household Panel Survey (BHPS). The first step in the process is to take individual records from the BHPS and to reweight them to provide distributions which are consistent with the known geographies of York. The assumption is that if census cross-tabulations are adequately represented, then the individual characteristics which are monitored by BHPS and not by the census are also transferable. Thus it is possible to represent geographies of income and benefits, health, values, and opinions, and histories of employment, fertility, and relationships.

Another benefit of the microsimulation approach is that it provides a basis for understanding policy impacts, both now and in the future. For example, Ballas et al. (2003) present examples showing the impact of various national policy initiatives such as working family tax credits, child tax credit, winter fuel payments, and minimum wage and income guarantees on relative poverty levels of individual households in York up to the year 2021.

Historically, microsimulation has been a popular approach for the analysis of policy impacts, particularly in relation to financial policy (e.g., Orcutt et al. 1986, Haveman and Hollenbeck 1980). The distinctiveness of the Leeds approach is partially in adding an explicit and detailed spatial dimension to such frameworks. Furthermore, the approach has been applied to domains such as education, health, labor markets, and retailing (Clarke 1996). A particularly interesting research challenge, which is especially relevant to problems relating to retailing and labor markets, is how to add activity variables to microsimulation models and thus to represent things like shopping behavior or access to employment opportunities. A mechanism to achieve this was proposed by Birkin and M. Clarke (1987) who provided a simple coupling between a microsimulation model and a spatial interaction model. A synthetic population of individuals and households was created from census data, and to this, spending patterns were added from the Family Expenditure Survey. From this model, aggregate estimates of expenditure by small area were derived as inputs to a spatial interaction model. The SIM was then used to compute interaction probabilities within each small area for different retail destinations. These interaction probabilities were then used to add shopping behavior (i.e., most probable retail destination) to the synthetic micropopulation. The method has recently been revived and extended by Nakaya et al. (2003).

The relationship between microsimulation and GIS has been, for the most part, at arm's length. In relation to the SimLeeds microsimulation environment,

Ballas and Clarke (2000) note that "SimLeeds outputs can be easily linked to proprietary GIS packages such as MapInfo Professional® or ArcInfo"(p. 321). A number of illustrations are used to support this argument. Nevertheless, there is a strong sense that the two environments are loosely coupled rather than fundamentally embedded. Thus the outputs from the models are essentially imported and then manipulated independently within the GIS—there is no two-way interaction. However, one recent project which seeks to develop the relationship between microsimulation and GIS to a new level is MicroMaPPAS (Stillwell et al. 2004). This project seeks to estimate micropopulations to support planning and policy development—for example, to identify disadvantaged or socially excluded groups. The criteria by which target groups are identified involves weighted sampling from aggregate census tabulations. The authors describe a weights controller interface, and the outputs can be evaluated through a Java mapping dialogue. Depending on the outcomes from this process, the models may be further refined or upgraded.

Another important question concerns the relationship between microsimulation and microagent simulations, not least because of the current popularity of agent methods. Some excellent examples of the application of agent-based methods to a spatial modeling problem can be found in the work of Nagel (2003) who has developed an approach showing the journey-to-work patterns of commuters across the whole of Switzerland in something like real time. The model is of considerable interest in practical terms—for example, queueing behavior can be studied in relation to the setup of traffic light controls at a particular junction or speed limits on individual stretches of road. In general, it may be fair to characterize agent approaches as mostly concerned with behavior at the individual level, microsimulation as concerned with questions of composition and structure. Additionally, in terms of the applications discussed above, agents may be more likely to address questions of short-term dynamics, microsimulation more with long-term forecasting. In this respect, another interesting question might be how the use of agents to study evolutionary processes in relation to the social behavior of biological populations (e.g., Noble and Franks 2003) might be applied to questions of spatial evolution.

A link between agent-based approaches and spatial interaction modeling was recently explored by Heppenstall et al. (2004). This research is distinctive in attempting to model the behavior and decision making of individual retailers. Specifically, the work looks at how petrol retailers continually change prices within a competitive market. It is argued that such changes can only be understood in combination with their effects on customer response within local geographic neighborhoods and that this behavior can be effectively represented, as ever, through the spatial interaction modeling approach. Thus these authors present and test a hybrid model, which combines microagent and spatial interaction models, with encouraging results.

What is clearly missing from the above discussion are examples showing the application of microsimulation methods within commercial planning environments.

Individual data has become an increasingly precious commodity within the commercial marketplace in recent years with the advent of sources such as the electoral roll, lifestyle data (for a definition and review, see Birkin 1995), shareholder registers, credit risk data, and loyalty card records. Such databases have been widely and effectively used in the construction of a new generation of profiling tools, like Prizm® (Claritas 2004) and Pixel™ (Experian 2004, Farr and Webber 2002). While Birkin et al. (2002, chapter 11) have speculated on the potential for application of microsimulation methodologies, particularly within the financial services sector, real examples simply do not exist at this time. Further speculation on the possible reasons for this are discussed in the *Micro–macro integration* section below.

SOME KEY TRENDS AND ISSUES

APPLICABILITY AND UTILITY OF THE MODELS

Around the millennium, there was much talk of Internet retailing and a space-less economy. For example, one report (quoted in Birkin et al. 2002, chapter 5) indicated that exponential growth in home deliveries could lead to this activity accounting for up to 10% of trade for leading supermarkets by 2010. A number of observations are probably relevant in response. In the first place, if home deliveries account for 10% of trade, then other (conventional?) channels of distribution still account for the remaining 90%. Secondly, much of the more vacuous chatter about changing delivery patterns has been rendered superfluous following the various dot-com disappointments around the millennium. Thirdly, what we have actually seen in most cases is the emergence of what many intelligent commentators always predicted as a *bricks and clicks* retail and service economy, in which it is the major players with strong existing distribution networks who have been best placed to sustain the infrastructure costs associated with Internet retailing. Amazon.com is a high-profile exception, but for every Amazon there is a Virgin Cars, a notable failure to deliver cars through a virtual channel, and a Halifax Direct, in which an existing retailer has simply welded on an Internet shopping arm (see also Birkin et al. 2002, chapter 5). In consequence, much Internet retailing now runs alongside traditional branch-based delivery, which in turn means that, for both customers and suppliers, distribution channels are more complicated than ever. In short, what this means is that retailers need better tools for understanding and planning their markets than ever before!

We have seen earlier that the models have been used for a variety of purposes, ranging from benchmarking and scenario building (*what if* modeling) through forecasting to strategic network planning. In general, we would argue that models are probably more effective for benchmarking than for precise impact analyses. This is because the benchmarking process, by its very nature, requires analysis and interpretation. In a similar way, any model prediction requires interpretation and an understanding of the circumstances in which the predictions are robust and when they need to be challenged. At the end of the day, spatial modeling remains as much an art as a science. For similar reasons, strategic network planning uses are among the more successful applications, as again the focus tends to be much more on general insights and less on specific predictions.

An assessment of the usefulness of models by sector would be another interesting topic for further debate and analysis. It is ironic that the technologies described here have enjoyed the most conspicuous success in the automotive industry (not just through GMAP, but also through competitors like CACI and Experian and specialist businesses like Urban Science and Polk), despite the fact that this is a sector where the predictive power of the models is probably weakest because of the importance of high-quality marketing and salesmanship in selling motor vehicles. Indeed, it may be precisely because of this that the benchmarking and strategic qualities of the modeling are more highly valued. Equally ironic is the fact that, although most research tends to be focused on retailing proper and retail trade flows are among the easiest to simulate accurately, a relatively low value is placed on modeling within this sector. This perhaps reflects an overall lack of strategic thinking among retailers as a breed, as well as a traditional concern over tight margins and cost minimization.

It may also be useful once again to reflect on why the models have been seen as even less applicable to public service problems. In part, this may be due to the scale of the problems and both the intellectual and financial cost required for their resolution. It may also reflect the lack of clear and quantifiable goals in public service provision (in contrast to the clear profit focus within commercial organizations). It is noticeable that the interest in modeling approaches has perked up considerably alongside an increased focus on best value and especially league tables.

DATA, CALIBRATION, AND VALIDATION

How accurate are model-based impact analyses, and how much confidence can therefore be placed in model predictions? This is such a fundamental question that it is, at face value, surprising that there exists no substantial canon of evidence to provide the answer. Admittedly, some limited evidence has been published, for example by Birkin et al. (1996, chapter 5) and Clarke and Clarke (2001), but in general such data is conspicuous by its absence. In this section we consider reasons why this might be so.

From the perspective of commercial organizations, one constraint is simply the difficulty of the process. In particular, the real world is not a laboratory and does not stand still. Comparisons of a set of predictions against one set of assumptions and outcomes actually generated against an ever-changing environmental backcloth are not straightforward. These problems are exacerbated by the length of time over which comparative work needs to be undertaken. For example, between starting to evaluate a site and actually completing the building of something like a retail supermarket would take at least three years, and probably nearer five, particularly if a stable pattern of trade needs to be established. Furthermore, it is highly unlikely that any useful comparative benchmarks will be available, so even if the models do not perform, what evidence is there that any other methodology would have served any better? Most important of all is the question of self-interest. Many organizations will not admit to any difficulty in the process of retail sales estimation or worse, will claim to be able to achieve infeasible levels of accuracy already. A market analysis business would be reticent to claim apparently inferior performance levels, while there is no benefit to the retail client to publishing results whether they are manifestly better or worse than the competition. There is no commercial motivation in publishing such analyses, and it is no coincidence that there exist similar lacunae, for example, in comparative performance between geodemographic systems for different products and promotions.

From an academic perspective, the question of model performance could be an interesting one and one where the independence of the observer could add value. However, academics will usually simply lack access to the data needed for such studies, while in their own research academics simply lack interest in broaching industrial-strength applications and are typically content to focus on ideas rather than outcomes.

SYSTEMS AND ARCHITECTURES

We argued above that over time the systems required to support model-based planning have tended to become less integrated and increasingly fragmented. One development which could help to counter this trend is the emergence of e-science and grid computing. The concept of computational grids owes its name to analogies with electrical power grids to the extent that they are predicated on a view that users will seek to access computational resources from the desktop with increasingly little regard for the origin of those resources (Foster 2003). Equally important, perhaps, is the notion of the *virtual organization,* which in essence means that users can assemble at will systems to tackle particular problems from a combination of spatially dislocated components, or grid services. The application of computational grid services to a spatial decision support problem, specifically the question of resource allocation within a local health service, has been explored within recent research at Leeds (Birkin et al. 2002). This research clearly demonstrates that different services for accessing data, running models, computational optimization, and reporting can all be implemented reasonably easily on a computational grid. This is not altogether surprising since these components largely mirror the kinds of system components which were previously integrated into decision support systems, prior to the fragmentation trend noted above.

The big advantage of such systems is that they permit simultaneous access and maintenance. For example, suppose that an organization like McDonalds wants to maintain a model-based planning capability for its global retail network. Chances are that, at the moment, this could mean a hundred or more desktop systems in each of its local headquarters around the world. Supporting these installations is a full-time job. A grid-based installation would allow all of this installation and maintenance to be controlled securely and easily from a central location. However, whether the adoption of grid computing will do much to affect long-term trends remains to be seen. Not only do such systems require much higher levels of software engineering, they also rely on levels of data sharing across organizations which again runs counter to all recent trends of data exchange and distribution.

Note that while some of this can be done over the Internet, the World Wide Web model is essentially orientated towards static data retrieval from a host to a client. In contrast, the grid service model seeks to support a more dynamic sharing of information and is thus well suited to activities such as scenario building and *what if* modeling. In the future, we might well envision grid-enabled systems which allow GIS and the associated decision-support systems to be packaged in a similar way to rudimentary Internet mapping systems such as MultiMap™ (MultiMap 2005). The user might select a country or study region, and a retail network, from within a Web browser. That browser would then automatically invoke services to access data from a variety of geographically dispersed sites and combine the data with appropriate modeling tools in order to produce benchmarks and scenarios. Such grid functions might be implemented as Internet services with restricted access from within an organization or as extranet applications which are accessible to a wider constituency of users under an appropriate business model.

Whether such an outcome could be achieved equally easily using a new generation of Web services is a point of some contention among computer scientists.

MICRO–MACRO INTEGRATION

Earlier, we identified much interesting academic research in the field of microsimulation with potential relevance to both commercial and public service organizations, but with little evidence that such value has yet been realized. Whether there is much prospect for change in the short to medium term is again dubious. In the first place, despite the apparent growth of individual-level data about customers and citizens, such data remains partial and incomplete. For example, supermarkets may have excellent information about their storecard customers in terms of their frequency of purchase, product preferences, basket size, and so on. However, they know much less about customers who are not storecard holders, about the shopping habits of their storecard customers at other retail outlets, or about that large and important group of customers with whom they have no relationship.

The availability of skills for the manipulation of microlevel data is much less widespread than is the case for aggregate data. Because of their very nature, microdatabases will tend to be large, but also messy and complicated. For example, a big issue with lifestyle databases is the incompleteness of responses. A respondent may not check a box indicating a liking for computer games, but this could indicate a genuine antipathy for such pastimes or just a laziness about filling in the form. Such issues make processing of individual level data nontrivial, and again it is perhaps unsurprising that the most popular products, like Prizm (see above), are those which explicitly simplify the data into a manageable form. Finally, all of these issues are compounded by the fact that there is a general dearth of tools and resources to support microscale modeling, particularly microsimulation, even within the research community. Therefore, these models are continually being reinvented, which limits their more widespread application and rapidity of development.

CONCLUSIONS

This chapter has reflected on the progress of a research stream with a strong applied dimension over a period of more than twenty years. One of our arguments has been that much has been learned from the application of classical techniques to real business problems, and one of our hopes is that a transfer of methods from business to public service problems may be productive in ongoing research. We have argued that further impetus will be provided by the availability of better methods and in particular, by the integration of micro-agent and simulation methods with meso-scale models of geographical interaction. The technical architectures of e-science, and especially the proliferation of richly-specified databases of organizational and customer behavior, may also enhance this process.

REFERENCES

Ashby, D. 2003. Evaluating crime and police performance by neighborhood type. AGI Annual Conference at GeoSolutions 2003, London, England. www.casa.ucl.ac.uk/ashby.

Ballas, D., and G. P. Clarke. 2000. GIS and microsimulation for local labor market analysis. *Computers, Environment and Urban Systems* 24: 305–30.

———. 2001. Towards local implications of major job transformations in the city: A spatial microsimulation approach. *Geographical Analysis* 33: 291–311.

Ballas, D., G. Clarke, D. Dorling, D. Rossiter, and B. Thomas. 2003. SimBritain: Simulating the geographies of well-being and health in Britain, 1991–2021. Paper presented at the International Microsimulation Conference on Population Aging and Health: Modeling Our Future, Canberra, Australia.

Birkin, M. 1994. Finding the right sites: The WH Smith approach. In *Proceedings: GIS in Business '94 Europe*, 211–12. Cambridge: Longman GeoInformation.

———. 1995. Customer targeting, geodemographics and lifestyles approaches. In *GIS for business and service planning*, ed. P. Longley and G. Clarke, 104–49. London: Longman.

Birkin, M., and G. Clarke. 1991. Spatial interaction in geography. *Geography Review,* 5 (4): 16–21.

Birkin M., G. Clarke, and L. Douglas. 2002. Optimising retail mergers and acquisitions geographically. *Progress In Planning* 58: 229–318.

Birkin, M., G. Clarke, and M. Clarke. 2002. *Retail geography and intelligent network planning.* Chichester: John Wiley and Sons.

Birkin M., G. P. Clarke, M. Clarke, and A. G. Wilson. 1996. *Intelligent GIS: Location decisions and strategic planning.* Cambridge: Geoinformation.

Birkin, M., and M. Clarke. 1987. Comprehensive models and efficient accounting frameworks for urban and regional systems. In *Transformations through space and time,* ed. D. Griffith and R. Haining, 169–95. The Hague: Martinus Nijhoff.

Birkin, M., P. Dew, and J. Wood. 2002. Spatial decision-support systems on the grid. e-Science All Hands Meeting, Sheffield, England.

Birkin, M., and A. Wilson. 1989. Some properties of spatial-structural-economic-dynamic urban models. In *Progress in the dynamic analysis of spatial systems,* ed. J. Hauer, H. Timmermans, and N. Wrigley, 184–200. Dordrecht: Reidel.

Cassidy, J. 2002. *Dot.con: The greatest story ever sold.* New York: HarperCollins.

Claritas. 2004. Adding intelligence to information. www/claritas.com.

Clarke, G., ed. 1996. *Microsimulation for urban and regional policy analysis.* London: Pion.

Clarke, G., and M. Clarke. 2001. Applied spatial interaction modeling. In *Regional science in business,* ed. G. Clarke and M. Madden, 137–58. Berlin: Springer.

Clarke, G., and R. Langley. 1996. The potential of GIS and spatial modeling for planning in the new education market. *Environment and Planning C, Government and Policy* 14: 301–23.

Experian. 2004. Goad retail property information. www.business-strategies.co.uk.

Farr, M., and R. Webber. 2001. MOSAIC: From an area classification to individual classification. *Journal of Targeting, Measurement and Analysis for Marketing* 87: 681–99.

Foot, D. 1981. *Operational urban models.* New York: Methuen.

Foster, I. 2003. The grid: Computing without bounds. *Scientific American* 288 (4): 78–85.

Fotheringham, A. S. 1986. Modeling hierarchical destination choice. *Environment and Planning A* 18: 401–18.

Geertman, S., and J. Stillwell, eds. 2002. *Planning support systems in practice.* Berlin: Springer.

Guy, C., G. Clarke, and H. Eyre. 2004. Food retail change and the growth of food deserts: A case study of Cardiff. *International Journal of Retail & Distribution Management* 32 (2): 72–88.

Haveman, R., and K. Hollenbeck. 1980. *Microeconomic simulation models for public policy analysis.* New York: Academic Press.

Heppenstall, A., A. Evans, and M. Birkin. Forthcoming. A hybrid multi-agent/spatial interaction model system for petrol price setting. *Transactions in GIS.*

Huff, D. 1964. Defining and estimating a trade area. *Journal of Marketing* 28: 34–38.

KSS. 2005. Pricing solutions for retail and petroleum industries. www.kssg.com.

Lakshmanan, T., and W. Hansen. 1965. A retail market potential model. *Journal of the American Institute of Planners* 31: 134–43.

Langston, P., G. Clarke, and D. Clarke. 1997. Retail saturation, retail location and retail competition: An analysis of British food retailing. *Environment and Planning A* 29: 77–104.

Leyshon, A., and N. Thrift. 1995. Geographies of financial exclusion: Financial abandonment in Britain and the United States. *Transactions of the Institute of British Geographers* 20: 312–41.

Majeed, A., M. Bardsley, D. Morgan, C. O'Sullivan, and A. Bindman. 2000. Cross-sectional study of primary care groups in London: Association of measures of socio-economic and health status with hospital admission rates. *British Medical Journal* 321: 1057–60.

Multimap. 2005. Multimap.com—online maps to everywhere. www.multimap.com.

Nagel, K. 2003. Traffic networks. In *Handbook of graphs and networks: From the genome to the Internet,* ed. S. Bornholdt and H. Schuster, 248–72. New York: John Wiley and Sons.

Nakaya, T., K. Yano, S. Koga, A. S. Fotheringham, D. Ballas, G. Clarke, and K. Hanoaka. 2003. Retail interaction modeling using meso and micro approaches. Paper presented at the 33rd Annual Conference of the Regional Science Association International, British and Irish Section, St. Andrews, Scotland.

Noble, J., and D. Franks. 2003. Social learning mechanisms compared in a simple environment. In *Artificial life VIII: The eighth international conference on artificial life,* ed. R. Standish, M. A. Bedeau, and H. A. Abbass. Cambridge, Mass.: MIT Press.

Orcutt, G. H., J. Mertz, and H. Quinke, eds. 1986. *Microanalytic simulation models to support social and financial policy.* Amsterdam: North-Holland.

Rees, P. H., A. S. Fotheringham, and A. G. Champion. 2003. Migration modeling for policy analysis. In *Applied GIS and spatial analysis,* ed. G. Clarke and J. Stillwell, 257–78. London: John Wiley and Sons.

Secta. 2002. Leeds Health Community: An Investigation into Variations in the Use of Secondary Care Services. Secta Consulting, Liversedge. (Copies available from the author.)

Simmonds, D. 2001. The objectives and design of a new land-use modeling package: DELTA. In *Regional science in business,* ed. G. Clarke and M. Madden, 159–88. Berlin: Springer.

Skipton Information Group. 2004. EuroDirect: The direct marketing professionals. www.gmap.com/Pages/EuroDirect%20Information.htm.

Snyder, K. 2002. Tools for community design and decision making. In *Planning support systems in practice,* ed. S. Geertman and J. Stillwell, 99–120. Berlin: Springer.

Stillwell, J., M. Birkin, D. Ballas, R. Kingston, and P. Gibson. 2004. Simulating the city and alternative futures. In *Twenty-first century Leeds: Geographies of a regional city,* ed. J. Stillwell and R. Unsworth, 345–64. Leeds: University of Leeds Press.

Tonks, D., and S. Clarkson. 1997. A geodemographic analysis of degree performance. *Higher Education Review* 30: 5–19.

van Maren, G. 2002. Key to virtual insight: A 3D GIS and virtual reality system. In *Planning support systems in practice,* ed. S. Geertman and J. Stillwell, 193–204. Berlin: Springer.

Verbree, E., G. van Maren, R. Germs, F. Jansen, and M. Kraak. 1999. Interaction in virtual world views—Linking 3DGIS with VR. *International Journal of Geographic Information Science* 13: 385–96.

WH Smith. 2004. The history of WH Smith. www.whsmithplc.com.

Williamson, P., M. Birkin, and P. Rees. 1998. The estimation of population microdata by using data from small area statistics and samples of anonymised records. *Environment and Planning A* 30: 785–816.

Wilson, A. 1967. A statistical theory of spatial distribution models. *Transportation Research* 1: 253–69.

———. 1970. *Entropy in urban and regional modeling.* London: Pion.

———. 1974. *Urban and regional models in geography and planning.* Chichester: John Wiley and Sons.

Chapter 12

Simulating Spatially Explicit Networks for Dispersion of Infectious Diseases

LING BIAN, DEPARTMENT OF GEOGRAPHY

DAVID LIEBNER, SCHOOL OF MEDICINE AND BIOMEDICAL SCIENCES

STATE UNIVERSITY OF NEW YORK AT BUFFALO

AMHERST, NEW YORK

ABSTRACT

WE PRESENT A STOCHASTIC APPROACH to examining the effect of network topology of human contact on spatial and temporal dispersion of infectious disease. This approach is based on an individual-based and spatially explicit conceptual framework. Discrete individuals and their locations in a home space and a workplace space are explicitly represented through a two-layer and two-scale network. The spread of infectious diseases depends on the properties and structure of the network, represented by six indices. These include the ratio of family and workplace size, transmission rate of disease, number of direct connections of an individual, covariance between home and workplace locations, the shortest path between individuals, and the length of infectious period. The effect of these parameters on the peak time of an epidemic, the total number of infected at the peak time, and the total number of infected during an epidemic is analyzed thorough a simulated influenza epidemic.

INTRODUCTION

In this chapter, we discuss the effect of network topology on the transmission of communicable diseases within a human population. Communicable diseases, by definition, are transmitted from individual to individual and follow a network of human contacts as they spread through space and time. Modeling these phenomena requires an individual-based and spatially explicit approach. However, this approach has not received adequate attention until very recently because of the prevalence of traditional epidemiology models that rely on a population-based and spatially implicit approach to modeling epidemics. The success of an individual-based and spatially explicit approach requires a sound conceptual framework and a corresponding analytical approach. We briefly discuss the conceptual framework, while focusing this chapter on the analytical approach to examining the effect of network topology on spatial and temporal dispersion of infectious diseases.

Results of this analysis may serve several goals. First, individual-based epidemiology models are in their infancy. Many basic elements, such as individuals, space, time, and the interplay between them, have not been considered (or considered in a different light) in previous models. A conceptual framework is necessary to establish assumptions, model structures, and represent these basic elements. The conceptual and analytical discussions in this chapter serve this goal. Second, this chapter provides a guideline for the design and implementation of a working version of individual-based and spatially explicit epidemiology model, although the actual development falls outside the scope of this chapter. In serving this goal, design principles specifically for a working model that can use GIS data are discussed toward the end of this chapter.

Third, the ultimate goal of individual-based and spatially explicit epidemiology models is to help decision making in public health policy. These models can help predict health outcomes in order to recommend preventive measures, such as vaccination, against the transmission of disease in a population. The individual-based and spatially explicit approach can offer realistic assessments of the spatial path of infectious diseases. This helps allocate limited resources to most critical communities in order to protect population.

In the remainder of the chapter, we first review a conceptual framework for individual-based and spatially explicit epidemiology models, with comparison to traditional models and some recent development. We then describe network topology in the context of dispersion of infectious diseases. Based on these discussions, we present a stochastic approach to analyzing the effect of network topology on the spatial and temporal dynamics of infection in a simulated influenza epidemic.

BACKGROUND

Traditional epidemiology models represent epidemics of communicable disease using a population-based, nonspatial approach. The conceptual framework for this approach is rooted in the general population model (Kermack and McKendrick 1927) which divides a population into susceptible, infected, and recovered population segments. The rates at which individuals move from the susceptible to the infected segment and from the infected to the recovered segment are assumed to be continuous and are usually described by partial differential equations. By adjusting the parameters in these equations, the models can reasonably approximate the observed health data (Anderson and May 1992). These population-based nonspatial models imply the following: (1) all individuals share identical attributes; (2) the spatial distribution of individuals is ignored; (3) the interaction between individuals is global; and (4) transmission rates of diseases between individuals are equal. The spatial dispersion of disease is not addressed, while time is always explicitly considered.

The spatial version of these models represents the dispersion of diseases in a ring-like fashion. That is, diseases spread from a center point in space and travel uniformly outward in all directions. On the crest of the ring are the infected individuals, while in front of the crest are the susceptible individuals and behind are the recovered (Cliff et al. 1981, Cliff et al. 2000, Cliff and Haggett 1990, Ferguson et al. 2001, Rhodes and Anderson 1997). Although space is explicit, these models do not change the assumptions of the traditional models. They simply locate the three population segments, each as a whole, in space.

This basic population model and its derivatives provide a foundation for modern epidemiology and have remained as a mainstay of epidemiology for over half of a century. In the past decade, however, these population-based nonspatial models have drawn increasing criticism. Despite the strengths of these models, they fail to produce realistic results, especially for complex systems (Holmes 1997, Koopman and Lynch 1999, Bian 2004).

Several recent efforts consider alternative approaches to modeling population health. One such approach is the *discrete individual transmission model* (Adams et al. 1998, Ghani et al. 1997, Koopman and Lynch 1999, Kretzschmar and Morris 1996, van der Ploeg et al. 1998, Welch et al. 1998). This model stresses that individuals are different from one another, and this simple fact should be a basic assumption for epidemiological modeling (Keeling 1999, Koopman and Lynch 1999). The discrete individual transmission model challenges the traditional models by explicitly considering discrete individuals and the interactions between them. Mostly built for sexually transmitted diseases, these models do not explicitly consider space.

A second alternative approach is represented by the *spatial adjacency model* (Holmes 1997). This model is based on the idea that disease transmission is an intrinsically spatial process. Individuals are represented as discrete entities with explicit spatial coordinates. The transmission of disease between individuals is assumed to be a local phenomenon, only occurring between susceptible and infected individuals who are spatially adjacent. Similar to the discrete individual transmission models, the conceptual framework of the *spatial adjacency model* deviates significantly from that of the traditional models. However, because individuals are assumed to be immobile in the spatial adjacency models, these models are inappropriate for modeling disease transmission between highly mobile and spatially dispersed humans.

A third approach includes various *subpopulation models*. These models focus on divisions within a population, such as by age, and the transmission of diseases between them (Ferguson et al. 1997, Grenfell and Harwood 1997, Schenzle 1984, Keeling 2000, Lloyd 1995, Rhodes and Anderson 1997, Szymanski and Caraco 1994, Torres-Sorando and Rodriguez 1997). These models are similar to the traditional models except for a greater number of subpopulations than the traditional three segments. The spatial version of the subpopulation model explicitly considers the location of a subpopulation, but individuals within a subpopulation are assumed identical, immobile, and homogeneously mixed. These models are most appropriate for high-density and immobile populations.

These aforementioned approaches reflect a recent shift away from population-based and towards individual-based modeling. This shift is widely supported in several disciplines, such as individual-based modeling in ecology (Bian 2000, DeAngelis and Gross 1992, Judson 1994, Tyler and Rose 1994, Westvelt and Hopkins 1999), micro-simulation in regional science (Amrhein and MacKinnon 1988, Benenson et al. 2002), and most recent, agent-based simulation in many disciplines (Bousquet et al. 2001, Gilbert and Conte 1995, Gilbert and Doran 1994, Lake 2000, Parker et al. 2003).

The stochastic approach described in this chapter is based on an individual-based and spatially explicit conceptual framework. This conceptual framework explicitly considers discrete individuals, the spatial distribution and mobility of these individuals, local and long-distance connections between them, and the heterogeneity of this network of connection. Similar to the discrete individual transmission models and spatial adjacency models described above, this conceptual framework differs from that of the traditional modeling by explicitly considering discrete individuals and their spatial location. It is most appropriate for modeling the dispersion of infectious diseases between mobile humans.

THE CONCEPTUAL FRAMEWORK

The individual-based and spatially explicit model considers conceptual issues in four aspects: (1) the modeling unit, (2) temporal dynamics, (3) spatial variation, and (4) interactions between individuals. Details of the conceptual framework are described in Bian (2004). We review the framework briefly below, with an emphasis on the interaction structure between individuals.

The model uses individuals as the basic modeling unit. Many aspects of an individual are important in the context of epidemiological modeling, such as the identification of individuals, their characteristics and behavior, the relationships between individuals, and the change of these characteristics and relationships through time and space. With the object-oriented approach, these can be readily represented.

The temporal dynamics of an epidemic are treated as discrete periods in this conceptual model. Each period begins and ends with an event. For example, the infectious period begins with the event of emitting infectious material and ends with the cessation of the emission. These periods are used to indicate the health states of an individual and serve as one of the individual's characteristics. This health state reflects the susceptibility of an individual to infection as well as his/her capacity to transmit infection. In addition, the length of a discrete period affects the pattern of spatial and temporal dispersion of diseases through a population.

The spatial variation of disease dispersion is represented according to the concept of time geography (Hägerstrand 1970, Kwan 1999, Lenntorp 1978, Löytönen 1998, Miller 2005, Pred 1977). Time geography represents an individual's daily activities at different locations as a trajectory in a space–time prism, or a life path. When several individuals form a group at a location, such as home or a workplace, their life paths intersect. When a group dissolves and individuals travel to different groups, they link groups into a network of connected population. Through this network, diseases may spread in space through both a local infection during group activities and a long-distance dispersion when an individual travels between locations.

The pattern of within-group interaction may vary depending on the environment. At home during evening, family members are often in full contact, leading to a full mix. In workplaces during daytime, the contact may be a partial mix. Presently, most health studies involving GIS focus only on the evening population, due partially to the availability of census or other evening population data, although the daytime population is equally at risk. The differences between the evening and daytime populations, and especially the link between the two populations, are critical in determining the spatial and temporal pattern of disease dispersion.

The above conceptual framework, regarding modeling unit, temporal dynamic, spatial variation, and interaction structure, leads to a two-scale and two-layer network of connections. A network consists of nodes and links. In this study, an individual or a group is a node in the network, and the interactions between individuals or between groups are the links. The two scales are within-group and between-group networks. The two layers represent different types of group, i.e., homes and workplaces, respectively. Within each layer is the within-group interaction, while between the layers is the between-group interaction realized by individuals' travel between groups (fig. 1). The within-group interaction may facilitate local infection, while the between-group interaction may facilitate long distance dispersion of diseases. This two-layer and two-scale network serves as the guideline for the subsequent simulation detailed later in the Simulation Design section.

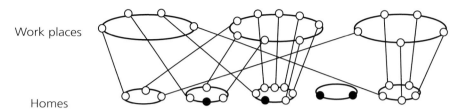

Work places

Homes

Figure 1. An illustration of a two-scale and two-layer contact network. The two layers represent homes and workplaces, respectively. Oval-shaped circles represent group nodes (homes or workplaces). A small open circle within a node represents an individual who has both family and workplace links. A small filled circle represents an individual who has family links only (the within-node links are not shown). A straight line indicates an identical individual at two different locations.

The individual-based and spatially explicit approach moves epidemiological modeling toward the stochastic approach and away from the deterministic approach commonly used in the traditional models. The stochastic prediction of individuals' health states relies on the probability of individual infection, the contact between individuals, the health states of group members, and network topology. The health outcome at the population level depends on the accumulative effect of these connected yet individualized infections. With this conceptual framework established, the following section discusses network topology in the context of dispersion of infectious diseases.

NETWORK TOPOLOGY

Network topology directly affects the performance of a network, i.e., how efficiently a network can support the transmission of information, capital, goods, diseases, etc. through the network. In the context of dispersion of infectious diseases, we represent network topology through three sets of indices, namely, (1) the attributes associated with nodes, (2) the direction and attributes of links, and (3) the structure of the network. Each set of indices is explained below.

There are two types of nodes in this study, the individual nodes and group nodes. This is in correspondence with the two-scale network structure established in the conceptual framework described above. These nodes have attributes. The attributes of individual nodes may include those that describe the health states of an individual, i.e. susceptible, infected, or recovered. The attributes of a group may include group size, the health states of each member, and the contact pattern within the group (full or partial mix). These attributes are one of the fundamental stochastic properties of the individual-based and spatially explicit epidemiology models. The spatial distribution of these properties, combined with other properties, ultimately determines the spatial and temporal pattern of disease dispersion.

Links in a network have both magnitude and a direction because infection not only carries a probability but also is a directional event. Infectious diseases are always transmitted from the infected to the susceptible individuals. This direction is important because it determines the temporal sequence of infection that begins with an individual, subsequently moves to other members of a group (local infection) or members of other groups (long-distance dispersion), and eventually to the entire population. One magnitude of a link is the probability of disease transmission, often represented as a transmission rate. This rate may vary depending on the susceptibility of an individual to infection.

Network structure determines how nodes are linked into a network. This structure plays a critical role in determining the temporal and spatial dispersion of disease through a population. Although network structure may vary greatly, several indices are commonly used to describe a structure. These include the number of direct links of a node, the degree of interconnection between nodes that are linked to a given node, and the minimum number of links between any two given nodes (Albert et al. 2000, Keeling 1999, Watts and Strogatz 1998). In the context of disease dispersion, the number of direct links of a node can be used to describe the number of family members and coworkers associated with an individual. For the degree of interconnection between nodes, we devised an index that describes the overlap between an individual's family members and his/her coworkers. In the situation of a family business, for example, the overlap value is high because family members may be also coworkers. This index thus corresponds to individuals' mobility, outlined in the conceptual framework, that links the evening and daytime populations together. The minimum number of links between any two given nodes can be used to describe the shortest path between an infected and a susceptible individual.

The aforementioned indices are used in this study to describe the topology of the two-layer and two-scale network of human contact. In addition, we also explicitly consider infection time, which represents the number of days an infected individual can transmit disease. The development of an epidemic is normally presented as a curve, with the number of infected individuals plotted against the time step through an epidemic. The dynamic of an epidemic is usually portrayed by three descriptors. These are the number of days for the epidemic to peak, the number of people affected at the peak, and the total number of people affected during the entire epidemic (Keeling 1999, Anderson and May 1992, Ferguson et al. 1997, Bailey 1975). An efficient network leads to an early peak, a high peak, and a large number of people affected during the epidemic. The effect of aforementioned node, link, network structure, and time indices on an epidemic is analyzed through a simulation as described below.

SIMULATION DESIGN

Based on the conceptual discussion above, we present a stochastic approach to evaluating the effect of network topology on the dispersion of infectious diseases. An influenza epidemic is simulated for the analysis. Influenza is chosen because it is readily communicable between individuals. The simulation involves 1000 susceptible individuals in an urban environment over a period of 75 days. These individuals participate in activities at home and most of them at workplaces on a daily basis. The population is assumed closed. That is, there is no birth, death, or migration during the epidemic, and the recovered individuals do not reenter the susceptible pool.

The simulated population follows the two-layer and two-scale network structure outlined in the conceptual framework. Each of the 1000 individuals is assigned to two spaces, a random location in a home space and a random location in a workplace space. The two spaces correspond to the two layers discussed in the conceptual framework. Each location represents a pseudo physical location in the space because in a true physical space, all family members or workplace colleagues would have occupied an identical location. Those individuals who are close to each other are linked into families or workplaces in the respective space. These are the within-group networks described in the conceptual framework. Because an individual may belong to both a family and a workplace, they link the two layers into one network, and these are the between-group networks in the conceptual framework. The average size is three for families and ten for workplaces. The latter is the number of people with whom an individual is in direct contact on a daily basis; thus, it may appear to be smaller than the actual size of a workplace.

The epidemic is simulated with the three sets of indices, namely nodes, links, and network structure. In order to evaluate the effect of each index, alternate values are assigned to the index, while holding other indices constant. For each given value of a given index, 500 realizations are simulated to obtain the average value of the epidemic descriptors, namely the peak date, number of infected at peak, and the total number of infected. For example, if three values are assigned to the index of transmission rate, it takes 500×3 realizations to evaluate the effect of this index. The values for these indices and related settings are described below, organized by (1) nodes, (2) links, (3) network structure, and (4) time.

NODES

For group nodes, we use group size as the primary attribute. Because in this study we keep the total number of connections within the population constant, the ratio of the number of workplace connections to family connections is used as a surrogate for group size. Three ratios, 1:1, 3:1, and 5:1, are used in different simulations to evaluate the effect of group size on the dynamic of an epidemic. For individual nodes, the attributes of an individual include the individual's home and workplace location, health state (susceptible, infected, or recovered), and associated group members. Although the effect of group attribute (group size) is the focus of interest, in actual computation, this attribute is attached to the individual nodes.

LINKS

The direction of a link is assigned from an infected to a susceptible individual. Infection is possible only at the presence of an infected individual on one end of a link and a susceptible individual on the other. The magnitude of a link is represented by the transmission rate of the disease. This value is set to vary from 0.1, 0.3, to 0.5 between simulations. This is to evaluate the effect of transmission rate on the development of an epidemic. A rate of 0.1, for example, means a 10% probability of transmission from an infected to a susceptible individual.

NETWORK STRUCTURE

We use the three indices discussed above to represent network structure: (1) the number of direct links of an individual, (2) the overlap between an individual's family members and coworkers, and (3) the minimum number of links between an infected and a susceptible individual. In this study, the number of direct links of an individual is the sum of family and workplace connections of an individual. This value is set to vary between 10 and 25 with an increment of 5 between simulations. We represent the overlap between family member and coworkers by the covariance between the home locations and workplace locations associated with individuals. The home and workplace locations are represented by their x- and y-coordinates in the corresponding space. Four covariance values, 0, 0.5, 0.8, and 0.99, are used in the simulation. A high covariance corresponds to a high degree of overlap between an individual's family members and coworkers. The minimum number of links between an infected and a susceptible individual is derived from the simulated population.

While altering the value of each index, other indices are held constant. The default values for these indices are set as follows: workplace to family connection ratio = 3:1, transmission rate = 0.1, average number of direct links of a node = 12, covariance of spatial locations between home and workplace spaces = 0.5, length of latent period = 1 day, and length of infectious period = 3 days. The figures displayed below represent the average of the 500 simulations that represents the overall trend in the simulated results.

Figures 2a–2c display one of the simulated populations. The three graphs show the simulated 1000 individuals, their locations in the family or workplace space, and the links between an individual and his/her family members or coworkers. The illustration for the number of direct links of an individual, to his/her family members or coworkers, is straightforward. The interconnection between family members and workplace colleagues is illustrated through different covariance values between the two spaces. With a low covariance between the two spaces, the two sets of locations associated with an individual differ greatly. The members of a family are widely dispersed in the workplace space. This indicates that the family members work at diverse places and interact with different groups of people at daytime. With a high covariance, the two sets of locations overlap greatly, and the workplace locations are clustered tightly. This indicates that the family members interact largely with themselves during both daytime and evening. When the family and workplace links are displayed simultaneously in figure 3, the difference in network structure is apparent. The network with a lower covariance shows a much more outreaching pattern outside a family than the one with a high covariance. The latter shows high interconnection within clusters and less connection between clusters. This difference in network structure is expected to have impact on the dispersion of infectious diseases. Note that the spaces are simulated in a circular shape. This is to assess distance between a first infected individual, who would be placed in the center of the space, to any susceptible individuals in the same space.

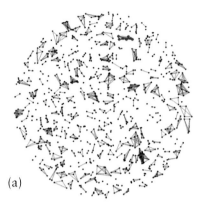

(a)

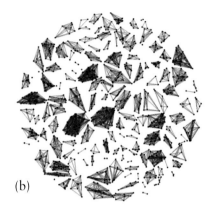

(b)

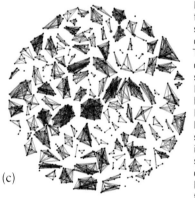

(c)

Figure 2. An illustration of the simulated 1000 individuals, the links between them in their home and workplace spaces, and links between the two spaces. (a) Locations of 1000 simulated individuals in the pseudo home space. The linked individuals form families, and the individuals of one family are highlighted in red. (b) Locations of the same 1000 individuals in the workplace space. The linked individuals indicate workplaces. Because the home space shown in (a) and this workplace space are linked with a low covariance = 0, the individuals of the highlighted family are widely dispersed in the workplace space. (c) Locations of the same 1000 individuals in another workplace space. This time, the home space and the workplace space are linked with a high covariance = 0.99. Consequently, the individuals of the highlighted family are located close to each other and to their locations in the home space.

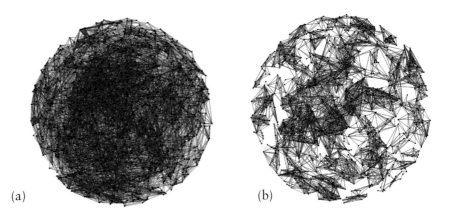

(a)   (b)

Figure 3. The family and workplace links of the 1000 individuals shown in the home space. Family links are in red, and workplace links are in gray. (a) Covariance = 0.8 between locations of the home space and the workplace space. (b) Covariance = 0.99 between locations of the home space and the workplace space. The network of lower covariance in (a) shows an outreaching pattern outside a family. The network of a high covariance in (b) shows a high degree of interconnection within clusters while a lesser degree of connection between clusters.

TIME

This is presented as the length of infectious period for an individual. Three lengths are used, 2 days, 4 days, and 8 days, in the simulation to evaluate the effect of length of infectious period. In addition, the simulation uses a latent period of one day.

When an epidemic begins, one infected individual is introduced into the center of the home space. The infection of the rest of population is simulated in three operational procedures. First, the family members and coworkers of the first infected individual are identified. Second, certain family and workplace members are assigned an infected state using a Monte Carlo process for a given transmission rate. Third, the individuals linked to these infected are identified, and some of them are assigned an infected state. The simulation continues through the entire population.

EFFECTS OF NETWORK TOPOLOGY

The development of the influenza epidemic is presented as an epidemic curve, with the number of infected individuals plotted against the time step through the epidemic. Specifically, the temporal dynamics of the epidemic are described by the number of days for the epidemic to peak, the number of infected individuals at the peak time, and the total number of individuals infected during the epidemic. The latter is expressed as individual*day, or the total area under the epidemic curve. The effect of the six indices representing node and link attributes and network structure on the dynamics of an epidemic is described in the following sections.

EFFECTS OF NODE ATTRIBUTE.

Figure 4 shows the effect of group size, expressed as the ratio of workplace connections to family connections, on the development of an epidemic. Each curve represents a simulated epidemic with a specific workplace/family ratio (1:1, 3:1, and 5:1). With a greater ratio, the epidemic peaks later with a lower peak and a lesser magnitude of individual*day during the epidemic. This is because small families become the bottleneck in the dispersion of disease. The susceptible pool quickly exhausts in a small family, thus preventing further dispersion of disease in the network. Consequently, the spread of disease largely depends on the workplace connections. Thus, it takes longer for the epidemic to peak and decline. With such an inefficient network, fewer individuals are infected at the peak time and throughout the entire epidemic.

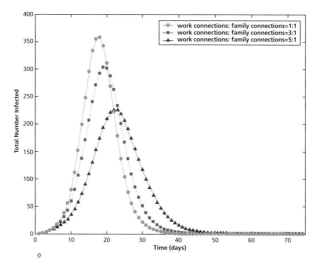

Figure 4. An illustration of the effect of group size on an epidemic. The group size is expressed as the ratio of the number of workplace connections to family connections of an individual. The vertical axis represents the number of infected individuals, and the horizontal axis represents the time step of an epidemic in days. The three curves represent the temporal dynamic of an epidemic with the workplace/family connection ratio = 1:1, 3:1, and 5:1, respectively.

EFFECTS OF LINK MAGNITUDE

Figure 5 illustrates the effect of transmission rate on an epidemic. Three epidemic curves are displayed with transmission rates of 0.1, 0.3, and 05, respectively. The effect is obvious, and the explanation is straightforward. A high transmission rate causes a great number of people to be infected soon after the first infection is introduced into the population. This leads to an early and high peak, an early decline, and a great number of people affected during the epidemic. The opposite is true when the transmission rate is low, and the epidemic may not even develop in the case of transmission rate = 0.1.

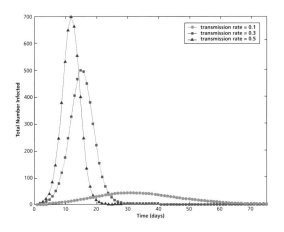

Figure 5. An illustration of the effect of transmission rate on an epidemic with the transmission rate = 0.1, 0.3, and 0.5, respectively.

EFFECT OF NETWORK STRUCTURE—NUMBER OF LINKS

Figure 6 shows the effect of the number of direct links of an individual. Similar to the effect of transmission rate, the more direct links an individual has, the greater number of individuals can be infected early in an epidemic. Thus, the epidemic tends to peak early, and a great number of people are affected at the peak time. Subsequently, a great number of people are affected throughout the epidemic. In the meantime, the epidemic tends to decline early because the susceptible pool exhausts quickly after the epidemic begins.

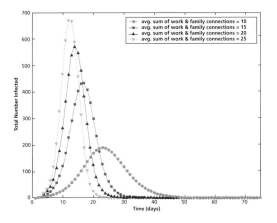

Figure 6. An illustration of the effect of the number of direct links of an individual on an epidemic. The number of direct links is the sum of family and workplace connections of an individual. The four curves show the effect of the number of links when its value = 10, 15, 20, and 25, respectively.

EFFECT OF NETWORK STRUCTURE—INTERCONNECTION

Figure 7 displays the effect of overlap between family members and coworkers. A great degree of overlap between the two groups (a high covariance) forms a network with many highly interconnected clusters but modest connections between these clusters (fig. 2). The dispersion of disease, once it reaches a group, can quickly affect all members in the group, but the between-group dispersion in such a network is inefficient because the infected clusters are relatively isolated. This effect is similar to that of the workplace/family connection ratio, resulting in a late and low peak and a lower total number of people affected.

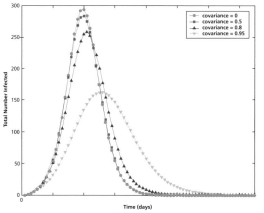

Figure 7. An illustration of the effect of overlap between family members and coworkers associated with an individual. The overlap is represented by covariance of locations between the individual's home space and workplace space. The four curves represent the dynamics of an epidemic when the covariance = 0, 0.5, 0.8, and 0.95, respectively.

EFFECT OF NETWORK STRUCTURE—SHORTEST PATH

Figures 8a and 8b demonstrate the effect of shortest contact path on the development of an epidemic, specifically, whether those individuals who have shorter contact paths to an infected individual can be infected earlier. Figure 8a shows the 1000 individuals in their home space with the first infected individual at the center of the space. Those individuals who have short paths to the infected individual and are located close to the center are family ties to the infected. Those who have short paths but are far away from the infected individual are the workplace ties. Figure 8b shows that all those who are infected early indeed have shorter paths than others do to the infected individual.

259

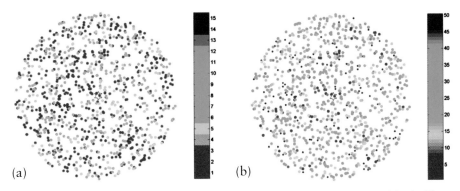

Figure 8. An illustration of the effect of shortest path between individuals on an epidemic. The 1000 individuals are in their home space with the first infected individual at the center of the space, indicated by a star. (a) The color scheme indicates the length of the shortest path, expressed as the number of links along a path, between an individual to the infected one. (b) The color scheme indicates the number of days for an individual to be infected. The small dark dots represent those who are not infected during an epidemic.

EFFECT OF LENGTH OF INFECTIOUS PERIOD

Figure 9 exhibits the effect of length of infectious period. Similar to the effects of number of direct links and transmission rate, an extended infectious period increases the number of infected individuals within a short time period. This leads to an early and high epidemic peak and a great number of people affected.

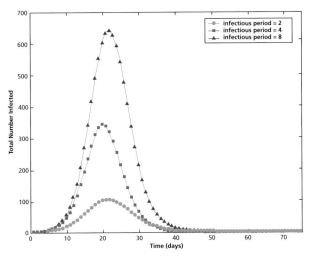

Figure 9. An illustration of the effect of length of infectious period on an epidemic with the length = 2, 4, and 8 days, respectively.

Results of the analysis can be summarized as follows. When holding all other indices constant, a lower ratio of workplace to family connections, a greater transmission rate, a greater number of direct links of an individual, a lower degree of interconnection, and a shorter path between individuals lead to a rapid development of an epidemic. Based on the analysis of individual indices, the health outcome of any combinations of these indices can be readily evaluated.

DESIGN PRINCIPLES FOR A WORKING MODEL

For analytical purposes, the simulation presented above is implemented in MATLAB. For a working model, the operational functions described in the *Simulation design* section can be implemented using a programming language in order to model a large number of individuals. The population, the network of contact, and network topology indices for the working model can be extracted from GIS and other data.

The basic design of such a model uses an object-oriented approach. That is, individuals are represented as objects, and each may have several attributes and behavior. Families and workplaces may be represented as separate object classes or attributes of individuals. To support the individual-based and spatially explicit principle, the attributes and behavior for an individual may include the following:

Attributes: Age: children, elderly, other adults at risk and associated transmission rate.

Occupation: With or without outside-group interaction.

Infection status: latent, infected, and recovered.

Location: home, workplace, and their associated spatial coordinates.

Time: nighttime, daytime, and associated time step.

Connections: family identification and associated family members, and workplace identification and associated coworkers.

Behaviors: Interaction: between- and within-group interactions, full or partial mix.

Infection and recovery.

Events: Receipt of infection, emission of infectious material, and end of emission.

Values of most of these attributes can be estimated from census data, such as TIGER data for the United States, and other sources of data. For example, the size, age composition, and locations of families and workplaces can be estimated from census data and other available data. Using the estimated location, street data, and travel time between home and workplace provided in the census data, the connection between families and workplaces can be estimated. The mixing pattern within a group and interaction between groups can be estimated according to the population statistics. Some of these estimations are not straightforward and may require either assumptions or further research. It is possible, of course, to link the outputs from MATLAB to various GIS using a loose coupling of outputs and inputs although stronger couplings can be considered. Linking mathematically intensive processes to GIS is in its infancy although, as many other chapters in this book show, there is rapid progress being made in effecting such coupling, as for example in the recent linking of the agent-based modeling languages RePast to ArcGIS.

CONCLUSIONS

We present a stochastic approach to examining the effect of network topology of human contact on spatial and temporal dispersion of infectious disease. This approach is based on an individual-based and spatially explicit conceptual framework. Discrete individuals and their locations in a home space and a workplace space are explicitly represented through a two-layer and two-scale network. The spread of infectious diseases depends on the properties and structure of the network, represented by six indices.

Various combinations of these indices may characterize communities of different family and workplace compositions and connections. An understanding of these effects helps foresee the spatial and temporal dispersion patterns of health threats in different communities and focus preventive measures on communities at high risk. For example, high priority may be given to communities that are characterized by large family size, diverse workplaces in a family, and a large number of connections of family members.

The individual-based and spatially explicit conceptual framework and the stochastic approach of exploring the effect of network show great promise to the study of population health. For future applications, the basic model outlined in this chapter can be extended to represent additional aspects of human contact, for example, the link between families and between workplaces. We hope that our work can stimulate further discussions of this approach and further development of individual-based epidemiology models.

ACKNOWLEDGMENTS

This research was funded in part by the National Institute of Environmental Health Sciences, National Institute of Health under Award No. R01 ES09816-01.

REFERENCES

Adams, L. A., D. C. Barth-Jones, S. E. Chick, and J. S. Koopman. 1998. Simulations to evaluate HIV vaccine trial designs. *Simulation* 71: 228–41.

Albert, R., H. Jeong, and A. Barabási. 2000. Error and attack tolerance of complex networks. *Nature* 406: 378–82.

Amrhein, C. G., and R. D. MacKinnon. 1988. A micro-simulation model of a spatial labor market. *Annals of the Association of American Geographers* 78: 112–31.

Anderson, R. M., and R. M. May. 1992. *Infectious diseases of humans: Dynamics and control.* New York: Oxford University Press.

Bailey, N. T. J. 1975. *The mathematical theory of infectious diseases and its applications.* New York: Hafner Press.

Benenson, I., I. Omer, and E. Hatna. 2002. Entity-based modeling of urban residential dynamics: The case of Yaffo, Tel Aviv. *Environment and Planning B* 29: 491–512.

Bian, L. 2000. Object-oriented representation for modeling mobile objects in an aquatic environment. *International Journal of Geographical Information Science* 14: 603–23.

———. 2004. A conceptual framework for an individual-based spatially explicit epidemiological model. *Environment and Planning B* 31: 381–95.

Bousquet, F., C. LePage, I. Bakam, and A. Takfoyan. 2001. Multiagent simulations of hunting wild meat in a village in eastern Cameroon. *Ecological Modeling* 138: 331–46.

Cliff, A. D., P. Haggett, J. K. Ord, and G. R. Versey. 1981. *Spatial diffusion: An historical geography of epidemics in an island community.* New York: Cambridge University Press.

Cliff, A. D., and P. Haggett. 1990. Epidemic control and critical community size: Spatial aspects of eliminating communicable diseases in human populations. In *Spatial epidemiology,* ed. R. W. Thomas. London Papers in Regional Science 21: 93–110. London: Pion.

Cliff, A. D., P. Haggett, and M. R. Smallman-Raynor. 2000. *Island epidemics.* New York: Oxford University Press.

DeAngelis, D. L., and L. J. Gross, eds. 1992. *Individual-based models and approaches in ecology: Populations, communities, and ecosystems.* New York: Chapman and Hall.

Ferguson, N. M., R. M. May, and R. M. Anderson. 1997. Measles: Persistence and synchronicity in disease dynamics. In *Spatial ecology,* ed. D. Tilman and P. Kareiva, 137–57. Princeton: Princeton University Press.

Ferguson, N. M., C. A. Donnelly, and R. M. Anderson. 2001. The foot-and-mouth epidemic in Great Britain: Pattern of spread and impact of interventions. *Science* 292: 1155–60.

Ghani, A. C., J. Swinton, and G. P. Garnett. 1997. The role of sexual partnership networks in the epidemiology of gonorrhea. *Sexually Transmitted Diseases* 24: 45–56.

Gilbert, N., and R. Conte, eds. 1995. Artificial societies: The computer simulation of social life. London: UCL Press.

Gilbert, N., and J. Doran, eds. 1994. Simulating societies: The computer simulation of social phenomena. London: UCL Press.

Grenfell, B., and J. Harwood. 1997. (Meta) population dynamics of infectious diseases. *TREE* 12: 395–99.

Hägerstrand, T. 1970. What about people in regional science? *Papers of the Regional Science Association* 24: 7–21.

Holmes, E. E. 1997. Basic epidemiological concepts in a spatial context. In *Spatial ecology*, ed. D. Tilman and P. Kareiva, 111–36. Princeton: Princeton University Press.

Judson, O. P. 1994. The rise of the individual-based model in ecology. *TREE* 9: 9–14.

Keeling, M. J., 1999. The effects of local spatial structure on epidemiological invasions. *Proceedings of the Royal Society of London B* 266: 859–67.

———. 2000. Metapopulation moments: Coupling, stochasticity and persistence. *Journal of Animal Ecology* 69: 725–36.

Kermack, W. O., and A. G. McKendrick. 1927. A contribution to the mathematical theory of epidemics. *Proceedings of the Royal Society of London A* 115: 700–21.

Koopman, J., and J. Lynch. 1999. Individual causal models and population system models in epidemiology. *American Journal of Public Health* 89: 1170–4.

Kretzschmar, M., and M. Morris. 1996. Measures of concurrency in networks and the spread of infectious disease. *Mathematical Biology* 133: 165–95.

Kwan, M. 1999. Gender and individual access to urban opportunities: A study using space–time measures. *Professional Geographer* 51: 210–27.

Lake, M. W. 2000. MAGICAL computer simulation of mesolithic foraging. In *Dynamics in human and primate societies*, ed. T. A. Kohler and G. J. Gumerman, 107–43. New York: Oxford University Press.

Lenntorp, B. 1978. A time-geographic simulation model of individual activity programmes. In *Human activity and time geography*, ed. T. Carlstein, D. Parkes, and N. Thrift, 162–80. New York: John Wiley and Sons.

Lloyd, A. 1995. The coupled logistic map: A simple model for the effects of spatial heterogeneity on population dynamics. *Journal of Theoretical Biology* 173: 217–30.

Löytönen, M. 1998. Time geography, health and GIS. In *GIS and health*, ed. A. C. Gatrell and M. Löytönen, 97–110. London: Taylor & Francis.

Miller, H. J. 2005. A measurement theory for time geography. *Geographical Analysis* 37: 17–45.

Parker, D. C., S. M. Manson, M. A. Janssen, M. J. Hoffmann, and P. Deadman. 2003. Multi-agent systems for the simulation of land-use and land-cover change: A review. *Annals of the Association of American Geographers* 93: 314–37.

Pred, A. 1977. The choreography of existence: Comments on Hagerstrand's time geography and its usefulness. *Economic Geography* 53: 207–21.

Rhodes, C. J., and R. M. Anderson. 1997. Epidemic threshold and vaccination in a lattice model of disease spread. *Theoretical Population Biology* 52: 101–18.

Schenzle, D. 1984. An age-structured model for pre- and post-vaccination measles transmission. *IMA Journal of Mathematics Applied in Medicine and Biology* 1: 169–91.

Szymanski, B. W., and T. Caraco. 1994. Spatial analysis of vector-borne disease: A four-species model. *Evolutionary Ecology* 8: 299–314.

Torres-Sorando, L., and D. J. Rodriguez. 1997. Models of spatio-temporal dynamics in malaria. *Ecological Modeling* 104: 231–40.

Tyler, J. A., and K. A. Rose. 1994. Individual variability and spatial heterogeneity in fish population models. *Reviews in Fish Biology and Fisheries* 4: 91–123.

van der Ploeg, C. P. B., C. Van Vliet, S. J. De Vlas, J. O. Ndinya-Achola, L. Fransen, G. J. Van Oortmarssen, and J. D. F. Habbema. 1998. STDSIM: A microsimulation model for decision support in STD control. *Interfaces* 28: 84–100.

Watts, D. J., and S. H. Strogatz. 1998. Collective dynamics of "small-world" networks. *Nature* 393: 440–2.

Welch, G., S. E. Chick, and J. S. Koopman. 1998. Effects of concurrent partnerships and sex-act rate on gonorrhea prevalence. *Simulation* 71: 242–9.

Westvelt, J. D., and L. D. Hopkins. 1999. Modeling mobile individuals in dynamic landscapes. *International Journal of Geographical Information Science* 13: 191–208.

Chapter 13

The Use of GIS in Transport Modeling

THOMAS ISRAELSEN AND RASMUS DYHR FREDERIKSEN

RAPIDIS

CHARLOTTENLUND, DENMARK

ABSTRACT

THIS CHAPTER DESCRIBES the structure of the typical transport modeling process, emphasizing how the four-step model based on trip generation, distribution, modal split, and assignment can be interfaced with geographical information systems technology. Various limits on the degree to which such models can be coupled to GIS are spelled out, but the use of contemporary GIS software, such as ArcGIS, makes it now possible to use the ModelBuilder functions within the suite to develop quite sophisticated transport models.

INTRODUCTION

Transport models are used for a wide range of purposes, from local traffic planning to examining infrastructure projects at a national level, as parts of other models (for instance, land-use models), and for providing the basis for evaluating the environmental impacts of traffic. Traditionally, transport modeling has been caried out using commercial stand-alone packages, custom software, or a mix of both, with GIS sometimes used not at all or for various supporting tasks (handling data, visualizing results, performing postcalculation analysis). In the terminology of various contributions in this book, hitherto, GIS has been loosely coupled to transport models. These models are also close in structure to those discussed by Wegener (2005, this volume), and many of the same issues involving their coupling to GIS arise in this context too.

This chapter focuses on how GIS has been used in conjunction with transport models and how this has changed and will continue to change as GIS technology evolves. We will deal with five main topics, beginning with definitions of what a transport model is, providing an overview and discussion of usage. We will then focus on how transport modeling work is carried out and what tools are necessary for this, how this work been done traditionally and how GIS has been used, what the options are currently and in the future, finishing with a summary of the key challenges that define the use of GIS in transport modeling.

DEFINING A TRANSPORT MODEL

A detailed definition of a *transport model* is beyond the scope of this chapter. Interested readers are therefore referred to the literature of the field, and a particularly good summary is contained in the book *Modelling Transport* by Ortuzar and Willumsen (2001). It is sufficient to say that a transport model is typically a mathematical model of a certain geographical area and the transportation system in this area, focusing on how traffic is generated in each subarea of the model, how it is distributed between origins and destinations of trips, and how it is assigned to the various networks that enable traffic to move between different origins and destinations. The size of the model area, the level of detail of the model, and the complexity of the mathematics involved can all vary substantially, depending on the purpose of the specific transport model.

In practical terms, the use of a transport model usually involves data preparation and data management, a number of calculation modules, and a dataflow between these calculation modules. In the following section, the overall structure of a transport model is discussed, while the actual tasks and tools involved in the practical use of a transport model are discussed below.

TYPICAL USES

In general, transport models are used to support planning and decision making in the field of transport. Good examples of their use and application are:

• Evaluating the short-term impact of a relatively simple infrastructure change (e.g., adding lanes to a highway or expanding an intersection).

- Producing long-term prognoses of travel demand and passenger flows, using a set of scenarios which describe varying assumptions regarding economic development, land use, demographic developments, changes to the transport system, etc.

- Using the output of a transport model as the basis of an environmental impact study (e.g., using modeled traffic flows as input to a noise propagation model).

- As an aid helping to evaluate the impact of proposed policy changes (e.g., the consequences of introducing road pricing).

Transport models for most of these purposes are developed at many different scales—from cities of 20,000 inhabitants, say, to major metropolitan areas of millions. In the last two decades, there has also been a move to develop national transport models. The challenges in having efficient working software for transport models are greatest with the larger models due to, among other things, the large amounts and many types of data used. For this reason, the main focus of this chapter will be on larger scale models.

In general, transport models have a wide range of uses and therefore, also vary greatly in complexity and data requirements. A good example of the scale of the traffic zoning systems and the public transport system network used for a large-scale transport model of the Copenhagen area is shown in figure 1 where the intensity of color shows accessibility by public transportation measured by travel time to the center of the city.

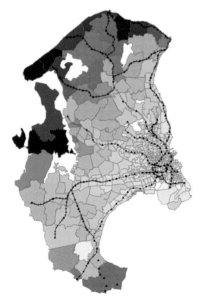

Figure 1. A large-scale transport model for the Copenhagen area, showing public transport travel times from the center of the city.

VARIOUS TYPES OF TRANSPORT MODELS

In the general field of transport modeling, a number of more narrowly focused models are used to model specific situations. Most transport models are built by combining such focused models in appropriate ways, and examples include:

- Linear regression models for estimating the amount of traffic generated by households.

- Gravity-style models for modeling travel patterns between zones, which is referred to as trip distribution.

- Logit- or probit-based choice models for choosing between alternative travel modes of travel, which are often combined with the gravity models used to allocate trips between origins and destinations.

- Static assignment models for calculating average network flows in a transportation system (e.g., a street network or a public transport system).

- Dynamic assignment models for simulating precise trips of every individual automobile on the streets and in the intersections of the study area, often embodying capacity constraints posed by congestion on the network.

The overall trend has been that most of the submodels used in transport models were originally implemented using heuristic approaches that have over time been replaced by more rigorous approaches. These models are based on a wide range of mathematical techniques, such as discrete choice modeling as developed in microeconomic theory, graph theory which is associated with network representation, and travel activity modeling which relates household behavior to time and space budgets for travel demand.

AN EXAMPLE

A fairly simple and widely used type of transport model is the four-step model, used to model the travel patterns and routes of travelers in an area (Banister 2002). The following is an overview of what a specific transport model might look like. The four-step model is used as an example and consists of a series of four steps that are carried out sequentially and often subject to iteration so that a balance between generation, distribution, modal split, and traffic assignment to the network is struck. In this overview, our focus is on the structure of the model, i.e., on what data and calculation modules are involved and the data flow between modules, and less on the actual work being done when using a transport model, for instance, gathering and preparing data.

The input data

The input data necessary to describe the area to be modeled can roughly be divided into the following elements:

- Socioeconomic data

- Transportation networks

- Travel patterns and descriptions of travelers' preferences

Typically, the study area is described in an aggregated manner, by dividing the area into a number of model zones. Socioeconomic data, such as number of inhabitants, number of workplaces, distribution of income among inhabitants, etc., is then easily described for each model zone. A good example of such data is pictured in the ArcMap™ representation in figure 2.

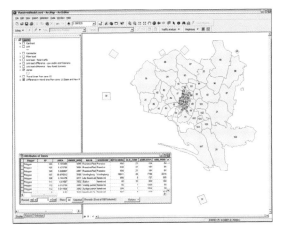

Figure 2. An area has been divided into a number of model zones.

Which *transportation networks* are included in a transport model and at what level of detail usually varies according to the intended use of the model and/ or other constraints (budget, availability of data). In some cases, it is only necessary to include the road networks (if, for instance, only car travelers' behavior is of interest and there is no significant public transport alternatives in the area), while in other cases road, public transportation, pedestrian, and cycle networks might be included in great detail. The example of figure 2 is shown in figure 3 with the road network illustrated.

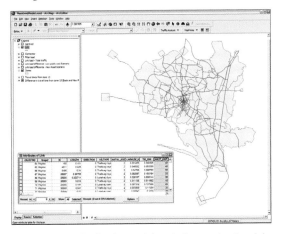

Figure 3. For this simple model, only the road network is used.

Ideally, if available, a description of existing *travel patterns* (in the form of zone-to-zone trip matrices) can also be included in the model. Again, determined by needs and constraints, this data can be detailed in varying degrees. For instance, the population of travelers might be segmented into groups for more detailed purposes of travel (home–work travelers, business-related travels, leisure, etc.) or divided into separate sets of data for distinct time periods (for instance, one travel pattern for the morning rush hour and one for the rest of the day, depending on what period of time is being modeled, e.g., a normal workday). These are usually represented as an origin and destinations matrix as we show in figure 4.

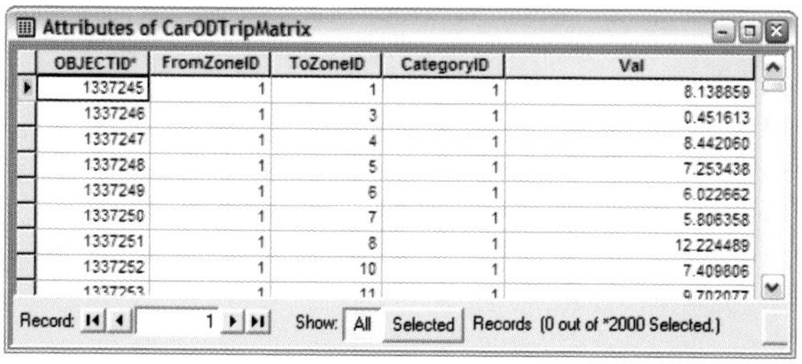
Attributes of CarODTripMatrix

OBJECTID*	FromZoneID	ToZoneID	CategoryID	Val
1337245	1	1	1	8.138859
1337246	1	3	1	0.451613
1337247	1	4	1	8.442060
1337248	1	5	1	7.253438
1337249	1	6	1	6.022662
1337250	1	7	1	5.806358
1337251	1	8	1	12.224489
1337252	1	10	1	7.409806
1337253	1	11	1	9.702077

Record: 1 Show: All Selected Records (0 out of *2000 Selected.)

Figure 4. Travel patterns described as a zone-to-zone matrix.

Finally, *travelers' preferences* (for transportation mode, for choice of route, etc.) need to be established and described.

The calculation modules

The calculation modules used in a typical four-step model either have to do with modeling *travel demand* or *traffic assignment*. The modules involved in modeling *travel demand* produce data representing travel patterns (trip matrices). These trip matrices are then in turn used by *traffic assignment* modules which use the trip matrices in combination with the relevant transportation networks to calculate the routes of all travelers and the resulting traffic flows (network loads).

Travel demand is modeled by the first three steps in a classic four-step model:

- *Trip Generation*—determining the overall demand for transport.
- *Trip Distribution*—determining the origins and destinations of the trips.
- *Modal Split*—determining the split between available transport modes of the generated and distributed trips.
- *Assignment*—modeling the route choices made by travelers, thereby converting the zone-to-zone trip matrices into network flows.

Trip Generation involves the calculation of the total number of trips generated and attracted by an analysis zone. This is often done by using socioeconomic variables, such as average number of residents per household, total number of workplaces, car ownership, income levels, etc., and combining these linearly with a set of model parameters (based on surveys and analysis of the area being modeled). The level of detail used can vary a lot (e.g., should an average income per resident be used or should incomes be divided into a number of categories?). The output is essentially two numbers per zone: the number of trips generated by the zone and the number of trips attracted to the zone.

Trip Distribution transforms the generations and attractions from the previous step into trip matrices. A classic approach to doing this is using a *gravity model,* that is, distributing the trips as a function of travel costs so that most trips happen between zones that are close. The function is calibrated using surveys and is usually exponential (i.e., it looks like the formula for gravitational attraction).

Modal Split is the process of splitting the trip matrices (number of trips from zone-to-zone) into a number of submatrices: one for each of the modes of transport being modeled (usually car, often transit, perhaps bike/walk). For each zone-to-zone pair, the total number of travelers is split into separate modes, based on how expensive (or competitive) the available modes of transportation are, relative to each other. This is done based on a set of parameters, again often established using surveys from the area being modeled. The choice of transport mode is a *discrete choice* problem, a type of problem very often modeled using *logit* models.

Assignment is performed using assignment models. Assignment models calculate network flows and can vary a lot in complexity, but in their most basic form, they involve determining the paths taken by travelers between each zone pair in the relevant transportation network and then adding *(assigning)* the traffic described in the relevant trip matrix to each of the links in these paths. As mentioned above, a number of transportation networks (and related sets of trip matrices) might be used in the transport model, thus requiring the use of a number of assignment models.

Data flow in models
Figure 5 below shows the modeling flow in the classic four-step model. Performing the complete calculations of a transport model usually involves among other things:

- a lot of data manipulation between calculation modules (This must of course be performed correctly.);
- the handling of both input data and various kinds of temporary data; and
- the handling and storage of the various calculation results.

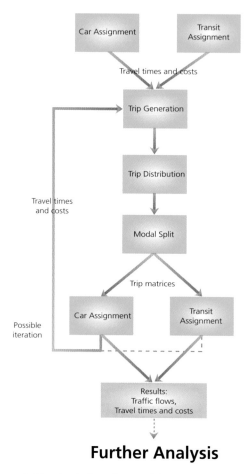

Further Analysis

Figure 5. The classic four-step model.

TOOLS NEEDED FOR A
COMPLETE TRANSPORT
MODELING STUDY

This section will attempt to identify the key software tools which are necessary in transport modeling studies. The tools are grouped into five major categories, each of which represents a different set of tasks or work processes in a modeling study:

- Editing Data
- Scenario Management and Comparison
- Control of Modeling Flow
- Presentation
- Storage and Integration

Additional calibration and calculation tools were discussed briefly in the previous section.

EDITING DATA

It is more often than not the case that editing data takes up more time than any other activity in a transport modeling study. This is due to the fact that most studies involve examining hypothetical scenarios. In order to be able to apply a model to such a scenario, the modeler first has to create a dataset representing the scenario. This is usually done by starting from another scenario which resembles what is needed or from a base scenario representing the present-day situation. Although it might be simple to describe the required scenario textually, the task of actually creating the necessary datasets can, in many cases, be very significant. This is more likely to be the case if the underlying model works on a detailed level. There are a number of ways in which one might categorize editing processes:

Creating the base scenario versus creating hypothetical scenarios

Creating the base scenario is mostly about compiling the data needed for modeling from a variety of different sources. Hence a lot of conversion work is needed. These conversions can be between different data formats, different levels of detail, or different times of collection (maybe the traffic counts in county A were done in one year and those in county B were done in another. In this case, they might need to be converted to the same year). In contrast, creating a hypothetical scenario is mostly about taking an existing dataset and modifying it to fit the requirements for the desired scenario. While this sounds simpler than creating the base scenario, it can easily be more time consuming. As an example, the study might require many hypothetical scenarios, and creating each scenario might also involve a lot of work, which often happens when public transport is involved.

Different types of data

Typical editing efforts for some of the most frequently used types of data are described here.

Street networks are essential for the vast majority of transport models. Although very high-quality street networks are commercially or freely available for most study areas, there is still usually a lot of work put into editing street networks. There are a few reasons for this:

- Existing street networks frequently do not include all the attribute data needed for transport modeling, so the missing data has to be acquired from another source and somehow transferred to the street network.
- For transport modeling purposes, it is usually desirable to include only those street segments in the network which play a significant role in the transport system. Commercial street networks generally include many more street segments (dirt roads, residential roads, etc). If such unnecessary street segments can be excluded, running times for various calculation tools will very often drop significantly.

The main challenges for street network editing tools are:

- To allow users to easily and intuitively make the changes they want.
- To have good editing performance.
- To enable users and other tools to easily query the network for connectivity information (what is connected to what).

Zone data. Usually transport models divide their study area into analysis zones on which they represent various socioeconomic data and possibly also land-use data. As such, zone-level data is essential for transport models. It is, however, usually not very difficult to edit.

Trip matrices relate to analysis zones and describe travel patterns within the study area. Usually the numbers of rows and columns in a trip matrix will equal the number of analysis zones in the study area. Trip matrices are rarely edited manually, but they do need to be viewed easily for quality assurance purposes.

Public transport. When attempting to include public transport in transport models, it is essential to have access to competent editing tools designed specifically for this purpose. This is due to the fact that public transport systems are inherently complex. Thus the data models which represent them tend to also be complex. Data models for public transport systems usually have relationships to infrastructure networks (roads for buses and railroad tracks for railroads), so editing tools should be able to manage these relationships efficiently.

Another challenge is to minimize the number of times users have to enter the same information. For example, a study area might have a large number of buses using the same sequence of streets in the same manner (stops in the same places, identical driving times). Users should be able to easily reuse such data. Editing tools for public transport data should be able to operate efficiently on different levels of detail as different users have different requirements for this. Some users need to be able to model the precise location of bus stops along streets while it is sufficient for other users to have bus stops always located at street intersections. Some users need to model every single departure from every single stop at precise times while other users can manage with just defining driving times between stops and general frequencies for lines.

SCENARIO MANAGEMENT AND COMPARISON

Most transport modeling studies examine a number of alternative scenarios. As a minimum, modelers need to have access to a tool which allows them to manage all the different datasets which constitute a scenario (like trip matrices, road network, transit network, and zonal data) as a unit and do things like copy scenarios, create new scenarios, delete scenarios, etc. It is also essential that it is easy for modelers to compare scenarios. This goes both for model input and model output and on a detailed and aggregate level. It can further be of benefit to modelers to be able have a form of connection between scenarios. This is relevant since scenarios in most models share the great majority of data (probably over 90%). Consequently, if modelers find data errors, they are quite likely to exist in many scenarios or every scenario. Thus it would be a great benefit for users to need to fix the error only once.

CONTROL OF MODELING FLOW

Most transport models are actually built from a combination of specific calculation tools. In other words, modelers usually need to execute a number of calculation tools in order to run their model for a specific scenario. This has to be done in the correct order, and data has to be properly transferred between the different calculation tools. Depending on the complexity of the model, the way in which the individual calculation tools need to work together can be quite simple or quite complex; hence, modelers tend to need a tool to manage the overall flow in the model. Some of the things such management tools take care of are:

- Running calculation tools in the proper order
- Transferring data between individual calculation tools
- Cleaning up intermediate results
- Providing feedback during a model run
- Allowing users to gracefully cancel a model run
- Allowing modelers to configure certain elements of the model

PRESENTATION

It is vital, for the quality assurance work that modelers do, to be able to present input data as well as results for transport models in a geographical view which highlights precisely the aspect that the modeler is interested in. This means that modelers need flexible and customizable presentation tools. In addition to quality assurance use, geographical presentation capabilities are also vital for modelers to be able to present model results to their customers.

STORAGE AND INTEGRATION

Transport models do not exist in vacuums. On the contrary, they are usually closely integrated with numerous other activities which organizations that employ transport models also engage in. This integration typically occurs in one of two ways:

- Data for base scenarios is acquired from a wide range of different sources, such as previous transport modeling projects, mapping or cartography departments, and public transport authorities and operators.
- The results from transport models are used in several other models. Some of these models are very tightly integrated with the transport model and actually need to be run right away for every transport model scenario run in order to properly evaluate the consequences of the scenario. Other models are less tightly integrated. For example, the models discussed by Wegner (2005, this volume) and by Batty and Xie (2005, this volume) can be interfaced with transport models to a greater or lesser degree, and the

database models of the planning system proposed by Hopkins, Kaza, and Pallathucheril (2005, this volume) is also adapted to take such transport models as one of its critical modules.

In order for modelers to be able to integrate transport models with various other models and systems, transport modeling tools need to support such integration. The most obvious and useful way to accomplish this is by having modeling tools support industry-standard data storage, such as relational databases or XML or text files with very simple formats (comma-separated values, for instance). Tools can support these formats either by providing import and export capabilities or by using these formats as the native data storage. From an integration standpoint, the latter is by far the preferred solution.

TRADITIONAL TRANSPORT MODELING

Traditionally, transport models were either custom built or implemented using a black-box-style software package or maybe (usually at great pains) a combination of the two. In neither case did GIS play any significant role. Some important reasons for the lack of integration were:

- The vendors which offered commercial modeling packages had not yet responded to the demand for GIS-like functionality in their products.
- The possibilities for getting data in and out of commercial tools were limited and cumbersome, so it was difficult to use the combination of a modeling package for calculations and a GIS for display.
- Although GIS packages had rich features for data exchange, it was difficult or impossible to integrate new models and functionality into their frameworks. This prevented modelers from building models based on GIS packages.

CURRENT OPTIONS

Some of the approaches to selecting a combination of software tools for building transport models are described below. They are certainly not the only ones and maybe even not the most common ones, but they are very illustrative of the options available to modelers.

USING OFF-THE-SHELF TRANSPORT MODELING PACKAGES

Firms like Caliper, INRO, Citilabs, and Ptv make software packages designed to handle all the requirements in transport modeling (TransCAD®, Emme/2®, Cube™, and Visum™ respectively). These packages are the most widely used out-of-the-box solutions for transport modeling and are, as such, representative of what is currently available. The following section is a discussion of how well the available packages support the various aspects of building and using transport models. Information about these models can be derived from the following Web sites:

Emme/2: www.inro.ca/en/products/emme2/e2brengl.pdf

TransCAD: www.caliper.com/TCTravelDemand.htm

Cube: www.citilabs.com/voyager/index.html

Visum: www.english.ptv.de/cgi-bin/traffic/traf_visum.pl

In general, all of the packages use some kind of fixed data model supported by a visual interface and various editing tools. The quality of the interface and tools varies to a surprising degree, from the very simple to the fairly sophisticated GIS-like. It is clearly an advantage for the user that the interfaces, editing tools, and implemented data models are all focused on handling the data used for transport modeling. On the other hand, in areas where the packages can be compared to a GIS, they are all less sophisticated than a real GIS. The underlying data models range from the very simplistic to the fairly complex and detailed. Most of the packages are based on a proprietary file-based data format. When working with network data in a transport model, users often run into problems regarding interdependence. For instance, splitting an edge in the road network could invalidate the descriptions of all bus routes using that road edge, unless these are also updated. Curiously, only one of the packages tries to handle these problems. In most of the packages, it is all too easy for a user to introduce invalid data. In addition, because of the lack of validation functions, these errors are too often only discovered when a calculation tool returns an error (or even worse, returns no error but produces erroneous results).

Nearly all of the packages provide some kind of support for scenario management of modeling data. In general the support is fairly simple, consisting of various tools that assist the user in handling the model data (copying all of the files making up some element of the model data, for instance), without offering more sophisticated features like comparison.

Support varies greatly. Some packages do not have any support at all, while others are entirely script based. Only one package offers a framework which is flexible (can among other things combine scripts and executable tools) and has a visual representation. On the other hand, this framework is based on the use of executables and the exchange of data using text files, which can make it difficult to find and correct errors.

All of the packages offer some kind of visualization; however, the sophistication of the implementations varies greatly. All of the packages have implemented proprietary solutions for visualization and presentation, and in general, even the best implementations fall short of a dedicated GIS. On the other hand, the implemented facilities are all focused on the data involved in transport modeling and support several types of data well (for instance matrices, transit routes, intersections) that are not normally handled in a standard GIS.

All of the packages use some kind of proprietary file-based data storage. To varying degrees, import and export tools to other data formats are supplied. In addition, some of the packages have added more integrated mechanisms for data exchange with ArcGIS. In most cases, some kind of API supports access to the data from external applications. However, as long as data storage is not based on some kind of open standard data storage (for instance, a relational database or XML-based files), access to data and integration with external applications is not as seamless as it could be.

USING A COMBINATION OF DIFFERENT TOOLS

The main alternative to using the packages mentioned previously is to build the model from a combination of tools from different vendors and/or tools custom made for the model. This approach offers significantly greater flexibility in picking the right tools for each task than when using a dedicated package. The downsides are usually reduced ease of use and/or significant costs for integrating the various tools. Frequently, the most complicated and demanding part of a transport model is traffic assignment. Hence, a commonly seen example of this strategy is to use a dedicated package for traffic assignment in conjunction with other packages or custom tools for different parts of a model.

The editing experience with a combination model is usually similar to that of using a dedicated package. This is due to the fact that the main challenges when editing have to do with editing street networks and public transport data, and in combination models this is frequently accomplished with a dedicated package.

Scenarios are frequently a serious challenge in combination models. Usually scenario management influences every part of a transport model. Hence, with a combination model, a coordinated system which takes into account all the different parts the model will have to be implemented.

Control of modeling flow is a challenge with a combination model. The solution usually depends on the complexity of the model, of the data it uses, of the requirements for varying flow of individual model runs, and of other issues. Normally the solution will be based on scripts and/or on one or more custom developed applications.

In combination models, base data and results are imported into a GIS, typically which is then used for creating presentations.

Attempts to integrate custom tools and or standard packages into one model usually cause a fair amount of difficulty with regard to data storage and conversion. This happens since most packages and custom tools only support a limited range of data formats, with the consequence that no one single common data storage format can be specified for a complete model. One might easily end up with using three different formats. In addition, many packages only support one (proprietary) format natively. The remaining supported formats are then a kind of import/export format. This type of arrangement necessitates a lot of extra conversion operations during model runs. This is not only cumbersome and time consuming but can even, in some cases, cause problems due to subtle differences in the degree to which certain modeling functionality is supported in internal and external data formats.

A decision to adopt a strategy of a combination model for a specific project comes down to weighing advantages against disadvantages. Usually the main advantage will be flexibility to choose precisely the best-suited modeling tool for each specific subproblem the model needs to address. The main disadvantage, conversely, will be difficulty in integrating a range of different tools into one model. This usually involves two main activities:

- Creating conversion routines which can automatically and reliably translate data between the formats required by the different tools.
- Creating a system for reliably executing the complete model by invoking calculation tools and translation routines in the proper order.

For sophisticated models, these two activities can easily consume a large part of the entire budget for the modeling project.

BASING THE MODEL ON A GIS

GIS or GIS-like functionality is used in almost every transport model, but the tasks for which GIS is generally used differ significantly from model to model. Most often GIS is used for presentation but also very often for data management and editing. While GIS packages do not include the calculation tools necessary for building a transport model out of the box, third-party extension components are emerging which provide calculation tools for transport modeling as completely integrated plug-ins for the GIS. Traffic Analyst™ from Rapidis is an example (www.rapidis.com/trafficanalyst.htm).

In many cases, it can be a sensible strategy for building a transport model to make a GIS the central component in the transport model. This is particularly the case when it is necessary to use several different calculation tools. Such a strategy typically involves the following:

- having a GIS-based central data repository
- using a GIS for all editing tasks
- using a GIS for presentations

In order to make this work, it is necessary to be able to transfer data between the GIS-based repository and the separate calculation tools. The complexity of this obviously depends on which storage formats are supported by the GIS and by the calculation tools. The main benefit of this solution over the one described in the previous section is the potential for significantly reducing the data conversion efforts. This should be possible for these reasons: Modern geographic information systems support industry-standard relational databases as their native storage format, and they support editing this data directly without any conversion. The consequence is that integrating custom tools becomes much easier as the open nature of relational databases makes them very easy to access. The wide range of import and export options available in GIS products and in relational databases also makes it surmountable to transfer data back and forth between the GIS and calculation tools, which do not support direct access to relational databases or common GIS formats.

The effort necessary for editing transport model data in a GIS depends on the type of the transport model. The most important distinguishing factor is whether or not the model needs to represent public transport. Modern GIS packages usually have adequate to excellent support for editing data for models without public transport (mainly street network data), whereas the support for editing stops, routes, and timetables is either nonexistent or inadequate.

Traffic Analyst includes plug-in transit editing tools for ArcGIS as shown in figures 6, 7, and 8 below.

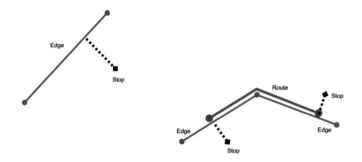

Figure 6. An example of a detailed representation of transit stops and routes.

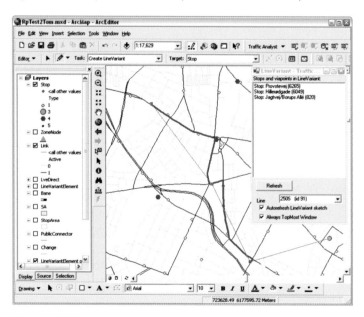

Figure 7. Editing a route using custom editing tools in ArcGIS (Traffic Analyst).

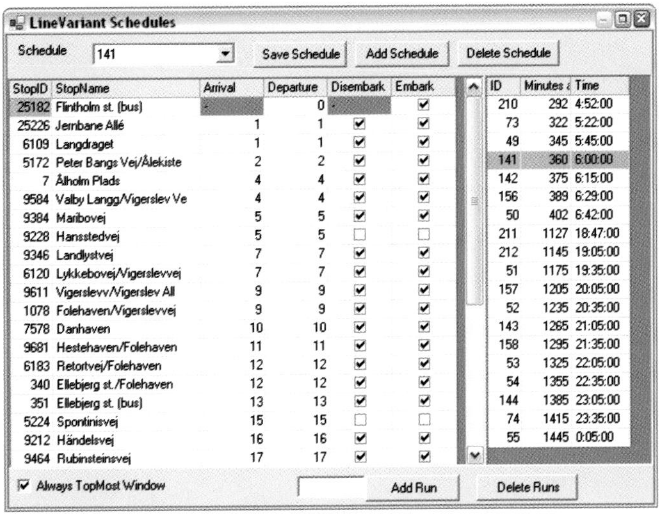

LineVariant Schedules

Schedule [141] | Save Schedule | Add Schedule | Delete Schedule

StopID	StopName	Arrival	Departure	Disembark	Embark		ID	Minutes	Time
25182	Flintholm st. (bus)	-	0	-	✓		210	292	4:52:00
25226	Jernbane Allé	1	1	✓	✓		73	322	5:22:00
6109	Langdraget	1	1	✓	✓		49	345	5:45:00
5172	Peter Bangs Vej/Ålekiste	2	2	✓	✓		141	360	6:00:00
7	Ålholm Plads	4	4	✓	✓		142	375	6:15:00
9584	Valby Langg/Vigerslev Ve	4	4	✓	✓		156	389	6:29:00
9384	Maribovej	5	5	✓	✓		50	402	6:42:00
9228	Hansstedvej	5	5	□	□		211	1127	18:47:00
9346	Landlystvej	7	7	✓	✓		212	1145	19:05:00
6120	Lykkebovej/Vigerslevvej	7	7	✓	✓		51	1175	19:35:00
9611	Vigerslevv/Vigerslev All	9	9	✓	✓		157	1205	20:05:00
1078	Folehaven/Vigerslevvej	9	9	✓	✓		52	1235	20:35:00
7578	Danhaven	10	10	✓	✓		143	1265	21:05:00
9681	Hestehaven/Folehaven	11	11	✓	✓		158	1295	21:35:00
6183	Retortvej/Folehaven	12	12	✓	✓		53	1325	22:05:00
340	Ellebjerg st./Folehaven	12	12	✓	✓		54	1355	22:35:00
351	Ellebjerg st. (bus)	13	13	✓	✓		144	1385	23:05:00
5224	Spontinisvej	15	15	□	□		74	1415	23:35:00
9212	Händelsvej	16	16	✓	✓		55	1445	0:05:00
9464	Rubinsteinsvej	17	17	✓	✓				

☑ Always TopMost Window | Add Run | Delete Runs

Figure 8. Editing public timetables in ArcGIS.

No GIS has native support for proper management of scenarios. ArcGIS, however, comes close, as its versioned Geodatabase supplies most of the necessary building blocks for this. Whereas the features for scenario management in ArcGIS are probably as good as those in some of the dedicated transport modeling packages, the price for such a solution and the amount of administrative work involved is probably prohibitive for its use in transport modeling projects with an average budget.

Uniquely in the GIS world, ArcGIS has an excellent system for control of modeling flow: Geoprocessing. The Geoprocessing framework in ArcGIS allows control of tools. These tools can be either:

- Built-in tools supplied with ArcGIS.
- Scripts in any COM-compliant scripting language, such as VBScript, JavaScript™, and Python.
- Executable programs.
- Batch files.
- Third-party tools developed by business partners and others (typically delivered in extension dll's).

This is what Traffic Analyst provides. These tools can all be invoked from the command line or from a script. The Geoprocessing framework also allows users to create models which use these tools through a graphical user interface as seen in figure 9, essentially a complete four-step model.

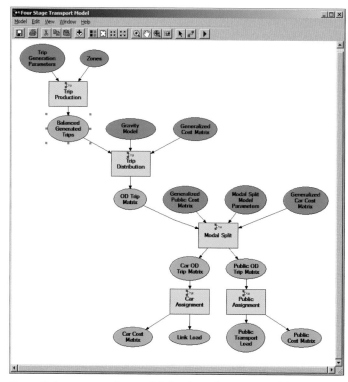

Figure 9. A geoprocessing model showing a four-step model.

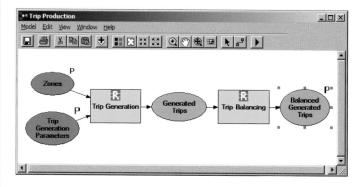

Figure 10. A closer look at the Trip Production submodel.

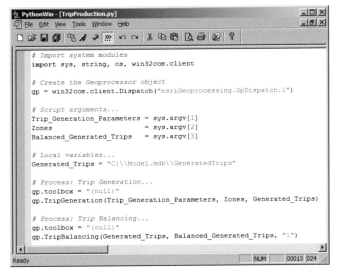

Figure 11. The Trip Production submodel converted to a script.

The Geoprocessing framework essentially lets users build transport models by creating a model or a script which represents a complete transport model and includes calls to a number of external or internal tools in order to execute the actual calculations involved in each step. This reinforces the idea that GIS is being developed as a platform for all kinds of spatial modeling as developed by Maguire (2005, this volume) in chapter 2. This application is a particularly good example of the way GIS systems are being adapted to contain and embed quite sophisticated models that previously were always treated in stand-alone terms.

GIS packages have excellent presentation capabilities, and when all or most of the data used in a transport model is stored in a format which is natively accessible from the GIS, the required presentations can be easily created without any data conversion.

As mentioned above, a GIS-centric data storage strategy has significant benefits for allowing easier access to data. This is not only the case for the various calculation tools involved in a transport model but also for other models, analysis projects, or applications which need to share data with the transport model. Examples of such uses are environmental impact models, economic models, and land-use models.

The key to whether or not a GIS-centric strategy can work smoothly for transport modeling is the degree of support for integrating the calculation tools which are to be used in the model. This integration is achieved most elegantly by using plug-in type tools, which are directly available inside the GIS application; this allows entirely seamless integration. If external tools are to be used, two types of interoperability are typically needed:

- The ability for invoking functional modules from outside the tool (through scripts, etc.)

- The ability for importing and exporting to and from industry-standard formats like relational databases, shapefiles, and text files. It should also be possible to invoke this import/export functionality in a script or something similar.

SUMMARY

The main advantage of using a dedicated transport modeling package is that transport models can be implemented and executed in one single integrated environment. The downside is that it is often difficult to integrate such models with other models or systems and that the options for tailoring the model to specific needs are limited to the features available in the package. In some cases, it can also be a problem that the GIS-like features available in the dedicated packages are insufficient for the specific needs for projects, necessitating the complementary use of a dedicated GIS.

Creating a transport model from a number of different tools or packages helps to overcome this limitation. The downside of this solution is that automating model runs and transferring data between the different tools in the model can become much more difficult and time consuming. Frequently, the editing process also becomes more difficult and error-prone in this scenario. This can occur when different data needs to be edited in different packages in a coordinated way.

Centralizing as many aspects of a transport model as possible in a GIS can alleviate some of these problems while retaining the flexibility of using the best-suited calculation tools through external use of these tools. In particular, editing and data transfer and presentation can be eased through the very robust features for this in packages like ArcGIS. Integration problems can be significantly further alleviated by using emerging plug-in calculation tools like Traffic Analyst.

FUTURE POSSIBILITIES

It is the firm conviction of the authors that the integration of GIS software into transport modeling is going to grow very significantly. This conviction is based on the significant work that has been done among the GIS vendors, particularly ESRI, during the past five years to improve on their software's capabilities for integration and embedding in other systems. The fact that it is now not only possible but actually surmountable to take various subsystems from a package like ArcGIS and embed them into transport modeling tools means that vendors of transport modeling tools will probably think twice in the future about whether to keep building such subsystems themselves or whether to use those provided by GIS vendors. An even more radical approach to integrating GIS and transport models is demonstrated by Traffic Analyst, which is a transport modeling solution, packaged entirely as an extension to an existing GIS product: ArcGIS. The following two sections go into a bit more detail on what specifically could be added to transport modeling packages and to ArcGIS in order to be able to provide users with a coherent solution which offers the best of both worlds.

POSSIBLE IMPROVEMENTS OF TRANSPORT MODELING PACKAGES

A number of things could be done in order to make it easier to integrate transport modeling packages with GIS and other applications and systems. Some of the more important ones are mentioned here.

For modelers who want their transport models to work in conjunction with other models and who are considering the use of an off-the-shelf modeling package for the transport model, it is usually very important that the package allows other applications and systems to access its internal data. The most obvious way to achieve this is to simply use an open industry-standard storage format such as a DBMS internally and to publish the schema.

For situations in which a modeler wants to use specific calculation tools from an off-the-shelf package, say as a part of a large custom-made transport model, it is not sufficient that the package uses industry-standard storage. In these situations, it is also important that specific tools from that package can be invoked separately from the main application in the package.

Most of the off-the-shelf packages have a significant way to go before they can fulfill this wish list, but in the opinion of the authors, they are well underway, and the vendors have significant focus on the integration needs of modelers.

IMPROVEMENTS IN ArcGIS

Due to its dedication to open data storage, industry standards, sophisticated editing and presentation facilities, and its framework for controlling modeling flows, ArcGIS is clearly the best GIS package for a modeler who wants a transport model to be based on a GIS. It does, however, have some shortcomings. The most important of these are outlined here.

Matrix data is essential in transport models and unfortunately is not very well supported by ArcGIS. Matrices can easily be stored in a regular tabular format, such as this:

From	To	Value
1	1	3.45
1	2	5.43
...	...	...

This, however, can easily become wasteful in disk-space consumption, and it does not facilitate editing or presentation. A more compact storage mechanism for matrices and a grid-style display, such as what is seen below, would be a very useful addition to ArcGIS.

	1	2	...
1	1.23	3.45	...
2	3.21	5.43	...
...	...	...	...

Using a transport model generally involves creating a number of datasets which should represent each of the hypothetical scenarios to be examined. When working with transport models, it is a significant benefit to have access to a system which can help in the administration of these scenarios. Presently, there are no facilities in ArcGIS for this. (One could, with a surmountable effort, build something useful on top of a versioned geodatabase, but the cost of ArcSDE just for the sake of scenario management is probably prohibitive). Some very useful scenario tools could be:

- Create a new scenario (consisting of a number of interrelated datasets)
- Compare two scenarios (join on id-field and calculate relative or absolute differences for value fields)

For users who want to build transport models in ArcGIS, the single biggest problem is probably the lack of calculation tools for some of the many methods and algorithms usually employed in transport models. Such tools (like Traffic Analyst) are emerging now, but it will probably be a while before the collection of tools that modelers have access to from inside ArcGIS is as comprehensive as what can be found in the very mature stand-alone transport modeling packages.

CONCLUSIONS

In the last half-decade or so, a number of developments in GIS technology have occurred which have implications for users and developers of transport models. These developments include:

- the use of relational databases for storage;
- the ability to create custom data models using a relational approach in combination with topological networks and the ability to formulate validation rules;
- the use of a software architecture that makes it possible to use a standard GIS as a development platform;
- and, most recently, the addition of a sophisticated framework for handling calculation processes.

These combine to offer strong potential benefits for users and developers of transport models. They also make it possible for the use of GIS to change from a secondary to a potentially primary role in the use of transport models.

The impact of this now primarily benefits projects involving custom-built transport models and will probably only later reach users of existing dedicated transport modeling packages, if and when the vendors of the dedicated packages decide to incorporate these or similar features in their products. In addition, products which make use of the improved GIS features listed above to provide transport modeling capabilities seamlessly to GIS users are emerging now. They provide an easy-to-use framework for building transport models and will be attractive for certain types of models.

In conclusion, the authors of this chapter are convinced that users of transport models will gain alternatives that offer seamlessly integrated GIS-based solutions for transport modeling. This will probably come about both through greater GIS-integration of existing stand-alone packages and from the introduction of new GIS-focused solutions. For users and developers, the end result will be the same: It will become possible to perform transport modeling from within a GIS framework, making it possible to leverage GIS technology fully.

REFERENCES

Banister, D. 2002. *Transport planning*. London: Spon Press.

Ortuzar, J., and L. G. Willumsen. 2001. *Modelling transport*. London: John Wiley and Sons.

Chapter 14

The Integration of Case-Based Reasoning and GIS in a Planning Support System

ANTHONY G. O. YEH

CENTRE OF URBAN PLANNING AND ENVIRONMENTAL MANAGEMENT

THE UNIVERSITY OF HONG KONG

HONG KONG, CHINA

ABSTRACT

ALTHOUGH THERE IS AN INCREASING TENDENCY to integrate planning models in geographic information systems (GIS), the loosely-coupled architecture in which data is exported from a GIS and transferred to an external modeling program and the modeling results are sent back to GIS for display and further analysis is still the most commonly used method in the integration of planning models with GIS. There are many advantages of using case-based reasoning (CBR) which uses previous cases to interpret and solve a new problem in a planning support system. The knowledge representation scheme of CBR is better than rule-based reasoning in recording and representing knowledge that is hard to express with explicit rules or is too case specific. It can overcome the black box inference process of rule-based reasoning. CBR can simulate the present working style of planners in dealing with development applications which is based on their knowledge of past application records. The results derived directly from real cases in CBR are more convincing and acceptable to planners. A system that integrates a CBR shell (ESTEEM[1]) and a GIS package (ArcView) was developed to demonstrate the usefulness of the integration of case-based reasoning and GIS as a planning support system to assist planners in the Planning Department of Hong Kong in handling planning applications in development control. Because it is case-based and not rule-based, the system is also applicable to other cities in dealing with development applications.

GIS serves both as a database and toolbox for urban planning (Yeh 1999; Hopkins et al. 2005, this volume). In a database-oriented GIS, spatial and textual data can be stored and linked using the georelational model. This supports efficient data retrieval, query, and mapping. Planners can also extract data from the databases and input it to other modeling and spatial analysis programs. When combined with data from other tabular databases or specially conducted surveys, GIS can be used to make effective planning decisions. As a toolbox, GIS allows planners to perform spatial analysis using geoprocessing functions such as map overlay, connectivity, and buffering (Berry 1987, Tomlin 1990).

Decision support systems (DSS) were developed as a response to the shortcomings of the management information systems (MIS) of the late 1960s and early 1970s which were not adequate support for analytical modeling capabilities and for facilitating the decision maker's interaction with the solution process. DSS provides a framework for integrating database management systems, analytical models, and graphics to improve decision-making processes. They are designed to deal with ill- or semi-structured problems which are poorly defined and partially qualitative in nature. The decision support system concept was extended to the spatial context in the development of spatial decision support systems (SDSS) (Armstrong and Densham 1990; Armstrong, Densham, and Rushton 1986; Densham 1991; Densham and Rushton 1988) to help decision makers make decisions on different locational alternatives (for example, optimal location of service centers). A parallel development in the planning field is the concept of planning support systems (PSS), first advocated by Harris (1989), which is a combination of computer-based methods and models that support the planning functions. PSS not only serve as a decision support system to decision makers, but they also provide the tools, models, and information used for planning (that is, the information technologies that planners use to carry out their unique professional responsibilities) (Harris and Batty 1993). PSS comprise a whole suite of related information technologies (e.g., GIS, spreadsheets, models, and databases) that have different applications in different stages of planning (Batty 1995, Klosterman 1995). GIS is becoming an increasingly important component of a PSS because of its geoprocessing, graphic display, database, and modeling capabilities (Brail and Klosterman 2001, Geertman and Stillwell 2003).

The database management, mapping, and spatial analysis functions of GIS have been very useful to many areas of urban planning (French and Wiggins 1990, Levine and Landis 1989). The main weakness of GIS in urban planning is the linkage with urban planning models (Douven 1993). There are different strategies for linking planning models with GIS, ranging from loosely-coupled, tightly-coupled, and fully-integrated architecture as in figure 1. Integration based on the loosely-coupled architecture involves importing and exporting data between GIS and the planning models. Data is exported from a GIS and transferred to an external program for execution. The modeling results are sent back to GIS for display and further analysis. Tightly-coupled architecture integration involves writing programs within the GIS environment, avoiding explicit data transfer between software packages. Although there is an increasing tendency to integrate planning models in GIS, the loosely-coupled architecture is the most commonly used in the integration of planning models with GIS (Wegener 2005, this volume). The California Urban Future Model (Landis 1995) uses the loosely-coupled approach in the integration of GIS with models. It makes use of GIS extensively for data manipulation and for displaying the results of external modeling packages. Such an approach is also used in multiple criteria decision-making planning methods (Jankowski 1995). A tightly-coupled approach has been used for residential location modeling in the Buffalo region (Batty and Xie 1994a, 1994b). Although currently there is an increasing trend toward the development of fully integrated planning models in GIS, such as the availability of location–allocation and spatial interaction models in ArcGIS, until most of the commonly used planning models are fully integrated in GIS, there is still a need for loosely-coupled and tightly-coupled architectures. This chapter presents an example to show how the integration of case-based reasoning with GIS can be developed into a powerful planning support system.

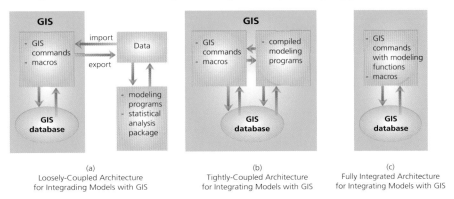

Figure 1. Integration of models with GIS. a) loosely coupled; b) tightly-coupled; c) fully integrated architecture.

CASE-BASED REASONING AND URBAN PLANNING

Urban planning often involves a huge amount of data, regulations, and guidelines from various sources. It also requires the experiences and expertise of planners and the assistance of planning models and analytical methods in a complicated decision-making process. But the capability of handling large amounts of information and the availability of experienced planners are often very limited. Therefore, computerized knowledge-based systems (KBS) or expert systems (ES), which have the capability of easy storage and retrieval of the required information and knowledge and "can reach a level of performance comparable to—or even exceeding that of —a human expert" (Turban 1995, p. 16), would be, at least theoretically, very helpful to planners in their work.

KBS and ES have aroused the interest of planners for many years. Many potential applications have been explored by researchers, and a few prototypes and even operational systems have been built (Kim, Wiggins, and Wright 1990). However, there are many limitations in using KBS in urban planning

(Barbanente et al. 1995, Borri et al. 1994, Han and Kim 1990b, Marchand 1993, Ortolano and Perman 1990). The two main obstacles in successfully applying KBS to urban planning are difficulties in building a practical KBS for planning and difficulties encountered in "inspiring confidence in the use of it" (Marchand 1993). Some of these problems can be overcome by the use of case-based reasoning (CBR) which uses previous similar cases to suggest solutions to new cases (Yeh and Shi 1999). In contrast to rule-based reasoning or model-based reasoning, CBR directly uses concrete knowledge, and its inference is basically the processes of retrieval and adaptation. These features allow CBR to avoid some of the problems in building KBS, such as knowledge elicitation bottlenecks, and they can help gain the confidence of users.

CASE-BASED REASONING (CBR)

Originating from the work of Schank and Abelson (1977), CBR has developed into a mature and important field of AI (Aamodt and Plaza 1994, Kolodner 1993, Schank and Leake 1989, Watson 1997). Increasingly, many domains are using CBR, such as architecture design, law, medicine, and customer services (help desk) (Watson 1997). The basic philosophy of CBR is to use previous similar case(s) to help to solve, evaluate, or interpret a current new problem (Kolodner 1993). It simulates human behavior in solving such new problems. When confronted with a new and difficult problem, it is natural for human problem solvers to look into their memories to find previous similar instances for help. An important reason why people can become experts is that they can remember and properly use suitable previous cases in solving new ones. In simulating the human brain in problem solving, a computerized case-based system (CBS) using CBR sees knowledge as encapsulated memories, and its knowledge base is a *case library* storing these memories in the form of concrete stories. After the user inputs the descriptions of a new problem into the computer, the computer will look for similar old cases in its case library according to the predefined matching algorithms. Cases which meet certain criteria will be retrieved and their solutions or any other parts of the stories required by the user will be either directly proposed to the user or, if necessary, be adapted to meet the new situation before being proposed. The user can evaluate or test whether the proposed solutions work well or not and modify them. When a satisfactory solution is obtained, the newly solved problem can be stored in the case library as a new case, and the knowledge of the system increases (for details of the techniques of CBR, see Aamodt and Plaza 1994; Kolodner 1993; Watson 1995, 1997). The CBR process can be typically represented by a schematic cycle comprising the four REs as in figure 2:

a)　RETRIEVE the most similar case(s);

b)　REUSE the case(s) to attempt to solve the problem;

c)　REVISE the proposed solution if necessary, and

d)　RETAIN the new solution as a part of a new case.

A new problem is matched against cases in the case library, and one or more similar cases are *retrieved*. The solution (transformational reuse) and the past method that constructed the solution (derivational reuse) of the retrieved cases are then *reused* and tested for success in application. Unless the retrieved case is a close match to the new problem, most likely the solution has to be *revised* in producing a new case that can be *retained*.

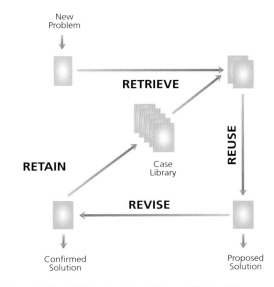

Figure 2. The CBR cycle (after Watson 1995, p.17).

ADVANTAGES OF CBR OVER RULE-BASED REASONING TO URBAN PLANNING

In building a practical KBS for urban planning, the main difficulties exist in the process of *knowledge acquisition* and *knowledge representation*. The successful construction of a practical KBS is largely based on the assumption that the domain knowledge for problem solving can be properly extracted and represented. Many efforts have been made to refine these processes. However, both knowledge acquisition and knowledge representation have always been the major difficulties in knowledge engineering. They are generally referred to as the *knowledge acquisition problem* (Musen 1993) and the *knowledge elicitation bottleneck* (Han and Kim 1990b, Kolodner 1993, Musen 1993, Watson 1995). Unfortunately, in urban planning, knowledge acquisition and representation seem to be even more difficult to overcome than other domains.

Knowledge acquisition

Many authors asserted that KBS (rule-based or model-based) is based on the assumptions that (adapted from Han and Kim 1990b):

a)   the problem can be clearly specified and is well-bounded;

b)   the relations between the factors or elements of the problem are known and can be expressed explicitly;

c)   problem-solving methods can be articulated; and

d)   experts agree on solutions, that is, the cause-effect relationships are clearly defined.

However, most of the problems in urban planning seem to deviate far from these assumptions. Firstly, as Han and Kim (1990b) pointed out, "Because of the distinctive nature of urban planning, practicing professional planners must deal with multidisciplinary activities that embrace social, economic, political, and even anthropological factors." There are often too many interweaving factors and relationships in the problem-solving process, and it is very hard to analyze them into clear, definite, and one-directional threads. Secondly, urban planning is also a domain in which many uncertain factors, such as politics, public opinions, personalities of planners, and other occasional situational factors, may play important roles in the problem-solving process. This makes the cause-and-effect relationships difficult to be predefined or even to be found before the event occurs. Thirdly, although urban planning is a kind of work largely guided by guidelines and regulations, many planners regard it as an art as well as a science (O'Harrow 1968). They would like to use their creativity in the work rather than just following prototypes. This will introduce many subjective factors into the problem-solving process.

Knowledge representation

Most existing KBS are rule-based or model-based. In a rule-based system, the knowledge is typically represented by *IF-Then* syntax and the control scheme constructed by rules-of-thumb. In a model-based system, more *in-depth knowledge* is required, and the knowledge is represented with causal models. To represent knowledge in these ways requires two prerequisites: 1) the relationships between a situation and its consequent situation can be explicitly predefined, and 2) the knowledge should be generalized and can be directly applied to routine situations. There are two main difficulties in representing some planning knowledge by *rules* and *models*. First, if the knowledge is difficult to articulate in natural language, as mentioned above, it will be more difficult to represent in the strict form as rules and models. Furthermore, there is often much *informal information* involved in planning, for example, personal judgments, hunches, intuition, hearsay, and personal experiences (Han and Kim 1990b), which is obviously not suitable to be recorded as rules or defined as causes and effects. Second, some knowledge, especially informal information, is usually very case specific and hard to abstract into a general rule. The abstract knowledge used by conventional KBS usually abandons these individual characteristics in order to reach a general rule.

Advantages of CBR over rule-based reasoning

From the perspective of a KBS builder, since CBS tends to store knowledge in the form of concrete instances rather than abstract and general rules or models, the system builder can largely avoid meeting the *knowledge elicitation bottleneck*. First, extracting knowledge "becomes a simple task of acquiring past cases" but not grasping the underlying reasoning in solving the problems (Watson 1995). Second, the knowledge-storing scheme of CBS provides a good way to record the *informal information.* This information can be easily recorded in the narration of a story, and because this narration is on the level of a concrete case and has no effect on other cases, the system builder does not need to worry about the problems related to generalization. Third, different solutions to different cases of a similar problem which are quite common in planning can be explicitly and conveniently represented. Finally, when the new problem is solved and the effects of the solution in the real world are known, the user can conveniently save this new case in the case library and increase the knowledge of the system. This learning method is very simple and can be performed by the users themselves in their daily work without the help of knowledge engineers. Even when conflicting cases are found, the experts can check what caused this conflict at the case level, while in a conventional KBS, the conflicts may cause a large modification to the whole knowledge base.

From the perspective of the users, the enlightening style of CBR may be more welcome to planners. There are five main reasons for this :

1) *The reasoning process is more visible to the users*—from the retrieved cases, the user can directly obtain solutions to previous similar problems and, more importantly, these results are based on actual past cases that can be presented to the user to provide more concrete support for the system's conclusions and recommendations (Leake 1996).

2) *The user can take part in the inference process*—rule-based reasoning tries to abstract the experts' problem-solving methods into some fixed routines, and its inference is largely a closed iterative process that will usually reach a final result. But the reasoning procedure of CBR can be open, and the user can take part in or even control the problem-solving process. For example, when planners have retrieved several similar cases for a new problem, it is easy for them to understand how the solution was generated, why it was successful or failed, and what might be the consequence of a solution.

3) *The way CBR provides help is not compelling*—CBR will not just tell the planner what he/she should do. Instead, it presents cases related to previously handled similar problems and suggests what has been done under similar situations, what are the consequences of the applied solutions, and what tips the precedents can provide for dealing with the current problem. This process is analogous to what often happens in our brains and is the way through which many experts teach novices to handle a difficult problem.

4) *The cases can provide knowledge about exceptions*—as discussed before, knowledge for handling exceptions is often what planners mostly require, particularly in a domain such as urban planning that is characterized

by uncertainty and subjectivity. While many conventional methods of knowledge representation try to omit the exceptions, a case record is all the knowledge about each concrete instance, including the exceptions (Kolodner 1993).

5)   *A real case is more inspiring than abstract knowledge*—in their practical work, planners often refer to previous real examples but not abstract guidelines or regulations to inspire their creativity. A computerized system that facilitates the retrieval of relevant cases and provides required information and tools for visualization, analysis, evaluation, and adaptation will relieve the burden of planners in trying to remember everything. It will help them to have more time to understand the cases.

In summary, CBS leaves much room for the intelligence of planners to recognize, understand, and generate creative solutions to a new problem while it provides raw but comprehensive and original information and tools to facilitate the decision-making process. By studying previous cases, new planners may broaden their experience in handling similar problems and get tips and lessons, while experienced planners, through reviewing the old cases, may recall their experience and knowledge and even generate inspirations in solving new problems.

USE OF CBS IN DEVELOPMENT CONTROL

Development control is an important function of urban planning. Processing planning applications is a daily work of government planning agencies, and there is a statutory regulation on the length of time in processing an application. Planning applications are especially important in the UK's planning system because all developments have to obtain planning permission from the planning authority (Bruton and Nicholson 1987). It is a relatively well-structured function of urban planning and, as a result, many attempts have been made to apply KBS to it (Leary and Rodriguez-Bachiller 1989, Borri et al. 1994). However, a rule-based KBS may still encounter difficulties similar to those in other fields of urban planning. One of the problems is knowledge acquisition. Some developers of KBS for development control found that "it is extremely difficult to find an expert who is able to formalise his/her decision processes and to communicate his/her knowledge in a satisfactory way, as a domain experience is often based on automatic physical and mental processes, and the expert is frequently led to mix facts and factors and to judge by his/her intuition and imagination" (Barbanente et al. 1995, p. 573). Although Leary and Rodriguez-Bachiller (1989) argued that this expertise was more structured and able to be articulated than expected, their decision tree method seems to have the following problems:

a)   often in development control, it is not easy to subdivide a goal into several definite subgoals;

b)   the decision tree may oversimplify the relationships among the subgoals; and

c)   the method tends to tell users what they should do or should not do, rather than how to do it.

Another problem is how to represent case-specific knowledge. Although the problems in development control and their solutions are largely well structured compared with problems in other fields of urban planning, special considerations and characteristics of a planning application case are often also important in making a decision. Borri et al. (1994) found that "different context stimuli or pragmatic suggestions arising from the analysis of relevant context elements may produce microchanges in the problem-solving scheme."(p. 36).

Finally, although development control is relatively well defined, it is far from being without uncertainty. Leary and Rodriguez-Bachiller (1989) pointed out that "officers and committees have discretion to interpret plans and policies"; also, "aesthetic and political judgements introduce an element of arbitrariness in the decision-making process," thus "layers of complexity and uncertainty" are added to "what at first glance is a rigid rule-based system" (p. 20). There are always grey areas in development control, and often these are the areas where the expertise and experience of the experts are most required. When dealing with such kinds of problems, the experts usually draw upon "previous experiences" or "the memory of how similar cases had been solved in the past" (Borri et al. 1994, p. 37). This is the type of problem that is most suitable for CBR.

The advantages of using CBS in development control are :

a) It is a retrieving tool that can help planners to find relevant cases quickly.

b) It is an intelligent library that can relieve the burden of experts' memory and also increase novices' memory. It is a corporate memory system that will retain knowledge of experienced experts even when they are absent or retired.

c) It will provide knowledge directly at the case level. At this level, the operations of the experts to a specific problem and their results, as well as the comments from the experts, are just descriptive records. There is no need to extract and generalize knowledge.

d) It will use concrete cases, instead of control branching, to demonstrate the templates of different routines or methods.

e) For problems with uncertainty, it will help planners to make further considerations. From similar cases, planners can get tips, hints, instructions, templates, or precedents, depending on what they need.

f) From the old cases, planners can learn HOW to do to a problem, not just what to do or what not to do.

SYSTEM ARCHITECTURE AND BUILDING

As a case study of building a CBS planning support system, a system that integrates a CBR shell, ESTEEM, and a GIS package, ArcView[2], has been developed to support planners in the Planning Department of Hong Kong in handling planning applications (Shi and Yeh 1999).

PLANNING APPLICATIONS IN HONG KONG

In Hong Kong, Outline Zoning Plans (OZP) are mainly used to control land development. These plans indicate areas that are zoned for various uses, for example, residential, commercial, and industrial. Attached to each plan is a Schedule of Notes which shows two columns of land uses that are permitted under different land-use zones. Column 1 contains land uses that are always permitted without the need to seek planning permission. Column 2 shows land uses that may be permitted with or without conditions on application to the Town Planning Board (TPB), the statutory body for making decisions on a planning application (table 1). The Board may either refuse the application or grant permission, with or without any conditions. If the proposed development is neither a column 1 nor a column 2 use, then it is not a permissible use under the zone.

RESIDENTIAL (GROUP A)

Column 1 Uses always permitted	Column 2 Uses that may be permitted with or without conditions on application to Town Planning Board
Ambulance Depot	Broadcasting, Television, and/or Film Studio
Ancillary Car Park	Commercial Bathhouse
Canteen	Educational Institution
Clinic/Polyclinic	Exhibition or Convention Hall
Government Refuse Collection Point (in public housing estate only)	Government Refuse Collection Point (other than in public housing estate)
Flat	Hospital
Cooked Food Center	Hotel
Government Staff Quarters	Massage Establishment

Table 1. Example of an explanatory statement of an Outline Zoning Plan (OZP) in Hong Kong.

Before a planning application is submitted to the Town Planning Board, it will first be inspected by the planners in the Planning Department. They will examine the new application according to the planning ordinances, regulations, and plans, collect opinions on this new application from relevant government departments, and prepare the evaluating documents for this new application. The application, together with the evaluating documents, will be submitted to the Town Planning Board that is composed of mainly nongovernment members who decide whether the application will be approved or not. The aim of the system is to help the planners in the Planning Department prepare reasonable, comprehensive, and consistent recommendations to the Town Planning Board for making decisions on planning applications.

SYSTEM ARCHITECTURE

CBS is a promising methodology for building and applying more practical KBS for planners (Yeh and Shi 1999). The integration of CBS with GIS will further enhance its usefulness as a planning support system for development control. In the integrated system, CBS will provide the method for decision support in providing relevant experiences, tips, lessons, and possible solutions in handling new problems based on past cases to the planners. The GIS of the system will provide the functions of storing, retrieving, and displaying spatial data. In the handling of spatial data, GIS can be a data generator, a DBMS, and a visualization tool. It can store, display, and generate spatial information related to a planning case. In spatial retrieval, GIS can locate the cases by their absolute positions, for example, to locate a case by its coordinates or its address. It can also retrieve an old case that has a similar spatial relationship with the new problem.

ESTEEM and ArcView were used to develop the integrated system because both of them are relatively inexpensive software and also can be easily integrated through the DDEs of Microsoft Windows. Figure 3 shows the framework of the integrated system. From the functional perspective, the system has four basic parts: the user interface, the GIS module (ArcView), the CBR module (ESTEEM), and the case library. With relatively high flexibility in building the input/output interface, ArcView was chosen to be the platform for the integration. Except for some special operations, such as creating a new template of retrieval method, all the user inputs will enter the system through ArcView, and all the retrieval or adaptation results from the system will be displayed by ArcView. The system provides two kinds of retrieval methods—spatial and nonspatial. For spatial retrieval, the system will let the user click within the outline of a specific case on an index map to retrieve that case. When the user clicks on that case, an identifying code is passed to the system, and ArcView will directly retrieve all the components of that case according to identification code from the case library and display them to the user. As for nonspatial retrieval, ArcView first receives from the user the formatted text or numeric descriptions of a new problem and then passes these descriptions to ESTEEM. ESTEEM looks for the similar cases through matching the descriptions of the new problem and the index values of the old cases. Then, ESTEEM returns the identifying codes of those matched cases to ArcView. With these codes, ArcView brings the components of these cases to the user. All the user interfaces and data exchange were built by programming with Avenue™ scripts.

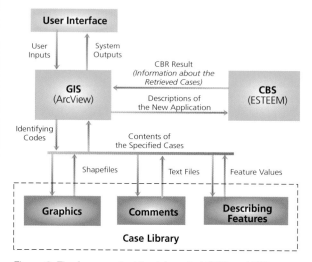

Figure 3. The framework of the integrated CBS and GIS system.

BUILDING THE CBS

The building of a CBS includes building the case library, defining the index for the cases, and building retrieval and adaptation methods (Kolodner 1993). For our system, we also developed a simple method for the user to do quantitative evaluation with the retrieved cases.

Case library

The case library is the knowledge base of a case-based system (CBS). It is the fundamental core of a CBS. Hence, the construction of the case library is the first and most important step in building a CBS. Two questions must be answered before building a case library: *What is a case in this domain? What should be used to describe a case or what is the content of a case?* In the domain of handling planning applications, it is natural to think that each submitted application is a case. But if a planning application has been rejected, its applicant might submit a modified version again, each some improvements in design or transportation. If we treated each of these applications as a single case, the planner will not get the whole history of the application. Furthermore, the system could not correctly evaluate the new problem. For example, if the application had been rejected several times but finally got the permission, when evaluating a new similar application, the system would draw the conclusion that the new application would tend to be rejected because the rejected cases are more than the approved cases. Therefore, in our project, a case is a whole procedure of an application story. If an application is a modified version of an old one, both the old and the new one will be included into a single case.

In our system, a planning application case contains three parts: graphics, tabular features, and comments as in figure 4.

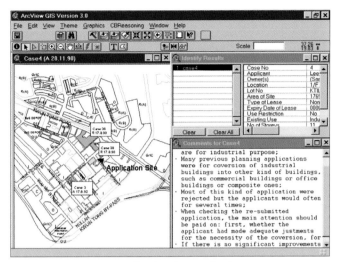

Figure 4. Representation of a planning application case.

Graphics—The documents of a planning application currently stored in the Planning Department usually include a map which shows the position and coverage of the land use referred to by the application. Often on this map, the nearby previous cases are also located and outlined with their results and dates labeled beside their sites. In our system, this basic map will be a shapefile of ArcView, and through the query and display functions of ArcView, this electronic map can provide or link to much more information than the original paper map as in figure 4. Also, the user can click on a specific old case outlined on the map to retrieve the materials of that case. In addition to this basic map, the documents of a planning application case sometimes also contain charts, photos, or other graphics. In our system, these graphics will be handled by ArcView.

Tabular features—Besides graphics, inevitably the case should include features (attributes) represented with numeric values or texts in tabular format. These features are listed in table 2. In our system, a planning application case includes four kinds of tabular features, although sometimes the boundaries between them are not very clear.

a) Features for organizing information: these features are used to manage the case library, that is to organize the whole case library, to identify cases, and to retrieve related documents. With these features, the case library can be well organized, and the efficiency of the system can be improved. The examples of this kind of features are *Case No.* and *Applicant.*

b) Features containing information about the problem itself: these features describe the application itself. Most of the items in table 2 belong to these kinds of features, for example, the applied land use, the planned land use, and the existing land use.

Feature Name	Feature Value
Planning Intention:	Industrial development, but the offices that need to be co-located with industrial operations tend to be permitted.
Traffic Aspect:	1. The site is close to the FFF MTR Station. This is a commuting convenience for the people working in the building. 2. The site is at the junction of YYY Rd. and XXX St., thus the provision of parking and loading/unloading space is required.
Lands Aspect:	The site is suitable for a composite industrial-office building.
Design Aspect:	The initial building plan was not up to the design requirements of the Board: 1. Separate entrances and lift lobbies for goods and passengers should be provided. 2. The prescribed window area and light angles were insufficient, on some floors by more than 65%. The applicant changed the building design: 1. The use of ground floor was changed from "storage, car parking, loading/unloading" to "car parking, loading/unloading, lobby." 2. The design of window area and light angle is modified.
Drainage Aspect:	N/A
Consultation:	N/I
Processing:	Two fresh applications were submitted, in which building design was modified according to the suggestions of the Board.
Planning Department's View	1. The application was in line with the Board's guidelines to permit offices that need to be co-located with industrial operations to be established in industrial buildings. 2. The site is suitable for such a composite industrial-office building because of its good commuting situation. 3. Every unit within a composite industrial-office building must be designed, constructed, and made suitable for both industrial and office uses. Where building design requirements for industrial and office buildings differ, the more stringent requirements under the Buildings Ordinance should apply. Board should pay attention to: • the window area and light angle design; • the provision and layout of parking and loading/unloading facilities.
C: approved with conditions N/A: not applicable N/I: no information	

Table 2. Example of representation of the tabular features of a planning application case.

c) Features containing solution information: this is one of the objectives of the user. The main solution of the problem of processing planning applications is the *Planning Department's View,* that is, the recommendations that should be submitted to the Town Planning Board.

d) Features containing outcome information: this is another objective of the user. The final result of the application, that is to be approved or rejected by the Town Planning Board, can be regarded as part of the *outcome* of the *solution.* Although the decision of the Town Planning Board does not totally depend on the opinions of the Planning Department, it is largely affected by these opinions.

The next question is how to record each feature in a computer-based case library. This is a question related to symbolization. The symbolization of a problem is an important work in building many AI systems (including CBS) because the reasoning performed by the computer has to be based on symbols

(Stefik 1995). However, for the time being, our system is primarily an aiding and advisory system. The main objective is to retrieve useful cases for the user, and it would not carry out much automatic inference work such as automatic adaptation (see Kolodner 1993, Leake 1996). We do not want the representation of our cases to be overly symbolic because the descriptions of the cases should be understandable as much as possible to users so that they can quickly and directly get lessons from the cases or detect the differences between current situation and the old cases, without much interpretation of the symbols. In addition, the cases should involve details, especially case-specific details, as much as possible because details are very important for distinguishing one case from another and will directly affect the final decision.

All these feature values are stored in a table file in *dbf* format. The table file is independent from both ArcView and ESTEEM. It is convenient for the user to modify the case library. The description of each case is a record in this table and can be identified by its identifying number *(Case No.)* when ArcView accesses the table.

Comments—The content of Comments is the advice on a case. It has two parts. One part contains any valuable tips about the case, including anything special to this application which cannot be processed in a routine way or should be paid more attention to, anything difficult to deal with, anything uncertain, any mistakes made, any tricks used, and anything else that deserves special attention. The other part of the comments is a list of cases that are relevant to this case which the user may be interested in examining. The comments of a case are stored in an independent text file and can be identified by its file name.

Case indexing

As discussed above, the description of the case is not described symbolically so that users can easily learn lessons from it. But such description is not suitable for computational matching and retrieving. Furthermore, using the whole description to do matching and retrieving is usually not efficient and practical. Thus, we need to develop an index for each case. The index of a case is the symbolized and simplified or partial description of the case. With the index, cases can be more efficiently and appropriately retrieved (Kolodner 1993). Two types of indexes are used in our system. The first index is a *spatial index* built with ArcView. With ArcView, the user can directly retrieve cases through the index maps. The second index is a *conventional index* of CBS by using ESTEEM. The vocabulary for indexing cases includes two parts—the dimensions describing the retrieving situation and the symbols describing each dimension (Kolodner 1993). The dimensions of the index for retrieving the cases with similar land uses to a new application and the data types of these dimensions are listed in table 3.

Dimension	Data Type	Value Range
Time of the End	Number*	1980 ~ 2000
Planned Use	One of a List (an element from a defined list)	- I (industrial) - C (commercial) - Ra (residential group A) - Rb (residential group B) - Rc (residential group C) - G/IC (government/institution/community) - CDA (comprehensive development areas) - V (village type development) - OS (open space) - GB (green belt) - OST (open storage) - SSSI (site of special scientific interest) - UU (unspecified use)
Existing Use	Text	(Simple words describing the existing land use, such as industrial, office, oil depot, residential, natural protection, vacant, warehouse, agriculture, and so on. If the information is not available, N/I will be assigned to this dimension.)
Applied Use	Text	(Simple words describing the proposed development, such as industrial, warehouse, office, low-density residential, recreational, kindergarten, comprehensive development, PFS (petrol filling station), oyster cultivation, and so on.)
Relationship (Applied – Existing)	One of a List	- Regularize - Conversion - New - Redevelop - Relaxation of Restriction
Relationship (Applied – Planned)	Number	- 1 (the applied use is very relevant or conformable to the planned use) - 2 (the applied use is somewhat relevant to the planned use) - 3 (the applied use is not relevant or inconformable to the planned use)
Justification	Yes or No	Yes, No
Review	Number	0, 1, 2, 3 …
Fresh Application	Number	0, 1, 2, 3 …
Petition	Number	0, 1, 2, 3 …
Result	One of a List	- R (rejected) - C (approved with conditions) - A (approved without conditions)
Reason for Rejection	One of a List	- U (because of concern on land use) - T (because of concern on traffic situation) - D (because of concern on design of the proposed development)
Tip	Text	(Simple words describing the handling, especially why the application was approved or why the Board's decision changed. The words may include: change design, compatible with planning intention, more justification, temporary permitted, compatible with environment, and so on.)
Approval Score	Number	0 ~ 1

Table 3. The dimensions of the index for retrieving cases with similar land uses.

These dimensions can be classified into two categories. The first-level dimensions are for what is called *partial matching*, that is, to find all the cases that are potentially applicable to the new application (Kolodner 1993; Leake 1996). These cases are at least similar in some aspects to the new problem, but not necessarily all of them will make real contributions to handling the new problem. The most useful one(s), if it (they) exist(s), should be among these partial-matching cases and will be picked up by further retrieving. In our system, the first-level dimensions include:

1) *Time of End:* the time that the final decision to the application is made;

2) *Planned Use:* the land-use type of the proposed site on the zoning plan;

3) *Existing Use:* the current use of the proposed site;

4) *Applied Use:* the proposed development for which the permission is applied by the applicant;

5) *Relationship (Applied–Existing):* the relationship between Applied Use and Existing Use can be *new, conversion, regularize, redevelop,* and so on;

6) *Relationship (Applied–Planned):* the relevance of the Applied Use to the Planned Use, represented by numbers, where 1 represents the most relevant uses.

These six dimensions were chosen as the first-level dimensions because they can basically classify cases and can be used to retrieve all the potentially applicable cases with similar land-use types. They are those that first come to the minds of planners when they want to look up the precedent cases with similar land-use types. When all the potential applicable cases are found by using first-level dimensions, users may want to further find out what is (are) the most useful one(s). Then the other dimensions (second-level) will be used. The second-level dimensions include four kinds of features:

1) Justifications of the applicant:

   Justification—whether the applicant made justifications for his/her/its application or not.

2) The features that describe the handling process:

   Review—how many reviews made during the process of the application. (According to the Town Planning Ordinance of Hong Kong, if applicants are aggrieved by the decision of the Town Planning Board, they can apply to the Board for a review of the Board's decision.)

   Fresh—how many fresh applications are there in a case after the initial one. (If the application had been refused in the initial application, the applicant may have applied for the same use on the same site more than one time.)

   Petition—whether the applicant made petition to the Appeal Board.

3) The features that describe the application result:

   Result—the final decision made to the proposed development, i.e., *approved* or *rejected.*

4) The features that describe the evaluation of the application:

Reasons for Rejection—the main reasons for the Board's rejection to some or all applications included in the case.

Tips—the reasons for the Board changed opinions, especially for the cases in which the proposed developments were initially rejected but finally approved.

Approval Score—the probability of approval which ranges from 0 (absolute rejection) to 1 (absolute approval).

These second-level dimensions will be able to help the user to find the most useful case(s) from the *partial-matching* set. In our system, we have the computer (ESTEEM) make retrievals just based on the most basic features (first-level dimensions) to find all the potential cases, while leaving the work to find the most useful case(s) based on second-level dimensions to the planning professionals. This is because the most similar case is not necessarily the most useful one (Leake 1996). To let users decide which case(s) is(are) the most useful one(s) may be the most efficient and effective way because only users exactly know what they really want to get further from the cases.

Retrieval methods

For performing the retrieval, the system should know how to match each feature (dimension) of a new application with an old case and how to evaluate the similarity between the new application and the old case. Figure 5 shows a similarity-assessment template to define the feature-matching method in finding the similarities of cases. This template was built with the *Similarity Definition Editor* of ESTEEM. In this template, the similarity-assessment methods for evaluating each feature and the whole case are defined, and the value of each parameter of the algorithms is set. Users can modify this template according to their experience. They can create more than one such template for different situations or tasks.

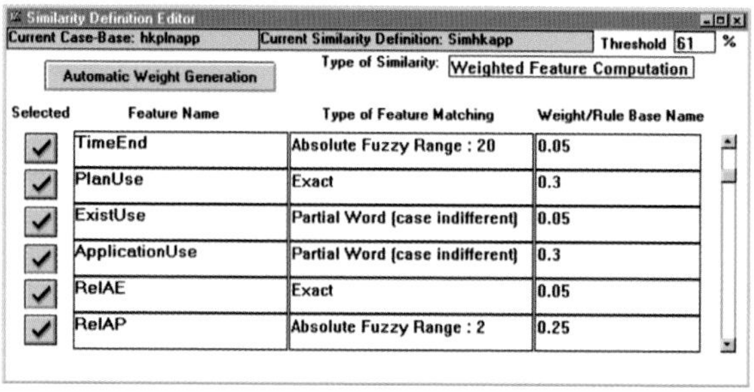

Figure 5. A similarity-assessment template for retrieving cases with similar land uses.

The Nearest Neighbor algorithm is used by the system to find the similarity between a new problem and an old case. It is one of the most popular algorithms for comparing cases in CBS (Kolodner 1993, Watson 1995). The Nearest Neighbor algorithm is defined using the following score:

$$s = \frac{\sum\limits_{i=1}^{n} w_i \times sim(f_i^I, f_i^R)}{\sum\limits_{i=1}^{n} w_i} \qquad (1)$$

where *s (Similarity Score)* is the sum of weighted similarities of each feature and only those cases whose *s* is larger than a predefined threshold (for example, 60%) will be retrieved as the similar cases; w_i is the importance of feature *i*, *sim* is the similarity assessing function for comparing feature f_i, and f_i^I and f_i^R are the values for feature *fi* in the input new case and the retrieved old case respectively (Kolodner 1993). The weights (w_i) used in the study are assigned by the authors on the advice from the planners in the Planning Department. They can be adjusted, modified, and refined as the system develops.

Adaptation methods

Apparently, a new planning application has little chance to be totally the same as an old case. Although the planners could learn a lot directly from similar old cases, they have to adapt this knowledge according to the particular context of the new problem. Automatic adaptation is one of the most challenging topics in CBR research (Leake 1996). In our system, the *Planning Department's View* of old similar cases can be modified to some extent to fit the new situation. Usually the *Planning Department's View* is composed of several opinions on a new planning application. Thus, the results of adaptation could be suggestions for modifying the old opinions, such as under the new condition, a new opinion may need to be added, an old opinion may not be needed any more, or an old opinion should be modified. The algorithms of adaptation can be represented with rules, for example:

> **IF** *new Location <> old Location*
>
> *and* *new Number of Car Parking Spaces > old Number of Car Parking Spaces*
>
> **THEN** *maybe the car parking problem is not so serious.*

Also, the *Approval Score* of the old case can be modified according to the new situation. For example:

> **IF** *new Location = a*
>
> **THEN** *old Approval Score = old Approval Score - 0.1 .*

Evaluation

The experimental system performs a very simple evaluation operation for the user. It will calculate the *Approval Score* of a new planning application based on the previous similar cases. It can be used for considering the consistence of the decisions. The new approval score *(NA)* is calculated by the following formula:

$$NA = \frac{\Sigma(((a_i - 0.5)s_i + 0.5)s_i^2)}{\Sigma s_i^2} \qquad (2)$$

where *NA* is the calculated new *Approval Score* of the new application, a_i is the *Approval Score* of each retrieved old case, and s_i is the *Similarity Score* of each retrieved old case (Similarity Score is automatically calculated by ESTEEM). The difference between a_i and 0.5 represents whether the application tends to be approved or to be rejected. For example, if the difference is positive, the application tends to be approved. The larger the difference, the more significant this tendency is. Because the old case is not totally the same as the new application and the similarity is represented by s_i, so the difference, $(a_i-0.5)$, should be discounted by multiplying s_i. The square of s_i is used as the weight of each case if more than one similar case is found. The more similar the case is, the more important it is to the calculation of the new Approval Score.

Learning process of the system

There is no special learning scheme in the system. Planners can add or delete cases at any time when they think it is necessary, and then the knowledge of the system is modified. A new planning application can be stored as a new case when the planners in the Planning Department finish handling it, or when the result (approved or rejected) has been obtained from the Town Planning Board, or when any further processing has been performed as in figure 6. The planner needs to make a judgment on what Approval Score, which ranges from 0 to 1, to input to the new case before it is stored in the case library. It is based on his judgment on whether the decision by the Town Planning Board is unanimous or not and whether it encounters any problems before approval or rejection. If it is unanimously approved or rejected, the approval score of the new case can be 1 or 0, respectively. An application that was approved quickly should have a higher score than one which was approved after reviews and appeals. If an applicant applied more than once for a development, the planner can combine these applications to form a single case after the final decision is made. After the case is stored in the case library, the planners can still modify it later with new knowledge about it, such as the consequences of the approval or rejection and any new similar cases stored in the case library. The planners can also delete obsolete cases when the situation changes. Because the cases are independent from each other, adding or deleting a case has no effect on the other cases. Thus, planners can easily make the system learn from the practical work. When put into daily work, this CBS can be improved by the planners themselves, even without the assistance of knowledge engineers.

IMPLEMENTATION OF THE SYSTEM

The operation of the system conforms to the four REs cycle of a typical case-based reasoning system. When the descriptions of a new application are input, the system will retrieve similar cases in the case library and adapt them according to the defined algorithms as in figure 6. Detail information of similar cases and the suggested solutions from adaptation will be displayed to users as in figure 7. When retrieving cases, the system calculates the similarities of the old cases in the case library. Only those cases whose similarity values are larger than or equal to a threshold set by users in the *Similarity Definition Editor* will be retrieved. If more than one similar case is found, the general information on them will be listed in a table, and users can choose from this table the cases which they are interested in looking up for further details. Users can also examine the retrieved cases to find hints and information and make their own judgment in addition to the suggestion of the system.

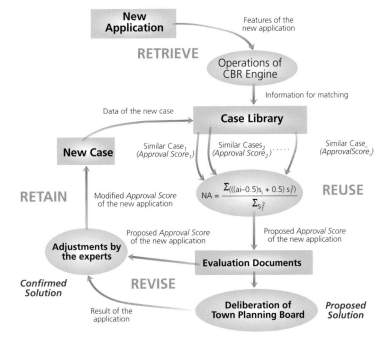

Figure 6. Flow diagram of the system.

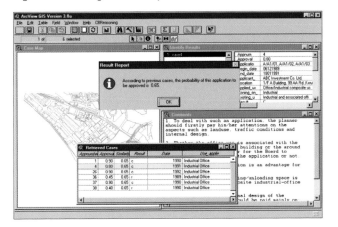

Figure 7. Retrieval of old cases and evaluation of the new application.

This chapter has shown how the integration of CBR and GIS can be used to handle planning applications in development control. The system simulates the way of handling planning applications in which the planner has to recall and make reference to similar planning application cases. Instead of doing it manually and having to rely on the experience of the planner who dealt with the case, the CBR system will help the planner to reuse previous similar cases in making decisions on the new applications, regardless of whether the planner is new or experienced. As all the relevant past cases are revealed to the planners to help them in making decisions using the recommend score of the system as a guide, this overcomes the black-box approach of a rule-based system. As the decision is vested with the planners, they can still be creative in making the final decision, but they have to justify why the decision deviates from the past cases that have been revealed by the system.

The system will be an effective and efficient PSS in helping planners to make consistent recommendations to the Town Planning Board and meeting the statutory time period in processing planning applications which is an important daily work of a planning department. As it is using past cases to give guidance to new application, it can help in making consistent decisions for similar applications. This is especially useful in developing countries in which development control is mainly done by planners. Planners have to justify why their decision on the application is different from previous similar cases as found by the system. This can avoid inconsistency and corruption in making decisions. Because it is case-based and not rule-based, once the system is developed, it can be applied to other cities in dealing with development applications by inputting the real cases of a particular city into the case library of the system.

The system is a corporate memory system (Smith et al. 2000; Stein 1995) which frees the planners from retaining a mental record of all past decisions which can be easily lost through oversight of the person involved or frequent change of staff. In addition to providing planning decision support to planners, it can also be used as an office automation system for easy retrieval of relevant past cases. It can be used to enhance the present database system which is being used for storing and retrieving past cases. Our system, which integrates the functions of CBS and GIS, can provide the ability to easily retrieve the required relevant cases, spatially or nonspatially. By integrating with GIS, it is also a visualization tool to bring the relevant graphics, data, and texts to planners.

This system is in its initial stage of development. Its capability for automatically adapting cases needs further exploration and development. For example, the system should automatically recognize the differences in the critical aspects between the new application and its precedent cases and make evaluation according to these differences and then propose modifications to the old solution. The capability of matching and adapting cases based on spatial similarities and relationships is another important topic that needs further research. For example, a pollution source has the spatial relationship of distance and direction to a residential building. The pollution source and residential building constitute a kind of spatial relationship. How to use GIS to automatically recognize this relationship and automatically retrieve cases with a similar pattern needs further research.

The use of case-based reasoning is not without limitations. One of the obvious limitations is the lack of cases for new problems and changes in the planning environment which makes previous cases irrelevant. In the absence of similar cases, the system will alert users so that they have to make a judgment without the assistance of previous cases as a general guideline. For a change in legislation, the system should alert users of such changes and delete related cases from the system's case library.

There is also a need to explore the integration of case-based reasoning with rule-based reasoning. Different reasoning engines can be complementary to each other (Bartsch-Sporl 1995, Smith et al. 2000, Kolodner 1993, Koton 1993). The integration of case-based reasoning with other KBS will make more powerful and efficient system by taking advantages of the strengths of the other techniques (Medsker 1995, p. 215). For example, case-based reasoning may be better at enlightening a user's own creativity while rule-based reasoning may be more efficient in dealing with routine processes. A rule-based system can be used when there are no cases in the CBS similar to the new application or when new regulations are introduced which make old cases in the case library irrelevant. The integration of these two reasoning engines may lead to a more powerful system for development control.

NOTES

1. ESTEEM is a registered trademark of Esteem Software, Inc.

2. ArcView is a registered trademark of ESRI.

REFERENCES

Aamodt, A., and E. Plaza. 1994. Case-based reasoning: Foundational issues, methodological variations, and system approaches. *AI Communications* 7 (1): 39–52.

Armstrong, M. P., and P. J. Densham. 1990. Database organization strategies for spatial decision support systems. *International Journal of Geographical Information Systems* 4(1): 3–20.

Armstrong, M. P., P. J. Densham, and G. Rushton. 1986. Architecture for a microcomputer-based decision support system. In *Proceedings of the 2nd international symposium on spatial data handling,* 120–21. Williamsville, N.Y.: International Geographical Union.

Barbanente, A., D. Borri, N. Maiellaro, and F. Selicato. 1995. Expert systems for development control: generalizing and communicating knowledge and procedures. In *Proceedings of 4th international conference on computer in urban planning and urban management,* ed. R. Wyatt and H. Hossain, 571–86. Melbourne, Australia.

Bartsch-Sport, B. 1995. Towards the integration of case-based, schema-based and model-based reasoning for supporting complex design tasks. In *Case-based reasoning research and development,* ed. M. Weloso and A. Aamodt, 145–56. Berlin: Springer-Verlag.

Batty, M. 1995. Urban planning and planning support systems. *Regional Development Dialogue* 16(1): v–viii.

Batty, M., and Y. Xie. 1994a. Modelling inside GIS: Part I. Model structures, exploratory spatial data analysis and aggregation. *International Journal of Geographical Information Systems.* 8(3): 291–307.

—. 1994b. Modelling inside GIS: Part II. Selecting and calibrating urban models using ARC-INFO. *International Journal of Geographical Information Systems* 8(5): 451–70.

Berry, J. K. 1987. Fundamental operations in computer assisted map analysis. *International Journal of Geographical Information Systems* 1(2): 119–36.

Borri, D., E. Conte, F. Pace, and F. Selicato. 1994. Norm: An expert system for development control in underdeveloped operational contexts. *Environment and Planning B: Planning and Design* 21:35–52.

Brail, R., and R. E. Klosterman, eds. 2001. *Planning support systems: Integrating geographic information systems, models, and visualization tools.* Redlands, Calif.: ESRI Press.

Bruton, M., and D. Nicholson. 1987. *Local planning in practice.* London: Hutchinson.

Densham, P. J. 1991. Spatial decision support systems. In *Geographical information systems: Principles and applications, vol. 1,* ed. D. J. Maguire, M. F. Goodchild, and D. W. Rhind, 403–12. New York: John Wiley and Sons.

Densham, P., and G. Rushton. 1988. Decision support system for location planning. In *Behavioral modelling in geography and planning,* ed. R. G. Golledge and H. Timmermans, 56–90. Beckenham: Croom Helm.

Douven, W., M. Grothe, P. Nijkamp, and H. Scholten. 1993. Urban and regional planning models and GIS. In *Diffusion and use of geographic information technologies,* ed. I. Masser and J. Onsrud, 317–37. Dordrecht: Kluwer.

French, S. P., and L. L. Wiggins. 1990. California planning agency experiences with automated mapping and geographic information systems. *Environment and Planning B* 17(4): 441–50.

Geertman, S., and J. Stillwell, eds. 2003. *Planning support systems in practice.* Berlin: Springer-Verlag.

Han, S. Y., and T. J. Kim. 1990. Intelligent urban information systems: Review and prospects. In *Expert systems: Applications to urban planning,* ed. T. J. Kim, L. L. Wiggins, and J. R. Wright, 241–61. New York: Springer-Verlag.

Harris, B. 1989. Beyond geographic information systems: computers and the planning professional. *Journal of the American Planning Association* 55: 85–92.

Harris, B., and M. Batty. 1993. Locational models, geographic information and planning support systems. *Journal of Planning Education and Research* 12: 184–98.

Jankowski, P. 1995. Integrating geographical information systems and multiple criteria decision-making methods. *International Journal of Geographical Information Systems* 9(3): 251–73.

Kim, T. L., L. L. Wiggins, and J. R. Wright, eds. 1990. *Expert systems: Applications to urban planning.* New York: Springer-Verlag.

Klosterman, R. E. 1995. Planning support systems. In *Proceedings of 4th international conference on computer in urban planning and urban management,* ed. R. Wyatt and H. Hossain, 19–35. Melbourne, Australia.

Kolodner, J. 1993. *Case-based reasoning.* San Mateo, Calif.: Morgan Kaufmann.

Koton, P. 1993. Combining causal models and case-based reasoning. In *Second generation expert system,* ed. J. M. David, J. P. Krivine, and R.Simmons, 69–78. Berlin: Springer-Verlag.

Landis, J. D. 1995. Imagining land use futures: Applying the California urban futures model. *Journal of the American Planning Association* 61(4): 438–57.

Leake, D. B. 1996. CBR in context: The present and future. In *Case-based reasoning: Experiences, lessons, and future directions,* ed. D. B. Leake, 3–30. Menlo Park, Calif.: AAAI Press/The MIT Press.

Leary, M, and A. Rodriguez-Bachiller. 1989. Expertise, domain-structure and expert system design: A case study in development control. *Expert Systems* 6(1): 18–23.

Levine, J., and J. D. Landis. 1989. Geographic information systems for local planning. *Journal of the American Planning Association* 55(2): 209–20.

Marchand, D. 1993. Expert system in urban planning: New tools or new toys? In *Systemes d'information geographique et systemes experts,* ed . D. Pumain, 88–91. Montpellier: GIP RECLUS.

Medsker, L. R. 1995. *Hybrid intelligent systems.* Norwell, Mass.: Kluwer.

Musen, M. 1993. An overview of knowledge acquisition. In *Second generation expert systems,* ed. J. M. David, J. P. Krivine, and R. Simmons, 405–27. Berlin: Springer-Verlag.

O'Harrow, D. 1968. Preface. In *Principles and practice of urban planning,* ed. W. I. Goodman and E. C. Freund, II. Washington, D.C.: International City Managers' Association.

Ortolano, L., and C. D. Perman. 1990. Applications to urban planning: An overview. In *Expert systems: Applications to urban planning*, ed. T. J. Kim, L. L. Wiggins, and J. R. Wright, 3–13. New York: Springer-Verlag.

Schank, R., and R. Abelson, eds. 1977. *Scripts, plans, goals and understanding.* Hillsdale, N.J.: Lawrence Erlbaum Associates.

Schank, R., and D. Leake. 1989. Creativity and learning in a case-based explainer. *Artificial Intelligence* 40(1-3): 353–85.

Turban, E. 1995. *Decision support systems and expert systems.* Englewood Cliffs, N.J.: Prentice Hall.

Tomlin, C. D. 1990. *Geographic information systems and cartographic modeling.* Englewood Cliffs, N.J.: Prentice Hall.

Shi, X., and A. G. O. Yeh. 1999. The integration of case-based systems and GIS in development control. *Environment and Planning B: Planning and Design* 26(3): 345–64.

Smith, H. G., F. V. Burstein, R. Sharma, and A. Sowunmi. 2000. Organisational memory information systems: A case-based approach to decision. In *Decision support systems for sustainable development*, ed. G. E. Kersten, Z. Mikolajuk, and A. G. Yeh, 277–90. Boston: Kluwer.

Stefik, M. 1995. *Introduction to knowledge systems.* San Francisco, Calif.: Morgan Kaufmann.

Stein, E. W. 1995. Organizational memory: Review of concepts and recommendations for management. *International Journal of Information Management* 15(1): 17–32.

Turban, E. 1995. *Decision support systems and expert systems.* Englewood Cliffs, N.J.: Prentice Hall.

Watson, I. 1995. An introduction to case-based reasoning. In *Progress in case-based reasoning: First United Kingdom workshop*, ed. I. D. Watson, 3–16. Salford, UK: Springer.

—. 1997. *Applying case-based reasoning: Techniques for enterprise systems.* San Francisco: Morgan Kaufmann.

Yeh, A. G. O., and X. Shi. 1999. Applying case-based reasoning to urban planning—A new PSS tool. *Environment and Planning B: Planning and Design* 26(1): 101–16.

Yeh, A. G. O. 1999. Urban planning and GIS. In *Geographical information systems: Principles, techniques, management and applications*, ed. P. Longley, M. Goodchild, D. Maguire, and D. Rhind, 877–88. New York: John Wiley and Sons.

Introduction to Section 4: Environmental Applications

MICHAEL F. GOODCHILD

NATIONAL CENTER FOR GEOGRAPHIC INFORMATION AND ANALYSIS

UNIVERSITY OF CALIFORNIA

SANTA BARBARA, CALIFORNIA

Many of the earliest roots of GIS were in environmental applications, including Tomlinson's Canada Geographic Information System of the mid-1960s and McHarg's overlay techniques of the 1970s. Although admirable progress has been made in recent years in extending GIS applications into the social and health sciences, in part through efforts such as those of the Center for Spatially Integrated Social Science (CSISS: www.csiss.org), environmental applications remain prominent and continue to drive the development of systems and tools. This section of the book includes six chapters that in various ways explore the application of spatial analysis and modeling to environmental issues, in the context of GIS.

The section begins with a chapter on hydrology, based on the extensive efforts beginning about six years ago to develop a specialized data model for hydrologic applications of ArcGIS that evolved into Arc Hydro. Maidment and his team at the University of Texas at Austin have done excellent work in developing Arc Hydro and promoting its use, and in chapter 15, they show how the approach has been used to underpin a series of sophisticated models of hydrologic system dynamics. ESRI has sponsored the development of specialized data models in many domains and vertical markets (for a current listing, see support.esri.com/datamodels), and one can imagine similar efforts to integrate dynamic models with specialized data models in areas as diverse as transportation and health.

The second chapter in the section, chapter 16, describes the work of a team at the University of Utrecht, led by Burrough, to develop a GIS for the specific purpose of dynamic modeling. As its name suggests, PCRaster models systems as layers of raster cells and includes a range of functions appropriate to dynamic modeling. Each time step of a system is represented as a separate raster layer, and in a simulation, the sequence of iterations becomes an ordered sequence of layers. The language used by PCRaster was developed in a notable dissertation by van Deursen and provides a succinct and efficient way to encode transformations and models. PCRaster has now been used to simulate a very impressive range of processes and systems, from the development of a fault-block landscape over millions of years to the dispersal of seeds over a few hours, and from scales of centimeters to hundreds of kilometers. PCRaster provides a convenient and powerful platform for the simulation of processes that are written as partial differential equations and solved using finite-difference methods and also for processes that can be simulated as cellular automata.

Chapter 17 provides a nice contrast by focusing on Idrisi, a GIS with roots in education and raster processing that has perhaps done more than any other development to advance GIS support for spatial decisions. Eastman has led the Idrisi team since its inception and has built up an extremely impressive collection of GIS applications in areas as diverse as New England and Nepal. The chapter focuses on land-cover change and on its prediction, using a range of analytic and modeling tools, and provides a very useful comparison of methods, evaluating their performance using appropriately chosen metrics.

The focus in all of chapters 15 through 17 is on modeling at the aggregate level, and it would indeed be absurd to try to model hydrologic systems using individual-agent methods applied to each independent molecule of water and grain of sand. But in chapter 18, Ahearn and Smith look at a very different system in which the individual agents are large, powerful, and rare—the habitat of *Panthera tigris*. In addition to being magnificent creatures, large carnivores are at the top of the food chain and as such are frequently viewed as indicator species that can reveal the health of an entire ecosystem. If the tiger is in trouble, it is argued, then the ecosystem that supports it must be in trouble as well Thus the management of tiger populations is particularly important, especially given the numerous threats that exist to their habitat and survival. Chapter 18 illustrates the power of individual-agent modeling, in which each tiger is in effect a processor, taking in information and exhibiting spatial behavior as a consequence. Ahearn and Smith detail the rules used in the model to characterize behavior and the basis on which these rules have been specified. Models such as this are of great value in allowing managers to examine alternative policies and scenarios, and ideally they would be constantly available and primed with current information so that the consequences of day-to-day management decisions could be investigated before they are made.

The agent-based models of chapter 19 by Parker are similar in concept, but very different in application. Decisions over land use are made by numerous individuals and agencies and often at locations that are substantially distant from the land in question. The consequences of these decisions are critical, however, to the survival of species that depend on access to defined areas of contiguous habitat. Thus the most important outputs of such models are predictions of landscape fragmentation. Parker reviews recent progress on agent-based models of land-use change and the use of GIS to support such modeling. The models raise important questions and issues. For example, how is it possible to ensure that the predictions of such models are accurate when the periods that are the subject of the predictions are well into the future? How can the behavior of the individual agents in the system be captured and represented as rules? What are the appropriate levels of temporal and spatial resolution for such models?

In the final chapter of this section, chapter 20, Duh and Brown look at land-use patterns from a different perspective, asking whether it is possible to use models to create patterns that have specific characteristics. This is, in a sense, the reverse of Parker's approach, starting with an ideal landscape and asking what behaviors would be needed to achieve it, rather than starting with behaviors and asking what landscapes result. Both are clearly valuable in planning and management, and tools for both approaches are slowly making their way from the research community to practitioners. GIS platforms provide an ideal foundation for both types, and it is heartening to note that GIS support for modeling is expanding at a rapid pace, as Maguire so clearly demonstrated in chapter 2.

Taken together, the six chapters of this section illustrate all of the major approaches to modeling in environmental science, with the possible exception of finite-element modeling. The latter field currently dominates modeling efforts in areas such as river and estuary hydrodynamics, the modeling of windflow and other atmospheric processes, and groundwater flow, all areas where processes are described by partial differential equations. At present, such modeling tends to use specialized software, and to date, there has been little progress in integrating it with GIS. Given the current rate of progress, however, there seems every reason to expect greater interaction between the two fields in the coming years.

Chapter 15   *Hydrologic Modeling*

DAVID R. MAIDMENT, OSCAR ROBAYO, AND VENKATESH MERWADE

CENTER FOR RESEARCH IN WATER RESOURCES

UNIVERSITY OF TEXAS AT AUSTIN

AUSTIN, TEXAS

ABSTRACT

HYDROLOGIC INFORMATION SYSTEMS require the integration of information in space and time with hydrologic models, and such integration is supported by the Arc Hydro data model for water resources in ArcGIS. Hydrologic processes such as conversion of rainfall to runoff or flow routing down rivers can be linked to ArcGIS by calling hydrologic simulation models as tools using the ArcGIS ModelBuilder. The interaction between the hydrologic models and ArcGIS is facilitated by constructing within the geodatabase a detailed Interface Data Model for each hydrologic model under consideration. A case study of flood simulation for Rosillo Creek in San Antonio, Texas, integrating Arc Hydro with HEC-HMS and HEC-RAS is presented to illustrate these concepts.

INTRODUCTION   The purpose of this chapter is to describe hydrologic modeling and its integration with ArcGIS using experience accumulated through many projects carried out at the Center for Research in Water Resources of the University of Texas at Austin. A conceptual framework for thinking about the integration of modeling and GIS in a hydrologic context is presented and illustrated using a case study of the development of a Regional Watershed Modeling System for San Antonio, Texas.

In general, hydrologic modeling is undertaken to address four types of water problems: floods, droughts, water pollution, and degradation of aquatic ecosystems. In all cases, what is needed first is a description of the physical environment through which the water flows and second, a simulation of water movement and the transport of constituents such as the sediment, dissolved chemicals, and bacteria that water carries as it flows. GIS is very useful for the first task, namely the description of the physical environment. This includes defining the shape of the land surface terrain, watershed and stream network delineation, description of soils and land-cover properties, and the three-dimensional depiction of channel and floodplain morphology. These quantities are spatially varying, often in a very detailed manner, but they change little in time.

Hydrologic modeling is used for the second task, namely simulation of water velocity, depth, discharge, and quality throughout a domain of interest, such as a watershed, river channel system, or groundwater aquifer. The modeled variables can fluctuate rapidly in time, as evidenced by the fact that the standard interval for recording of streamflow discharge is every fifteen minutes, and for radar remote sensing of rainfall, the standard sampling interval is even shorter, on the order of every six minutes. By contrast, a few hydrologic investigators even seek insight in geological records of floodplain deposits to assess the severity of floods going back millennia in geologic time! Thus, the representation of geospatial information over many time scales is necessary to support hydrologic modeling.

The earth's waters move continuously through the hydrologic cycle (fig. 1), in which water evaporated from the oceans and the land surface flows over the earth as part of atmospheric circulation, returns to the earth as precipitation, runs off into streams and rivers, soaks into the soils and groundwater aquifers, is stored in lakes and reservoirs, and eventually flows back out into the sea again. The manner and speed at which water flows in the atmosphere, in surface water, and in groundwater differ so much from one another that hydrologic models are normally applied just for one part of the hydrologic cycle and typically just to address a single kind of water problem (e.g., flooding).

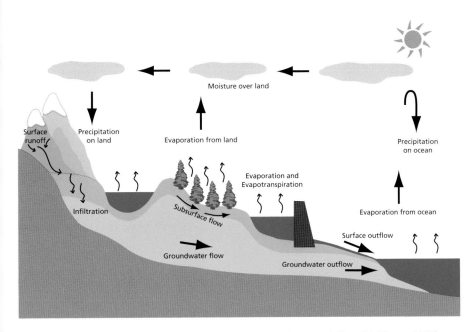

Figure 1. Hydrologic cycle—the circulation of the waters of the earth (from Maidment 2002).

HYDROLOGIC INFORMATION SYSTEM

A hydrologic information system is a synthesis of geospatial and temporal data and hydrologic models that supports hydrologic analysis and decision making (fig. 2). A hydrologic information system can be built from a geographic information system, provided that capabilities are added to represent time-varying data, three-dimensional spatial features, and the operation of hydrologic models. While it is theoretically possible to carry out hydrologic modeling within GIS, the lack of both robust time-varying data structures and an internal dynamic modeling system mean that most hydrologic modeling is still carried out using external hydrologic models which exchange information with the GIS (Djokic et al. 1995, Sui and Maggio 1999). An exception to this rule is the modeling of time-invariant systems, such as estimation of mean annual runoff and pollutant loads, which can be carried out completely within GIS.

Hydrologic information system

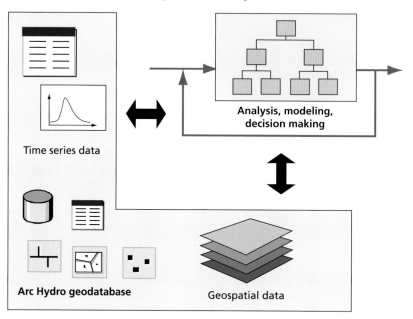

Figure 2. A hydrologic information system combines geospatial and temporal information with hydrologic models (from Maidment 2002).

Further complicating this situation is the fact that representation of both discrete entities and continuous fields is needed. Atmospheric water knows no boundaries except the land surface, atmospheric properties vary continuously in three dimensions, and the hydrologic interaction of the atmosphere with the land surface is described by two-dimensional spatial fields of precipitation and evaporation. These spatial fields are intimately tied to similar two-dimensional fields describing the energy balance of solar radiation and heat at the land surface. All these fields vary continuously through time.

Surface water flow in streams and rivers has sculpted the shape of the earth's surface since time immemorial. The domain of a surface water hydrology model is typically defined by a watershed boundary delineated along the drainage divide that separates flow draining into the stream network of interest from that draining away from those streams. Stream and river networks are represented in GIS by connected sets of line segments, and watershed and water bodies by sets of polygons. Streamflow gauging stations and water quality monitoring sites are represented as points, and the water flow and water quality data measured at these gauges is stored as tables. Soils and land-cover data is represented as rasters or polygon features. Thus, GIS is well suited to depicting the geospatial domain of surface water hydrology models, provided that a suitable arrangement for the attachment of tables of water observations is included in the database.

Groundwater flow takes place very slowly through soil and rock strata called hydrogeologic units that are either aquifers (allow significant water flow) or aquitards (allow very little water flow). The thickness and properties of these units vary spatially, sometimes smoothly, sometimes abruptly. For groundwater flow, the fundamental geospatial entities are arbitrarily shaped volume features.

So, if the whole picture of atmospheric water, surface water, and groundwater is considered, a hydrologic information system needs to be able to support discrete entities as points, lines, areas, and volumes. It also needs to be able to support 2D and 3D continuous spatial fields of information, and some of the variables or attributes of discrete objects described on these domains must be represented as time-varying. Fortunately, it turns out that, with appropriate application development and with new core software engineering presently being done for ArcGIS, a reasonable hydrologic information system can be constructed using ArcGIS as the core platform.

TIME AND SPACE

When a hydrologic modeling project is set up, three basic questions have to be answered: (1) What is the spatial domain of the model and how will that domain be subdivided into analysis units? (2) What is the time horizon for the model and into what intervals will this horizon be subdivided for modeling purposes (e.g., hourly, daily, monthly, annual intervals)? (3) What variables will the model determine (e.g., rainfall, evaporation, streamflow, groundwater flow, water quality constituents)? One can imagine that these considerations can be described on a *data cube* (fig. 3), in which the three principal axes are space, time, and variables, indexed by L, T, V, respectively, and that a particular data value D is a function of what feature it describes, what time it represents, and what variable it is, D(L,T,V).

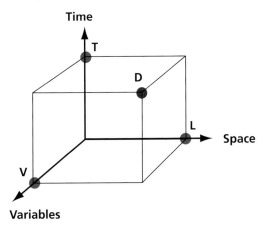

Figure 3. Data for a variable measured at a particular point in space and time (from Maidment 2002).

This conceptual data cube is the basis for the tabular time series model used in the Arc Hydro data model (Maidment 2002). In Arc Hydro, all geospatial features throughout a geodatabase have a unique identifying number, their HydroID, that is generated using Arc Hydro tools in such a manner that once issued, the same HydroID is never used again in a particular geodatabase. In Arc Hydro time series tables, the HydroID of the feature is stored as an attribute FeatureID so as to support a one-to-many database relationship between the feature and the time series describing that feature, such as streamflow values measured at a particular gauging station. Similarly, the type of time series data (e.g., streamflow, rainfall) is indexed by a TSType table that also specifies the time interval, the origin of the data (measured or simulated), whether the data is regularly or irregularly recorded in time, and a specification of the abstract character of the time series—is it an instantaneous value valid at this time instant or a value defined over the interval between this time instant and the next?

All time series data in Arc Hydro is time-stamped with an attribute, TSDateTime, that is an instantaneous time value valid at the beginning of a time interval. Each individual data value is labeled as a TSValue, and thus, the abstract model D(L,T,V) is actually implemented as a four-column table TSValue (FeatureID, TSDateTime, TSTypeID). In this manner, a single table can store time series data for multiple spatial features from several feature classes and multiple types of time series data. In effect, each time series is really a collection of time-indexed data table records, so this structure supports both regularly and irregularly recorded time series data. Figure 4 shows an Arc Hydro time series table, which also includes a fifth field, ObjectID, which is a standard field that indexes the records in all ArcGIS tables.

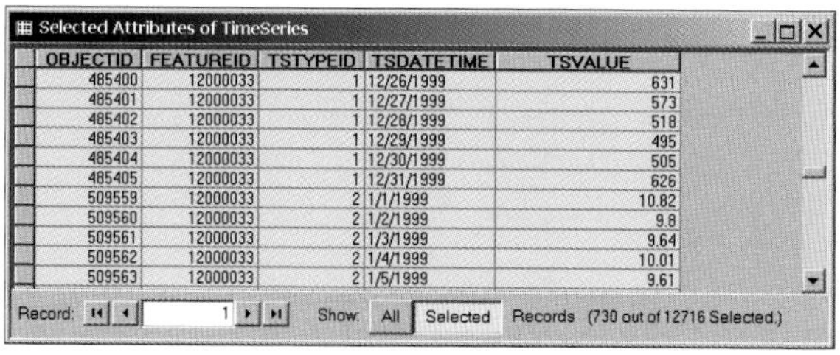
Selected Attributes of TimeSeries

OBJECTID	FEATUREID	TSTYPEID	TSDATETIME	TSVALUE
485400	12000033	1	12/26/1999	631
485401	12000033	1	12/27/1999	573
485402	12000033	1	12/28/1999	518
485403	12000033	1	12/29/1999	495
485404	12000033	1	12/30/1999	505
485405	12000033	1	12/31/1999	626
509559	12000033	2	1/1/1999	10.82
509560	12000033	2	1/2/1999	9.8
509561	12000033	2	1/3/1999	9.64
509562	12000033	2	1/4/1999	10.01
509563	12000033	2	1/5/1999	9.61

Record: 1 Show: All Selected Records (730 out of 12716 Selected.)

Figure 4. An Arc Hydro time series table for daily streamflow (TSTypeID = 1) and water level (TSTypeID = 2) at the gauging station of the Guadalupe River at Victoria, Texas (FeatureID = 12000033), during January and February 1999 (from Maidment 2002).

The tabular Arc Hydro time series model works well for describing time-varying information on discrete features, and data tables containing up to five million records have been constructed. Database performance diminishes as the size of the data tables increases, but performance is acceptable in a personal ArcGIS geodatabase with data tables of the order of 100,000 records. For larger databases, the time series information should be split among several tables or stored in a fully relational database such as SQL/Server or Oracle using Enterprise ArcGIS.

While the geospatial time series model just described is adequate for storing tabular data on discrete features, hydrologic modeling requires a more complete description of space and time and in particular, how to convert between continuous and discrete space–time data. One way of thinking more broadly is illustrated in figure 5, which shows four different types of time series representations developed in a study of flood inundation of the Kissimmee River in Florida (Sorenson et al. 2004): Time series, Attribute series, Raster series, and Feature series.

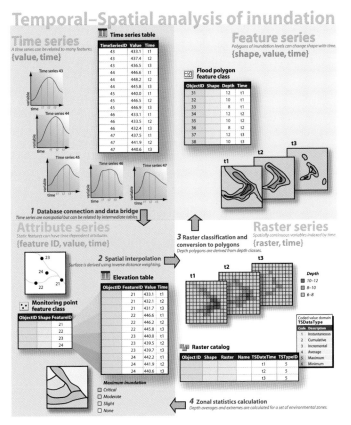

Figure 5. Temporal–spatial analysis of inundation (from Arctur and Zeiler 2004).

Beginning with the top left panel of this diagram, one can think of a time series as being simply a set of {value, time} pairs that may have loose spatial connections or no spatial connection at all, such as the Dow-Jones industrial index of stock prices. In this event, it is convenient to index the time series simply by an arbitrary number TimeSeriesID. Variants of this concept are used in many hydrologic modeling systems, including the Hydrologic Engineering Center's Data Storage System (DSS) (USACE 1995), a time series inventory that underlies all the HEC models; the WDM file system used in the Hydrologic Simulation Program Fortran; and the DSF file system that underlies the hydrologic models of the Danish Hydraulic Institute. The South Florida Water Management District manages its water observation data in a very large corporate database in which each time series is indexed by a randomly generated five-character text string called the *dbKey*. This database includes records of water-surface elevation versus time measured at gauges in the Kissimmee River flood plain.

Moving to the lower left portion of figure 5, suppose that each gauge observation record is associated with the gauge as a spatial feature; that is, a triplet {featureID, value, time} is thus formed where now the feature class of water level gauges has an attribute, the water-surface elevation that changes through time. This type of time series can be termed an Attribute series because it represents the time-varying values of a map attribute, and a comparable series of time-varying values exists for each gauge feature in the feature class. Arc Hydro time series are thus Attribute series under this definition.

Attribute series are defined on discrete features, but an equivalent representation can be constructed in the raster domain by spatially interpolating the water-surface elevations at the gauges onto a raster showing the water-surface elevation over the floodplain. Each raster is indexed by its time point to form the pair {raster, time}, and these pairs are stored in an ArcGIS Raster catalog, as shown in the lower right panel of figure 5.

If the water-surface elevation rasters are classified into depth zones using a classification table, each raster can be converted into a set of classified features whose geometry evolves through time as the inundation of the floodplain advances and recedes during a flood season. This type of time series, now having spatially varying feature geometries, is here termed a Feature series, as shown in the upper right portion of figure 5. These features form a triplet {shape, value, time}. Under these definitions, an Attribute series represents geographic features whose shape is fixed in time but whose attributes vary, while a Feature series represents geographic features whose shape and attributes can both vary through time.

If one takes a Raster series and lays it over a set of points, lines, or areas, Zonal statistics can be used to summarize the values of the Rasters overlying discrete spatial features. Thus, an Attribute series can be produced from a Raster series, as indicated at the bottom of figure 5, where the inundation time series occurring on particular habitat-zone polygons is quantified. The interaction between Attribute series and Raster series has proven particularly valuable to accomplish data transformations in many hydrologic modeling projects undertaken at CRWR.

Raster series can also be directly ingested from other continuous spatial representations of data. For example, the U.S. National Centers for Environmental Prediction has produced a North American Regional Reanalysis of climate, which contains a representation of the climate of North America on a 32 km grid at 3-hour time intervals from 1979 to 2003 (wwwt.emc.ncep.noaa.gov/mmb/rreanl/index.html). Variables describing atmospheric conditions and fluxes are presented as 2D and 3D time-varying grid maps. The 2D grids of energy and water fluxes at the land surface can be converted to Raster series and thus brought into the GIS environment.

**INTEGRATION OF
HYDROLOGIC MODELS**

Hydrologic simulation models are usually developed independently of GIS, and they are based on a set of binary and ASCII files whose form is very specific to the model being represented. Arc Hydro is a geographic data model for water resources features of the landscape—it does not know the details about how these features are represented or generalized for a particular hydrologic model. It is possible, however, to generate within the geodatabase an exact representation in tabular form of the information content of the ASCII and binary files supporting a hydrologic model. This is called an Interface Data Model because it stands at the interface between the GIS and the hydrologic model.

Interface Data Models have been developed at CRWR for the HEC-HMS and HEC-RAS hydrologic models produced by the U.S. Army Corps of Engineers Hydrologic Engineering Center (HEC). The Hydrologic Modeling System (HMS) transforms rainfall into streamflow (USACE 2000a) and the River Analysis System (RAS) transforms streamflow into water-surface elevations along the river system (USACE 2000b). By exchanging information through their respective Interface Data Models, it is possible for both hydrologic models to communicate with the Arc Hydro geodatabase and also for information to flow from one model to the other, as shown in figure 6.

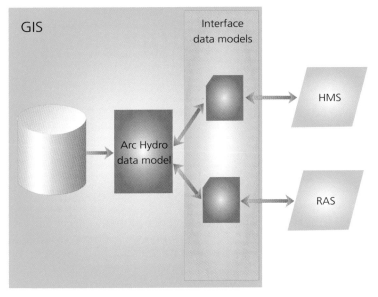

Figure 6. Information interchange among Arc Hydro and the hydrologic models HMS (Hydrologic Modeling System) and RAS (River Analysis System).

Map2Map is an application built using the ArcGIS ModelBuilder environment that integrates Arc Hydro, HEC-HMS, and HEC-RAS to automatically transform a NEXRAD radar rainfall map into a flood inundation map. Map2Map is part of a larger project called the Regional Watershed Modeling System undertaken by a coalition of water agencies in San Antonio, Texas, coordinated by the San Antonio River Authority (SARA). As shown in figure 7, the overall idea of this modeling system is to *bring the models together* for flooding, water quality, groundwater, water supply, and other issues using a common geospatial data framework compiled by the cooperating agencies and common rainfall and model-calibration data for flows and water quality. The intent is then to use the resulting integrated modeling system to support a variety of water planning and management functions. Given the individual and very specific nature of each of the different types of hydrologic models involved, this is no small task!

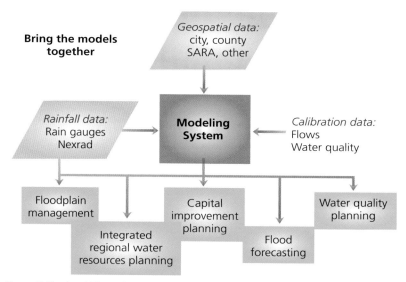

Figure 7. Regional Watershed Modeling System for San Antonio.

The manner in which the geospatial connections are made among Arc Hydro and the two hydrologic models is illustrated in figure 8. Arc Hydro contains in its framework model a set of watersheds and a stream network for the drainage basin of Salado Creek and a set of stream cross sections for Rosillo Creek, a subarea within the Salado Creek basin. Arc Hydro also has tools that create a Schematic Network of points and lines over the landscape. The green points and lines in figure 8 symbolize the connection between the watersheds and points on the stream channel at their outlets; the red points and lines in figure 8 symbolize point-to-point connections along the stream network. This Schematic Network is an exact replica of the topological arrangement of the hydrologic objects within the hydrologic model, HEC-HMS.

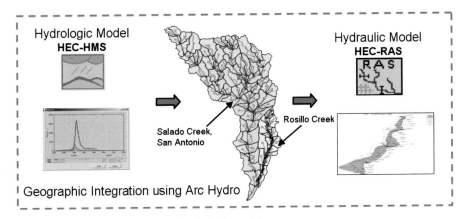

Figure 8. Geographic integration of hydrologic models.

Similarly, for Rosillo Creek, the set of stream cross sections in Arc Hydro corresponds exactly to the stream cross sections in the HEC-RAS hydraulic model (hydraulic models are those that take stream discharge and convert that into flow velocity and water-surface elevation). Arc Hydro has a HydroJunction feature class whose features mark points of interest along the stream network—in this study, the HydroJunctions are located at each red dot in figure 8. By establishing database relationships between the HydroJunction and the corresponding Schematic Node, CrossSection, and time series of flow and water-surface elevation produced by the models at a given point in the stream network, the flow of information among the three systems is accomplished. The points where this occurs in the landscape are called Information Exchange Points.

Map2Map is implemented in the ArcGIS 9 ModelBuilder environment. This environment provides functions to process sequential geoprocessing tasks automatically on spatial datasets. This environment not only uses standard ESRI geoprocessing tools but can also use customized scripts that perform specialized tasks needed for integration and are not available as standard tools in GIS.

The general procedure for Map2Map is composed of eight components:

1. Transfer time series from NEXRAD files into the geodatabase

2. Transfer time series from NEXRAD polygons in the geodatabase to watersheds

3. Create an input DSS file for HEC-HMS using watershed rainfall time series from the geodatabase

4. Run HMS to produce runoff hydrographs

5. Transfer time series of streamflow from the HMS output to the geodatabase and then to a DSS file for HEC-RAS

6. Run RAS to produce water-surface elevations at each cross section

7. Create a water-surface raster using cross section water-surface elevations

8. Subtract the land-surface raster from the water-surface raster and create a polygon representing inundated area

The implementation of these steps using the ModelBuilder environment is shown in figure 9.

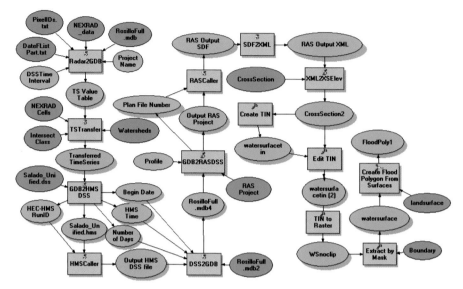

Figure 9. Workflow automation of the transformation of NEXRAD rainfall maps to flood-inundation maps.

In the ModelBuilder environment, each blue oval represents an input GIS dataset, a green oval represents an output dataset, and a yellow rectangle represents a processing tool. A processing tool with a hammer symbol represents a generic GIS tool, and a tool with a script symbol represents a custom tool that employs user-defined scripts. The tools labeled HMSCaller and RASCaller in figure 9 are custom-built tools that directly call the hydrologic model codes from within ArcGIS ModelBuilder without needing to use the graphical user interfaces for the hydrologic models. Thus, a hydrologic model operates as a tool embedded within the ArcGIS ModelBuilder environment.

NEXRAD radar rainfall is defined using 4 km cells as shown in figure 10. For these cells, rainfall data is available for each hour during the several days that this particular storm occurred over San Antonio. The flood-inundation map is a static image that represents the highest elevation that the water reached in the creek at any time during the storm period. Flood mapping is a complex task where the sensitivity of the flood map to details of the representation of the flood plain terrain is critical (Noman et al. 2001). Map2Map achieves a great saving in time through workflow automation, executing in minutes what would otherwise take hours or even days to accomplish. The resulting floodplain maps need to be checked for authenticity against high-water marks observed during the flood events depicted.

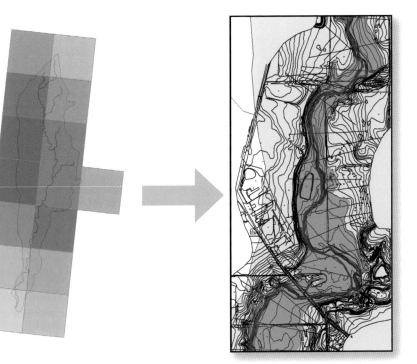

Figure 10. Time-varying NEXRAD radar rainfall over the watershed is converted into a flood-inundation map along Rosillo Creek.

CONCLUSIONS

The integration of hydrologic modeling and GIS has to confront many complexities, including the need to integrate time-varying information on water movement through the landscape with static information about the character of the landscape. Another complex task is to integrate file-based hydrologic simulation models with database-oriented GIS. Detailed attention to geodatabase design, accommodation of time-varying data tables within GIS, and workflow automation using ArcGIS ModelBuilder, in which hydrologic models are called as GIS tools, are useful steps in this process.

ACKNOWLEDGMENTS

The authors wish to acknowledge the financial support of this research by the San Antonio River Authority and the collaboration in carrying out the study of the consulting firm PBS&J, Austin.

REFERENCES

Arctur, D. and M. Zeiler. 2004. *Designing geodatabases: Case studies in GIS data modeling*. Redlands, Calif.: ESRI Press.

Djokic, D., A. Coates, and J. E. Ball. 1995. GIS as integration tool for hydrologic modeling: A need for generic hydrologic data exchange format. *1995 ESRI user conference*, 22–6. Redlands, Calif.: ESRI.

Maidment, D. R., 2002. *Arc Hydro: GIS for water resources*. Redlands, Calif.: ESRI Press.

Noman N. S., E. J. Nelson, and A. K. Zundel. 2001. Review of automated floodplain delineation from digital terrain models. *Journal of Water Resources Planning and Management* 127(6): 394–402.

Sorenson J., J. Goodall, and D. Maidment. 2004. Arc Hydro time series framework for defining hydroperiod inundation. AWRA Spring Specialty Conference, May 17-19, 2004, Nashville, Tenn.

Sui, D. Z., and R. C. Maggio. 1999. Integrating GIS with hydrological modeling: Practices, problems, and prospects. *Computers, Environment and Urban Systems* 23: 33–51.

U.S. Army Corps of Engineers (USACE). 1995. *HEC-DSS, user's guide and utility manuals, user's manual*. CPD–45. Davis, Calif.: Hydrologic Engineering Center.

U.S. Army Corps of Engineers (USACE). 2000a. *HEC-HMS hydrologic modeling system, user's manual*. Davis, Calif.: Hydrologic Engineering Center.

U.S. Army Corps of Engineers (USACE). 2002b. HEC-RAS: River analysis system. *Hydraulic reference manual*. Version 3.1. Davis, Calif.: Hydrologic Engineering Center.

Chapter 16
Environmental Modeling With PCRaster

PETER A. BURROUGH AND DEREK KARSSENBERG

UTRECHT CENTRE FOR ENVIRONMENT AND LANDSCAPE DYNAMICS

UTRECHT UNIVERSITY

UTRECHT, THE NETHERLANDS

WILLEM VAN DEURSEN

PCRASTER ENVIRONMENTAL SOFTWARE

UTRECHT, THE NETHERLANDS

ABSTRACT

MODERN GIS ARE WELL DEVELOPED for dealing with information on the spatial distribution of static objects and continuous fields, but most lack the ability to deal with the change of patterns or collections of objects over time. Consequently, they may be poorly equipped to deal with dynamic space–time processes such as flooding, erosion, plant growth, tectonics, or diffusion of plants and animals. Although raster GIS are often used to link stand-alone dynamic models of spatial change to geographic databases, few incorporate the process modeling in the GIS itself.

Developments during the past ten years show that GIS toolkits can be developed to address many of the generic aspects of space–time modeling. Temporal changes in attributes of cell values can be computed for single cells or locations, for neighborhoods of varying size and shape, for transport of materials over a network, or for action at a distance. Extreme flexibility in space–time modeling is given by writing the basic operations in easy-to-understand commands. Once the model has been set up and run, the changes can be visualized as a film, providing the user with extra understanding of the processes being modeled.

This chapter discusses the basic ideas behind space–time modeling using embedded GIS generic commands, in particular the PCRaster toolkit. It starts with a simple model of rainfall-runoff interaction over a small catchment for which each attribute of the model is given by a single raster layer. The ideas are extended to large-scale landscape change ranging from landscape building (a volcano) to landscape degradation (gulley-forming and erosion). It also shows how the generic toolkit may itself be used as a computer modeling language and how simple and complex geographic models can be created. Finally, the chapter introduces new developments in PCRaster that provide special facilities for modeling the sedimentation and erosion of material on three-dimensional stacks of cells.

INTRODUCTION: A GENERIC APPROACH TO ENVIRONMENTAL MODELING

Modern geographical information systems (GIS) provide a consistent and mature technology for storing, organizing, retrieving, and modifying information on the spatial distribution of plants, natural resources, forest areas, land use, land parcels, utilities, and many other natural and anthropogenic features (Burrough and McDonnell 1998). Although GIS offers a well-established and well-defined framework for the analysis of the spatial component of geographic problems, support for the analysis of the temporal or dynamic component of these issues is largely lacking. This chapter deals with the development and applications of a generic approach for such a dynamic framework.

With respect to their representation of space, GIS are often divided into *raster* GIS (based on a tesselation of space) and *vector* GIS (detailed geographic representation of boundaries of well-defined objects). The raster representation is often ideal for spatial analysis because it provides a common and consistent basis for computing new attributes from existing data. This aspect of raster spatial data analysis was developed by Dana Tomlin (1990) in his Map Analysis Package, which forms the basis of the ArcView Spatial Analyst. The ideas behind the methods of cartographic algebra that were embodied in the Map Analysis Package are based on the view that space can be divided into regular, orthogonal cells or grids which can be subjected to well-defined, generic, and primitive transformations. As in ordinary algebra, these transformations can be linked together in sequence to compute more complex functions. For example, using a gridded digital elevation model, it is possible to compute a slope hazard map by computing the slope of the land at every cell as a function of the elevations of the cells surrounding it and then to select and display those cells for which the slope exceeds a given value.

Raster GIS are often used to supply data to and display results from stand-alone models that run on databases external to the GIS. This has often been deemed necessary for computer models of processes that involve the use or input of time-related data. Increasingly, however, people have perceived the need for GIS toolkits that are equipped with generic suites of algorithms for spatial and temporal analysis and modeling. These GIS toolkits (known variously as Map Algebra or Map Calculus) provide a computational scripting language based on simple, easy-to-understand mathematical operations for which various classes of primitive operation can be distinguished (Burrough 1998, Eastman 2003, Tomlin 1990, Pullar 2003, Takeyama and Couclelis 1997). The main classes of spatial operations found in these GIS toolkits are:

i.   Operations on single cells or locations (point operations or local functions)

ii. Operations in which a value is computed for a cell that lies at the center of a surrounding circular or rectangular block of cells (neighborhood operations or focal functions)

iii. Operations that compute the flux of material over a topologically linked route (network functions; e.g., water over a river network)

iv. Operations that involve action at a distance (surface functions; e.g., a viewshed or area that can be seen from a given point or the amount of solar radiation falling on a surface at a given time of day and year)

v.   Operations calculating statistics of an attribute for each area (zonal functions; e.g., the average soil contamination for each land-use type)

FROM SPACE TO TIME: THE BASIC PRINCIPLES OF DYNAMIC SPATIAL MODELING

In many environmental problems (such as rainfall-runoff interactions, soil erosion, dispersion of plants and animals, water quality variations, land cover, and landform change) where patterns change in response to external forces, it is essential to include the time component in the analysis. This gives rise to a dynamic spatial model, which is defined as a mathematical representation of a real-world process in which the state of a geographic field or object changes in response to variations in the driving forces. Any system for modeling space–time processes must include procedures for discretizing space–time and for the computation of new attributes for the spatial and temporal units in response to the driving forces.

Like space, time can be divided in different ways. Computationally, the easiest way is to discretize time into equal steps, and that is the procedure followed in PCRaster. When discretizing both time and space, the choice of the size of the interval or cell is extremely important because variations that occur within the dimensions of the cell will not be registered by either the data or the process. Therefore, it is essential to choose the correct spatial and temporal resolution.

Dynamic modeling involves computing the temporal change of the *state* of an entity in response to information from *driving forces* (or inputs) and the *processes* that act in the system being modeled. In a dynamic modeling program, temporal change is represented by discrete time steps, applying the following equation for each time step:

$$\mathbf{z}_{t+1} = f(\mathbf{z}_t, \mathbf{i}_t) \qquad \text{for each } t \qquad (1)$$

The equation shows that the change in the state *(z)* of an entity from a specific time step *t* to the next time step *t*+1 is a function of the processes (*f*) in the system and the driving forces (**i**). The state of each entity (object or grid cell) is described by three kinds of information, namely *what is it? where is it?* and *what is its relation to other entities?* The nature of an entity is given by its *attributes,* its whereabouts by its geographic *location* or *coordinates,* and the spatial relations between different entities in terms of *proximity* and *connectivity* (topology).

In a dynamic model, the processes (*f* in equation 1) in the system causing changes in *z* from each time step *t* to *t*+1 are represented in an iterative modeling program using standard spatial operations, combining operations from the five standard groups of spatial operations described earlier. Note that this set of operations is the same for each time step, since in most cases it can be assumed that the kind of processes occurring in the system does not change through time. These mathematical operations are described in detail by Burrough and McDonnell (1998) and are to be found in many standard GIS. A dynamic GIS expands the capabilities of these operations by allowing them to be placed in an interactive loop that represents the temporal behavior of the processes *f*.

In addition to these standard groups of spatial operations to represent *f*, additional operations are provided in dynamic modeling to represent the driving forces or inputs **i**. These *timeinput operations* are used to read driving forces as inputs to the model, for each time step and for each grid cell. In most cases, the driving forces are derived from time series of observations sampled at points or over areas. Dynamic modeling also requires efficient data storage and retrieval to access and use intermediate results and to report them to file. These files can be displayed as time series plots and animated 2D maps or 2.5D drapes to provide the user with dynamic visual output. In addition, the dynamic modeling of surface changes (transport of material from place to place) may not only require all of the usual raster GIS functionality but also the specific ability to derive surface topology and use that information to transfer data from cell to cell.

A TOOLKIT FOR DYNAMIC SPATIAL MODELING—PCRASTER

Many scientists have approached the problem of modeling dynamic aspects of environmental processes by writing individual models using standard languages such as FORTRAN or C++ which could be interfaced with GIS. These models are often difficult to maintain and modify, particularly if the original author is no longer working in the team.

PCRaster (Van Deursen 1995, PCRaster 2004, Wesseling et al. 1996) was the first widely available raster GIS to incorporate a dynamic, generic modeling tool that takes Map Algebra beyond the static timeless spatial analysis model.

This has been made possible by the development of a modeling language with a large number of basic analysis operations that can be linked in programs (i.e., scripts). Many of these operations extend existing Map Algebra concepts with the notion and control of time.

PCRaster is a dynamic modeling language that fills the gap between standard nondynamic or nontemporal commercial GIS and the off-line dynamic model or the once-off program. It operates in the raster domain, providing a large selection (>150) of standardized, generic operations for spatial and temporal analysis, including a full set of mathematical tools for computing new attributes from the original attributes of each cell. It also includes a wide range of operations for modeling spatial dispersion (neighborhood interactions) and directed transport over topological networks. These operations can be driven by data from 1D or 2D time series to provide interactive dynamic models of spatial and temporal processes with feedback loops. Visual output of results is in the form of 1D graphs or 2D (and 2.5D) stacks of maps.

A model written in PCRaster should adhere to the four precepts of good modeling given by Casti (1997), namely *simplicity, clarity, freedom from bias,* and *tractability.* Figure 1 provides a conceptual overview of the structure of a PCRaster program, and further details are given in Table 1. The dynamic database of time series and stacks of grid maps can easily be obtained from conventional GIS such as ArcView, remote sensing imagery, or interpolation.

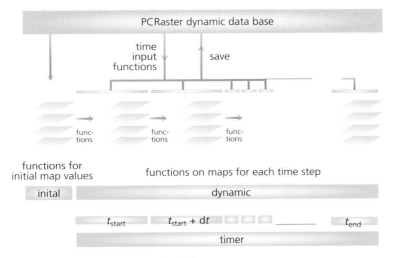

Figure 1. Conceptual overview of a PCRaster program.

A PCRaster program has 5 main sections called **binding, areamap, timer, initial**, and **dynamic.**

The **binding** section links the external file names or parameter values to the internal variable names used in the program; by simply changing file names, the same model can be run with different data.

The **areamap** section defines the geographic extents of the gridded input files that will be addressed by the model—the default is the whole area.

The **timer** section specifies and controls the number of iterations for the dynamic section of the program.

The **initial** section defines the starting values of all attributes, either by directly reading from file or by creating derived attributes (e.g., the slope of a digital elevation surface) that will be used only once in the program. All of the allowed mathematical operators can be used to prepare the data in the initial section.

The **dynamic** section contains the code for all the mathematical operations for one cycle of the model. Intermediate results may be saved to time series or to stacks of gridded attribute files. The output of one cycle forms the input for the next. For example, when modeling erosion and sedimentation, each new sedimentary layer computed can be stored as a new data file so the whole set of maps forms a 3D sediment packet.

Table 1. The structure of a PCRaster program.

Once the model has been run, the results can be displayed as static or dynamic 2D or 3D (2.5D) displays. In the latter case, the display resembles a movie. This enables the user to see exactly how the dynamic model has created the patterns and how these patterns change with time. By changing the model parameters and rerunning the program, the effect of changing the value of single parameters, or combinations of parameters, on the results can easily be seen and evaluated, as is demonstrated in the remainder of this chapter.

A SIMPLE EXAMPLE OF DYNAMIC MODELING WITH PCRASTER

This example illustrates the use of PCRaster for modeling surface water runoff. We have deliberately chosen a naïve model so that the functioning of PCRaster can be more easily understood. This example models the inputs of rain to a surface and its division into infiltration into the soil and overland flow. Rainfall, recorded at three rain gauges, is extrapolated to Thiessen polygons to provide water inputs to each cell. If the infiltration of water is too great, there is no runoff; if insufficient, then overland flow is generated. The topology of flow is computed to yield the directions for surface drainage. In the dynamic (iterative) part of the model, incident rainfall is partitioned into infiltration and overland flow, depending on the balance between inputs, infiltration, and outputs per cell. Finally, the state of the cells is recorded (report operation) every time step to provide a means to display the results of the model as a 2.5D + time visualization.

Table 2 contains the model script built on the structure given in Table 1. The first section is the *binding*, which links the internal variable names to the names of the external files or attributes supplying the data. Note that a 2D grid map has the extension *.map*, a time series the extension *.tss*, and a lookup table the extension *.tbl*. Note also that the value of constants or starting values for single attributes can be defined in the binding. The second section is the *areamap*, which defines the grid used for mapping (location, resolution, direction of counting, numbers of rows and columns). The third section is the timer, which simply gives the number of iterations to be used in the model.

```
binding      # Defines inputs and outputs
# Inputs
RainStations = rainstat.map;   # map with location of rain stations
RainTimeSeries = rain.tss;   # timeseries with rain at rainstations (mm/3h)
SoilInfTable = infilcap.tbl;   # table with infil. cap. of soil types (mm/3h)
SoilType = soil.map;        # soil map
DEM = dem.map;             # Digital elevation map
SamplePlaces = samples.map;   # map with runoff sampling locations
ConvConst = 36000;            # conversion constant, mm/3hours -> m3/s
# Outputs
SampleTimeSeries = runoff.tss;  # timeseries runoff at sample loc's
areamap      # Defines area to be operated on by model clone.map
timer      # Defines number of time steps in model 1 56 1
initial      # Computes initial values for whole area
# Compute surface topology
report Ldd = lddcreate(DEM, 1E34, 1E34, 1E34, 1E34);
# Coverage of meteorological stations for the whole area
report RainZones = spreadzone(RainStations,0,1);
# Create a map of infiltration capacity (mm/3hours), based on a soilmap
InfiltrationCapacity = lookupscalar(SoilInfTable,SoilType);
dynamic      # Iterations of the model
# Add rainfall to surface (mm/3h)
SurfWater = timeinputscalar(RainTimeSeries,RainZones);
# Runoff per time step as water input to cell minus infiltration,
# and actual infiltration (mm/3h)
report Runoff, Inf =
    accuthresholdflux, accuthresholdstate(Ldd,SurfWater,InfiltrationCapacity);
# Runoff (converted to m3/s) at each timestep for selected locations
report SampleTimeSeries = timeoutput(SamplePlaces,Runoff/ConvConst);
# report log of Runoff over whole area for visualisation
report LogRun = log10((Runoff+0.001)/ConvConst)
```

Table 2. Model for simple simulation of precipitation, infiltration, and overland flow for 56 time steps of 3-hour intervals, modeling time one week.

The initial section sets and computes initial map values. The example in Table 2 shows the derivation from the DEM of topology (Ldd, *local drain direction,* map, fig. 2) for routing flow, the creation of Thiessen polygons (RainZones) to define the coverage for each rain station as a *spread* operation (fig. 3), and the use of a lookup table to derive potential soil infiltration (InfiltrationCapacity) from the soil type map shown in figure 2.

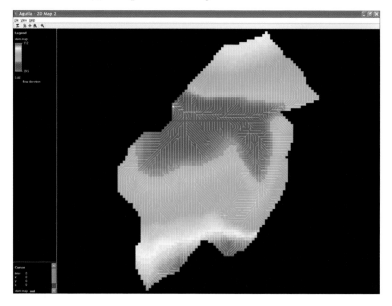

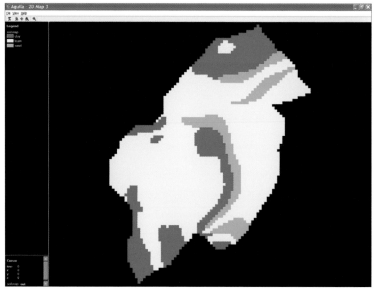

Figure 2. Top, digital elevation model (Dem, m, purple: low, red: high) with Local Drain Direction Map (Ldd white lines); Bottom, soil map (SoilType), red: clay, yellow: loam, green: sand.

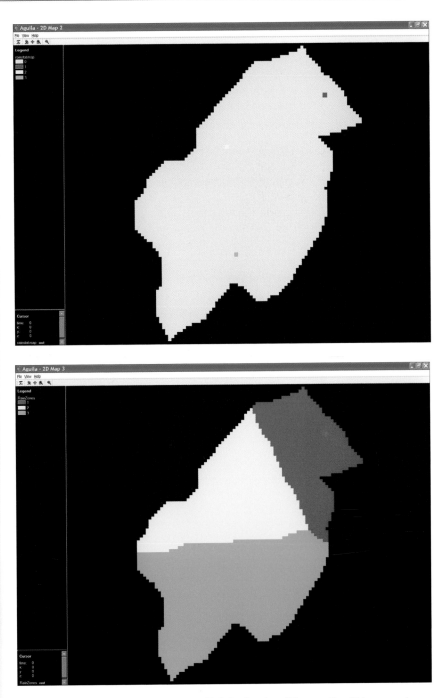

Figure 3. The map with the rain stations (RainStations) and the resulting Thiessen polygons (RainZones) created with the operation report RainZones = spreadzone(RainStations,0,1).

The *dynamic* section contains the model iterations representing the change through time. First the precipitation from the rain gauges (fig. 3 and 4) is extrapolated to the whole area of the Thiessen polygon surrounding any given rain gauge. This is done with the *timeinputscalar* operation, which for each time step and for each rain zone in RainZones reads a value from the time series file RainTimeSeries (fig. 5). The overland flux of runoff is determined by the *accuthresholdflux* operation, which computes flow to the next downstream cell only when the input of water, which is rain plus runon from upstream cells, exceeds the infiltration capacity of the cell. Maps of the distribution of overland flow are obtained by saving the maps of runoff for each time step. These values are converted to logarithms for ease of display, and the resulting series of maps can be shown as a movie using the PCRaster visualization software (fig. 6). The sequence of flux is written as an output time series file for the sites indicated on sample.map in the binding (fig. 7). Note that, to minimize run times, model results are only saved when the statement is preceded by a *report* command.

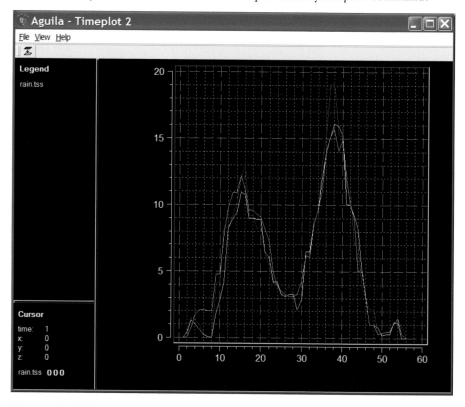

Figure 4. Rainfall time series. Rainfall measured at three rain stations shown on figure 3. X-axis shows time steps, each with a duration of 3 hours.

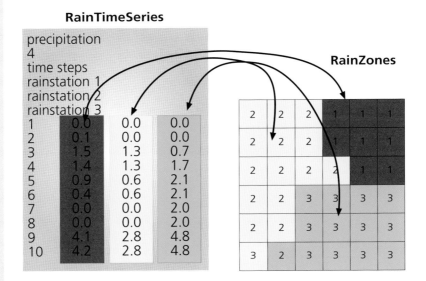

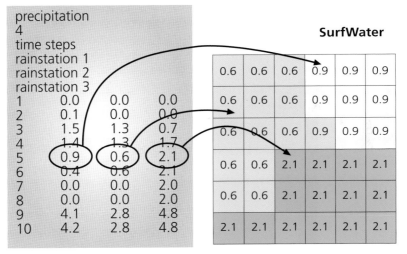

Figure 5. Left: heading and upper part of the time series file RainTimeSeries. First column: time steps, second up to fourth column: rainfall measured at first, second, and third rain station. Top-right: zoomed area of the RainZones map with three rain zones associated with the three rain stations. The arrows in the upper figure show that each column in the rainfall time series is linked to an area on the RainZones map. The operation

SurfWater = timeinputscalar(RainTimeSeries,RainZones)

reads for each time step a row of values from the time series file and assigns these values to the SurfWater map for that time step, as shown in the lower figure for Time Step 5.

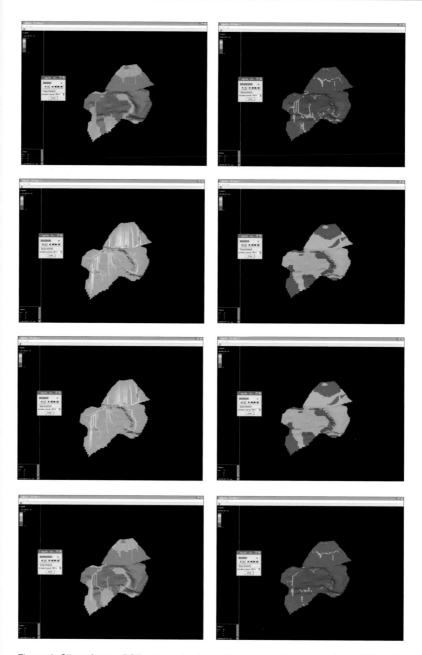

Figure 6. Slices from a PCRaster animation of the temporal change of runoff (LogRun, left), and actual infiltration (Inf, right). From top to bottom, the time steps 30, 35, 40, and 45 are shown, representing the second rainfall event on the rainfall time series (fig. 4) occurring over a period of 45 hours. Note that the areas with high actual infiltration rates are associated with sandy soils on the soil-type map shown in figure 2. At Time Steps 30 and 45, runoff occurs only on the clay soil type having the lowest infiltration capacity.

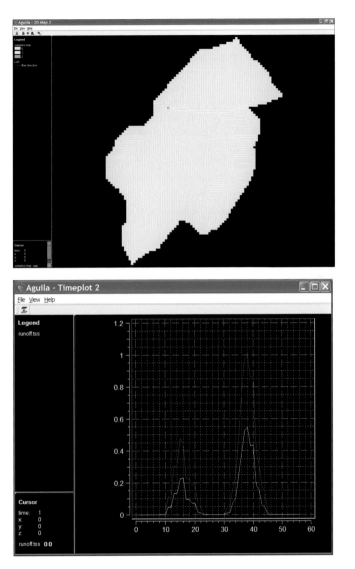

Figure 7. Left: sample locations (SamplePlaces) and right: runoff simulated at these sample locations as stored in a time series file (SampleTimeSeries) using a timeoutput operation. The sample locations are located in the main streams as can be seen from the local drain direction pattern (Ldd) draped over the SamplePlaces map.

In this example the soil water balance is represented in a simplified way. In reality, the inputs per cell would consist of precipitation and runon minus evapotranspiration. The amount of water held in the soil will also have an effect on infiltration and runoff. Consequently, for each time step there is a feedback between the moisture remaining in the soil after runoff and infiltration, which means that the moisture input to cells in later cycles of the model must take account of what happened in the previous cycle. The feedback loop may be computed by modifying the model script by adding two extra lines of code, as seen in Table 3. This model script represents a well-known approach to dealing with feedback in soil water infiltration and flow, known as the Green-Ampt equation (Green and Ampt 1911), which needs merely two additional lines of PCRaster code (see Table 3). First, the cumulative infiltration (InfCum) is recorded for each time step by adding the actual infiltration (Inf) for each time step to InfCum. Second, the potential infiltration is modeled as a function of this cumulative infiltration, with three parameters (Ks, B, and DTau) used in the Green-Ampt equation. Karssenberg (2002b) gives an example of a more complicated rainfall-runoff model and discusses the value of PCRaster for hydrological modeling.

dynamic   # Iterations of the model

Add rainfall to surface (mm/3h)

SurfWater = timeinputscalar(RainTimeSeries,RainZones);

cumulative infiltration (mm)

InfCum=InfCum+Inf;

potential infiltration per time step (mm/3h)

InfiltrationCapacity = Ks * ((-B*Dtau+InfCum)/ InfCum);

Runoff per time step as water input to cell minus infiltration,

and actual infiltration (mm/3h)

report Runoff, Inf = accuthresholdflux(Ldd,SurfWater, InfiltrationCapacity)

Table 3. Model component with feedback regarding infiltration.

EXAMPLES OF PCRASTER APPLICATIONS

MODELING CUMULATIVE CHANGES IN LANDSCAPES: THE GROWTH OF VOLCANOES AND THE EFFECTS OF EROSION AND SEDIMENTATION.

Processes such as erosion and deposition in a landscape may be difficult to appreciate because they operate over geological, rather than human, time scales, but they are similar in concept to the phenomenon of surface water transport in which material is moved downslope along a path of least resistance. Consider the formation of volcanoes, for example. Essentially these landforms develop by discharge of volcanic lava from a central chamber, which then flows over a steepest downhill path. The lava cools, solidifies, and modifies the landform in such a way that the next lava discharge must take another path. As the paths accumulate, so does the characteristic conic form develop.

A PCRaster model may provide useful insights into processes of erosion and deposition. For example, formation of simple volcanoes can easily be modeled by starting with a random amount of lava discharged per cycle from a central vent. The paths taken by the lava are determined by the surface over which it flows so the Ldd function may be used to route the lava flow over the cone. As the cone cools and solidifies, it modifies the form of the underlying DEM and hence, the possible surface over which lava may flow. Adding a small amount of uncertainty to the surface of the growing cone to indicate that deposition of molten lava is not confined to a single path ensures that the average growth of the cone is much the same, and a symmetrical feature evolves. Figure 8 illustrates some of the steps in the simulation and compares the final result with the processes operating on real volcanoes such as Aranal in Costa Rica and Vesuvius in Italy.

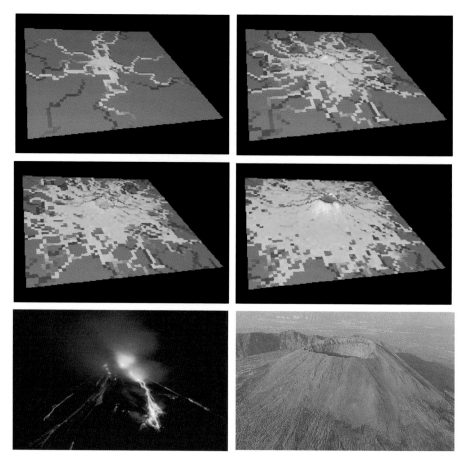

Figure 8. Modeling the development of a volcanic cone (4 steps selected from 250.) Compare process and results with Aranal (left bottom) and Vesuvius (right bottom). (Photo: Aranal – R. Sluiter)

The growth of a volcano only entails the addition and distribution of new material over the growing landscape. In many situations, the land surface is subject to both erosion and deposition. Figure 9 illustrates the formation of simple gullies on a uniform slope covered with a uniform soil. Clearly, the feedback in the model resembles the kinds of erosion seen in the field in which an initially linear system is transformed into a nonlinear result (gullies varying in depth down the field). Figure 10 illustrates the same process, but this time for a landscape in which there is a buried, resistant rock layer, such as a basalt flow or a layer of limestone or hard slate. At the start of the simulation, the hard rock layer cannot be seen and has no effect on the process because it is buried under layers of softer sediments. After a certain period of time, however, the hard rock layer becomes exposed to the elements, but as it erodes much more slowly than the other sediments, the landform changes in response to its presence.

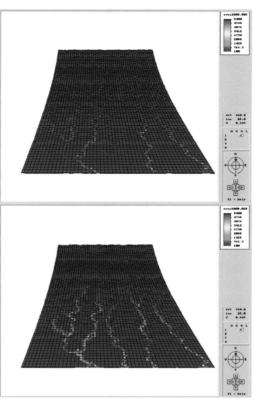

Figure 9. Example of modeling gully erosion on a sloping paddock.

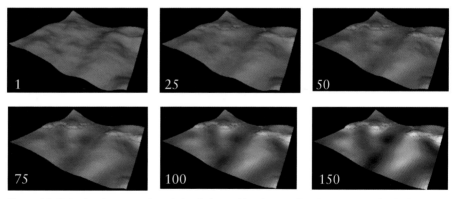

Figure 10. Selection from a series of simulations of landscape development as a buried hard rock layer becomes exposed. Light yellow colors indicate erosion, dark blue colors indicate deposition. Numbers indicate numbers of model cycles.

All these examples illustrate the value and the role of creating positive and negative feedback loops in PCRaster to deal with situations for which the end result can only be known by running the simulation—the results of these models are difficult to predict as the processes are nonlinear, both in time and space.

USER MODELS BUILT WITH PCRASTER: THE LISEM AND LISFLOOD MODELS

PCRaster has been used in several studies for flood management and erosion control. For water routing and erosion and deposition mentioned above, the PCRaster models use the *accu* family of functions, which route all available material in one time step through the catchment. The *accu* approach is insufficient when flood routing becomes important, when the time step of the model approaches the average travel time through a cell, or when the number of pixels along the transport path is large. In these cases, a more detailed approach is needed. This approach can be found in the conventional algorithms for flood routing such as the kinematic wave approximation and the diffusion wave model (Chow, Maidment, and Mays 1988, Fread 1993, Singh 1996). The kinematic wave was implemented as an extra PCRaster function using the following syntax:

Q2 = **kinematic**(*Ldd, Q1, Input, Alpha, Beta, DtSecs, CellLengthMetres*);

The new discharge *Q2* at a certain location within the flow network (defined by *Ldd*) is calculated from the discharge *Q1* from the previous time step at the same location and using *Q2* from neighboring upstream pixels. The kinematic wave can be used for hydrologic catchment models for overland flow routing and for channel routing under certain conditions. Extensions of the kinematic wave, which include backwater effects, are found in the new dynamic wave equation modules, which are currently being tested in PCRaster. These functions further expand the PCRaster capabilities for physically based models.

The LISFLOOD distributed catchment model (De Roo, Wesseling, and van Deursen 2000) was written in PCRaster to investigate the origin and causes of flooding and the influence of land use, soil characteristics, and antecedent catchment saturation. LISFLOOD simulates runoff and flooding in large river basins as a consequence of extreme rainfall; it is a distributed rainfall-runoff model taking into account the influences of topography, precipitation amounts and intensities, antecedent soil moisture content, land use type, and soil type. LISFLOOD is a major extension of LISEM, an earlier PCRaster model that was developed for simulating soil erosion in Limburg, the Netherlands (De Roo 1996), and also in Mediterranean countries and China.

Processes that can be simulated in LISFLOOD are precipitation, interception, snowmelt, evapotranspiration, infiltration, percolation, groundwater flow, lateral flow, and surface runoff (fig. 11). LISFLOOD uses rainfall and temperature time series as input. Data from many meteorological stations can be used. Inundation extents may be computed by extrapolating predicted water levels onto a DEM, or LISFLOOD can be linked to an existing 2D or 3D model for detailed floodplain routing. Infiltration is simulated using a two-layer Green-Ampt equation. The LISFLOOD model contains around 200 lines of code, which is considerably less than a model written in FORTRAN or C++.

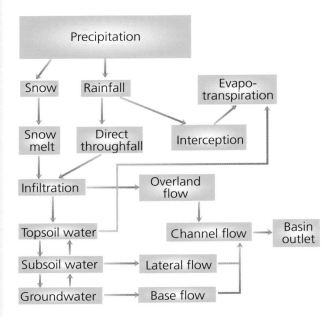

Figure 11. Flowchart of the LISFLOOD model.

Outputs of LISFLOOD are time series of discharge at user-defined catchment outlets and suboutlets. Furthermore, final maps of source areas of water, total rainfall, total interception, total infiltration, etc. can be produced, as well as a series of maps showing changes in time of certain variables, such as the water depth in each pixel.

The LISFLOOD model has been used in pilot studies to investigate flooding problems in two transnational European river basins, namely the Meuse catchment, covering parts of France, Belgium, and the Netherlands, and the Oder basin, covering parts of the Czech Republic, Poland, and Germany. The Meuse suffered from extreme flooding in December 1993 and January/February 1995. The Oder area was flooded in July 1997 (De Roo and Schmuck 2002). In these catchments, LISFLOOD was tested, calibrated, and validated by stream flow data from gauging stations before a detailed analysis of the causes of flooding could be examined. SAR images were used to validate the (maximum) extent of the flooded area in the floodplain.

NEW APPROACHES TO MODELING RECENTLY ADDED TO THE TOOLKIT

MODULES FOR SIMULATING ALLUVIAL ARCHITECTURE

New modules can be added to the PCRaster software in order to extend the application field of the software to a wider range of environmental systems and modeling approaches. While the existing PCRaster software comes with many functions for hydrological modeling, several recent applications of PCRaster have also been in the field of large-scale sedimentological modeling. One example is the group of models referred to as alluvial architecture models that have been developed to understand the processes driving delta evolution and to predict the nature of hydrocarbon and water reservoirs consisting of deposits from rivers (Karssenberg, Törnqvist, and Bridge 2001, Mackey and Bridge 1995). This group of models simulates the landscape evolution of a floodplain or river delta over time periods of thousands to millions of years. The aim of these models is to simulate the temporal evolution of the channel network on a river delta, the spatial pattern of sedimentation and erosion as a function of this continuously changing channel network, and the resulting three-dimensional architecture of the different types of sediments deposited through time.

To provide model builders with the appropriate suite of tools to develop these kinds of models, several tools are currently being added to the PCRaster software. One of these is a new water (and sediment) routing algorithm that can deal with divergent flow patterns. Most standard GIS, including PCRaster, include functions to derive the local drain direction (Ldd) network from a digital elevation model. While this network is very powerful for representing flow patterns in hilly catchments, it is insufficient to represent divergent flows in relatively flat terrain such as a river floodplain. This limitation of the Ldd network is due to the use of single flow directions assigned to each cell (fig. 12, left and fig. 13, left). As a result, channel confluences can be represented, but channel divergences cannot. To solve this problem, new, experimental functions for flow routing have been added that use multiple flow directions for each cell, resulting in channel networks that can include both channel confluences and divergences (fig. 12, right and 13, right). This group of functions can also be used for constructing hydrological and erosion models for hilly catchments in which multiple flow directions are currently widely applied (Burrough and McDonnell 1998), replacing the single flow direction algorithm. These functions are still in a prototype phase. In addition, a new module is currently being developed to deal with three-dimensional layering in sedimentological models (Karssenberg, de Jong, and Burrough 2000; Karssenberg 2002a; Karssenberg and de Jong, forthcoming). This module provides functions for operating on three-dimensional blocks of data consisting of stacks of voxels with variable thickness and attribute values (fig. 14). When sedimentation occurs, voxels are added at the top of this block; when erosion occurs, voxels are removed or sliced. Compaction of sediments can be simulated by decreasing the thickness of individual voxels. Although this module is still in the prototype phase, the aim is to provide a wide range of functions operating on this three-dimensional data type, integrated with existing PCRaster modeling tools using two dimensional data (maps).

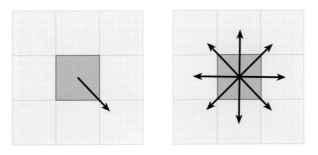

Figure 12. Flow direction(s) shown for a single cell on a map. Left: approach used in the local drain direction network of standard GIS; each cell has a single flow direction to one of its neighboring cells, and material is moved to that single cell only. Right: approach where each cell may have flow to each of its 8 neighbors and where material can, therefore, flow in multiple directions.

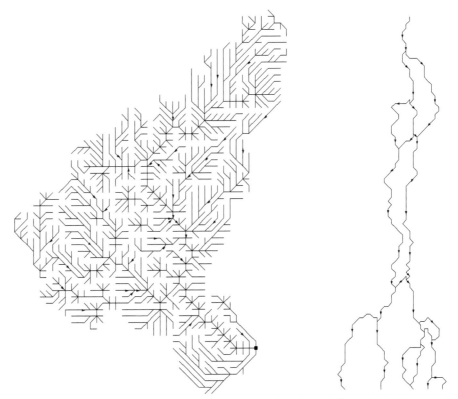

Figure 13. Resulting drainage networks from the approaches shown in figure 12. Left: approach used in local drain direction network of standard GIS, with single flow directions resulting in convergent flow only. Right: approach with multiple flow directions for each cell, used to represent convergent and divergent flow. Note that the right figure shows only the flow directions for the main channels.

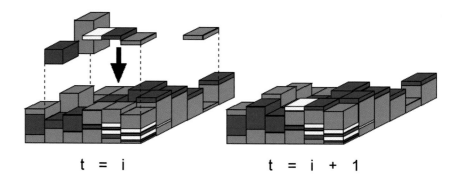

Figure 14. Three-dimensional block containing stacks of voxels with variable thickness. Deposition of material between t = i and t = i+1 is represented by addition of voxels at the top of the block.

GEOSTATISTICS AND DYNAMIC MODELING

There are many situations in dynamic modeling which are incompletely known and where a geostatistical approach is appropriate. PCRaster is linked to a full suite of methods for geostatistical interpolation (Gstat) and conditional or unconditional spatial simulation (Pebesma and Wesseling 1998) that is now also incorporated in the R suite of statistical methods (Bivand and Gebhardt 2000). The module for spatial simulation can be used for calculating error propagation in models built with PCRaster, using the approach of Monte Carlo simulation. To make error propagation modeling with Monte Carlo simulation available to a wider audience of modelers, prototype language extensions are being developed with new functions for Monte Carlo simulation with dynamic models (Karssenberg 2002a).

OPENMI

PCRaster was developed as a general-purpose simulation language, but it is becoming increasingly clear that many specialist models (including hydrodynamic models) have been written and maintained by other workers. These models might provide useful material for expanding PCRaster functionality, but it would require a prohibitively huge effort to translate them into PCRaster. This is a generic problem that extends beyond the PCRaster environment: several organizations have already invested quite some time and effort in the development of models, and although they don't want to lose their investments, they would like to offer their models to the outside world to be linked with other models. There are several ongoing international projects that are aimed at providing generic frameworks for linking models. As an example, PCRaster is participating in the HarmonIT framework, a research project funded by the

European Commission aiming at the development and implementation of a European Open Modelling Interface and Environment (OpenMI) that will simplify the linking of hydrological and related models.

REFERENCES

Bivand, R., and A. Gebhardt. 2000. Using the R statistical data analysis language on GRASS 5.0 GIS data base files. *Computers and Geosciences* 26: 1043–52.

Burrough, P. A. 1998. Dynamic modeling and geocomputation. In *Geocomputation: A primer*, ed. P. A. Longley, S. M. Brooks, R. McDonnell, and B. MacMillan. Chichester: John Wiley and Sons.

Burrough, P. A., and R. A. McDonnell. 1998. *Principles of geographical information systems*. Oxford: Oxford University Press.

Casti, J. 1997. *Would-be worlds*. New York: John Wiley and Sons.

Chow, V. T., D. R. Maidment, and L. W. Mays. 1988. *Applied hydrology*. New York City: McGraw-Hill.

De Roo, A. P. J. 1996. The LISEM project: An introduction. *Hydrological Processes* 10: 1021–26.

De Roo, A. P. J., and G. Schmuck. 2002. ODER-LISFLOOD: Assessment of the effects of engineering, land use and climate scenarios on flood risk in the Oder catchment. European Commission, EUR 20276.

De Roo, A. P. J., C. G. Wesseling, and W. P. A. Van Deursen. 2000. Physically-based river basin modelling within a GIS: The LISFLOOD model. *Hydrological Processes* 14: 1981–92.

Eastman, R. 2003 Idrisi. Clark Labs. Worcester, Mass.: Clark University.

Fread, D. L. 1993. Flow routing. In *Handbook of hydrology*, ed. D. R. Maidment, 10.1–10.36. New York: McGraw Hill.

Green, W. H., and G. A. Ampt. 1911. Studies on soil physics: Flow of air and water through soils. *Journal of Agricultural Science* 4:1–24.

Karssenberg, D., 2002a. Building dynamic spatial environmental models. *Nederlandse Geografische Studies* 305. Utrecht: KNAG/Faculteit Ruimtelijke Wetenschappen Universiteit Utrecht. www.library.uu.nl/digiarchief/dip/diss/2003-0414-125023/inhoud.htm.

———. 2002b. The value of environmental modelling languages for building distributed hydrological models. *Hydrological Processes* 16: 2751–66.

Karssenberg, D., and K. de Jong. Forthcoming. Dynamic environmental modelling in GIS: Modelling in three spatial dimensions. *International Journal of Geographical Information Science*.

Karssenberg, D., K. de Jong, and P. A. Burrough. 2000. A prototype computer language for environmental modeling in the temporal, 3D spatial and stochastic dimension. In *International conference on integrating geographic information systems and environmental modeling: Problems, prospectus, and needs for research.* www.colorado.edu/research/cires/banff/pubpapers/192.

Karssenberg, D., T. E. Törnqvist, and J. S. Bridge. 2001. Conditioning a process-based model of sedimentary architecture to well data. *Journal of Sedimentary Research,* 71: 868–79.

Mackey, S.D., and J. S. Bridge. 1995. Three-dimensional model of alluvial stratigraphy: Theory and application. *Journal of Sedimentary Research* B65: 7–31.

Pebesma, E., and C. G. Wesseling. 1998. GSTAT—A program for geostatistical modelling, prediction and simulation. *Computers and Geosciences* 24: 17–31.

PCRaster. 2004. pcraster.geo.uu.nl.

Pullar, D. 2003. Simulation modelling applied to runoff modelling using MapScript. *Transactions in GIS* 7: 267–83.

Singh, V.P.. 1996. *Kinematic wave modeling in water resources.* New York: John Wiley and Sons.

Takeyama, M., and H. Couclelis. 1997. Map dynamics: Integrating cellular automata and GIS through Geo-Algebra. *International Journal of Geographical Science* 11:73-92.

Tomlin, C. D. 1990. *Geographic information systems and cartographic modeling.* Englewood Cliffs, N.J.: Prentice Hall.

Van Deursen, W. P. A. 1995. Geographical information systems and dynamic models: Development and application of a prototype spatial modelling language. PhD thesis, University of Utrecht. www.carthago.nl (under Publications).

Wesseling, C. G., D. J. Karssenberg, P. A. Burrough, and W. P. A. Van Deursen. W. P. A. 1996. Integrating dynamic environmental models in GIS: The development of a Dynamic Modeling Language. *Transactions in GIS* 1: 40-48.

Chapter 17 Transition Potential Modeling for Land-Cover Change

J. RONALD EASTMAN

CLARK UNIVERSITY

WORCESTER, MASSACHUSETTS

LUIS A. SOLÓRZANO AND MEGAN E. VAN FOSSEN

CONSERVATION INTERNATIONAL

CARACAS, VENEZUELA

ABSTRACT

A COMMON INGREDIENT to most predictive GIS-based models of land-cover change is the empirical modeling of transition potentials—the likelihood that land would change from one cover type to another, based on factors such as the suitability of land for the transition in question and the presence of driving forces of change. However, there are many different approaches currently in use for the empirical modeling of transition potentials. In this study, we undertook a comparative evaluation of twelve empirical procedures using case study data over three time periods from Bolivia. Performance in predicting the third period from modeling the transitions between the first two periods was tested using a Peirce skill score (PSS) and an associated performance chart, and a relative operating characteristic (ROC) statistic and associated curve. Despite very strong differences in the outputs from the twelve models, the commonly used ROC statistic suggested that all performed well and with a similar level of skill. However, it was determined that this arose primarily because the ROC statistic interprets persistence as skill. The PSS showed a very different picture, with strong differences in skill between the procedures. The only technique that performed well in all tests was the back propagation multilayer perceptron neural network. The most commonly used technique of logistic regression was found to perform well in determining the relative transition potential, but poorly in establishing absolute transition potentials. Another prominent technique, weights-of-evidence, was also found to perform poorly because it has no means of gauging interaction effects.

INTRODUCTION

Land-cover change is one of the most immediate impacts of the human use of land, with significant environmental consequences. Natural habitats are changed, resources are modified, and exchanges between the land and the atmosphere are altered in ways that can potentially have impacts over extensive regions. Although land-use and land-cover change has long been a focus of geographers and economists (e.g., the models of Von Thünen and Ricardo), it is only recently that geographic information systems (GIS) have become a critical ingredient to the understanding of land-cover change and the rational allocation of land resources. At national and regional levels, it has generally been the practice to monitor and model land-cover change using nonspatial models based on statistical data from administrative districts. However, recently there has been a sustained emphasis on the development of what are known as *spatially explicit* land-cover change models. The reasons for this are several:

1. a general recognition that land-cover change arises from the decision of a multitude of individual spatially dispersed household and business units and the need to understand the relationship between public policy and individual decision making;

2. the wide-scale availability of digital remotely sensed imagery that permits the monitoring of land-cover change at a highly detailed spatial resolution; and

3. the growing analytical sophistication of GIS.

Today, virtually all spatially explicit land-cover change models are paired with one or more GIS. For example, the CLUE system is paired with ArcView and Idrisi, LTM is paired with ArcView, Lucas is paired with GRASS, Geomod2 is paired with Idrisi, and Dinamica is paired with SPRING and Idrisi. Further, the operations they perform outside the GIS are in most cases inherently GIS operations[1]. Add to this the increasing availability of fundamental land cover analysis support routines within existing GIS (such as the inclusion of the Geomod2, Markov, LOGISTICREG, and CA_Markov modules into Idrisi), and it is clear that land cover change modeling is emerging as a major vertical application.[2] Of concern to the GIS community.

COMPONENTS OF LAND-COVER CHANGE MODELS

The rationale for constructing a land-cover change model is threefold: to act as a testbed for understanding the driving forces and the dynamics of land-cover change, to understand the future economic and environmental implications of current conversion processes, and to serve as a means of projecting the impact of policy changes on the current trajectory (Pijanowski et al. 2002). In all cases, the model must therefore be able to predict change based on an assessment of current conditions.

Land cover change models generally consist of three major components: a *change demand* submodel, a *transition potential* submodel, and a *change allocation* submodel. Change demand modeling is concerned with establishing how much change will take place over a specified period of time. Transition potential modeling is concerning with determining the likelihood that land would change from one cover type to another, based on factors such as the suitability of land for the transition in question and the presence of driving forces of change. Finally, change allocation submodels are concerned with the decision of which specific areas will change, given the demand and potential surfaces.

The primary focus of this chapter is transition potential modeling. Clearly, if one can determine transition potentials well, the change allocation process can be quite simple since the potential locations of change will have been largely determined—an approach taken by many models of land-cover change. However, it is equally the case that if the change allocation process is carefully modeled, then the transition potential modeling component can be very simple. Thus there is an interdependency between the two. Similarly, if the change demand is modeled spatially, then it has direct implications for transition potential. Consequently, we will briefly review the character of change potential and change allocation submodels in current use before a more detailed consideration of transition potential models.

SYSTEMS EVALUATED   As a basis for this review, a total of nine systems were examined:

1. Geomod2 (Pontius, Cornell, and Hall 2001)
2. CA_Markov (Eastman 1999)
3. CLUE (Verburg et al. 1999)
4. CLUE-S (Verburg et al. 2002)
5. SLEUTH Urban Growth Model (Clarke and Gaydos 1998)
6. LOV—LeefOmgevingsVerkenner (White and Engelen 2000)
7. Lucas (Berry et al. 1996)
8. Dinamica (Soares-Filho, Pennachin, and Cerqueira 2002)
9. LTM (Pijanowski et al. 2002).

This list was not intended to be exhaustive, but representative of the range of approaches in use today. As mentioned above, most are linked to a GIS to undertake selected analytical tasks and spatial data management and display. However, all share one common characteristic: they are all raster-based systems and are inherently GIS-like in their operation and output.

CHANGE DEMAND MODELING

Change demand models lie at the interface between transition potential models and change allocation models. Their purpose is to estimate the rate of change between each pairwise combination of land-cover types. The results are summarized in a *transition probability matrix* that expresses the rate of conversion from each land-cover type to each other. Not all systems provide tools to establish this matrix (e.g., Dinamica, Geomod2) while others (e.g., SLEUTH) make no attempt to determine this explicitly but allow the quantity of change to be completely dictated by the parameters of the change allocation model. However, of those that do, approaches may be either empirical (e.g., CA_ Markov and its use of the Markov module in Idrisi and the procedure discussed by Brown, Pijanowski, and Duh 2000, as used with LTM) or theoretical in nature (e.g., CLUE, Lucas). The usual empirical approach is to assume a Markovian or semi-Markovian process (see Baker 1989; Brown, Pijanowski, and Duh 2000) while theoretical approaches are typically economic or socio-economic (e.g., White and Engelen 2000).

CHANGE ALLOCATION MODELING

Change allocation is essentially a decision process. Current models range from simple deterministic procedures to complex dynamic systems that mimic individual decision making through autonomous agents. In addition, some systems model only binary land-cover classifications (such as Geomod2 which is intended for modeling deforestation) while others can model changes in multiple land-cover classes. In addition, some can only model changes that are unidirectional rather than bidirectional (e.g., again, Geomod2 where deforestation is understood to be a state of disturbance which can never return to an undisturbed state). Regardless, there is substantial variation in the techniques that are used to allocate change across space.

RANK/THRESHOLD PROCEDURES

The simplest change allocation procedure depends upon a strong transition potential model. On the assumption that the pixels that will change at a particular time are those that have the highest potential, an allocation can simply be achieved by ranking them and then selecting the top ranks according to the area required. Some systems (such as CA_Markov) literally rank-order the pixels and then set a rank threshold with a reclassification operation. However, this requires an extremely rapid ranking procedure. An alternative approach (such as is used by CLUE-S) is to use an iterative process of thresholding the transition potential value directly (without ranking). After each thresholding operation, the amount of over- or under-allocation is assessed, and the threshold is adjusted for the next iteration. This is also computationally intensive but can produce an exact ranking. LTM uses a third approach—to approximate a ranking by reclassifying the transition potential map into percentile ranges and then choosing a threshold percentile. This leads to some imprecision in the area allocated but has the advantage of being fast.

CONSTRAINED RANK/THRESHOLD PROCEDURES

Among those that use a rank/threshold procedure, it is very common to incorporate constraints that serve to limit the pool from which pixels are chosen. Both CLUE-S and Geomod2 offer the ability to specify upper-level strata that constrain pixel-level allocations. One logical application of these strata is to apply different regional development rates. Geomod2 also offers the option of specifying a spatial constraint such that top ranks are chosen only within a buffer specified around existing areas of the land cover being transitioned into. When the buffer is extremely small (e.g., one pixel in width) and iterated over time, the system is similar in outcome to a cellular automata model as will be discussed below.

ALLOCATION OF RESIDUALS PROCEDURE

The CLUE system uses a rather unusual method for allocating change. Its transition potential modeling is based on a multiple regression between the proportions of various land covers and a set of driver variables. It then allocates change to areas that exhibit residual errors between the actual proportional land cover and the surface predicted by the regression equation, thereby progressively reducing the residuals. The authors state that they make the assumption that all of the explanatory variables are known and that the residuals exist because of land competition. By allocating change to residuals, the landscape will progressively look more like the predicted proportional land cover.

STOCHASTIC CHOICE

Lucas uses an allocation system that can be described as stochastic choice. Transition potentials are modeled as transition probabilities using multinomial logit models of historical data. In a projection into the future, the present cover type along with situational characteristics of the pixel (elevation, proximity to infrastructure, etc.) are fed into a set of equations covering all possible transitions to determine the probability that the pixel will change to any other cover type. Any unaccounted residual from 1.0 is the probability that the current cover type will persist. These transition probabilities can be arranged as a stack. A random number is then generated from a uniform distribution, and its location within this stack then determines the transition that will occur. Without further modification, a stochastic choice procedure tends to be rather ungeographic in character (it lacks the spatial dependence normally associated with geographic data). Of special importance to the discussion in this chapter, however, this technique also requires that the absolute value of the probabilities realized be highly accurate in order for both the total quantity and relative distribution of change to properly reflect reality.

PROCESS-SPECIFIC ALLOCATION MODELS

It is generally recognized that there are varying processes of change. Although a general typology has not been developed (Mertens and Lambin 1997), there are some common allocation procedures that address commonly recognized types:

Spontaneous change

SLEUTH's Urban Growth Model recognizes the possibility of change that occurs without any spatial logic. Thus it allows a small amount of change at randomly assigned locations.

Patch change

Patch change accommodates the change of large blocks of contiguous land. Dinamica and SLEUTH both incorporate the ability to develop new free-standing patches. In SLEUTH, a proportion of cells selected for spontaneous growth are designated as new spreading centers and are allowed to change two neighbors (thus acquiring the critical mass necessary to be a growth center). With Dinamica, however, a very rich patch development process is incorporated in which both the size and shape characteristics of patches can be manipulated. However, this process is not blind but uses the underlying transition potentials as a critical ingredient to the selection of pixels that will be clumped together. The process, unfortunately, is not well documented (Soares-Filho et al. 2003).

Edge expansion

Edge expansion is a common form of growth and is almost always modeled with some variant of a cellular automata process. Of the models considered here, Dinamica, CA_Markov, and SLEUTH incorporate such a component, while LOV incorporates neighborhood effects that would favor edge growth. With the exception of SLEUTH, which uses a simple dominance logic (a specified proportion of cells with three or more adjacent urbanized cells will change to urban), all the others use prevalence of land covers within a cell's neighborhood to modify its original transition potential—cells at a distance from existing cells of that type thus have a lower potential of being changed.

Road-related growth

While most systems recognize the extreme importance of roads to occurrence of change, few explicitly incorporate an allocation model that addresses it. Dinamica incorporates a Road Constructor model that produces new roads which in turn influence the process of change. However, SLEUTH actually models a process where urbanized cells can take a random walk down existing roads to colonize new sites.

Clearly there is a variety of change allocation procedures in use. However, what is clear is that, in most instances, transition potential modeling forms the underlying basis of the allocation procedure and that, in many instances, selection is based on the relative (rank ordered) rather than the absolute transition potential.

TRANSITION POTENTIAL MODELING

In the predictive modeling of land-cover change, the majority of models include a component in which an attempt is made to model the suitability of land for transition from one cover type to another. This component may be expressed in various ways (suitabilities, probabilities, propensities, likelihoods, etc.), but all are concerned with establishing the degree to which locations might potentially change in a future period of time. Thus we have chosen to use the term also used by Pijanowski et al. (2002), *transition potential modeling,* to cover all of these approaches.

The typical logic of transition potential modeling is to establish a set of explanatory variables that can be considered as predictive of the location of change and then to determine the relationship through empirical testing. These explanatory variables are of two types: *suitability variables* (such as slope or soil type) that describe the inherent capability of the land to support the transition in question and *driver variables* (such as proximity to infrastructure) that capture the historical context that establishes some locations as being more likely to change than others. Areas of known change are commonly used as training sites for the empirical calibration of the models, and driver variables are frequently updated in successive iterations to capture the changing geographical context.

From an examination of the literature, we have found that a surprisingly diverse set of analytical procedures has been used to develop transition potential models, with no clear guidelines regarding their comparative strengths. Thus in this study, we have undertaken a comparative evaluation of the major approaches along with some additional procedures that we felt may be relevant.

MODELING PROCEDURES EVALUATED

From an examination of recent studies, two main groups of modeling procedures were encountered: those that evaluated the relationship between explanatory variables and change separately and then aggregated the results to yield a single statement of transition potential and those that undertake a holistic multivariate analysis.

Independent evaluation of explanatory variables with subsequent aggregation
One approach to establishing the relationship between a single explanatory variable and change involves a *binning* of the driver variable into discrete ranges (classes) with a subsequent examination of the relative frequency of change within each bin to establish the probability of change (e.g., Geomod2). Alternatively, one can examine the relative frequency of each bin within areas of change. The result is thus the calculation of the likelihood function of change. Figure 1 illustrates the difference between these approaches, which we will refer to as *empirical probabilities* versus *empirical likelihoods.*

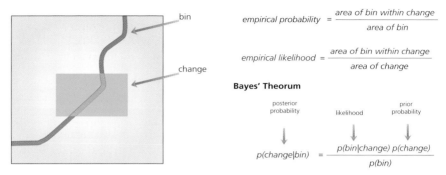

Figure 1. Calculation of empirical probabilities and likelihoods. The bin is a subrange of the explanatory variable, such as a range of elevations on a DEM. Bayes' Theorum allows for the determination of posterior probability given a likelihood and the projected prevalence of change (i.e., its prior probability) and the relative frequency of the bin.

Empirical probabilities are valid statements only for the specific time and location examined. For example, a simple shift in the study region boundary may yield different results since the probabilities calculated are dependent on the areas of the bins and the amount of change present. In contrast, empirical likelihoods are independent of the areas of the bins and the absolute amount of change and are thus transferable over space and time. They express a relationship between the change and the bin and can be converted into probabilities for any specific location and time by the application of Bayes' Theorem (fig. 1). Because of their generality, our expectation was that as an expression of relative transition potential, empirical likelihoods would probably outperform empirical probabilities.

The relationship between an explanatory variable and change may also be established on a theoretical basis, either using an empirical fit to a known utility, value, or fuzzy set function or using previously established parameters (e.g., White and Engelen 2000). However, for simplicity of comparison, we have used empirical probabilities and likelihoods (where appropriate) in this study. Accordingly, the following techniques were evaluated.

Averaging/Weighted averaging

This is a commonly used approach for the aggregation of factors. For example, it is the basic aggregation operator of Multi-Criteria Evaluation (MCE), as is commonly used for suitability mapping, and is one of the procedures suggested for aggregation of fuzzy factors for use with the CA_Markov land-cover change model of the Idrisi software system. It is also supported by the LTM model. In this instance, we examine the manner in which it is used in the Geomod2 land-cover change modeling system, where the user supplies binned driver variable maps and the system calculates a weighted average of empirical probabilities. An averaging operator always produces a result that is intermediate to the input values.

Product

This is another common aggregation operator such as is found in the LOV model as used by White and Engelen (2000). In this instance, we have tested its use in producing the intersection of empirical probabilities. A product operator always yields a result that is smaller than any of its inputs.

Dempster's Rule

One of the problems with the product operator is that as evidence is added, the result keeps getting smaller. Thus, for example, if potential on the basis of proximity to roads is 0.6 and potential on the basis of slopes is 0.7, the aggregated result is 0.42. Similarly, an averaging operator can only yield a value between 0.6 and 0.7 depending upon the weights. Dempster's Rule of Combination (see Gordon and Shortliffe 1985) is the basic aggregation operator of Dempster-Shafer Theory and has an interesting property in this context. When both inputs are above 0.5, the aggregated result is higher than either input; if both are less than 0.5, the aggregated result is lower than either input; and if one is higher and the other is lower, the result is intermediate to the two. Thus the aggregation of 0.6 and 0.7 yields 0.78!

Weights-of-evidence/Bayesian aggregation

The *weights-of-evidence* (Bonham-Carter, Agterberg, and Wright 1989; Bonham-Carter 1994) approach is a modified form of Bayesian analysis that is currently used by the Dinamica land-cover change model. In its most common use, empirical likelihoods derived from Boolean map layers are used as inputs to a log odds ratio recasting of Bayesian aggregation. However, Dinamica does allow (and would most commonly use) multibin driver maps (what is commonly known as a *grayscale* weights-of-evidence model). Although there is inherent value in some contexts to examination of the weight maps produced, it is far more efficient to calculate the transition potentials using Bayesian aggregation in the context of land-cover change. Figure 2 illustrates the formula used and its derivation from binned data.

$$p(change \mid X_1 \cap X_2) = \frac{p(change) * p(X_1 \mid change) p(X_2 \mid change)}{p(X_1) p(X_2)}$$

Figure 2. Bayesian aggregation of evidence.

Multivariate evaluation of driver variable relationships

In contrast to the group above, techniques using a multivariate evaluation of driver variable relationships assess the relationship of all variables at the same time rather than assessing each separately, followed by aggregation. In this context, we examined eight additional techniques, of which only a few are commonly encountered in change transition modeling.

All combination empirical probabilities

With this procedure, a crosstabulation is created of all combinations of all bins of all driver maps. Empirical probabilities are then calculated for these smaller bins in the normal way. The major limitation here is that there is a trade-off between bin size (and thus precision) and the number of driver variables. As the number of driver variables increases, the number of combinations of all possible bins increases exponentially, and the spatial extent of bins decreases similarly. There is thus a risk of undersampling. The advantage, however, is that these bins can pick up interaction effects that would otherwise be lost.

All combination empirical likelihoods

In a similar manner, empirical likelihoods are calculated for all combinations of all bins of all drivers, with the same limitations and opportunities.

Logistic regression

Logistic regression is a very popular choice for transition suitability modeling since it can relate presence/absence land-cover data with data of any form of explanatory variable and yields a probability statement that can be interpreted as a transition potential. It was used in the past (before a change to weights-of-evidence) with Dinamica. It is offered as an option in LTM and is a permissible input to CA_Markov. Further, it is the main tool used in the CLUE-S and Lucas (through its multinomial extension) models.

Bayesian soft classification (Equal priors)

Bayesian soft classification (Eastman 2003) is a soft variant of the maximum likelihood classifier that is used extensively in remote sensing. A maximum likelihood classifier evaluates the posterior probability of a pixel belonging to each candidate class using a multivariate normal model developed from training data. In its traditional use, the output of a maximum likelihood classifier for each pixel is the identifier of the class with the maximum posterior probability. However, with a soft classifier, no hard decision is made, and maps of posterior probability are output for each class. They are normally used as a means of examining uncertainty in the classification process (Wang 1990, Eastman and Laney 2002). However, in this case the posterior probability image for the disturbance class is used as a measure of transition potential. In this variant, equal prior probabilities of change and no change are assumed.

Bayesian soft classification (Markovian priors)

This variant is identical to the one above, except that the priors are set at those values expected from a Markov chain analysis. To provide the fairest possible evaluation, the Markovian projection was set to the actual relative frequencies of change/no change for the period evaluated (1989–1992).

Mahalanobis soft classifier

The Mahalanobis (Mahalclass) soft classifier (Eastman 2003) is very similar to the Bayesian soft classifier. In this case, however, the output is the *typicality* of the pixel. Typicality expresses the probability of finding a pixel with a Mahalanobis distance greater than or equal to that of the pixel being evaluated (Foody et al. 1992). The Mahalanobis distance is thus the multivariate equivalent of a z-score and can be used to evaluate how typical a pixel is of any multivariate normal class being evaluated.

Fuzzy soft classifier

The fuzzy soft classifier evaluated here, Fuzclass (Eastman 1999), evaluates the membership grade of each pixel in each class using a modified form of *Minimum Distance to Means* classifier. Specifically, the normalized distance (assuming a zero covariance) of each pixel to the mean in explanatory variable space is computed as a z-score and compared to a user-defined limit of zero membership. In this study, the limit was set as a z-score of 2.58. Assuming a zero covariance, membership is zero at a z-score of 2.58 and increases linearly, reaching a membership of one when the pixel at a z-score of 0 (i.e., is identical to the mean).

Neural network

The final procedure evaluated was a back propagation neural network (BPN) model as implemented in the Idrisi software system (Eastman 2003). Several research groups have explored the potential of this neural network for modeling transition potentials (Yeh and Li 2002; Li and Yeh 2001, 2002; Pijankowski et al. 2002; Wang 1994). A back propagation neural network is a multilayer perceptron in which training data is fed forward through a network consisting of an input layer and output layer and one or more hidden node layers, and errors are propagated backwards to adjust the weights at each node associated with an activation function (Tso and Mather 2001). In its use for land-cover transition potential modeling, known areas of change are used as training areas to develop the relationship between a set of explanatory variables and activation levels of the output nodes. Once the training has been completed, new data is fed to the network, and the activation levels can be mapped out for each class. Thus the activation level maps act as statements of the degree of support the model finds for the land-cover change being considered.

THE CASE STUDY TEST SITE

To evaluate the differences between these procedures, a case study was developed for the region of Santa Cruz, Bolivia. The case study site (fig. 3), encompassing the municipalities of San Javier and Concepción (located in the province of Ñuflo de Chávez), and its associated datasets (applied in this investigation) formed part of a prior microscale landscape simulation study carried out by researchers at the Noel Kempff Mercado Natural History Museum in Bolivia and the Andean CBC of Conservation International. The municipalities of San Javier and Concepción were established by Jesuit priests between 250 to 300 years ago (Killeen et al. n.d.). The expansion rates for these municipal sites, initially driven economically by smallholder subsistence agriculture, timber extraction, and cattle ranching operations, have undergone a substantial change over the past thirty years. Major increases in municipal expansion rates have been attributed, in large part, to roadway improvement and construction activities that have improved accessibility to market centers and that have helped to initiate a general agricultural growth trend that favors mechanized production (Killeen et al. n.d.). Consequently, this study region has experienced and is expected to continue experiencing inflated growth rates.

Figure 3. Landsat ETM composite of bands 357 (San Javier and Concepción, Bolivia 2000).

METHODOLOGY

All analyses in this case study were undertaken with the Idrisi Kilimanjaro GIS and Image Processing software system (Eastman 2003). Primary data layers used included binary land-cover maps of forest versus anthropogenic disturbance (deforestation without consideration of regeneration) for the years 1986, 1989, and 1992, previously developed from Landsat TM imagery by researchers at the Noel Kempff Mercado Natural History Museum. From these, change maps were generated for the 1986–1989 and 1989–1992 intervals. Using the 1986–1989 change map, crosstabulations were run with a series of potential explanatory variables as an initial screening technique[3]. In the end, three explanatory variables were selected[4]—proximity to existing development in 1986, proximity to roads in 1986, and elevation (developed from SRTM data).

Because we expected significant intercorrelations between the three explanatory variables and we knew that some of the procedures to be evaluated would be sensitive to this, a principal components analysis was run to develop a series of uncorrelated factors. We had anticipated that this might reduce the number of independent variables to two, but in fact, three meaningful components were found to exist (see fig. 4).

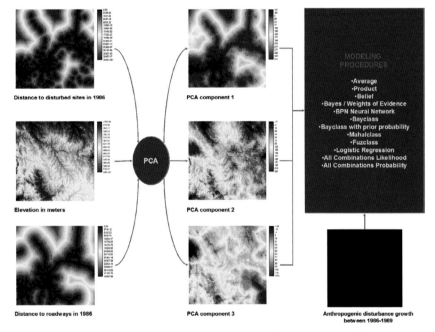

Figure 4. Data processing and modeling procedure inputs for the calculation of transition potentials.

In the development of the transition potential models, the areas that changed between 1986 and 1989 and the areas that could have changed, but did not, formed training areas. For most techniques, only the change areas were required, but the classifiers all required examples of areas that did not change. In these cases, a sample of forest areas that did not change was chosen roughly equal in size to that of forest areas that did change.

Figure 5 shows each of the transition potential maps developed for the case study region, for which the map of areas that changed from 1989–1992 was used for validation purposes. The major issue encountered here was how to make this comparison. Forecast verification is still an area of active research (Jolliffe and Stephenson 2003). Although a number of indices of forecast performance or skill have become commonplace in specific scientific contexts, the differences between them are not well understood. Among land-cover change modelers, the relative operating characteristic (ROC) is perhaps the most widely used. However, our intuitive consideration of the analytical problem at hand led us also towards consideration of the Peirce skill score (PSS). To our initial surprise, they present very different portraits of the character of these transition potential measures. However, these differences point to very different aspects of their character.

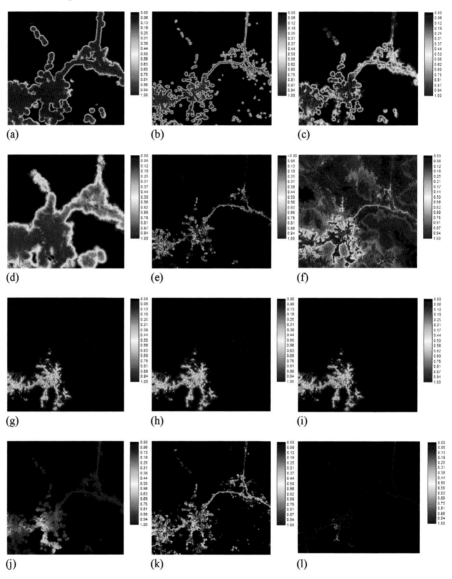

Figure 5. The transition potential maps produced by: (a) Bayclass (b) BPN Neural Network (c) Mahalclass (d) Fuzclass (e) All Combinations Likelihood (f) Average (g) Product (h) Bayes / WofE (i) Belief (j) Bayclass with Prior Probability (k) All Combinations Probability (l) Logistic Regression.

PSS

Intuitively we felt that to be successful a transition potential model should have judged the pixels that truly did change to have a high potential and those that did not change to have had a low potential. This is essentially the logic of the Peirce skill score. In the context of binary forecasts (change/not change), a correct forecast of change is known as a *hit,* and an incorrect forecast of change is known as a *false alarm.* If one tabulates the proportion of hits (H) and the proportion of false alarms (F) in a set of forecasts, the Peirce skill score is defined as:

$$PSS = H - F$$

In this study, the forecasts are soft rather than hard. Thus the equivalent of the hit rate is the relative weight of potential allocated to areas of change, and the false alarm rate is equivalent to the relative weight of potential allocated to areas of no change, which are in turn equivalent to the mean potential in the areas of change and the mean potential in the areas of no change. These are easily calculated in a GIS (in this case using the Extract module in Idrisi).

For a perfect predictor, the PSS takes on a value of 1.0 while one that performs no better than random will yield a value of 0. Negative values are also possible, indicating a measure that is systematically incorrect.

ROC

The *receiver operating characteristic,* now more commonly called the *Relative Operating Characteristic* after Swets (1973), is also based on an examination of hits and false alarms (see Mason 2003, Pontius and Schneider 2001). If one considers the transition potential map as a surface, the ROC evaluates the relative proportion of hits and false alarms as a horizontal decision plane lowered vertically downward to intersect this surface. At a high threshold, only the peaks of the transition potential surface will have been intercepted, and we would expect (if the surface is a good predictor) that most of these hill tops would be found to be hits rather than false alarms. However, as the decision surface is lowered further and further, we would expect the number of false alarms to increase. If one plots a set of points on an x,y graph at each vertical position of the decision surface, with the false alarm rate (F) on the x-axis and the hit rate (H) on the y-axis, the points present a series of vertices that can be joined to create the *ROC curve* (see fig. 6). A highly predictive measure will produce a curve that rises rapidly from the lower left to a point near the upper left corner and then moves slowly near the upper edge of the graph to reach the upper right hand corner. Conversely, a measure with no predictive ability at all would be expected to encounter equal rates of hits and false alarms at each threshold, yielding a straight line from the lower left to the upper right. A common summary statistic to describe the ROC curve is thus to calculate the area under the ROC curve (now frequently called the *ROC Statistic*). In this case, a measure with perfect predictive power would yield a value of 1.0 while one with no power (random) would yield one of 0.5. Values less than 0.5 indicate a measure that is systematically incorrect.

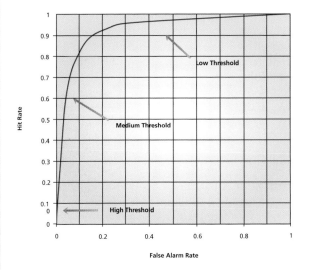

Figure 6. The construction of an ROC curve. The curve joins vertices that indicate the hit rate versus false alarm rate as the transition potential surface is thresholded at various levels. Three general levels are illustrated, but in practice, generation of a smooth curve may require hundreds of thresholds (after Mason 2003, p. 69).

RESULTS

Figures 7 and 8 present the results of evaluating the transition potential measures examined with the PSS and ROC statistics respectively. The results are clearly different.

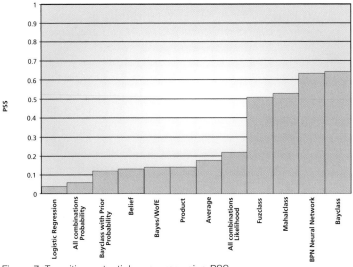

Figure 7. Transition potential measures using PSS.

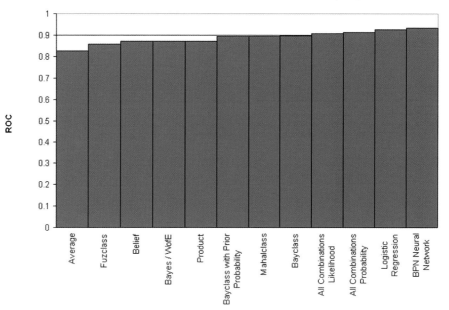

Figure 8. Transition potential measures using ROC.

PSS

Looking at the PSS, what is most striking is the separation between the group of classifiers (Bayclass, BPN, Mahalclass and Fuzclass versus all other techniques. These are all multivariate techniques, and it would be expected that they would perform better than the aggregated univariate procedures if significant interaction effects were present. However, four of the multivariate procedures did less well: the All Combinations Likelihoods, All Combinations Probabilities, Bayclass with Prior Probabilities, and Logistic Regression. Thus there needs to be another explanation.

To explore the results of the PSS further, we developed a series of performance charts that illustrate the cumulative distribution of transition potentials in areas that truly changed from 1989 to 1992 versus areas that did not change. Figure 9 presents the performance chart for the back propagation neural network as an illustration of its function. The red line depicts the cumulative proportion of pixels (y-axis) that have values lower than the transition potential specified on the x-axis within change areas. A perfect predictor would yield a line looking like a backwards L. The green line shows a similar cumulative proportion curve in areas that did not change. In this case, a perfect predictor would produce a line like an inverted (upside-down) L. A completely unskilled predictor would produce a cumulative proportion curve like the yellow line (a diagonal). An interesting feature we discovered about this performance chart is that the area between the red and green curves is equal to the Peirce skill score.

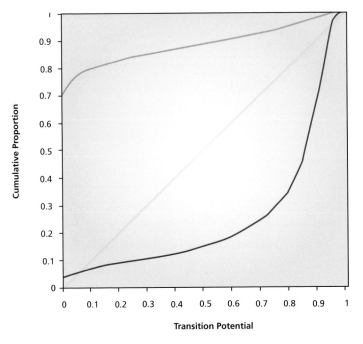

Figure 9. Performance chart for Back Propogation Neural Network.

Figure 10 presents performance charts for all of the indices tested. The reason for the sharp division between the performance of the classifiers versus the others is immediately apparent. All of the classifiers (with the exception of Bayclass with Prior Probabilities) perform as one would hope with an approximation of the backwards/inverted L-shaped curves of a strong performer. However, all of the other indices show a systematic problem with the distribution of potentials in areas that actually changed. They are all positively skewed—i.e., they have a high frequency of low transition potentials and a low frequency of high potential values. In contrast, the four strongly performing classifiers are all negatively skewed—a highly desirable quality.

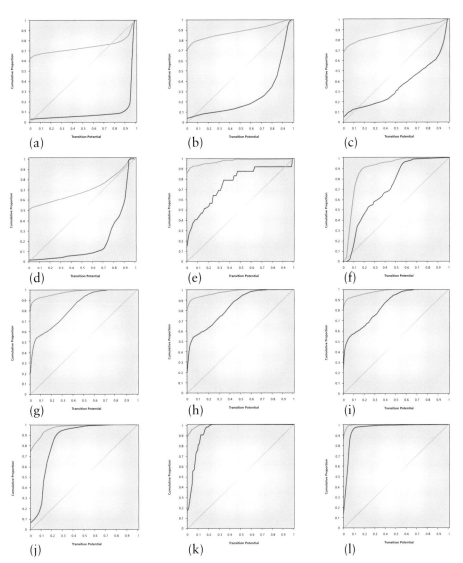

Figure 10. Performance charts for: (a) Bayclass (b) BPN Neural Network (c) Mahalclass (d) Fuzclass (e) All Combinations Likelihood (f) Average (g) Product (h) Bayes / WofE (i) Belief (j) Bayclass with Prior Probability (k) All Combinations Probability (l) Logistic Regression.

The most extreme case of positive skew occurs with the logistic regression result. It is interesting to note that this positive skew was also noted by Mertens and Lambin (2000) who also used logistic regression for transition potential modeling. In a study of deforestation in Cameroon, they noted that only 8 percent of the deforested area fell within areas with a predicted probability of 0.8 or greater and that to correctly predict as much as 80% of deforestation required a threshold as low as 0.5. This is very consistent with the observations of this study.

The difference between the Bayclass and the Bayclass with Priors results is very interesting with respect to this observation of skew. When equal priors are used (Bayclass), a negative skew in the transition potentials exists. However, when the prior probabilities accurately reflect the true proportion of change/no change (0.005/0.995) the Bayclass with Priors result becomes positively skewed. Of the twelve techniques tested, the eight that exhibit a positive skew are all concerned in one way or another with modeling the underlying probability or likelihood of change. However, the four that exhibit a negative skew do not consider the relative distribution of change to no change. As such, they appear to express more the concept of plausibility rather than probability. Although this term has a specific means of determination in the context of Dempster-Shafer theory (see Gordon and Shortliffe 1985), we use it here because of its consistency of interpretation.

What is interesting in this result is that areas that truly changed from 1989 to 1992 tended to have a high plausibility even if a low probability as measured by other techniques. This clearly indicates that errors tend to occur in areas that did exhibit appropriate characteristics for change. A possible interpretation of this is to conclude that there are multiple possible outcomes from a given context of change and that the pattern observed is only one of those realizations. This will be pursued further below.

ROC

Looking at the ROC statistics, a somewhat different picture emerges. Using this measure, all of the indices appear to have done very well, with all the multivariate measures outperforming the aggregated univariate measures with the sole exception of Fuzclass. Figure 11 illustrates the ROC curves for all of the techniques. What is most evident is that the most of the curves are quite similar and indicate a strong performance, confirming the general nature of the data presented in figure 7. The ROC would thus suggest that the various indices tested are quite similar and that they all act as good predictors of change—a rather different conclusion from the PSS.

Although not widely recognized, the ROC is a measure of relative performance while the PSS measures absolute performance. Thus, for example, indices with widely different absolute values can yield the same ROC statistic if they produce the same rank order (Fawcett 2003). This would suggest that if one were to rank order the transition potentials, all of the techniques would tend to exhibit high scoring ranks in the areas that truly changed. This would be a very interesting conclusion (which we test below) since most of the procedures examined use some variant of a rank and threshold change allocation process.

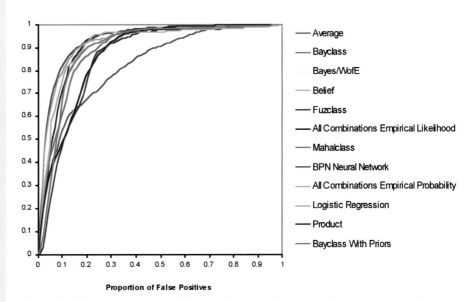

Figure 11. ROC curves for each of the transition modeling approaches based on the hit and false alarms rates using the 1989-1992 change validation map.

It is also interesting to note that there are some differences between the techniques on the ROC and that, in some cases, this is consistent with their score on the PSS and in other cases, quite inconsistent. For example, the BPN performed highly on the ROC as well as the PSS while WofE/Bayes performed in a mediocre to poor fashion on both measures of skill. Of those that changed, the All Combinations Likelihoods, All Combinations Probabilities, Bayclass with Prior Probabilities, and Logistic Regression procedures, which all performed poorly as measured by the PSS, all performed well with respect to the ROC.

To illustrate the difference between the performance of these measures in an absolute sense and a relative one, figure 12 shows the result of thresholding each of the indices at 0.5 while figure 13 shows the result of rank ordering the potentials and thresholding the result at the rank required to yield an area equal to that which actually changed from 1989–1992. In the former, the graphs are ordered according to their performance on the PSS while in the latter they are ordered with respect to their ROC statistic (from best to worst in left-to-right/top-to-bottom order).

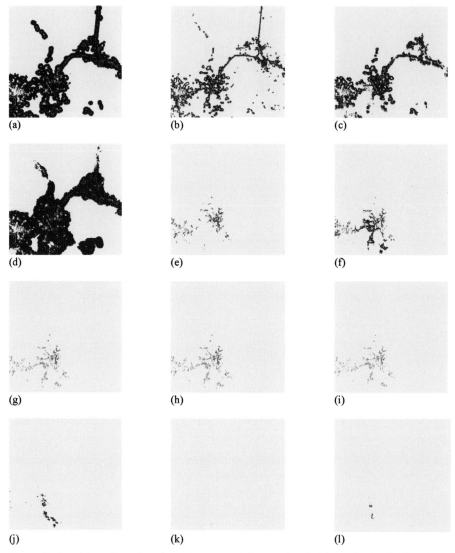

Figure 12. Spatial configuration of transition potential maps thresholded at 0.5 for: (a) Bayclass (b) BPN Neural Network (c) Mahalclass (d) Fuzclass (e) All Combinations Likelihood (f) Average (g) Product (h) Bayes / WofE (i) Belief (j) Bayclass with Prior Probability (k) All Combinations Probability (l) Logistic Regression.

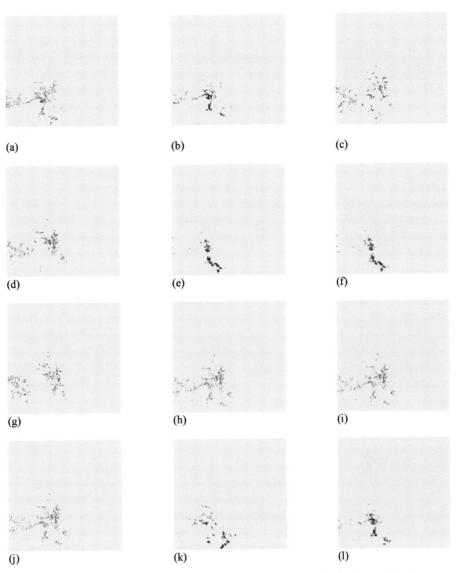

Figure 13. Spatial configuration of transition potential maps thresholded at the rank level necessary to produce the correct amount of change in the top ranks for: (a) BPN Neural Network (b) Logistic Regression (c) All Combinations Probability (d) All Combinations Likelihood (e) Bayclass (f) Mahalclass (g) Bayclass with Prior Probability (h) Product (i) Bayes / WofE (j) Belief (k) Fuzclass (l) Average.

Looking at figure 12, the effects of the negative skew among the first four and the positive skew among the rest are clearly evident. However, figure 13 does not present a convincing argument that all procedures performed similarly. There is clearly a relationship between the ROC and the areas selected. However, the results are not highly uniform.

PREDICTED CHANGE

To explore the ROC further, the hardened predictions depicted in figure 13 were crosstabulated with areas that truly changed from 1989–1992. Figure 14 examines the prediction accuracy by showing the hit rate and false alarm rate for each index. Note that the Peirce skill score is the difference between these two bars. Since they all experienced roughly the same false alarm rate, their skill (as measured by the PSS) is almost perfectly correlated with their hit rate. Figure 14 also plots their ROC values as markers using the secondary (right) y-axis.

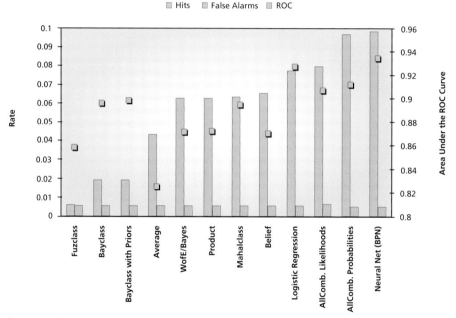

Figure 14. Comparison of predicted (using a rank/threshold allocation) to actual change, 1989–1992. The Peirce skill score is equal to the difference in the Hit and False Alarm rates (primary y-axis). The ROC is superimposed using the secondary y-axis.

What is evident in this graph is that while the ROC did serve as an approximate predictor of relative performance under this rank and threshold test, the absolute value of the ROC statistic (which measures the area under the ROC curve) was not a good predictor of absolute performance. For this group of indices, the ROC statistic ranged from 0.825 to 0.934, and yet the hit rate never exceeded 10% and went as low as 1%.

The ROC statistic is widely used in the land-cover change community. However, it was not a good indicator of the results of this test. Why this discrepancy? The area under the ROC curve describes the performance of the entire index. It is clearly high in all cases because all indices did a good job of predicting where change would not occur (the large expanses of undisturbed forest). However, our test was concerned less with where change would not occur as with where it would. The quantity of change being predicted was quite small in comparison to the area as a whole. Thus our concern is with the region of the ROC curve to the bottom left. Figure 15 shows a zoomed view of the region in which hit and false alarm rates were actually experienced (0–0.1 for the hit rate and 0–0.007 for the false alarm rate). The ordering of the curves in this portion of the ROC chart is a very good predictor of performance. Thus the problem is less with the ROC chart as it is with its generalization using a single statistic (the area under the ROC curve).

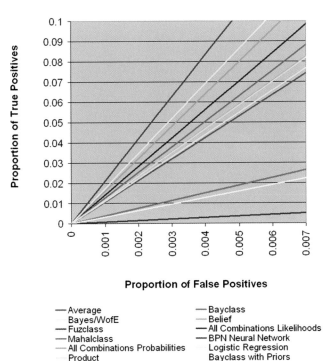

Figure 15. A zoomed view of the lower-left portion of the ROC chart in Figure 11. Note that the x-axis is scaled differently to highlight differences between the curves.

DISCUSSION AND CONCLUSIONS

From the results discussed above, a number of important conclusions can be reached:

1. Although a wide variety of techniques are currently in use for the modeling of transition potentials, they are not interchangeable.

2. The manner in which one assesses the predictive power of a transition potential model is not independent of how it will be used. For change allocation procedures that use an absolute threshold (such as the application of Mertens and Lambin 2002 or the change allocation procedure of Lucas), the PSS or similar measure of absolute performance will be appropriate while those that use a relative threshold (such as the large group of rank

and threshold allocation procedures) should use a measure of relative performance such as the ROC.

3.   Summary statistics (such as the ROC Area Under the Curve statistic) may not be good predictors in a specific instance. However, performance graphs such as the ROC curve, or the performance charts introduced here for examination of the basis of the PSS, can provide valuable information.

4.   Of all the techniques tested, the only index that consistently performed well on all tests was the back propagation neural network (BPN). The commonly used procedure of logistic regression worked fairly well in tasks that required the relative potential of transition but performed poorly in an absolute sense. Another technique currently in vogue, weights-of-evidence, was generally a mediocre to poor performer. We note that this technique aggregates independently evaluated criteria and thus has no means of gauging interaction. However, we are unable in this evaluation to assess whether this is the cause of its performance.

5.   In an absolute sense, indices that indicate the plausibility of change may outperform those that indicate the probability of change. One possible conclusion (such as is drawn by Pijanowski et al. 2002, in their assessment of the use of a back propagation neural network for transition potential modeling) is to say that we seem to be doing better at predicting where change won't happen than where it will. In this study, the performance of the indices that map the plausibility of change suggest an alternative hypothesis—that there are multiple outcomes at any point in history and that any specific scenario is only one of several (many?) possible realizations.

Both perspectives raised in this last point are consistent with each other. However, they point to a research trajectory in another possible direction. If there are multiple possible outcomes, then the likelihood of a successful prediction is slim and will get progressively worse over time. This is certainly consistent with general experience. However, consider the case of the back propagation neural network (BPN) for the problem of making a specific prediction (fig. 13) versus a soft prediction of the plausibility of change (fig. 2). The Peirce skill scores for these two tasks are 0.09 and 0.64 respectively. Should we not consider the possibility of making soft rather than hard predictions? In many planning contexts, this is really all that is needed, and there is a strong suggestion here that this approach may produce more accurate predictions in the long run.

NOTES

1. We consider that any analytical operation that takes one or more spatially explicit inputs and produces a spatially explicit output is truly a GIS operation, even if it is not currently offered within an existing GIS).

2. Horizontal applications are meant to serve many applications while vertical applications are oriented to a single application.

3. The technique requires that any quantitative driver maps be reclassified into a series of equal interval classes. The CROSSTAB module in Idrisi provides the Cramer's V measure of association along with a Chi-Square test of significance as a rapid screening procedure for the potential predictive power of each potential driver.

4. Note that our intention was not to develop a definitive model of land-cover change, but an adequate model for the purpose of comparing the transition potential modeling procedures reviewed.

REFERENCES

Baker, W. L. (1989). A review of models of landscape change. *Landscape Ecology* 2: 111–33.

Berry, M. W., B. C. Hazen, R. L. MacIntyre, and R. O. Flamm. 1996. LUCAS: A system for modeling land-use change. *IEEE Computational Science and Engineering* 3(1): 24–35.

Bonham-Carter, G. F., F. P. Agterberg, and D. F. Wright, 1989. Weights of evidence modeling: A new approach to mapping mineral potential. In *Statistical applications in the earth sciences,* ed. F. P. Agterberg and G. F. Bonham-Carter, 171–83.Geological Survey of Canada Paper 89–9.

Bonham-Carter, G. F. 1994. *Geographic information systems for geoscientists: Modelling with GIS.* New York: Pergamon.

Brown, D. G., B. C. Pijanowski, and J. D. Duh. 2000. Modeling the relationships between land use and land cover on private lands in the Upper Midwest, USA. *Journal of Environmental Management* 59: 247–63.

Clarke, K. C., and L. J. Gaydos. 1998. Loose-coupling a cellular automaton model and GIS: Long-term urban growth prediction for San Francisco and Washington/Baltimore. *International Journal of Geographical Information Science* 12:699–714.

Eastman, J. R. 1999. *IDRISI 32 : IDRISI for workstations.* Worcester, Mass.: Clark University.

———. 2003. *IDRISI : The Kilimanjaro edition.* Worcester, Mass.: Clark University.

Eastman, J. R., and R. Laney. 2002. Bayesian soft classification for subpixel analysis: A critical evaluation. *Photogrammetric Engineering and Remote Sensing* 68 (11): 1149–54.

Fawcett, T. 2003. ROC graphs: Notes and practical considerations for data mining researchers. HP Labs Tech Report HPL-2003–4. www.hpl.hp.com/techreports/2003/HPL-2003-4.pdf.

Foody, G. M., N. A. Campbell, N. M. Trodd, and T. F. Wood. 1992. Derivation and applications of probabilistic measures of class membership from the maximum likelihood classification. *Photogrammetric Engineering and Remote Sensing* 58 (9): 1335–41.

Gordon, J., and E. H. Shortliffe. 1985. A method for managing evidential reasoning in a hierarchical hypothesis space. *Artificial Intelligence* 26: 323–57.

Joliffe, I. T., and D. Stephenson. 2003. *Forecast verification: A practitioner's guide in atmospheric science.* Hoboken, N.J.: John Wiley and Sons.

Killeen, T., Z. Villegas, L. Soria, and B. S. Soares-Filho. (n.d.) Tendencias de la Deforestacion en los Municipios de San Javier y Concepcion, Santa Cruz-Bolivia. www.museoneolkempff.org/informacionDis/pdf/escenarioAmazon/Tend-Defor.pdf.

Li, X. and A.G. Yeh. 2001. Calibration of cellular automata by using neural networks for the simulation of complex urban systems. *Environment and Planning A* 33: 1445–62.

———. 2002. Neural-network-based cellular automata for simulating multiple land use changes using GIS. *International Journal of Geographical Information Science* 16(4): 323–43.

Mason, I. B. 2003. Binary events. In F*orecast verification: A practitioner's guide in atmospheric science,* ed. I. T. Joliffe and D. Stephenson, ch. 3. Hoboken, N.J.: John Wiley and Sons.

Mertens, B., and E. F. Lambin. 1997. Spatial modeling of deforestation in southern Cameroon. *Applied Geography* 17: 143–62.

———. 2000. Land-cover-change trajectories in Southern Cameroon. *Annals of the Association of American Geographers* 90 (3): 467–94.

Pijanowski, B. C., D. G. Brown, B. A. Shellito, and G. A. Manik. 2002. Using neural networks and GIS to forecast land use changes: A land transformation model. *Computers, Environment and Urban Systems* 26 (6): 553–75.

Pontius, R. G., Jr., J. D. Cornell, and C. A. S. Hall. 2001. Modeling the spatial pattern of land use change with GEOMOD2: Application and validation for Costa Rica. *Agriculture, Ecosystems and Environment* 1775: 1–13.

Pontius, R. G., Jr., and L. Schneider. 2001. Land-use change model validation by an ROC method for the Ipswich watershed, Massachusetts, USA. *Agriculture, Ecosystems and Environment* 85: 239–48.

Soares-Filho, B. S., C. L. Pennachin, G. Cerqueira. 2002. DINAMICA—A stochastic cellular automata model designed to simulate the landscape dynamics in an Amazonian colonization frontier. *Ecological Modelling* 154 (3): 217–35.

Soares-Filho, B. S., L. Corradi-Filho, G. C. Cerqueira, and W. L. Araujo. 2003. Simulating the spatial patterns of change through the use of the Dinamica model Anais, Simposio Brasileiro de Sensoriamento Remoto, XI, Belo Horizonte, Brasil: INPE 721–28.

Swets, J. A. 1973. The relative operating characteristic in psychology. *Science* 240: 1285–93.

Tso, B., and P. M. Mather, 2001. *Classification methods for remotely sensed data*. New York: Taylor and Francis.

Verburg, P. H., G. H. J. de Koning, K. Kok, A. Veldkamp, and J. Bouma. 1999. A spatial explicit allocation procedure for modeling the pattern of land use change based on actual land use. *Ecological Modelling* 116: 45–61.

Verburg, P. H., W. Soepboer, A. Veldkamp, R. Limpiada, V. Espaldon, and S. A Sharifah Mastura. 2002. Modeling the spatial dynamics of regional land use: The CLUE-S Model. *Environmental Management* 30(3): 391–405.

Wang, F. 1990. Fuzzy supervised classification of remote sensing images. *IEEE Transactions on Geoscience and Remote Sensing* 28 (2): 194–201.

———. 1994. The use of artificial neural networks in a geographical information system for agricultural land-suitability assessment. *Environment and Planning A* 26(2): 265–84.

White, R., and G. Engelen, 2000. High-resolution integrated modeling of the spatial dynamics of urban and regional systems. *Computers, Environment and Urban Systems* 24: 383–400.

Yeh, A. G., and X. Li. 2002. Urban simulation using neural networks and cellular automata for land use planning. In *Advances in spatial data handling*, ed. D. Richardson and P. van Oosterom, 451–64. Berlin: Springer-Verlag.

## Chapter 18

Modeling the Interaction between Humans and Animals in Multiple-use Forests: A Case Study of *Panthera tigris*

SEAN AHEARN

CENTER FOR ADVANCED RESEARCH OF SPATIAL INFORMATION (CARSI)

HUNTER COLLEGE, CITY UNIVERSITY OF NEW YORK

NEW YORK, NEW YORK

J. L. DAVID SMITH

DEPARTMENT OF FISHERIES, WILDLIFE AND CONSERVATION BIOLOGY

UNIVERSITY OF MINNESOTA

ST. PAUL, MINNESOTA

▶ ABSTRACT

THE LOSS OF ANIMAL HABITAT AND THE GREATER USE OF FORESTS by humans in various parts of the world have increased the conflict between humans and wildlife, especially for those animals with geographically large home ranges. As a result, much effort has gone into preserving a network of reserves of the last remaining prime habitat. Biologists, however, have realized that these areas alone are not sufficient to sustain populations and that the multiple-use regions that surround these core areas are essential for species' survival (Smith, Ahearn, and McDougal 1998). While the concept of multiple use is attractive, finding the right balance between competing uses is difficult or impossible without a computational framework in which to analyze these competing uses. The advent of object-based geographic data structures has given scientists such a framework and has spawned a number of dynamic individual-based models for analyzing the interaction of animals with their environment. One of the most difficult challenges associated with these models is the simulation of movement and the relationship between movement and behavior. Various analytic models have been proposed, and implementation of state-based movement has been designed using knowledge from domain experts. With the recent use of GPS collars for tracking animals, scientists now have quantitative information on the nature of animal movement. This quantitative data offers an unprecedented opportunity to better understand the relationship between an animal's state and its behavior at different spatial and temporal scales. The findings from these analyses can be used to calibrate and test the individual-based object models in an effort to understand the short- and long-term consequences of geographically specific management proposals and practices. This chapter explores these issues in the context of the tiger as a prototype for modeling the interaction between humans and animals in the wild.

INTRODUCTION

Over the past thirty years, there has been significant emphasis on establishing protected areas for conservation of the best remaining habitat. However, for keystone species like tigers, *Panthera tigris*, which often require large geographic areas for their survival, these protected areas may not be enough. Studies have shown that protected areas only account for 17–25% of all tiger habitat and that 75–83% of tiger habitat is in multiple-use forests with significant human activity (Smith, McDougal, and Sunquist 1987; Wikramanayake et al. 1999). The concept of multiple use is an often-cited solution by policy makers for balancing human activities in forests with conservation needs. However, the development of a quantitative framework for balancing the various needs in a multiple-use forest is in its early stages (Ahearn et al. 2001). Additionally, information on human–animal interaction is limited, especially for large carnivores like tigers (Kenney et al. 1995, MacKinnon, Mishra, and Mott 1999). In fact, resource selection by individual animals, a prerequisite for understanding this interaction, is notoriously difficult (Garshelis 2000) and has only recently been approached within an analytic framework (Franke, Caelli, and Hudson 2004; Jonsen et al. 2003; Brillinger et al. 2004). The fundamentals of animal movement and its relationship to behavior are the subject of this discussion. To provide context for this discussion, the movement and behavior of the tiger *(Panthera tigris)* will be examined in the context of the new analytic frameworks.

MODELING MOVEMENT AND BEHAVIOR OF ANIMALS

Early models for animal movement employed random walk models (Brownlee 1911) and diffusion models (Dobzhansky and Wright 1943). However, these models assumed spatial isotropy of movement and were considered too simple as a general principle of animal movement (Turchin 1998). Dice and Howard (1951) and Skellum (1951) examined dispersal movements to calculate neighborhood size. Metapopulation models proposed by Levins (1970) extended Wright's shifting-balance theory by creating an implicit spatial structure among populations. Hanski (1991) and McCullough (1996) extended metapopulations to include spatially explicit and individually based realistic models of animal movement among subpopulations that have been used to examine the effects of fragmented habitat connected by corridors. Siniff and Jessen (1969) were the first to realistically simulate animal movement and emphasize the importance of space as a medium for ecological interaction. Turchin (1998) proposed four general types of movement by animals. They include simple random walk, random walk with directional persistence, random walk with directional bias, and random walk with persistence and directional bias. Individual-based movement models (IBMMS), which have been widely adopted by ecologists, use these principles of movement to model individuals and their interaction with each other and their environment. An example of a spatially explicit individual-based model is TIGMOD (Ahearn et al. 2001). It used general principles of movement and behavioral information from tiger field studies to model the interaction between tigers and humans and to analyze tiger survivability given different levels of human interaction and prey abundance and varying management practices.

With the advances in GPS, there is now a plethora of data on animal movement at very high spatial and temporal scales (Moen et al. 1996. Schlecht et al. 2004). This data has resulted in phenomenological studies that describe the pattern of habitat use (Merrill 2000, Blake et al. 2001) and has been used by a limited number of researchers to develop spatiotemporal models to predict movement. Some of the models have used stochastic differential equations calibrated from the GPS data to simulate animal movement (Brillinger et al. 2004), while others have used Markov models to infer the behavior and sequences from GPS data and to generate movement based on the state probabilities, state transitions, and state observations (Franke, Caelli, and Hudson 2004; Jonsen et al. 2003). At issue with respect to these quantitative models is how well the models capture the complexity of the movement and behavior of individuals as it relates to the environment in which they move, the other individuals with whom they interact, and their own geographic strategies for resource usage.

At this point, it may be useful to distinguish between an animal's state and its behavior. We use *state* to define an animal's physiological condition (e.g., its age, whether in estrus, pregnant, hungry, alive), and *behavior* is an animal's actions in response to its state and its environment.

A CONCEPTUAL MODEL FOR TIGER BEHAVIOR

While the acquisition of high-resolution spatial and temporal information regarding animal movement is a recent phenomenon, a wealth of behavioral information has been acquired from field studies over the years that has led to an understanding of the relationship between behavior and movement at coarse spatial and temporal scales. From these studies, conceptual models for behavior have been developed which describe general strategies for resource usage, mating, hunting/foraging, and homerange delineation. In the following discussion, we will describe a conceptual model for the tiger.

TIGER BEHAVIOR AND MOVEMENT

Our conceptual model for tigers is based on the field research of Smith (1993), Smith, McDougal, and Sunquist (1987), Smith, McDougal, and Miquelle (1989), Smith and McDougal (1991), Smith, Ahearn, and McDougal (1998),

Seidensticker and McDougal (1993), Sunquist (1981), Karanth and Sunquist (1995), Chundawat, Gogate, and Johnsingh (1999), and Miquelle et al.(1999) that provides detailed information on predatory, reproductive, territorial, and dispersal behavior. Each of these behaviors can be further subdivided based on an animal's state. For example, there are a variety of behaviors that fall under reproductive behavior that are a function of an animal's changing reproductive state. Scent marking intensifies during a female's pre-estrus state, and she gradually marks throughout her entire home range. Once estrus occurs, her movement becomes more rapid and continuous as she begins repeated calling, day and night, to help the resident male to find her. Thus, we have a set of different behaviors, each in response to a changing physiological state. Each behavior has a specific movement pattern associated with it, which can be described by rate of movement and degree of directional persistence.

Tiger home ranges are established based on resource availability and sex. Home ranges tend to be fuzzy boundaries that are sometimes breached by small forays beyond a territorial boundary or in response to changing resource needs or conditions. Male tiger homerange spans vary from 35–150 km² in the Royal Chitwan National Park (Smith, McDougal, and Sunquist 1987) to >800 km² in the Russian far east (Miquelle et al. 1999). The male homerange circumscribes 2 to 7 female home ranges. Prey are killed on average every seven days if the animal is at least 200 kilograms (i.e., *Cervus unicolor*) but can be of higher frequency if the prey size is smaller. The tiger will remain near its kill for 2–3 days and begin hunting again between 3 and 5 days after it last fed (Sunquist 1981; Chundawat, Gogate, and Johnsingh 1999). Females with cubs will increase their frequency of hunting until cubs are 16–17 months old, at which time their rate of killing has doubled or tripled. Male tigers visit their females three to five times a month. If the female is fertile, the male will remain to mate with her for 2 to 3 days and copulate over 100 times. If not, he may just spend a few minutes with her and move to the next female. Females become fertile every 20–30 days on average and give birth to 2–5 cubs after 102 days. Cubs remain with their mother until they are 18–22 months old.

Movement by tigers can be characterized by the direction and distance a tiger travels per unit time and is functionally dependent upon its state. A male tiger has an external bias to its direction when moving to the next hunting area or visiting the next female. Once a male enters a female's home range, his movement will slow as he seeks his mate, and his movement may be characterized as a random walk. If he is within 1 kilometer of the female, he is likely to roar and move directly towards her. If she is not fertile, he assumes a random walk through her home range until he meets her or moves on to his next female. If he is hunting, he assumes a random walk once he enters his hunting area and searches for prey. After prey is killed, the tiger will remain near the kill until it is finished.

HUMAN INTERACTION AND CATTLE GRAZING

Human interaction with tigers takes various forms from poaching of tigers and their prey, to loss of habitat, or poisoning of tigers by villagers whose cattle have been killed by tigers. Human behavior toward tigers is complex. In multiple-use forests, one of the primary human uses for these forests is cattle grazing. The problem with cattle grazing is that it cascades through the ecosystem to eventually affect tiger viability. Grazing reduces regeneration, resulting in forest degradation and eventually forest fragmentation. This deterioration of habitat quality reduces the natural prey base and increases the likelihood that a tiger will kill domestic prey. If a sufficient number of prey are killed within a given geographic region, a domestic carcass will be laced with an insecticide by the owner, and when the tiger comes back to finish its meal, it will be poisoned and die. The motivation to poison tigers is dependent on the number of kills a tiger makes in an area and the number of kills in turn depends on local grazing pressure. At higher domestic stocking rates, a tiger is more likely to remain in the area, killing cattle.

An important management question concerning tigers and other large area-sensitive predators is: What is the probability of dispersal across a real, human-dominated landscape? (Smith 1993). Estimating the probability of dispersal is a vexing problem that field biologists have not been able to address because the dispersal of a single individual is too rare an event to hope to observe, even with intensive monitoring. However, it is not difficult for field biologists to observe and document the behavior of a tiger living in poor-quality habitat typical of a potential habitat corridor and then use this behavior or sets of behavior to model an individual animal's movement through a corridor. Such modeling also can help managers explore the effects of various management actions designed to increase the likelihood of successful dispersal.

TIGMOD REVIEW

INTRODUCTION

The principles behind individual-based movement models (IBMM) are that each individual is an autonomous entity that is behaviorally and physiologically distinct and that interaction among individuals is localized (Franke, Caelli, and Hudson 2004). GIS software constraints until recently have stymied efforts to create robust, extensible, geographically based IBMM (Raper and Livingstone 1995, Westervelt and Hopkins 1999, Ling 2000). With the advent of object-oriented (OO) geographic systems in the last ten to fifteen years, these constraints have disappeared. The critical difference from previous generations of GIS software tools is that OO systems make the object the unit of analysis, not its geometry. The result of this paradigm shift is that location and time are treated as explicit properties of an object, permitting the frequent updating of space–time attributes. It also results in the creation of an autonomous individual that can interact in a unique fashion with other individuals (Ahearn et al. 2001). In the case of the tiger in TIGMOD, the tiger objects have two geometry fields, location (a point) and home range (a polygon). TIGMOD was created to give an analytic framework for the enormous amount of behavioral data that has been collected for tigers in order to better understand its behavioral dynamics and to demonstrate that an IBMM could be used effectively to analyze the proper balance to strike in multiple-use forests. It was designed, however, not with a specific analytic task to be performed but with the goal of capturing the patterns of behavior and interactions needed to model the system. Once these aspects are correctly captured, questions concerning changes to the system could be answered (Ahearn et al. 2001).

Key features of TIGMOD are that it supports mobility of objects, variable spatial attributes and temporal resolutions, interaction with other individual objects, the creation of new individuals, and the propagation of change in the state of one object through the system in space and time to affect all related objects. Model inputs include: an array of information on movement (rate and direction) as a function of ten unique states of the tiger, a three-probability estimate on the likelihood of tiger poisoning, a rate of hunger, a probability of hunting success, and an input for temporal resolution (fig. 1).

Time

| days per move | 0.5 |

Hunger

hunger index trigger hunting	60%
hunger index increase daily	30%
stress index increase daily	3.33%

Movement Rate

"random"	2000 m/day
feeding	400 m/day
hunting	1500 m/day
male mating outside	3000 m/day
male mating inside	1500 m/day
female fertile	1000 m/day
female fertile	1000 m/day
female pregnant	800 m/day
female with cubs	

Hunting success

| domestic prey | 0.75 |
| wild prey | 0.25 |

Probability of poisoning

1 other cattle killed <1km	0.05
2 other cattle killed <1km	0.10
3 other cattle killed <1km	0.25
4+ other cattle killed < 1km	0.50

Movement direction

| "random" persistence | 0.75 |
| male mating bias | 0.85 |

Kill forgotten

| days after which villagers forget about the kill | 60 |

Figure 1. Input parameters for TIGMOD with default values (from Ahearn et al. 2001).

DATA MODEL

Tiger and prey are represented as objects that have physical, behavioral, and geometric characteristics, all being fields in the description of the respective object. Age, weight, and whether alive are examples of physical characteristics; feeding, hunting, mating, and giving birth are examples of behavioral characteristics; and location and home range are examples of geometric characteristics. Class hierarchies were created with animal as a super class, prey and tigers as sub-classes, wild and domestic prey as subclasses of prey, and male and female as subclasses of tiger. All methods were inherited from the super classes above any subclass. Closely coupled objects are modeled with relational joins. A male tiger can have one or more females in its home range, females can have two or more male and female cubs, and tigers can be hunting 0 or 1 prey.

TIGMOD is a dynamic model that is driven by the tiger's internal state and its relationship with its environment. In some instances, states are dependent on the environment (e.g., a male tiger stays longer with a female if she is fertile), and sometimes they are not (e.g., a female becomes fertile every ~20–30 days). A change in time drives the model affecting state-based relationships (e.g., relationship between hunger and desire to hunt), functional events (e.g., a female becomes pregnant if she is fertile and within close proximity of a male), and scheduled events (e.g., she gives birth ~102 days after conception (fig. 2). These in turn determine the pattern of tiger movement (Table 1). Movement is characterized by rate and direction. Rate and direction of movement is functionally dependent on state. Distance traveled in a time step is modeled as a chi squared random variable. Direction is modeled as four different behaviors: direct movement when the tiger is going directly to a spotted prey or toward a female's calling; directed movement when a tiger heads back toward its kill; random movement with a directional bias when a tiger cruises its home range; cruises and random movement with an external bias when a male heads toward a female home range.

Figure 2. Diagram of the dynamic interactions in TIGMOD (from Ahearn et al. 2001).

Movement Characteristics with default values		
Behavior	Rate (distance per day) μ = mean rate of movement σ = standard deviation of movement rate	Direction μ = mean direction of movement σ = standard deviation of movement direction
Looking for prey	χ^2 random variable (μ = 1500 meters, σ = 1500 meters)	Random with bias: moves in a random direction with a probability of bias of 0.75 in a direction selected from a normal random variable with μ = direction of prey and μ = 10 degrees
Found prey	Moves to the location of prey	Moves in the direction of the prey
Feeding	χ^2 random variable (μ = 400 meters, σ = 400 meters)	Movement is directed to prey location as selected from a normal random variable with μ = direction to prey and σ = 5 degrees
"Random"	χ^2 random variable (μ = 2000 meters, σ = 2000 meters)	Random with persistence: moves in a random direction with a probability of persistence of 0.75 in a direction selected from a normal random variable with μ = previous direction and σ = 10 degrees.
Mating (male): outside female domain	χ^2 random variable (μ = 3000 meters, σ = 3000 meters)	Random with directional bias: moves in a random direction with a probability of bias of 0.85 in a direction selected as normal random variable with μ = direction of female and σ = 10 degrees
Mating (male): inside female domain	χ^2 random variable (μ = 1500 meters, σ = 1500 meters)	Random with directional bias: moves in a random direction with a probability of bias of 0.85 in a direction selected as a normal random variable with μ = direction of female and σ = 10 degrees.
Mating (male): within 400 meters of female	Moves distance to female	Moves in the direction of female
Fertile (female)	χ^2 random variable (μ = 1000 meters, σ = 1000 meters)	Random with persistence: moves in a random direction with a probability of persistence of 0.75 in a direction selected from a normal random variable with μ = previous direction and σ = 10 degrees.
Pregnant (female	χ^2 random variable (μ = 1000 meters, σ = 1000 meters)	Random with persistence: moves in a random direction with a probability of persistence of 0.75 in a direction selected from a normal random variable with μ = previous direction and σ = 10 degrees.
With cubs (female)	χ^2 random variable (μ = 800 meters, σ = 800 meters)	Random with persistence: moves in a random direction with a probability of persistence of 0.75 in a direction selected from a normal random variable with μ = previous direction and σ = 10 degrees.

Table 1. Movement characteristics for different tiger behavior (from Ahearn et al. 2001).

Human interaction is modeled for one aspect of cattle grazing at the forest boundary: the likelihood that a cow killed by the tiger will be poisoned by villagers. The first aspect of interaction deals with the likelihood of a cow being killed by a tiger based on the difficulty of killing. This is determined by the method for grazing by the villagers. In some instances, cows are guarded, resulting in a lower probability of kill, and other village groups just send their cows into the forest unguarded, resulting in a higher probability of kill. The other two factors that determine the likelihood of poisoning are probabilities based on the number of kills within a geographic region (e.g., 1 km radius) and the length of time villagers are annoyed about the kill. All probabilities related to all three factors are user inputs and can change depending on geographic location and the level of education of the villagers. For instance, if the villagers know that tigers bring in tourist money, then they may be more tolerant of cattle kills and the probably of poisoning is reduced.

TIGMOD can be run at different time-step increments and for different durations. Ahearn et al. (2001) also ran the model with differing amounts of domestic and wild prey densities in order to understand tiger viability.

MODELING COMPLEXITY: A NEW SOURCE OF DATA

TIGMOD was developed as an IBMM using expert knowledge of the relationship between the tiger's state and its relationship to other tigers and its environment. While this model proved effective in simulating tiger behavior and tiger viability as a function of different management conditions, it has several limitations: (1) it wasn't calibrated with spatio–temporal geographic information for tiger movement, (2) it made significant assumptions about the nature of tiger movement given different behavioral states, and (3) it modeled a subset of tiger behavior.

The availability of high-resolution spatial and temporal information from GPS collars on animals provides us with a new source of spatio–temporal data and enables us to understand better the relationship between an animal's state and its behavior at different spatial and temporal scales. As discussed above, there have been a number of studies that have used GPS to examine the pattern of habitat use (Merrill 2000, Blake et al. 2001) and a limited number that have used it to measure quantitatively the nature of movement and its relationship to behavior (Brillinger et al. 2004; Franke, Caelli, and Hudson 2004; Jonsen et al. 2003). The critical question is: How well do these models capture the complexity of the movement and behavior of individuals as they relate to the environment in which the animals move, the other individuals with whom they interact, and their own geographic strategies for resource usage? For this discussion, we will concern ourselves with the Hidden Markov Model (HMM), as this type of model has the interesting properties of imputing behavior and movement characteristics from a spatio–temporal signal, although it is recognized that other models (e.g., Brillinger et al. 2004) show equal promise.

HMM

Hidden Markov Models (HMM) are in a class of stochastic signal models that characterize the statistical properties of a signal. They are an extension to the idea of discrete Markov chains, which characterize the probabilities of state transition sequences. In Markov chains, each state relates to an observable, physical event. In contrast, in HHM the observation is a probabilistic function of the state, which results in a doubly stochastic process where one process is observable and one is hidden. The ergodic HMM assumes that every state can be reach from any other state (Rabiner et al. 1989).

An HMM is characterized by N, the number of states in the model; M, the number of distinct observations; $\mathbf{A}$, a state transition matrix; $\mathbf{B}$, the observation probability distribution; and π, the initial state distribution. HMM is often described by:

$$\lambda = (\pi, \mathbf{A}, \mathbf{B}).$$

The three problems for HMMs include: 1) generating estimates of observations and state sequences, 2) determining the most likely state sequence given λ and an observation sequence, and 3) updating the model given new observation data (Rabiner et al. 1989; Franke, Caelli, and Hudson 2004).

For theoretical reasons, good initial estimates of λ are necessary to ensure optimal model parameterization, with particular importance given to good initial estimations of $\mathbf{B}$. There are various techniques for making estimates, including manual segmentation of observation sequences, maximum-likelihood segmentation with averaging, and segmentation with k-means clustering (for a definitive review of HMM, see Rabiner et al. 1989). As we discuss below, selecting the number of states for the A matrix often requires significant information on the state and associated behavior of the animal being modeled.

CARIBOU EXAMPLE OF HMM

Franke, Caelli, and Hudson (2004) implemented a HMM for caribou using GPS data acquired every 15 minutes for 12 caribou. They examined three *hidden states* (**A** matrix, as probabilities), feeding, bedding, and relocating, which typically occupy over 90% of the caribou's activity. They selected distance between locations and turn angle as observations that encapsulate movement as related to behavior. Distance was assigned to four intervals: stationary, short, medium, and long; turn angle was assigned four categories: ahead, left, right, back (the **B** matrix, as probabilities).

They compared their model with a traditional time series method and found much greater PC (percent correct) and significantly less AAD (average absolute difference) for the HMM when used to predict an observation sequence from λ. Perhaps more important, the state transition probability matrices (A matrix) showed that caribou tended to forage for short periods and bed and relocate for longer periods and that the animals were most likely to bed after relocating and forage after bedding. Both of these behaviors of movement and transition are supported by field observation. Through examination of the transition matrices,

Franke, Caelli, and Hudson (2004) also were able to deduce the differing land-use strategies of the individual caribou. In summary, they believed their model was very effective for predicting behavior but recognized that resource selection is scale dependent, and their implementation of HMM avoided integration across ecological scales. Nevertheless, Franke, Caelli, and Hudson (2004) have made a strong argument for using HMM for the derivation of behavioral states and generating observation sequences for the woodland caribou.

HMM FOR TIGER MODELING

The conceptual model for the tiger described above reveals the complexity of the relationship between the tiger's state and its behavior. In considering the use of HMM for imputing tiger behavior from movement and in generating movement from λ, several issues are at hand: Can a tiger's movement be described by a first-order Markov process? How are different temporal scales accommodated? Are there state changes that result in the generation of different movement rates and patterns for the same behavior? Are certain behaviors, and therefore movement patterns, dependent on the state of other entities?

Can a tiger's movement be described by a first-order Markov process? A first-order Markov process assumes that the current state is wholly dependent on the previous state. This is not as limiting as it sounds as dependencies propagate through the model. However, not all behaviors are first order. There is a significant amount of research that indicates that animals may possess a cognitive map of their environment (Poucet 1993, Bennett 1996) and that animals may use that map to develop geographic strategies of resource use. Our own preliminary analysis of GPS data obtained in the Royal Chitwan National Forest in Nepal indicates that the tiger may have a hunting strategy that minimizes disturbance between hunts and maximizes usage of her home range by sequencing hunts in different geographic regions of her home range over a one-month period (fig. 3). The strategy may also be part of her establishing and maintaining her home range.

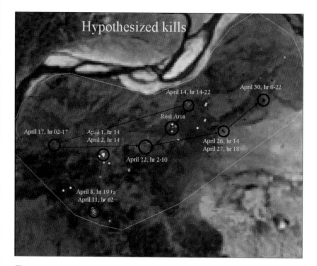

Figure 3:   Hypothesized hunting/kill areas

Are there state changes that result in the generation of different movement rates and patterns for the same behavior? For the tiger, the answer is yes. When a tiger's state starts to change from satiated to hungry, her behavior becomes that of a hunter. The rate at which she becomes hungry and her strategies for hunting may be a function of her reproductive state. When she is pregnant, she gets hungrier sooner. When she has cubs, her hunting increases until she is essentially hunting continuously when the cubs are 12 to 18 months old. Between the cubs' birth and when they are two months old, her home range is reduced by 50% (Smith 1993). Thereafter, she carries or leads the cubs from place to place until they are big enough to follow her and assist in the hunt.

Are certain behaviors and therefore movement patterns dependent on the state of other entities? The answer for the tiger is yes. The clearest example is the behavior of the male toward his females. If a visited female is not fertile, he may spend only minutes with her. If she is fertile, he will spend several days.

How are different temporal scales accommodated? Tigers operate at numerous temporal scales. Hunting occurs at 5–7 day intervals, home range traversal occurs every 24–28 days, and dry and wet season variation occurs biannually. Males also visit their females periodically. A model that truly mimics tiger behavior must operate at these multiple temporal scales.

DISCUSSION

The above analysis suggests that it may be difficult to use a single HMM to incorporate the complex states and corresponding behaviors of a tiger. Perhaps multiple HMMs, which correspond to different states, might be more appropriate. However, determining these states is no small task. It requires detailed, close-range, behavioral observations, information on rates, variability, and directional persistence of movement, and observation of anecdotal data such as presence of a kill or tracks of another tiger. Together, this information provides clues to an animal's behavioral rules. For example, finding a kill and determining the GPS time when the tiger reached the kill site allows one to infer the behavior (hunting) prior to the kill time. Similarly, behavior post feeding can be inferred to be either territorial patrolling or long-range movements designed to take a tiger to another potential hunting site.

To obtain behavioral data needed to model movement, it is important not to disturb an animal when making continuous close-range observations. However, in dense vegetation, sound attenuates rapidly, and it is often possible to approach a tiger close enough to hear the crunching of bones as it feeds on its prey or the sharp copulatory growls a female makes while mating. Following an animal closely provides opportunity to gather a variety of data from which an animal's behavioral state may be assessed. For example, patrolling can be distinguished from long-distance movements between hunting localities based on data on rates of movement versus rates of scent marking and inspection of scent marks which can determined by observing tracks going up to scent marks (Smith, McDougal, and Maquelle 1989). Having both the behavioral information from following a tiger and the GPS data, which provides quantitative information on movement, will enable us to evaluate the number and type of HMMs that may be need to model tiger movement. It will also help us to calibrate the HMM by determining the number of states needed for the A matrix, the initial approximations for the B matrix, and estimates of π.

CONCLUSIONS

This chapter has reviewed individual-based models as a framework for understanding the interaction of animals and humans in multiple-use forests. It has also examined the potential for using GPS data to calibrate these models and to provide new insight into the relationship between animal movement, behavior, and an animal's physiological state. TIGMOD, an individual-based model for emulating the behavior of tigers in multiple-use forests, was a first attempt to capture different movement patterns in response to behavior and physiological states. This conceptual model has begun to capture some of the complexity of animal movements. Statistical models such as the HMM can strengthen the movement dynamics of individual-based models, but there are limitations to the use of HMM. Stochastic events such as the appearance of another tiger (e.g., an estrous female, a male challenger) can alter the matrices describing the HMM.

What is clear is that modeling this complexity is a key challenge if we are to create individual-based models for animals that can be used for understanding both resource allocation and the interactions between humans and animals in multiple-use forests. The key to making advances is a close reiterative interaction between modeler and field biologist. For an endangered species where sample sizes are limited, management problems are site specific, and there simply is not time to examine the outcome of experimental management scenarios, modeling may be the only alternative for exploring management options.

ACKNOWLEDGMENTS   The authors would like to thank the editor and anonymous reviewers for their insightful comments. We would also like to thank Professor Edward Binkowski, Department of Mathematics and Statistics, Hunter College, for his review of this manuscript.

REFERENCES   Ahearn, S. C., J. L. D. Smith, A. R. Joshi, and J. Ding. 2001. TIGMOD: An individual-based spatially explicit model for simulating tiger/human interaction in multiple use forests. *Ecological Modeling* 140: 81–97.

Bennett, A. T. 1996. Do animals have cognitive maps? *Journal of Experimental Biology* 199: 219–24.

Blake, S., I. Douglas-Hamilton, and W. B. Karesh. 2001. GPS telemetry of forest elephants in Central Africa: Results of a preliminary study. *African Journal of Ecology* 39: 178.

Brillinger, D. A., H. K. Preisler, A. A. Ager, and J. G. Kie. 2004. An exploratory data analysis (EDA) of the paths of moving animals. *Journal of Statistical Planning and Inference* 122: 43–63.

Brownlee J. 1911. The mathematical theory of random migration and epidemic distribution. *Proceedings of the Royal Society of Edinburgh* A31: 262–89.

Chundawat, R. R. S., N. Gogate, and A. J. T. Johnsingh. 1999. Tigers in Panna: Preliminary results from Indian tropical dry forest. In *Riding the tiger: Tiger conservation in human-dominated landscapes,* ed. J. Seidensticker, S. Christie, and P. Jackson. Cambridge: Cambridge University Press.

Dice, L. R., and W. E. Howard. 1951. Distance of dispersal by prairie deer mice from birthplaces to breeding sites. *Contributions of the Laboratory of Vertebrate Biology, University of Michigan* 55: 1–23.

Dobzhansky, T., and S. Wright. 1943. Genetics of natural populations. X dispersion in Drosophila pseudoobscura. *Genetics* 28: 304–40.

Franke, A., T. Caelli, and R. J. Hudson. 2004. Analysis of movements and behavior of caribou (Rangifer tarandus) using hidden Markov models. *Ecological Modeling* 173: 259–70.

Garshelis, D. L. 2000. Delusions in habitat evaluation: Measuring use, selection and importance. In *Research techniques in animal ecology: Controversies and consequences,* ed. L. Boitani and T. K. Fuller, 111–64. New York: Columbia University Press.

Hanski, I. 1991. Single species metapopulation dynamics: Concepts, models and observations. In *Metapopulation dynamics,* ed. M.E. Gipin and I. Hanski, 17–38. London: Academic Press.

Jonsen, I. D., R. A. Myers, and J. M. Flemming. 2003. Meta-analysis of animal movement using state–space. *Ecology* 84: 3055–63.

Karanth, K. U. and M. E. Sunquist. 1995. Prey selection by tiger, leopard and dhole in tropical forests. *Journal of Animal Ecology* 64: 439–50.

Kenney, J., J. L. D. Smith, A. M. Starfield, and C. McDougal. 1995. The long-term effects of tiger poaching on population viability. *Conservation Biology* 9:1127–33.

Levins, R. 1970. Extinction. In *Some mathematical questions in biology,* ed. M. Gerstenharber. Lectures on Mathematics in the Life Sciences, vol. 2. Providence, R.I.: American Mathematical Society.

Ling, B. 2000. Modeling fish growth in a three-dimensional aquatic system using object-oriented design. *International Journal of Geographical Information Science* 14(7): 603–23.

MacKinnon, K., H. Mishra, and J. Mott. 1999. Reconciling the needs of conservation and local communities: Global Environmental Facility support for tiger conservation in India. In *Riding the tiger: Tiger conservation in human-dominated landscapes,* ed. J. Seidensticker, S. Christie, and P. Jackson. Cambridge: Cambridge University Press.

McCullough, D. R. 1996. *Metapopulations and wildlife conservation.* Washington, D.C.: Island Press.

Merrill, S. B. 2000. Details of extensive movements by Minnesota wolves (Canis lupus). *American Midland Naturalist* 144: 428–33.

Miquelle D. G., E. N. Smirnov, T. W. Merrill, A. E. Myslenkov, H. B. Quigley, and M. G. Hornocker. 1999.Hierarchical spatial analysis of Amur tiger relationships to habitat and prey. In *Riding the tiger: Tiger conservation in human-dominated landscapes,* ed. J. Seidensticker, S. Christie, and P. Jackson. Cambridge: Cambridge University Press.

Moen, R., J. Pastor, Y. Cohen, and C. Schwartz, 1996. Effect of moose movement and habitat use on GPS collar performance. *Journal of Wildlife Management* 60(3): 659–68.

Poucet, B. 1993. Spatial cognitive maps in animals: New hypotheses on their mechanisms. *Psychological Review* 100(2): 163–82.

Rabiner, L. R., C. H. Lee, B. H. Juang, and J. G. Wilpon. 1989. HMM clustering for connected word recognition. *Acoustics, Speech, and Signal Processing* 1: 405–8.

Raper, J., and D. Livingstone. 1995. Development of a geomorphological spatial model using object-oriented design. *International Journal of Geographical Information Systems* 9: 359–83.

Schlecht, E. C. Hulsebusch, F. Mahler, and K. Becker. 2004. The use of differentially corrected global positioning system to monitor activities of cattle at pasture. *Applied Animal Behaviour Science* 85: 185–202.

Seidensticker, J., and C. McDougal. 1993. Tiger predatory behavior, ecology and conservation. *Symposia of the Zoological Society (London)* 65: 105–25.

Siniff, D. B. and C. Jessen. 1969. Simulation model of animal movement patterns. *Advances in Ecological Modelling* 6: 185–219.

Skellum J. G. 1951. Random dispersal in theoretical populations. *Biometrika* 38: 196–218.

Smith, J. L. D. 1993. The role of dispersal in structuring the Chitwan tiger population. *Behaviour* 124: 165–95.

Smith, J. L. D., C. McDougal, and D. Miquelle. 1989. Scent marking in free-ranging tigers (Panthera tigris). *Animal Behavior* 37: 1–10.

Smith, J. L. D., C. McDougal, and M. E. Sunquist. 1987. Female land tenure system in tigers. In *Tigers of the world: The biology, biopolitics, management and conseration of an endangered species*, ed. R. L. Tilson and U. S. Seal, 97–109..Park Ridge, N.J.: Noyes Publications.

Smith, J. L. D. and C. McDougal. 1991. The contribution of variance in lifetime reproduction to effective population size in tigers. *Conservation Biology* 5: 484–9.

Smith, J. L. D., S. C. Ahearn, and C. McDougal. 1998. Landscape analysis of tiger distribution and habitat quality in Nepal. *Conservation Biology* 12: 1–9.

Sunquist, M. E. 1981. The social organization of tigers *(Pantera tigris)* in Royal Chitwan National Park, Nepal. *Smithsonian Contributions to Zoology* 336: 1–98.

Turchin, P., 1998. *Quantitative analysis of movement: Measuring and modeling population redistribution in animals and plants.* Sunderland, Mass.: Sinauer Associates.

Westervelt, J. D., and L.,D. Hopkins. 1999. Modeling mobile individuals in dynamic landscapes. *International Journal of Geographical Information Systems* 13: 191–208.

Wikramanayake, E. D., E. Dinerstein, J. G. Robinson, K. U. Karanth, A. Rabinowitz, D. Olson, T. Mathhew, P. Hedao, M. Connor, G. Hemley, and D. Bolze. 1999. Where can tigers live in the future? A framework for identifying high-priority areas for the conservation of tigers in the wild. In *Riding the tiger: Tiger conservation in human-dominated landscapes,* ed. J. Seidensticker, S. Christie, and P. Jackson. Cambridge: Cambridge University Press.

Chapter 19

Integration of Geographic Information Systems and Agent-Based Models of Land Use: Prospects and Challenges

DAWN C. PARKER

GEORGE MASON UNIVERSITY

FAIRFAX, VIRGINIA

ABSTRACT

INTEREST IS GROWING IN AGENT-BASED MODELS of land-use and land-cover change (ABM/LUCC). Such models combine agent-based representations of the decision makers influencing a land-use system with a cellular landscape and are appropriate when complex dynamics are present in the system under study. This chapter reviews conceptual challenges related to integrating ABM/LUCC and geographic information systems (GIS) and progress to date in meeting those challenges. Since the design of a model must take into account how it is likely to be used, the needs and possible activities of two hypothetical ABM/LUCC users, an end user and a researcher, are discussed. Three levels of possible integration of ABM/LUCC and GIS—no integration, initialization with real-world data, and full integration—are presented, and key ongoing research projects using each approach are reviewed. The review reveals a large number of ongoing projects and promise for continued rapid development of integrated ABM/LUCC GIS, especially given recent development of tools that integrate vector-based GIS with ABM. Drawing on input from the modeling community, functionality desired in an integrated ABM/LUCC-GIS model is discussed, including tools for programming, modeling, mathematical operations, verification and validation, and use of standard algorithms. Options for software implementation of such a model in terms of user interface, component integration, and software licensing are presented. Finally, a call for development of a standardized, component-based conceptual framework for ABM/LUCC is made. Such a framework would serve to facilitate communication of model mechanisms, comparisons across models, and derivation of standard results for ABM/LUCC models and would help ABM/LUCC transition to a mature scientific discipline.

Interest in agent-based models of land-use and land-cover change (ABM/LUCC) is growing, and many researchers are choosing to adopt such models for the study of coupled human-biophysical interactions related to land-use change. Agent-based models (ABMs) are microlevel simulation models that directly represent decision-making entities and their interactions with their social and physical environment. ABMs have been applied in a variety of social science domains, including economics, sociology, political science, and geography (Berry, Kiel, and Elliot 2002). Closely related individual-based models focus on nonhuman entities and their behavior (Grimm and Railsback forthcoming). ABM/LUCC combine agent-based representations of the key decision-making entities in the land-use system with a spatial model of the landscape under study. Decision-making agents can represent stakeholders at multiple scales, from individual parcel managers to village households to local planning boards. Interaction environments can include social networks, markets, and political institutions. Examples of feedbacks between agents and their environment include hydrologic balance, soil fertility and erosion, changes in species abundance, and spread of invasive species.

In contrast to techniques traditionally used in social science modeling, such as microeconomic, game-theoretic, and system dynamics models, ABM/LUCC are simulation-based, not equilibrium-based. Although models may reach an equilibrium, that equilibrium is the result of interactions among lower-level entities. As well, like cellular automaton models, ABM/LUCC may not reach an equilibrium. For the interested reader, many other works focus on potential roles for, applications of, and conceptual challenges related to development of ABM models of human–environment interactions (Bousquet and Le Page 2004; Janssen 2003; Janssen and Ostrom forthcoming; Parker, Berger, and Manson 2002b; Parker et al. 2003; Verburg et al. forthcoming).

One important challenge for the development of ABM/LUCC models is integration of geographic information systems (GIS) functionality with ABMs. This challenge was first discussed by Gimblett (2002a), following a 1998 workshop, and was also identified by participants at the 2001 Special Workshop on ABM/LUCC models (Parker, Berger, and Manson 2002a, 2002b). This chapter again focuses on needs for integration of ABM/LUCC models with GIS, the current state of integration, additional functionality desired by the user community, and various options for accomplishing integration. The goal of the chapter is both to report on current activities and to serve as a point of departure for continuing dialog within the community. While the chapter focuses most closely on development of agent-based land-use models, it draws on examples of other spatially explicit models, both agent-based and land-use, which face similar concerns and challenges. This chapter summarizes the activities, concerns, and challenges of developers and end users of ABM/LUCC. Readers are directed to other works for discussions of conceptual and technical integration of ABM and GIS (Brown et al. forthcoming-a, Torrens and Benenson forthcoming, Westervelt 2002).

While users of ABM/LUCC are a diverse group, for purposes of illustration, this section outlines the needs of two hypothetical representative users of ABM/LUCC. The first is an end user of an existing ABM/LUCC model. He or she may be a student in a modeling class or a policy maker interested in conducting scenario analysis. The end user may possess limited knowledge of programming but is likely to be comfortable with a wide variety of software applications, including GIS. The second is a researcher developing an ABM/LUCC from scratch, potentially as part of a larger research team or project. He or she is likely to have a moderate level of programming expertise, often linked to a particular programming language. The project's goals may include theoretical exploration, hypothesis generation and testing, developing land-use projections, and scenario analysis. Results are likely to be published in peer-reviewed academic literature. Often, individuals will progress from the first role to the second as their knowledge of and interest in ABM/LUCC increases.

END USERS

The end user will most likely begin by running a demo version of a simple model in order to become familiar with the basic model mechanisms and their results. As part of this process, he or she may find graphical documentation of the model helpful. He or she may then experiment by changing model parameters and observing how this leads to changes in outcomes, may also want to compare the results of different assumptions regarding agent decision-making mechanisms, and may then wish to develop a simple model of his or her own, using existing model components. The end user will likely want to view spatial model outcomes, as well as graphs and statistics generated from model output.

RESEARCHERS

An ABM/LUCC researcher embarking on a new modeling project will undertake a more complex series of tasks. First, a conceptual model will be specified that elucidates the component parts of the ABM and potential interactions between the parts. The set of software tools most useful for the particular project will be identified. This decision may be driven by the role of the model (Berger and Parker 2002), the available input data, the need for advanced mathematical functionality, the decision to use a vector or raster landscape representation, and the need for GIS functionality. The researcher will design agent decision modules, potentially choosing from a wide variety of decision algorithms, and will build spatial and temporal interactions among agents and between agents and their environment. He or she may input real-world data from GIS, surveys, and statistical models in order to parameterize his or her model. While initial model verification and exploratory analysis may be conducted through manually changing parameter settings and rerunning output, at some point the researcher is likely to conduct multiple model runs by incrementally sweeping the parameter space for purposes of model calibration, hypothesis generation, or model validation. Data from these multiple runs would be saved in a database for subsequent optimization or statistical analysis. Both spatial and aspatial outcomes are likely to be of interest. Finally, the researcher will likely want to compare generated and real-world outcomes, again focusing on both spatial and aspatial outcomes. To facilitate communication with other researchers and review of his or her work, the researcher may need to provide detailed model metadata, potentially including graphical descriptions of model structure and mechanisms.

CURRENT LEVELS OF INTEGRATION WITH GIS

Several different levels of integration of ABM/LUCC with GIS are possible. Models may run on abstract cellular landscapes, implementing simple spatial functionality within the ABM. Models may read in real-world spatial data from a GIS and also potentially write output into a format readable by GIS. When significant GIS functionality is required at run time, integrated models—those that implement both ABM and GIS functionality dynamically—may be constructed. Three approaches to such models are identified here: models that use separate GIS and ABM programs/libraries and communicate via files written to disk, models that use separate programs but communicate via a shared database or virtual memory, and stand-alone models that implement GIS functionality within the ABM model. (These definitions are related to, but do not exactly parallel, characterizations of model coupling discussed by Westervelt 2002, and Brown et al., forthcoming-a.)

ABSTRACT CELLULAR LANDSCAPES

Many ABM/LUCC researchers begin by developing models that operate over an abstract landscape, even when their longer-term goals include application to real-world landscapes. Roles for abstract ABM/LUCC models are discussed by Parker and colleagues (Parker, Berger, and Manson 2002 a,b; Parker, Manson, and Berger 2002; Parker et al. 2003), and the advantages of a progression from abstract to empirical are discussed by Berger and Parker (2002). Balmann and colleagues (Balmann 1997; Balmann et al. 2003) have developed spatially explicit models of structural change in agriculture. The RePast-based (repast. sourceforge.net) SLUDGE model (Parker and Meretsky 2004) examines the relationship between negative spatial externalities, landscape fragmentation, and economic efficiency. The SWARM-based (www.swarm.org) FEARLUS model explores the evolution of cropping patterns and land holdings in an agrarian setting (Gotts, Polhill, and Law 2003).

GIS INITIALIZATION /OUTPUT DISPLAY

Many currently developed ABM/LUCC models input either abstract or real-world raster landscapes and export output to files suitable for viewing in raster GIS. Berger (2001) models the influence of information networks and resource markets on adoption of new efficient irrigation technologies in Chile. The LUCIM model (Evans and Kelley 2004) focuses on the relationship between land-owner decision making, landscape heterogeneity, and the process of deforestation and reforestation. Landscape statistics similar to those produced by FRAGSTATS (McGarigal and Marks 1994) are calculated for the raster-based model output. The RePast-based LUCITA model (Deadman et al. forthcoming) focuses on the behavior of heterogeneous agricultural land owners in the Brazilian Amazon. The SWARM- and RePast-based SLUCE model focuses on the influence of landscape amenities on development on the ex-urban fringe (Brown et al. forthcoming-b). Caruso, Rounsevell, and Cojocaru (forthcoming) have developed a related model that focuses on the impact of both positive and negative local spatial influences on the expansion of the ex-urban fringe. The SWARM-based VILLAGE project models migration and settlement patterns of Anasazi populations in the U.S. Southwest. In addition to initializing the model with GIS landscapes, the model also uses GIS at the validation stage (Kohler et al. 2000; Reynolds, Kohler, and Kobti 2003).

A large number of ABM/LUCC applications has been developed using the Cormas platform (Bousquet et al. 2003). These applications are often designed through stakeholder participation and are used for role-playing games with stakeholders to develop strategies for sustainable resource use. Cormas allows users to import existing vector and raster GIS layers and create layers interactively. Abstract landscape-based applications include comparison of multiscaled agent representations (Bousquet and Gautier 1998); fuel wood management and deforestation in Burundi (Bousquet et al. 2000); negotiations between foresters and herdsmen over forest and pasture management in the French Mediterranean forest (Etienne 2003a); and land and water management in a periurban water catchment (Ducrot et al. 2004). Raster applications include land-use conflicts between fishers, hunters, herdsmen, and farmers in Senegal (d'Aquino et al. 2003); use of common groundwater in Tunisia (Feuillette, Bousquet, and Le Goulven 2003); the impacts of institutional change on mountain agrarian systems in Vietnam (Boissau and Castella 2003); multiple land-use interactions in the Rhone delta (Mathevet et al. 2003); water management in Northern Thailand (Becu et al. 2003); and wild game hunting in Cameroon (Bousquet et al. 2001). Vector applications include soil erosion risk in Thailand (Trébuil et al. 2002). Cormas can create composite objects, facilitating potential implementation of agents at differing spatial scales and cross-scale feedbacks.

INTEGRATION VIA FILES WRITTEN TO DISK

Westervelt and colleagues have developed a series of integrated agent-and-individual based models that explore interactions between mobile human and endangered animal species (Harper, Westervelt, and Trame 2002; Westervelt 2002; Westervelt and Hopkins 1999). Their modeling framework integrates SME (chapter 7, this volume) and SWARM with GRASS GIS (grass. itc.it) via files written to disk at run time. Gonçalves, Rodrigues, and Correia

(2004) simulate the spatial distribution of residues from stone-cutting operations, using a Java-based model coupled with Geotools open-source GIS (www.geotools). Etienne, Le Page, and Cohen (2003b) use a simplified Cormas-based ABM to support a role-playing game focused on the problem of pine invasion into open space in the south of France. Their model uses MapInfo to initialize the raster-based model and to display updated landscapes every five time steps.

RUN-TIME COMMUNICATION

Manson has developed the C++ DS3 system that integrates Idrisi GIS (www.clarklabs.org), SQL database functionality, embedded agent-based models, Monte Carlo tools for uncertainty analysis, and spatial validation tools into a dynamic modeling system. The SYPR model (Manson 2000, 2002; Manson forthcoming), which focuses on smallholder agricultural decision-making in the southern Yucatán peninsula, is implemented in DS3.

Several fully integrated ABM-GIS models utilize the Java-based RePast programming libraries. GeoGraphs (Dibble and Feldman 2004), a set of software libraries for use with RePast, initializes model landscapes through GIS input, including DEM and network layers. Modeling capabilities allow agents to move and interact via rugged 2D and 3D networks and include run-time 3D visualization capabilities. Applications include epidemiology, civil violence, and hierarchical social networks. The vector-based Tactical Sensor and Ubiquitous Network Agent-Modeling Initiative (TSUNAMI) (Brown et al. forthcoming-a; North, Rimmer, and Macal 2003) of peer-to-peer communication networks between mobile objects facilitates agent movement, sensing of surroundings, and communication using Openmap™ GIS (www.openmap.net). The Infrastructure SimSuite (Brown et al. forthcoming-a; Thomas et al. 2003) represents interactions between independent public utility infrastructure units. The model uses ArcGIS to initialize topological information and update feature attributes. Two recent extensions to the RePast libraries facilitate integration with ArcGIS through the Agent Analyst extension and with Openmap (Brown et al. 2004; Najlis and North 2004).

INTERNAL GIS FUNCTIONALITY IN ABM

The Recreation Behavior Simulator (RBSIM) models simulate the movement of recreational users in outdoor environments (Itami et al. 2004). The Visual Basic models import GIS layers from MapInfo and ESRI GIS, but also embed GIS functionality through a topological database structure, a network object model, and a terrain model. Mobile agents possess both line-of-sight and ability to calculate distances (Gimblett, Richards, and Itami 2002; Gimblett et al. 2002; Itami 2002; Itami et al. 2000).

Torrens and Benenson have developed an abstract geographic automata system (GAS), a conceptual framework for linking automaton-based urban models to geographic information systems (Torrens 2003; Torrens and Benenson forthcoming). The framework has been implemented in a variety of languages, including Starlogo, Java, and C++. The Object-Based Environment for Urban Systems (OBEUS) model (Benenson, Aronovich, and Noam forthcoming), written in C++, inputs MapInfo GIS files and implements a wide range of GIS functionality, including networks, georeferencing, and neighborhood relationships. Software implementation is discussed by Benenson and Torrens (2004).

The above examples and additional feedback from the modeling community indicate that a broad range of GIS functions are useful with ABM/LUCC models. These include topological functions such as neighborhood calculations, buffering, and spatial connectivity; complex network representations and travel-cost calculations; terrain functions such as DEMs, viewsheds, and line-of-sight calculations; and calculation of landscape-based spatial statistics. As well, although the majority of models are now implemented as rasters or other regular tesselations, many researchers have emphasized the need to create vector-based models, which may require the topological data structure provided in a GIS.

A WISH LIST FOR MODEL INTEGRATION

As seen in the *Needs and activities of ABM/LUCC Modelers* section, a researcher developing an ABM/LUCC model will engage in a wide variety of tasks, which may require extensive mathematical and software functionality. In an informal poll by the author of researchers developing a diverse set of fine-scale models of natural resource use, researchers expressed desire for a wide range of functionality within an ideal coupled ABM/GIS modeling environment (Maspace mailing list, Sept. 2003, csiss.ncgia.ucsb.edu/mailman/listinfo/maspace).

PROGRAMMING/MODELING FUNCTIONALITY

From a programming standpoint, researchers expressed a preference for an object-oriented structure that allows a range of event sequencing mechanisms, including synchronous, asynchronous, and event-driven (Brown et al. forthcoming-a; Najlis, Janssen, and Parker 2002; Torrens and Benenson forthcoming). Researchers have noted that ABMs are, by their nature, dynamic models, whereas GIS's traditional database structure does not facilitate dynamic modeling and generation of output statistics related to time as well as space (Brown et al. forthcoming-a; Gimblett 2002b; Manson 2002; Torrens and Benenson forthcoming). Researchers expressed a desire to interface with other temporally and spatially dynamic models, such as hydrology, transport cost, and erosion models. Modeling of mobile objects (see chapters 8, 12, and 17) was desired, as was the ability to model and visualize in 3D.

MATHEMATICAL FUNCTIONALITY

Researchers expressed a desire for a high degree of advanced mathematical functionality. This functionality is potentially needed for constructing agent decision-making algorithms, especially those based on optimizing behavior, for model calibration, and for coupling ABMs with environmental process models. Specific functions desired include finite-element modeling and complex and robust optimization algorithms such as spatial integer programming, genetic algorithms, and simulated annealing.

VERIFICATION AND VALIDATION TOOLS.

Researchers expressed the need for tools to support model verification and validation: "the correctness of model construction and the truthfulness of a model with respect to its problem domain" (Parker et al. 2003). Requests for verification tools included real-time visualization, the ability to conduct *on the fly* sensitivity analysis by changing model parameters, generation of good quality temporal and spatial output graphics, and the ability to save and export animations in standard formats. Requests for validation tools included the ability to call individual functions and components in batch mode, potentially for multiple runs that do Monte Carlo-style sweeps of the model parameter space, the ability to store model parameters and output for any execution, and the ability to analyze generated output using standard statistical models.

BUILT-IN STANDARD FUNCTIONS

Related to these needs, researchers expressed a desire for a wide range of built-in standard functions, including transparent and well-documented algorithms for agent behavior, spatial processes, calibration, verification, and validation; process-based models including flows, fluxes, transport, and reactivity; and spatial and landscape statistics functions, including standard land-use modeling validation statistics and nonparametric statistics.

POSSIBLE PATHWAYS FOR SOFTWARE DEVELOPMENT

As in the previous sections, this section takes the perspective of the individual or team responsible for instantiating a conceptual ABM/LUCC model in computer code through development of a project-specific software model. There are many possible paths through which development of this software model (hereafter *model*) could proceed. Here, the main choices are broken down into three relevant dimensions: single program vs. hybrid, graphical user interface (GUI) vs. scripted, and commercial vs. open source. Any single solution would utilize at least one option in each dimension. Each option within these dimensions has advantages and disadvantages, some specific to the type of model user, as discussed in the *Needs and activities* section.

SINGLE PROGRAM VS. HYBRID

Single-program options range from a model created entirely within a stand-alone application using the application's own scripting language, such as ArcInfo AML™ (Irwin and Bockstael 2002), to development of a project-specific stand-alone application in a lower-level language such as C++ (Berger 2001). The potential advantages of a single-program approach include reduced complexity of model development and decreased run time (Itami 2002).

Hybrid program options range from instantiation in a single programming language, utilizing specialized ABM and GIS libraries (Najlis and North 2004; North, Rimmer, and Macal 2003) to the use of a lower-level language to integrate functionality from a series of applications (Manson 2002). The strongest advantage of the hybrid approach is the ability to use optimized and well-verified specialized mathematical, statistical, and GIS functions. The disadvantages lie in increased model complexity, which may include increased development time required to program in and integrate multiple applications, the need to update the model as individual application elements are updated, and increased run time. Brown et al. (forthcoming-a) note, however, that the increased efficiency offered by previously optimized GIS algorithms may compensate for the increased complexity due to calling multiple applications.)

GUI VS. SCRIPTED.

While most higher-level applications designed for ABM can run in both GUI and scripted mode, a discussion of the role played by each could be helpful to developers with limited resources. GUIs are especially useful for the end users described previously, as their major advantage is that they do not require specialized programming ability. Such an interface can also be quite useful for advanced researchers for model verification and exploratory analysis. GUI systems that record user commands in a format that can be examined, saved, edited, and rerun are particularly useful. Graphical modeling languages such as Simile (www.simulistics.com) provide additional utility by facilitating a direct connection between the underlying conceptual model and its instantiation in programming code, enhancing model communication and replicability.

Scripted models can include those written in noncompiled scripting languages such as Python and compiled languages such as C++ and Java. For research and documentation purposes, there are many advantages to scripted models. Large numbers of model runs can be completed with little initial effort by the modeler, creating a database of model output for scenario analysis and validation. Such models create exact records of the research conducted and allow for replication of model-based experiments. Scripted models can facilitate communication of model mechanisms between researchers sharing a proficiency in that language and, when code is made available, create building blocks that can then be adopted and customized by other researchers.

COMMERCIAL VS. OPEN-SOURCE.

Integrated ABM/LUCC models can be developed as stand-alone commercial packages (Kwartler and Bernard 2001) or make use of commercial software (Brown et al. forthcoming-a, Thomas et al. 2003). Use of commercial software can have some advantages, especially for the end user. Commercial software is often widely available via site license agreements and can be easily installed by a system administrator or end user. Such software often contains extensive online help facilities, and training in the base software is often available to end users, reducing start-up time for researchers interested in investigating ABM/LUCC models. Because of the software's wide use, its available functions and algorithms may be well understood. Finally, when development of a model requires a large up-front investment of time and money beyond what is generally provided through research and educational funding, commercial development may be a practical alternative (Westervelt 2002).

Models can also be developed using only open-source licensed software (Itami et al. 2004), or developers may choose to provide newly developed code under an open-source license (Brown et al. forthcoming-b). Open-source licensing of land-use models has many potential advantages (Agarwal et al. 2002). The greatest advantage is that any modeler or end user can access and modify the model's source code. This facilitates transparency and replicability of models used for research and policy purposes. It also means that modelers can build on the previous work of other researchers, thus substantially shortening model development time and cost. A large and active user community can further speed software development and debugging time. These reduced development costs can potentially facilitate a high degree of individual customization by individual researchers that would not be profitable for commercial software developers (Westervelt 2002). The low cost of open-source models could potentially lead to wider model dissemination and use, particularly for users in developing countries. Research models possess important characteristics of what are referred to in economics as *public goods*—the benefits generated through their use are potentially nonrival, meaning that one user's benefits from the model are not diminished if others are concurrently using the model (Perman et al. 2003).[1] These public good characteristics may justify public investments in the often substantial start-up costs required to develop the basic infrastructure needed for a new modeling environment.

A CALL FOR A STANDARD BASE MODELING FRAMEWORK FOR ABM/LUCC

As seen from earlier sections of this chapter, a wide variety of ABM/LUCC models has been developed, using a mix of software options. In this sense, substantial progress is occurring in the development of integrated ABM/LUCC and GIS models. Yet substantial challenges remain with respect to developing a shared modeling vocabulary and understanding of the theoretical effects of various assumptions. In traditional analytical mathematical modeling, this shared vocabulary and understanding is provided through the language of mathematics. In statistical land-use modeling, it is provided through standard statistical regression models, including limited dependent variable models (Long 1997), spatial econometrics models (Anselin 1988), and combinations of both (Fleming 2004).

One pathway towards this shared vocabulary and understanding is development of a standard generic ABM/LUCC modeling framework that could be implemented in a variety of software environments. Such a framework would form a *conceptual design pattern* that might nest a number of representative project-specific models. A large number of specialized models could be implemented within this framework through invoking particular modeling components and parameter settings. The framework could serve as a point of reference for comparison of alternative modeling platforms and could also be used to develop a set of standard results for ABM/LUCC models, including the effects of alternative agent decision-making algorithms and the qualitative influence of changes in drivers of land-use change on land-use composition, pattern, and location. Finally, it would serve as a valuable resource for teaching and as a start-off point for new modeling projects. A similar role is served by the Sugarscape model (Epstein and Axtell 1996), originally implemented in Ascape (Parker 2001), and subsequently implemented in SWARM, RePast, and Cormas, with planned implementation in MASON (Luke et al. 2003). Jackson (1994) proposes a similar integrative framework for regional science.

An ideal version of such a generic framework would strike a balance between simplicity and realism sufficient to incorporate the major drivers of land-use change identified by the LUCC research community (Anas, Arnott, and Small 1998; Angelsen and Kaimowitz 1998; Briassoulis 1999; Geist and Lambin 2002; Irwin and Bockstael forthcoming; Kaimowitz and Angelsen 1998; Lambin, Geist, and Lepers 2003). These drivers include agent behavior and preferences; parcel accessibility and transportation costs; positive and negative local spatial externalities; biophysical properties of the parcel, such as slope, elevation, and soil quality; social relationships and norms, information availability, population growth and other demographic changes; and external institutional factors such as market prices, taxes and subsidies, land-tenure regimes, and zoning constraints. In order to represent these potential influences, the generic model requires a minimum set of ABM and GIS functionality:

- an agent decision model capable of implementing optimizing, boundedly rational, and rule-based decision models for a heterogeneous group of agents;
- a network model capable of representing both social and transport networks;
- a model that expresses both positive and negative local spatial influences, flexible with respect to the impact radius, and the functional form of diffusion;
- the ability to input spatial layers representing institutional, socioeconomic, and biophysical data and constraints;
- the ability to input relevant global socioeconomic and biophysical parameters; and
- the ability to link to separately developed biophysical process models.

In principle, such a framework should be inclusive of the major concerns of a diverse set of researchers, and a determination of whether this list of features is sufficient should be made in collaboration with the research community. It should be sufficiently well documented and specific to be replicable in a variety of software models. Since a one-size-fits-all generic model is not likely to be a good fit for any individual empirical research project, the model should be customizable and extensible, arguing in favor of an object-oriented representation (Gimblett 2002b; Jackson 1994; Najlis, Janssen, and Parker 2002). Specific options for representation might include the Discrete Event System Specification (DEVS) formalism and/or Unified Modeling Language (UML) (Fowler and Scott 2000; Gimblett 2002b; Gonçalves, Rodrigues, and Correia 2004). At least one software implementation of the framework should use open-source tools that are available across computing platforms at low or no cost. This implementation should have the ability to call basic GIS functions in a loosely coupled way that allows for integration with a number of GIS packages. Ideally, the implementation would also include a graphical modeling environment, facilitating use by nonprogrammers and seamless model replication.

Development of such a generic framework could provide a needed research and teaching infrastructure item for the ABM/LUCC community. Because of the lack of a shared mathematical or statistical language for ABM modeling discussed above, a coordinated effort to develop such infrastructure may be especially critical to help ABM/LUCC develop into a mature scientific discipline. Grimm and Railsback (forthcoming) cite difficulties in model communication as a factor that has inhibited development of the related field of individual-based modeling. Support for such infrastructure development is often difficult to obtain through traditional grant programs. Two relevant models for support for such infrastructure development exist, however. The LUCC (Land-Use and Land-Cover Change) project (www.geo.ucl.ac.be/LUCC/lucc.html), a program element of the IGBP and IHDP programs, has supported specialist workshops, related publications, learning workshops, and large conferences related to land-use change analysis and modeling. A variety of development activities for spatial statistical modeling has been supported by CSISS (the Center for Spatially Integrated Social Science) at UC Santa Barbara, including summer workshops, specialist meetings, and development of open-source tools for spatial data analysis. (See chapter 5 in this volume.) This effort has been supported by a series of general overview publications (for example, Anselin 2002) and learning workshops at professional meetings. The ABM/LUCC community has itself benefited from support from both organizations for specialist meetings, publication, and educational activities and development of communication infrastructure (for more details, see www.csiss.org/resources/maslucc).

CONCLUSIONS

The ABM/LUCC modeling field is young but rapidly developing, given increased interest in modeling human-environment interactions, increased computing power and availability of specialized programming tools, critical support from several senior researchers, and development of an enthusiastic cadre of young researchers. Much progress has already been made in terms of identifying key challenges and research priorities for the field. As well, as evidenced by the large number of well-developed projects cited here, substantial development of software infrastructure is occurring. A lens through which to focus this development, in terms of development of a generic integrated ABM/LUCC and GIS modeling framework, could ensure continued coordination between researchers and could contribute to the integration of new researchers into the ABM/LUCC community.

ACKNOWLEDGMENTS

The author acknowledges useful input from Maspace list members, fellow participants at the 2003 ESRI Modeling and GIS workshop, and student participants in the author's land-use and spatial agent-based modeling classes. The section Possible *pathways for software development* draws on white papers developed with Robert Najlis for NSF Biocomplexity in the Environment grant SES008351. Helpful comments on the first draft from Robert Muetzelfeld, Francois Bousquet, Derek Robinson, Gary Polhill, and the volume editors are also acknowledged. Thanks to Julie Witcover for excellent technical editing. All errors, misrepresentations, and omissions are the author's responsibility.

NOTES

1. The public good characteristics of open-source software imply that the success of many open-source projects contradicts the standard, static theoretical prediction that public goods will be underprovided in the marketplace. Thus, open-source licensing regimes are a potentially exciting area for research in public economics.

REFERENCES

Agarwal, C., G. M. Green, J. M. Grove, T. Evans, and C. Schweik. 2002. A review and assessment of land-use change models: Dynamics of space, time, and human choice. Publication NE-297. Burlington, VT: USDA Forest Service Northeastern Forest Research Station. www.fs.fed.us/ne/newtown_square/publications/technical_reports/pdfs/2002/gtrne297.pdf.

Anas, A., R. Arnott, and K. A. Small. 1998. Urban spatial structure. *Journal of Economic Literature* 36 (3): 1426–64.

Angelsen, A., and D. Kaimowitz. 1998. Rethinking the causes of tropical—deforestation: Lessons from economic models. *The World Bank Observer* 14 (1): 73–98. www.worldbank.org/research/journals/wbro/obsfeb99/pdf/article4.pdf.

Anselin, L. 1988. *Spatial econometrics: Methods and models.* Studies in Operational Regional Science series. Norwell, Mass.: Kluwer Academic.

———. 2002. Under the hood: Issues in the specification and interpretation of spatial regression models. *Agricultural Economics* 27 (3): 247–67.

d'Aquino, P., C. Le Page, F. Bousquet, and A. Bah. 2003. Using self-designed role-playing games and a multi-agent system to empower a local decision-making process for land use management: The selfcormas experiment in Senegal. *Journal of Artificial Societies and Social Simulation* 6 (3). jasss.soc.surrey. ac.uk/6/3/5.html.

Balmann, A. 1997. Farm-based modelling of regional structural change. *European Review of Agricultural Economics* 25 (1): 85–108.

Balmann, A., K. Happe, K. Kellermann, and A. Kleingarn. 2003. Adjustment costs of agri-environmental policy switchings: A multi-agent approach. In *Complexity and ecosystem management: The theory and practice of multi-agent approaches,* ed. M. A. Janssen. Northampton, Mass.: Edward Elgar Publishers.

Becu, N., P. Perez, B. Walker, O. Barreteau, and C. Le Page. 2003. Agent-based simulation of a small catchment water management in northern Thailand: Description of the catchscape model. *Ecological Modelling* 170 (2-3): 319–31.

Benenson, I., S. Aronovich, and S. Noam. Forthcoming. Let's talk objects: Generic methodology for urban high-resolution simulation. *Computers, Environment and Urban Systems.*

Benenson, I., and P. Torrens. 2004. *Geosimulation: Automata-based modeling of urban phenomena.* London: John Wiley and Sons.

Berger, T. 2001. Agent-based spatial models applied to agriculture: A simulation tool for technology diffusion, resource use changes, and policy analysis. *Agricultural Economics* 25 (2-3): 245–60.

Berger, T., and D. C. Parker. 2002. Introduction to specific examples of research. In *Meeting the challenge of complexity: Proceedings of the special workshop on agent-based models of land-use/land-cover change.* Santa Barbara, Calif.: CIPEC/CSISS. www.csiss.org/maslucc/ABM-LUCC.htm.

Berry, B. J. L., L. D. Kiel, and E. Elliot. 2002. Adaptive agents, intelligence, and emergent human organization: Capturing complexity through agent-based modeling. *Proceedings of the National Academy of Sciences* 99 (Supplement 3): 7178–88.

Boissau, S., and J. C. Castella. 2003. Constructing a common representation of local institutions and land use systems through simulation-gaming and multi-agent modeling in rural areas of northern Vietnam: The SAMBA-Week methodology. *Simulations and Gaming* 34 (3): 342–7

Bousquet, F., F. O. Barreteau, P. d'Aquino, M. Etienne, S. Boissau, S. Auber, C. L. Page, D. Babin, and J. C. Castella. 2003. Multi-agent systems and role games: An approach for ecosystem co-management. In *Multi-agent approaches for ecosystem management,* ed. M. A. Janssen.Northampton, Mass.: Edward Elgar Publishers.

Bousquet, F., and D. Gautier. 1998. Comparaison de deux approches de modélisation des dynamiques spatiales par simulation multi-agents : Les approches spatiales et acteurs. *CyberGéo* 89. 193.55.107.45/modelis/bousquet/bousquet.htm.

Bousquet, F., and C. Le Page. 2004. Multi-agent simulations and ecosystem management: A review. *Ecological Modelling* 76 (3-4): 313–32.

Bousquet, F., C. Le Page, M. Antona, and P. Guizol. 2000. Ecological scales and use rights: The use of multiagent systems. Paper presented in the session-Forest and Society: The Role of Research. Subplenary session XXI. IUFRO World Congress 2000, Kuala Lumpur.

Bousquet, F., C. LePage, I. Bakam, and A. Takforyan. 2001. Multi-agent simulations of hunting wild meat in a village in eastern Cameroon. *Ecological Modelling* 138 (1-3): 331–46.

Briassoulis, H. 1999. *Analysis of land use change: Theoretical and modeling approaches.* Morgantown, W.V.: Regional Research Institute, West Virginia University. www.rri.wvu.edu/WebBook/Briassoulis/contents.htm.

Brown, D., M. North, D. Robinson, R. Riolo, and W. Rand. Forthcoming-a. Spatial process and data models: Toward integration of agent-based models and GIS. *Journal of Geographic Systems.*

Brown, D., R. Riolo, D. Robinson, W. Rand, M. North, and K. Johnston. 2004. Toward integration of spatial data models and agent-based process models. Paper presented at GIScience 2004: Third International Conference on Geographic Information Science, University of Maryland.

Brown, D. G., S. E. Page, R. Riolo, M. Zellner, and R. W. Forthcoming-b. Path dependence and the validation of agent-based spatial models of land use. *International Journal of Geographic Information Science.*

Caruso, G., M. Rounsevell, and G. Cojocaru. Forthcoming. Exploring a spatio-dynamic neighbourhood-based model of residential behaviour in the Brussels periurban area. *International Journal of Geographical Information Science.*

Deadman, P., D. Robinson, E. Moran, and E. Brondizio. Forthcoming. Effects of colonist household structure on land-use change in the Amazon rainforest: An agent-based simulation approach. *Environment and Planning B.*

Dibble, C., and P. G. Feldman. 2004. The GeoGraph 3D Computational Laboratory: Network and terrain landscapes for RePast. *Journal of Artificial Societies and Social Simulation* 7 (1). jasss.soc.surrey.ac.uk/7/1/7.html.

Ducrot, R., C. Le Page, P. Bommel, and M. Kuper. 2004. Articulating land and water dynamics with urbanization:an attempt to model natural resources management at the urban edge. *Computers, Environment and Urban Systems* 28 (1-2): 85–106.

Epstein, J. M., and R. Axtell. 1996. *Growing artificial societies: Social science from the ground up.* Washington, D.C.: Brookings Institution Press.

Etienne, M. 2003a. Sylvopast: A multiple target role-playing game to assess negotiation processes in sylvopastoral management planning. *Journal of Artificial Societies and Social Simulation* 6 (2). jasss.soc.surrey.ac.uk/6/2/5.html.

Etienne, M., C. Le Page, and M. Cohen. 2003b. A step-by-step approach to building land management scenarios based on multiple viewpoints on multi-agent system simulations. *Journal of Artificial Societies and Social Simulation* 6 (2). jasss.soc.surrey.ac.uk/6/2/2.html.

Evans, T. P., and H. Kelley. 2004. Multi-scale analysis of a household level agent-based model of landcover change. *Journal of Environmental Management* 72 (1-2): 57–72.

Feuillette, S., F. Bousquet, and P. Le Goulven. 2003. Sinuse: A multi-agent model to negotiate water demand management on a free access water table. *Environmental Modelling and Software* 18 (5): 413–27.

Fleming, M. 2004. Techniques for estimating spatially dependent discrete choice models. In *Advances in spatial econometrics,* ed. L. Anselin and R. J. G. M. Florax. New York: Springer.

Fowler, M., and K. Scott. 2000. *UML distilled: A brief guide to the standard object modeling language.* Reading, Mass.: Addison Wesley Longman.

Geist, H., and E. F. Lambin. 2002. Proximate causes and underlying driving forces of tropical deforestation. *Bioscience* 52 (2): 143–50.

Gimblett, H. R., ed. 2002a. *Integrating geographic information systems and agent-based modeling techniques for simulating social and ecological processes.* Oxford: Oxford University Press.

———. 2002b. Integrating geographic information systems and agent-based technologies for modeling and simulating social and ecological phenomena. In Integrating geographic information systems and agent-based modeling techniques for simulating social and ecological processes, ed. H. R. Gimblett, 1–20. Oxford: Oxford University Press.

Gimblett, H. R., M. T. Richards, and R. Itami. 2002. Simulating wildland recreation use and conflicting spatial interactions using rule-driven agents. In *Integrating geographic information systems and agent-based modeling techniques for simulating social and ecological processes,* ed. H. R. Gimblett, 211–44. Oxford: Oxford University Press.

Gimblett, H. R., C. A. Roberts, T. C. Daniel, M. Ratcliff, M. Meitner, S. Cherry, D. Stallman, R. Bogle, D. K. Allerd, and J. Bieri. 2002. An intelligent agent model for simulating and evaluating river trip scenarios along the Colorado River in Grand Canyon National Park. In *Integrating geographic information systems and agent-based modeling techniques for simulating social and ecological processes*, ed. H. R. Gimblett, 245–76. Oxford: Oxford University Press.

Gonçalves, A. S., A. Rodrigues, and L. Correia. 2004. Multi-agent simulation within geographic information systems. Paper presented in the 5th Workshop on Agent-Based Simulation, ABS04, Lisbon, Portugal.

Gotts, N. M. G., J. G. Polhill, and A. N. R. Law. 2003. Aspiration levels in a land use simulation. *Cybernetics and Systems* 34 (8): 663–83.

Grimm, V., and S. F. Railsback. Forthcoming. Chapter 1: Introduction. In *Individual-based modeling and ecology*, ed. V. Grimm and S. F. Railsback. Princeton, N.J.: Princeton University Press.

Harper, S. J., J. D. Westervelt, and A.-M. Trame. 2002. Management application of an agent-based model: Control of cowbirds at the landscape scale. In *Integrating geographic information systems and agent-based modeling techniques for simulating social and ecological processes*, ed. H. R. Gimblett. Oxford: Oxford University Press.

Irwin, E., and N. Bockstael. 2002. Interacting agents, spatial externalities, and the evolution of residential land use patterns. *Journal of Economic Geography* 2 (1): 31–54.

—. Forthcoming. The spatial pattern of land use in the U.S. In *A companion to urban economics*, ed. R. Arnott and D. McMillen. Oxford: Blackwell.

Itami, R. 2002. Mobile agents with spatial intelligence. In *Integrating geographic information systems and agent-based modeling techniques for simulating social and ecological processes*, ed. H. R. Gimblett, 191–210. Oxford: Oxford University Press.

Itami, R., R. Raulings, G. MacLaren, K. Hirst, R. Gimblett, D. Zanon, and P. Chladek. 2004. Simulating the complex interactions between human movement and the outdoor recreation environment. *Journal of Nature Conservation* 11 (4): 278–86.

Itami, R. M., G. S. MacLaren, K. M. Hirst, R. J. Raulings, and H. R. Gimblett. 2000. RBSIM 2: Simulating human behavior in National Parks in Australia: Integrating GIS and Intelligent Agents to predict recreation conflicts in high use natural environments. Paper presented in the 4th International Conference on Integrating GIS and Environmental Modeling (GIS/EM4). Banff, Alberta, Canada. www.colorado.edu/research/cires/banff/pubpapers/57.

Jackson, R. W. 1994. Object-oriented modeling in regional science: An advocacy view. *Papers in Regional Science* 73 (4): 347–67.

Janssen, M. A., ed. 2003. *Complexity and ecosystem management: The theory and practice of multi-agent approaches.* Northampton, Mass.: Edward Elgar Publishers.

Janssen, M. A., and E. Ostrom. Forthcoming. Governing social-ecological systems. In *Handbook of computational economics II: Agent-based computational economics,* ed. K. Judd and L. Tesfatsion. North-Holland.

Kaimowitz, D., and A. Angelsen. 1998. *Economic models of tropical deforestation: A review.* Jakarta, Indonesia: Centre for International Forestry Research.

Kohler, T. A., J. Kresl, C. V. West, E. Carr, and R. H. Wilshusen. 2000. Be there then: A modeling approach to settlement determinants and spatial efficiency among late ancestral pueblo populations of the Mesa Verde region, U.S. Southwest. In *Dynamics in human and primate societies,* ed. T. A. Kohler and G. J. Gumerman, 145–178. New York: Oxford University Press.

Kwartler, M., and R. N. Bernard. 2001. CommunityViz: An integrated planning support system. In *Planning support systems integrating geographic systems, models, and visualization tools,* ed. R. K. Brail and R. E. Klosterman. Redlands, Calif.: ESRI Press.

Lambin, E. F., H. Geist, and E. Lepers. 2003. Dynamics of land-use and land-cover change in tropical regions. *Annual Review of Environmental Resources* 28: 205–41.

Long, J. S. 1997. *Regression models for categorical and limited dependent variables.* Thousand Oaks, Calif.: Sage Publications.

Luke, S., G. C. Balan, L. Panait, C. Cioffi-Revilla, and S. Paus. 2003. MASON: A Java multi-agent simulation library. Paper presented in the Agent 2003 conference: Challenges in Social Simulation, Chicago, Ill. agent2003.anl.gov/proc.html.

Manson, S. M. 2000. Agent-based dynamic spatial simulation of land-use/cover change in the Yucatán peninsula, Mexico. Paper presented in the Fourth International Conference on Integrating GIS and Environmental Modeling (GIS/EM4). Banff, Canada. www.tc.umn.edu/~manson/Resources/Manson_2000_GISEM4_ADSS_www.pdf.

———. 2002. Integrated assessment and projection of land-use and land-cover change in the Southern Yucatán Peninsular Region of Mexico. PhD diss., Clark University.

———. Forthcoming. The SYPR integrative assessment model: Complexity in development. In *Final frontiers: Understanding land change in the Southern Yucatán Peninsular Region,* ed. B. L. Turner II, D. Foster, and J. Geoghegan. Oxford: Claredon Oxford University Press.

Mathevet, R., F. Bousquet, C. Le Page, and M. Antona. 2003. Agent-based simulations of interactions between duck populations, farming decisions and leasing of hunting rights in the Camargue (Southern France). *Ecological Modelling* 165 (2-3): 107–26.

McGarigal, K., and B. J. Marks. 1994. FRAGSTATS: Spatial Pattern Analysis Program for Quantifying Landscape Structure. General Technical Report PNW-GTR-351. Portland, Ore.: U.S. Dept. of Agriculture, Forest Service, Pacific Northwest Research Station.

Najlis, R., and M. North. 2004. RePast for GIS. Paper presented in the Agent 2004 Conference on Social Dynamics: Interaction, Reflexivity, and Emergence, Chicago, IL. agent2004.anl.gov/proc.html.

Najlis, R. I., M. A. Janssen, and D. C. Parker. 2002. Software tools and communication issues. *Meeting the Challenge of Complexity: Proceedings of the Special Workshop on Agent-Based Models of Land-Use/Land-Cover Change.* Santa Barbara, Calif.: CIPEC/CSISS. www.csiss.org/maslucc/ABM-LUCC.htm.

North, M., M. Rimmer, and C. M. Macal. 2003. Why the Navy needs TSUNAMI. Paper presented in the Swarmfest, South Bend, Ind.

Parker, D. C., T. Berger, and S. M. Manson, eds. 2002a. *Meeting the Challenge of Complexity: Proceedings of the Special Workshop on Agent-Based Models of Land-Use/Land-Cover Change.* Santa Barbara, CA: CIPEC/CSISS Publication CCR-3. www.csiss.org/maslucc/ABM-LUCC.htm.

———. 2002b. Agent-Based Models of Land-Use/Land-Cover Change: Report and Review of an International Workshop. Bloomington, IN: LUCC Focus 1 Publication 6. www.indiana.edu/~act/focus1/FinalABM11.7.02.pdf.

Parker, D. C., S. M. Manson, and T. Berger. 2002. Potential strengths and appropriate roles for ABM/LUCC. In *Meeting the challenge of complexity: Proceedings of the special workshop on agent-based models of land-use/land-cover change.* Santa Barbara, CA: CIPEC/CSISS. www.csiss.org/maslucc/ABM-LUCC.htm.

Parker, D. C., S. M. Manson, M. A. Janssen, M. Hoffmann, and P. Deadman. 2003. Multi-agent systems for the simulation of land-use and land-cover change: A review. *Annals of the Association of American Geographers* 93 (2): 314–37.

Parker, D. C., and V. Meretsky. 2004. Measuring pattern outcomes in an agent-based model of edge-effect externalities using spatial metrics. *Agriculture, Ecosystems and Environment* 101 (2-3): 233–50.

Parker, M. T. 2001. What is Ascape and why should you care? *Journal of Artificial Societies and Social Simulation* 4 (1). jasss.soc.surrey.ac.uk/4/1/5.html.

Perman, R., Y. Ma, J. McGilvray, and M. Common. 2003. *Natural resource and environmental economics.* New York: Pearson Addison Wesley.

Reynolds, R., T. A. Kohler, and Z. Kobti. 2003. The effects of generalized reciprocal exchange on the resilience of social networks: An example from the Prehispanic Mesa Verde region. *Computational & Mathematical Organization Theory* 9 (3): 227–54.

Thomas, W. H., M. North, C. M. Macal, and J. P. Peerenboom. 2003. *From physics to finances: Complex adaptive systems representation of infrastructure interdependencies.* Dahlgren, V.A.: Naval Surface Warfare Center Publication.

Torrens, P. 2003. Automata-based models of urban systems. In *Advanced spatial analysis,* ed. P. A. Longley and M. Batty, 61–81. Redlands, Calif.: ESRI Press.

Torrens, P., and I. Benenson. Forthcoming. Geographic automata systems. *International Journal of Geographic Information Science.*

Trébuil, G., F. Shinawtra-Ekasingh, F. Bousquet, and C. Thong-Ngam. 2002. Multi-agent systems companion modeling for integrated watershed management: A Northern Thailand experience. Paper presented in the 3rd International Conference on Montane Mainland Southeast Asia (MMSEA 3), Lijiang, Yunnan, China.

Verburg, P. H., P. Schot, M. Dijst, and A. Velkamp. Forthcoming. Land-use change modeling: Current practice and research priorities. *GeoJournal.*

Westervelt, J. 2002. Geographic information systems and agent-based modeling. In *Integrating geographic information systems and agent-based modeling techniques for simulating social and ecological processes,* ed. H. R. Gimblett. Oxford: Oxford University Press.

Westervelt, J. D., and L. D. Hopkins. 1999. Modeling mobile individuals in dynamic landscapes. *International Journal of Geographic Information Science* 13 (3): 191–208

Chapter 20

Generating Prescribed Patterns in Landscape Models

JIUNN-DER (GEOFFREY) DUH
PORTLAND STATE UNIVERSITY
PORTLAND, OREGON

DANIEL G. BROWN
UNIVERSITY OF MICHIGAN
ANN ARBOR, MICHIGAN

ABSTRACT

The development of spatial optimization and simulation techniques in geographic information systems (GIS) can greatly improve the quality and efficiency of maps generated to pursue spatial pattern objectives in landscape design and planning. This chapter describes how pattern optimization and simulation can be useful in visualizing alternative possible landscapes and for evaluating landscape planning and design scenarios. It also describes various approaches that can be used to generate prescribed landscape patterns. Analyses are presented of performance benchmarks and external factors that affect optimal landscape patterns, using simulated-annealing-based algorithms on hypothetical two-dimensional gridded landscapes. The use and value of landscape simulation in environmental GIS applications is discussed.

INTRODUCTION

There has been considerable recent interest in developing GIS applications that incorporate landscape pattern criteria in land-use and land-cover planning and designs (Cova and Church 2000; Brookes 2001; Aerts and Heuvelink 2002; Xiao, Bennett, and Armstrong 2002, Church et al. 2003). The emphasis of spatial pattern characteristics in landscape design and planning is partly because spatial pattern is an important objective in habitat design and in other applications, such as watershed management, forestry, and local authority planning (Brookes 2001), and partly because new computer algorithms and platforms to deal with such applications have become available (Church 2002). While the field of landscape ecology tries to understand the ways in which landscape patterns affect habitat quality (e.g., Henein and Merriam 1990; O'Neill et al. 1992; Turner et al. 1993; Lamberson et al. 1994; McAlpine and Eyre 2002; Liu, Nishiyama, and Kusaka 2003), landscape design and planning projects are using landscape patterns as planning objectives to promote ecological benefits (e.g., Fedorowick 1993, Barrett and Peles 1994, Nassauer and Caddock 1996, Arendt 1999, Brooker 2002). GIS tools capable of analyzing landscape patterns and incorporating pattern information into a spatial decision support framework for siting and placement of landscape features have great potential to further encourage the integration of landscape ecology and ecological landscape design.

Generating landscape maps with the most favorable patterns is intrinsically computationally intensive. The fact that patterns are formed by the simultaneous effects of siting multiple spatial entities makes finding good solutions difficult or impossible with functions available in existing commercial GIS packages. The problem of finding the most favorable patterns in land allocation belongs to a group of optimization problems known as combinatorial optimization, which, when the size of the problem is relatively big, becomes intractable using the complete enumeration approach or exact optimization algorithms (e.g., linear programming) and requires the use of metaheuristic optimization algorithms such as simulated annealing or genetic algorithms (Revees 1993). Metaheuristic methods use stochastic processes that are based on a local search procedure, which finds the optimal solution by trial and error but incorporates some strategies (i.e., metaheuristics) to explore the solution space efficiently. Despite successful examples of using metaheuristic algorithms in solving land-allocation problems (Brookes 2001; Aerts and Heuvelink 2002; Xiao, Bennett, and Armstrong 2002), however, large problems lead to computational complexity and poor performance of the trial-and-error mechanism of metaheuristic algorithms, hampering the utility of spatial optimization to support scientific investigations and decision making. Recent efforts to solve spatial optimization have been made by developing approaches that use auxiliary rules (i.e., heuristics; e.g., Church et al. 2003). Heuristic approaches, if used appropriately, can greatly improve the performance and utility of spatial optimization algorithms in landscape design and interactive planning.

This chapter describes how pattern optimization techniques can be useful in visualizing alternative possible landscapes and for evaluating landscape design scenarios. We review various approaches that can be used to generate prescribed landscape patterns. We also demonstrate how the use of heuristics can reduce the computational complexity and improve performance of an algorithm to solve spatial pattern optimization problems. Lastly, we summarize the results and present conclusions and recommendations for future work.

Spatial simulation and spatial optimization are complementary tools for supporting normative landscape design. Landscape design assembles a number of landscape elements to compose landscape patterns that will satisfy some design goals (Ahern 1999). In this context, the purpose of a spatial simulation method is not to reproduce a particular landscape pattern exactly, but to generate realizations that account for the information that is relevant for the goals under consideration (Gotway and Rutherford 1996). The process of finding the most favorable landscape patterns under specified goals is referred to as *spatial optimization*. Although formal optimization approaches rarely generate good designs and some planners contend that optimization is not a reasonable objective of planning (Harris 1998), spatial optimization still has many practical uses in landscape design. For example, with an understanding of their strengths and weaknesses, planners can use optimization methods to conduct a crude first pass in design but should be prepared to go beyond them.

Spatial optimization, or optimization in general, can provide several functions for planning. The first is that it facilitates comparative evaluation of alternatives. The level of optimality achieved by optimization algorithms, because of their mechanical and objective nature, is reliable for comparing alternative planning scenarios in reference to some evaluation criteria. That is why, for some time, optimization approaches in the general area of resources planning have been seen as indicative, rather than prescriptive, tools (Cocklin 1989).

A second function of spatial optimization is as a tool for multilevel evaluation. Multilevel evaluation is important where the objectives of a plan are measured at multiple scales. These objectives can affect one another in a way that can only be detected when they are evaluated simultaneously. Landscapes are known to exhibit hierarchically structured patterns as suggested by ecological hierarchy theory (Allen and Starr 1982; O'Neill, Johnson, and King 1989). Based on the principle of suboptimization, that is, that the objectives at lower levels must be suboptimized in order to optimize the objective at a higher level, one can apply optimization analysis to explore how actions (i.e., suboptimization) at one level affect the optimality at a higher level. The results should provide knowledge on how the objectives at one level can be integrated into a higher-level objective in a way that is relevant to both levels.

Spatial optimization is also a useful tool for sensitivity assessment. The term *optimal* could be broadened to refer not only to solutions but also to the persistence and robustness of solutions, depending on the way an objective of a problem is specified (Pressey et al. 1996). Analysis of optimal solutions, derived from alternative plans that are administered with controlled variation from an initial plan, can identify landscape features that are of consistent importance to planning goals (Pressey, Possingham, and Margules 1995; Church, Stoms, and Davis 1996). Similarly, planners can calibrate the impacts of planning criteria on a planning objective and adjust criteria that have little impact on the objective more freely and restrain the alterations of criteria that have large impacts. This type of optimization is especially useful when the scope of the planning problem cannot be clearly defined. Most of all, spatial simulation and optimization are objective ways of visualizing spatial information specified by planners. The maps generated by these techniques can be used as effective tools for initiating discourses on subjective goals among planners, decision makers, and the public.

SPATIAL PATTERNS AS DESIGN OBJECTIVES

Landscape design tends to focus on aesthetic or economic rather than on ecological and environmental goals, partly because of the inadequacy of landscape design curricula in incorporating ecological science (Nassauer 2002) and partly because of the lack of tools needed to create a sustainable synthesis of nature and culture (Forman 2002). However, the growing importance of sustainability issues related to global warming, diminishing fossil fuels, and habitat loss has inadvertently raised the prominence of ecological and environmental goals in landscape design. Many measures to alleviate these problems require drastic changes in landscape patterns and urban forms (Wegener 1998, Alberti 1999). Landscape patterns can be useful to make inferences about underlying ecological processes (Urban 1993) and can be managed to support certain ecosystem functions or prevent potential hazards.

One goal of ecological or environmental landscape design is to identify landscape patterns that support necessary ecosystem functions in an optimal way. The ecosystem functions are evaluated based on some criteria, which are considered for optimization. To employ spatial optimization techniques in generating prescribed patterns, the chosen criteria have to be quantifiable so that the most favorable landscape patterns can be selected. One approach is to use as criteria spatial pattern descriptors that are correlated with the ecosystem functions of concern.

Some commonly used pattern descriptors include: texture descriptors, such as Markov random field models (Cross and Jain 1983, Geman and Geman 1984, Derin and Elliott 1987, Saura and Martínez-Millán 2000); points pattern descriptors, such as the lacunarity index (Dale 2000, McIntyre and Wiens 2000); spatial autocorrelation descriptors, such as the semivariogram (Deutsch and Journel 1992, Goovaerts 1997); multiscale pattern descriptors, such as those provided by spectral (Ripley 1978) and wavelet analysis (De Bonet and Viola 1997); descriptors of landscape composition and configuration, such as landscape ecological pattern metrics (McGarigal and Marks 1995). For a review of methods commonly used for landscape pattern quantification, see Gustafson (1998).

Landscape pattern descriptors are widely used by landscape ecologists to relate landscape patterns to ecological or socioeconomic processes (e.g., Schumaker 1996; Otto 1996; McIntyre and Wiens 1999; Griffiths, Lee, and Eversham

2000; Vos et al. 2001; Schmid-Holmes and Drickamer 2001; McAlpine and Eyre 2002; Liu, Nishiyama, and Kusaka 2003), but they are sensitive to the quality of landscape data (Antrop and van Eetvelde 2000, Brown et al. 2000), particularly in complex and very heterogeneous landscapes, and to scale (Gustafson 1998). Nonetheless, there is a continuing interest in using landscape pattern descriptors as ecological indicators in spatial planning (e.g., Löfvenhaft, Björn, and Ihse 2002). As Opdam, Foppen, and Vos (2002) suggest, by creating generalized knowledge of species' responses to landscape patterns as a mechanistic basis for applying landscape ecology in design and planning, planners and designers can use landscape ecology in a form that does not require detailed understanding of ecological processes. Therefore, future landscape plans are not tested against criteria based on ecological processes; instead, they are evaluated by their manifested patterns.

In landscape design projects whose ecological objectives are specific and can be clearly defined, using spatial process models for evaluating design goals could be more appropriate than using pattern descriptors. This involves, first, generating a design configuration and, then, applying a spatial model to analyze the ecological system response to the established design configuration. Such an approach has been used in linking, for example, land-use change and transportation pollution models (e.g., Young and Bowyer 1996), land-use change and hydrological impact (e.g., Nicklow and Muleta 2001, Seppelt and Voinov 2002), land-cover change and the viability of species (e.g., Lindenmayer et al. 2001; Chave, Wiegand, and Levin 2002), resource management and quality of natural habitat (e.g., Bettinger, Boston, and Sessions 1999; Loehle 2000). The advantage of using spatial models as design criteria in spatial optimization is clear: the design criteria used are directly and specifically related to the design goals to be optimized. As a result, the solutions can be easily interpreted and compared with one another.

While spatial models provide specificity in analysis, they reduce the generality of the findings. Many planning projects, such as residential subdivision developments, usually do not have clear and specific definitions of, for example, what species are to be protected or what ecosystem functions are to be maintained. Further, even when ecological objectives are clearly defined, their high level of specificity makes them unsuitable for uniform application across a large or diverse region. For example, in the Pacific Northwest, at least 22 different models were used to characterize forest growth and yield because no single model could satisfy all the needs of such a large and diverse landscape (Ritchie 1999). Also, using spatial models as evaluation criteria adds a significant amount of additional effort to the already computationally intensive process of optimization. Finally, models can be abused if planners who apply them in optimization do not have a clear understanding of their assumptions, limitations, and uncertainties.

SPATIAL OPTIMIZATION FOR GENERATING PRESCRIBED PATTERNS

When generating prescribed patterns in landscape design, the evaluation of the objective functions depends not only on the land type (e.g., land-use/cover) of a location but also on the types in the rest of the landscape or at neighboring locations. Tomlin (1990) uses the term *holistic* to describe location problems that have pattern objectives, in contrast with *atomistic* location problems that do not have pattern objectives. Holistic allocation problems are those that require treating groups of locations as integrated wholes, whereas atomistic allocation problems are those that can be addressed on a location-by-location basis (i.e., atoms of space). Brookes (2001) used the terms *dynamic* and *static* to categorize such differences in the context of stochastic spatial optimization. Dynamic objectives, in which locations are spatially coupled, need to be evaluated for every alternative realization. Static objectives, where locations are not spatially coupled, only require one evaluation at the beginning of the optimization. Holistic or dynamic resource allocation problems are usually more complex to solve.

Finding the most preferred patterns in a land-allocation problem, referred to here as a spatial pattern optimization problem (SPOP), involves examining all possible combinations at all coupling locations. For a gridded landscape with N cells and only two categories (e.g., patch and background matrix) and where the patch category occupies M cells $(M < N)$, the search space is of size $_NC_M$ $(= \frac{N!}{M!(N-M)!})$, that is, the combinatorial function of "N choose M," regardless of order. In the case of $N = 100$ and $M = 50$ (i.e., a 10 by 10 grid with half of the cells occupied by, say, tree cover), the size of its search space is larger than 10^{29}. A naïve approach to solving an instance of a spatial pattern optimization problem is simply to list all the feasible solutions of a given problem, evaluate their objective functions, and pick the best. However, it is obvious that this approach of complete enumeration is grossly inefficient and, in practice, it is not practical.

Metaheuristic methods are usually employed to find good (i.e., near-optimal) but not necessarily guaranteed optimal solutions in such problems (Pressey, Possingham, and Margules 1996). The effectiveness of metaheuristic methods depends upon their ability to adapt to a particular constraint, avoid entrapment at local optima, and efficiently exploit the basic structure of the problem (Revees 1993). Building on these notions, various metaheuristic search techniques have been developed that have demonstrably improved the ability to obtain good solutions to difficult combinatorial optimization problems. Some of the most promising of such techniques include simulated annealing, genetic algorithms, and Tabu search. Details of these algorithms follow.

SIMULATED ANNEALING

The ideas that form the basis of simulated annealing (SA) were first published by Metropolis et al. (1953) in an algorithm to simulate the cooling of material in a heat bath —a process known as annealing. Later, Kirkpatrick, Velatt, and Vecchi (1983) demonstrated that this type of simulation could be used to search the feasible solutions of an optimization problem, with the objective of converging to an optimal solution. SA has provided solutions for large-scale problems in areas of natural resources allocation (e.g., Trap and Helles 1997, Stoms 2001, Aerts and Heuvelink 2002). It is a random search method that avoids getting trapped in local optima by accepting, in addition to solutions that improve on the value of an objective function, solutions corresponding to a deteriorated objective function value as well. The latter is done in a limited way by means of a probabilistic acceptance criterion controlled by the annealing temperature (Floudas and Pardalos 2001). In the course of the annealing process, the probability of accepting deteriorated solutions descends slowly as the temperature drops. These deteriorations make it possible for SA to move away from local optima and explore the feasible solution space in its entirety.

The scheme controlling the decreasing probability for accepting deteriorations is called a cooling schedule, which is found to be a key parameter for determining whether SA finds good solutions (Hajek 1988). If the temperature is fixed at infinity, then all candidate solutions are accepted, and the SA approximates a purely random search with a uniform distribution. At the other extreme, if the temperature is fixed at zero, then only improving solutions are accepted, and the SA is a hill climbing (in the case of maximization) or greedy search. A cooling schedule, which starts at a high temperature and decreases toward zero as the search progresses, allows SA to freely explore the solution space in the beginning of an optimization process and to fully exploit the most promising region in the solution space as temperature drops. Several commonly used cooling schedules include Boltzmann (logarithmic), Cauchy (logarithmic distribution with a delayed cooldown at later times compared with the Boltzmann distribution), and quenching (exponential) schedules (Ingber 1993). The Boltzmann schedule is regarded as a standard cooling schedule for SA and has been proven to suffice for obtaining global optima with a large enough initial temperature (Geman and Geman 1984) but results in a slow process of identifying a solution and sometimes is impractical for applications. Cauchy and quenching schedules lead to a faster convergence to optima but have the risk of converging too fast to reach global optima.

SA is conceptually simple and offers great flexibility by accounting for different kinds of constraints and complex cost functions in the objective function (Goovaerts 1997). This advantage makes SA suitable for solving SPOPs because most pattern objective functions have complex mathematical forms that are difficult to implement with other optimization algorithms. The main drawback of SA is that it is CPU-intensive because it relies on a blunt, repetitive trial-and-error mechanism for finding global optima.

GENETIC (OR EVOLUTIONARY) ALGORITHMS

Genetic algorithms (GA) are modeled after the processes that drive biological evolution. By emulating the biology of natural selection and sexual reproduction, the computer derives the most fitted *organism* survived under *environmental* constraints in iterative reproduction and mutation processes (Bennett,

Wade, and Armstrong 1999). A surviving organism carries a fitted *phenotype*, which is a set of *indices* that document how well specific alternatives meet stated objectives, representing a feasible solution to the problem (Back, Hammel, and Schwefel 1997). The likelihood that an alternative will survive and be used to create a new generation of alternatives depends on its fitness value, which is a composite score derived from its phenotype. Ideally, the phenotypes of survived instances in early generations represent a wide range of possible solutions, and their reproduction and mutation allow the GA to explore the full range of the solution space. As generations evolve through selection of the fittest phenotypes at each generation, the GA exploits the solution space by directing the search towards phenotypes containing highly fit regions of the solution space. These phenotypes are called *schemas*. Since the GA always operates on finite-sized populations (i.e., those instances that survived), there is inherently some sampling error in the search for optima, and in some cases the GA can magnify a small sampling error, causing premature convergence (Goldberg 1989).

Formulation of an effective GA representation (i.e., schema) that explores the solution space of SPOPs is nontrivial (e.g., Brookes 2001; Xiao, Bennett, and Armstrong 2002; Stewart, Janssen, and van Herwijnen 2004). In the study of Xiao, Bennett, and Armstrong (2002), patch contiguity was used as a pattern constraint on the location problem, rather than as an objective to be optimized. Brookes (2001) proposed a novel multipatch parameterized region growing (MPRG) algorithm and used it in tandem with GAs to solve multiobjective location problems. The MPRG algorithm grows patches using a one-dimensional string of parameters that defines the location, size, and ideal shape of patches. The algorithm then translates these strings, which are compatible with the GA process, into two-dimensional maps that can be evaluated to provide feedback that drives the optimization process. MPRG grows patches cell by cell, starting at a seed and adding the cell with the highest suitability score at each iteration. Such an approach fails to account for the coupled nature of pattern objectives by evaluating location fitness sequentially. The solutions of intermediate iterations, before a patch grows to its intended size, usually do not qualify as feasible solutions. These difficulties, along with the requirement for one- to two-dimensional translation, limit the utility of GAs to solve SPOPs. Recently, Stewart, Janssen, and van Herwijnen (2004) formulated novel reproduction and mutation rules for a GA that directly uses generated maps as two-dimensional GA schemas. The effectiveness and generality of applying these rules on SPOPs need further examinations.

TABU SEARCH

Tabu search (TS) employs a somewhat different philosophy from SA and GA for avoiding being trapped in local optima. It downplays the importance of randomization on the assumption that intelligent search should be based on more systematic forms of guidance. The guidance derives from the history of *moves*, particularly as manifested in the recency, frequency, quality, or influence of past moves in generating past solutions (Glover and Laguna 1997). A move is an operation on an existing solution that transforms the solution into a *neighboring* solution. TS escapes local optima by systematically imposing and releasing constraints that operate in several forms, both by direct exclusion of certain moves in the solution space, classed as forbidden, and by translation of these constraints into modified evaluations and probabilities of selection (Reeves 1993). TS maintains a memory of the states encountered during the search and modifies the neighborhood structure of the current state by using the memory to determine the next move. Application of TS for SPOPs requires that meaningful syntactic information, that can be used in a TS memory from 2-dimensional maps, be extracted through a process that lacks theoretical basis and clear guidelines.

KNOWLEDGE-INFORMED SPATIAL PATTERN OPTIMIZATION

Auxiliary knowledge of the nature and structure of spatial configurations has been used to make solving SPOP more efficient or, in some cases, possible. Sometimes algorithms using such auxiliary knowledge are referred to as heuristic algorithms. We use the term *knowledge-informed*, instead of heuristic, to prevent confusion with metaheuristic optimization algorithms, and refer to spatial optimization algorithms that use auxiliary knowledge in solving optimization problems as *knowledge-informed* spatial optimization algorithms. Knowledge-informed spatial optimization is a promising approach to improving the efficiency and effectiveness of SPOP solutions. These improvements are sometimes critical to making it feasible to use spatial optimization in interactive spatial decision-support systems (Pressey et al. 1995).

Knowledge-informed spatial optimization algorithms, similar to the metaheuristic algorithms presented earlier, lack the ability to confirm global optimality. However, correctly specified knowledge-informed algorithms have been reported to drastically reduce the data structure size and computation time required to solve location problems (Rosing, ReVelle, and Rosing-Vogelaar 1979; Pressey et al. 1995; Sorensen and Church 1996). The main purpose of using auxiliary knowledge in metaheuristic algorithms is twofold: the auxiliary knowledge can reduce the search space, preventing unproductive search, or it can alter the structure of the solution space, making it easier to navigate to areas in the solution space where global optima are located. Empirical evidence indicates that optimization problems can thus be solved faster and easier (Glover and Laguna 1997). However, excessive use of inappropriate knowledge can generate significant errors in solving location problems (Sorensen and Church 1996) and, very often, can result in suboptimal solutions with different initial conditions (Church and Sorensen 1996).

In this section, we demonstrate and compare the use of two spatial optimization algorithms, simulated annealing (SA) and knowledge-informed simulated annealing (KISA), in solving a single-objective SPOP. Our objective is to identify the landscape with the most compact landscape patterns by maximizing a landscape pattern metric, PFF (Riitters et al. 2000). The landscape was an 18 by 18 gridded two-dimensional discrete space (i.e., raster data format) with fixed proportions of two land-cover types. In practice, the proportion information may be defined based on design objectives. For demonstration purposes, the landscape was specified as composed of 50% patch cells and 50% background cells. The proportions of land-cover types were maintained throughout the optimization process.

The optimization objective function, PFF, was developed to quantify forest fragmentation and is defined as the average proportion of cells among the eight neighboring cells of any cell of the same type. Figure 1 presents landscape patterns with (near)-maximal and (near)-minimal values of PFF. PFF has a theoretical range of 0 to 1. PFF equals 0 when all cells of a cover type, if there are any, are isolated, and 1 when the landscape is completely covered by a seamless cover of that cover type. A higher PFF value in general is indicative of a less fragmented landscape. Fragmented patches, which are usually formed by the encroachment of high-density human activities, are more likely to lose species because of small patch size and high frequency human disturbance (Harcourt, Parks, and Woodroffe 2001). Preserving large and compact patches is generally preferred in ecological landscape design.

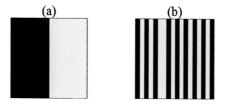

Figure 1. Examples of maps with extreme values of PFF on an 18 by 18 cells landscape with 50% patch cells (dark color): (a) (near-)maximum PFF (0.958), (b) (near-)minimum PFF (0.277).

KISA enhances the SA algorithm by using auxiliary knowledge, based on the pattern objectives specified, to improve the exploration and exploitation of the solution space. We designed and implemented two KISA rules: the *compactness rule* (KISA-Cmp) and the *contiguity rule* (KISA-Cnt). These rules govern the generation of neighboring solutions in the annealing process so that the perturbed cells tend to relocate at locations that promote the specified cell arrangement, that is, compactness or contiguity. Whereas SA swaps the cover type on two randomly selected locations to generate neighboring solutions, KISA-Cmp and KISA-Cnt preferentially move a randomly selected patch cell to a location that promotes patch compactness, that is, one with a high number of neighboring patch cells, or patch connectivity, that is, one with one or more neighboring patch cells. PFF increases greatly when a patch cell is placed on a location where most neighbors are of the same cover type. Such an allocation not only increases the individual PFF for the patch cells being moved but also increases the individual PFF of the neighboring cells. Both KISA rules should improve the performance in maximizing PFF and KISA-Cmp is expected to perform more efficiently than KISA-Cnt.

Ten random landscapes, with 50% of patch cells, were used as initial maps. Each initial map was optimized ten times under each of four cooling schedules by SA, KISA-Cmp, and KISA-Cnt. The four cooling schedules used were: Boltzmann, Cauchy, Exponential, and Greedy. Their definitions are:

Boltzmann (logarithmic) schedule:

$$T(k) = \frac{T_0}{\ln k}, k > 1.$$

Cauchy (modified logarithmic) schedule:

$$T(k) = \frac{T_0}{k}, k > 0.$$

Quenching (exponential) schedule:

$$T(k) = T_0 \exp((c-1)k), c = 0.9966.$$

Greedy:

$$T(k) = 0.$$

In the equations above, T_0 is the initial temperature and k is an index of annealing time, which was defined as the number of processed iterations. The initial temperature in SA applications is usually defined arbitrarily, as long as it is high enough to allow SA to escape from local optima (by accepting deteriorated solutions) and to fully explore the solution space. As a rule of thumb, T_0 should be chosen so that initially about 80% of the deteriorated solutions are accepted (Van Laarhoven 1987). SA stops when there is no better solution found after sampling a certain number of neighboring solutions in the solution space. To choose this number, the objective function values (OFVs) for forty simulations, obtained using hill climbing for each number of neighbors between 10 and 500, were averaged and plotted (fig. 2). When the number of searched neighbors is small, the hill-climbing stops prematurely. However, as the number of attempts increases, the improvement of OFV diminishes. Given this trade-off, we selected an arbitrary cutoff value of 200.

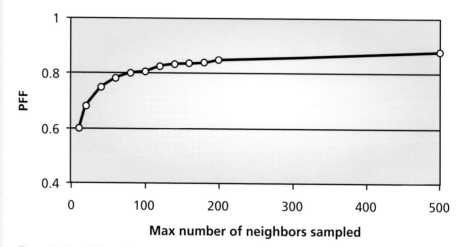

Figure 2. Max PFF reached under different numbers of neighbors sampled in hill climbing runs (solid lines are interpolated).

To compare performance among SA, KISA-Cmp, and KISA-Cnt, we recorded the OFVs (i.e., PFF) during each optimization run at a constant interval of every 100 iterations (i.e., every 100th solution was generated and evaluated). Two indices, Max Objective Function Value (MAXOFV) and Weighted Performance Index (WPI), were recorded. MAXOFV is the best OFV ever achieved in each run. WPI is the average of weighted OFVs using a linearly decreasing weighting scheme, which gives more weight to the OFVs in the earlier stage of runs and is derived from summation of the products of the difference between maximal iteration number and iteration number and the OFV at each recording interval divided by the sum of all iteration numbers. MAXOFV measures the effectiveness of the method used for approximating the optimal solutions while WPI measures the efficiency. Both MAXOFV and WPI vary with the length of the SA runs, and thus the benchmark results might change. In the case of maximization and at the annealing time of 10000 iterations, a hypothetical method (A) has a higher MAXOFV than another hypothetical method (B), while Method B approximates the optimal OFV faster than Method A. If we set the cutoff annealing time to 5000 for this comparison, then Method B is both more effective and efficient than Method A in finding a solution (fig. 3). The performance indices presented in this chapter are all based on an arbitrary cutoff annealing time of 25,000 iterations. This reflects the practical aspect of applying spatial optimization techniques in a group decision-making process, which usually requires timely evaluations of alternative solutions. The cutoff annealing time of 25,000 iterations equals roughly 30 seconds for an 18 by 18 map solved on an Intel® Pentium® 4 3.2 GHz computer.

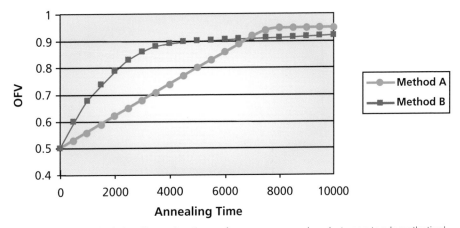

Figure 3. Hypothetical data illustrating the performance comparison between two hypothetical optimization methods.

RESULTS

A total of 1200 runs was carried out in the experiment, 100 runs for each of the twelve combinations of the cooling schedules and SA algorithms in solving the SPOP. The stochastic process in these algorithms was implemented using the Visual Basic RND random number generator. All algorithms found near-optimal solutions (PFF > 0.94) and conspicuous suboptimal solutions (PFF < 0.88) in some runs (fig. 4). For most annealing settings, the average PFF at 25,000 iterations was about 95% of the best PFF ever achieved at the maximal number of iterations (Table 1). The data confirm that most runs had converged at 25,000 iterations, and the use of 25,000 iterations as the cutoff range for measuring MAXOFV and WPI was reasonable. KISA-Cmp converged the fastest and SA converged the slowest in maximizing PFF (fig. 5).

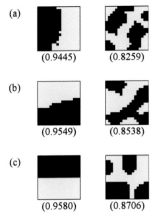

Figure 4. Better (left column) and worse (right column) solutions and their PFF values (in parentheses) of maximizing PFF of patch class (dark color). These solutions are generated using (a) SA, (b) KISA-Cnt, and (c) KISA-Cmp. They are differentiated by algorithms but not by the cooling schedules used.

Algorithm / Schedule	SA	KISA-Cnt	KISA-Cmp
Boltzmann	0.8921 (0.9446)	0.9284 (0.9562)	0.9386 (0.9580)
Cauchy	0.9139 (0.9139)	0.9120 (0.9508)	0.9338 (0.9557)
Exponential	0.8957 (0.9340)	0.9382 (0.9549)	0.9440 (0.9565)
Greedy	0.9048 (0.9171)	0.9353 (0.9531)	0.9542 (0.9580)

Table 1. The averaged maximal PFF reached in 25,000 iterations versus the maximal PFF ever reached in 150,000 iterations (in parentheses).

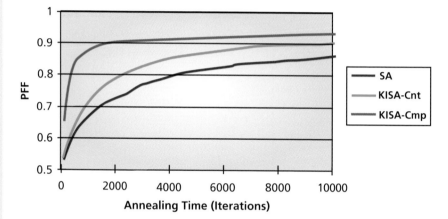

Figure 5. Averaged OFV curves of maximizing PFF (showing only the solutions solved using the Boltzmann cooling schedule).

We calculated the MAXOFV and WPI of all runs and used one-way ANOVA to test the significance of variations among different annealing settings. The results show that the performance of maximizing PFF varies among different combinations of SA algorithms and cooling schedules (fig. 6). When using the same cooling schedule, KISA-Cmp performed the best, that is, with higher MAXOFV and WPI values, and the conventional SA performed the worst. This is as predicted in our earlier discussions on KISA rules. For each algorithm used, the Boltzmann and the Exponential schedules were most effective but least efficient in generating the (near-)optimal solutions, whereas Cauchy and Greedy schedules, though more efficient in converging to optimal solutions, were not generating solutions as good as those generated using Boltzmann or Exponential schedules. Both KISA-Cmp and KISA-Cnt significantly improved the efficiency and effectiveness for all cooling schedules used. Boltzmann and Exponential schedules were more effective than Cauchy or Greedy. KISA-Cmp and KISA-Cnt were equally effective in maximizing PFF. However, KISA-Cmp was more efficient than KISA-Cnt. The data suggests that using KISA-Cmp with a Boltzmann or an Exponential cooling schedule is the most effective and efficient annealing setting for maximizing PFF.

(a)

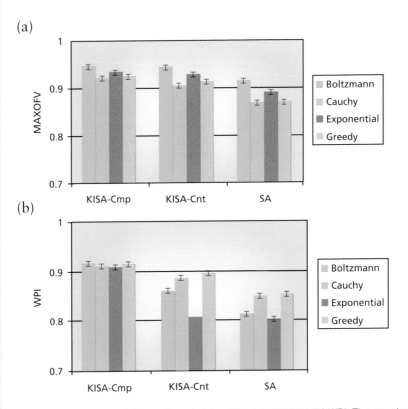

(b)

Figure 6. Performance indices of maximizing PFF: (a) MAXOFV, (b) WPI. The error bars of ± 2 standard errors of the mean are included.

CONCLUSIONS

Rapid urbanization has massively transformed landscapes and increased the tension between development and conservation at urban fringes. The adoption of ecological landscape designs in development is a practical method to balance development and conservation. The idea of ecological landscape design is not so much to exclude development as to distribute it in a way that minimizes disruption of ecological processes (McHarg 1969). Given the complexity and multidisciplinarity involved in evaluating ecological landscape design, the spatial optimization techniques presented in this chapter can potentially make the evaluation more efficient and comprehensive. No matter how complicated a problem, the optimization algorithms can generate design alternatives that might be overlooked by human cognition.

An important role for GIS is its capability to integrate diverse information resources in multidisciplinary collaborations. However, for GIS to play such a role successfully requires collaboration across disciplines. Using spatial optimization in landscape planning and design requires input from and dialogue between landscape architects and landscape ecologists to define the optimization objective clearly. Therefore, although spatial optimization is not a tool to automate the planning process or suggest solutions, the maps created by spatial optimization or simulation are media for visual communication and spatial inferences that can involve both objective and subjective evaluations. Generation of objective solutions to quantitative goals can iterate with subjective evaluation of the means and consequences of achieving those goals.

We presented a knowledge-informed simulated annealing (KISA) approach to improving the performance of solving spatial pattern optimization problems (SPOP). Simulated annealing is flexible and versatile in dealing with complex pattern objective functions, and empirical results indicate that KISA further improved its performance in solving SPOPs, making the approach of combining auxiliary information and simulated annealing desirable for similar applications. The computational time was significantly reduced by KISA. On a computer equipped with an Intel Pentium-4 3.2 GHz CPU, the SA program we implemented in a Microsoft Visual Basic program that generated and evaluated maps with a size of 324 cells at a rate of 45,000 per minute. It took about 14 seconds for KISA-Cmp to get a solution as good as one generated by SA in 220 seconds (3.7 minutes) on the same computer and for the same landscape. Although computer speed has doubled every couple of years, for more realistic problems, say, with a map size of 500 by 500 cells, the difference of times required to generate a near-optimal solution for decision making could be hours and minutes between SA and KISA. This makes spatial simulation more practical to use in interactive spatial decision making.

In addition to the compactness objective characterized by the PFF metric, there are other pattern objectives, such as connectivity. Corresponding KISA rules for these pattern objectives need to be designed, implemented, and evaluated. The performance of KISA rules in multiobjective problems, which are often encountered in planning and design, also requires further study.

ACKNOWLEDGMENTS   This research was supported by the USDA Forest Service North Central Research Station (#02-JV-11231300-037) and by the Eugene and Emily Grant Scholarship of the School of Natural Resources and Environment of the University of Michigan.

REFERENCES

Aerts, J. C. J. H., and G. B. M. Heuvelink. 2002. Using simulated annealing for resource allocation. *International Journal of Geographical Information Science* 16: 571–87.

Ahern, J. 1999. Integration of landscape ecology and landscape design: An evolutionary process. In *Issues in landscape ecology,* eds. J. A. Wiens and M. R. Moss. Snowmass Village, Colo.: International Association for Landscape Ecology, Fifth World Congress.

Alberti, M. 1999. Urban patterns and environmental performance: What do we know? *Journal of Planning Education and Research* 19: 151–63.

Allen, T. F. H., and T. B. Starr. 1982. *Hierarchy: Perspectives for ecological complexity.* Chicago: University of Chicago Press.

Antrop, M., and V. Van Eetvelde. 2000. Holistic aspects of suburban landscapes: Visual image interpretation and landscape metrics. *Landscape and Urban Planning* 50: 43–58.

Arendt, R. 1999. *Growing greener: Putting conservation into local plans and ordinances.* Washington, D.C.: Island Press.

Back, T., U. Hammel, and H. Schwefel. 1997. Evolutionary computation: Comments on the history and current state. *IEEE Transactions on Evolutionary Computation* 1: 3–17.

Barrett, G. W., and J. D. Peles. 1994. Optimizing habitat fragmentation—an agrolandscape perspective. *Landscape and Urban Planning* 28: 99–105.

Bennett, D. A., G. A.Wade, and M. P. Armstrong. 1999. Exploring the solution space of semi-structured geographical problems using genetic algorithms. *Transactions in GIS* 3:51–71.

Bettinger, P., K. Boston, and J. Sessions. 1999. Combinatorial optimization of elk habitat effectiveness and timber harvest volume. *Environmental Modeling and Assessment* 4(2-3): 143–53.

Brooker, L. 2002. The application of focal species knowledge to landscape design in agricultural lands using the ecological neighbourhood as a template. *Landscape and Urban Planning* 60: 185–210.

Brookes, C. J. 2001. A genetic algorithm for designing optimal patch configurations in GIS. *International Journal of Geographical Information Science* 15: 539–59.

Brown, D. G., B. C. Pijanowski, and Duh, J.-D. 2000. Modeling the relationships between land-use and land-cover on private lands in the Upper Midwest, USA. *Journal of Environmental Management* 59: 247–63.

Chave, J., K. Wiegand, and S. Levin. 2002. Spatial and biological aspects of reserve design. *Environmental Modeling and Assessment* 7: 115–22.

Church, R. L. 2002. Geographical information systems and location science. *Computers and Operations Research* 29: 541–61.

Church, R. L., and P. Sorensen. 1996. Integrating normative location models into GIS: Problems and prospects with the p-median model. In *Spatial analysis: Modeling in a GIS environment,* ed. P. Longley and M. Batty. Cambridge: GeoInformation International.

Church, R. L., D. M. Stoms, and F. W. Davis. 1996. Reserve selection as a maximal covering location problem. *Biological Conservation* 76: 105–12.

Church, R. L., R. A. Gerrard, M. Gilpin, and P. Stine. 2003. Constructing cell-based habitat patches useful in conservation planning. *Annals of the Association of American Geographers* 93: 814–27.

Cocklin, C. 1989. Mathematical programming and resource planning I: The limitations of traditional optimization. *Journal of Environmental Management* 28: 127–41.

Cova, T. J., and R. L. Church. 2000. Contiguity constraints for single-region site search problems. *Geographical Analysis* 32: 306–29.

Cross, G. R., and A. K. Jain. 1983. Markov random field texture models. *IEEE Transactions on Pattern Analysis and Machine Intelligence* 5: 25–39.

Dale, M. R. T. 2000. Lacunarity analysis of spatial pattern: A comparison. *Landscape Ecology* 15: 467–78.

De Bonet, J., and P. Viola. 1997. A non-parametric multi-scale statistical model for natural images. In *Advances in neural information processing, vol. 9.* Cambridge, Mass.: MIT Press.

Derin, H., and Elliott, H. 1987. Modeling and segmentation of noisy and textured images using Gibbs random fields. *IEEE Transactions on Pattern Analysis and Machine Intelligence* 9: 39–55.

Deutsch, C. V., and A. C. Journel. 1992. *GSLIB: Geostatistical software library and user's guide.* Oxford: Oxford University Press.

Fedorowick, J. M. 1993. A landscape restoration framework for wildlife and agriculture in the rural landscape. *Landscape and Urban Planning* 27: 7–17.

Floudas, C. A., and P. M. Pardalos, eds. 2001. *Encyclopedia of optimization.* Dordrecht: Kluwer.

Forman, R. T. T. 2002. The missing catalyst: Design and planning with ecology roots. In *Ecology and design,* ed. B. R. Johnson and K. Hill. Washington, D.C.: Island Press.

Geman, S., and D. Geman. 1984. Stochastic relaxation, Gibbs distribution and the Bayesian restoration in images. *IEEE Transactions on Pattern Analysis and Machine Intelligence* 6: 721–41.

Glover, F., and M. Laguna. 1997. *Tabu search.* Boston: Kluwer.

Goldberg, D. E. 1989. *Genetic algorithms in search, optimization, and machine learning.* Reading, Mass.: Addison-Wesley.

Goovaerts, P. 1997. *Geostatistics for natural resources evaluation.* New York: Oxford University Press.

Gotway, C. A., and B. M. Rutherford. 1996. The components of geostatistical simulation. In *Proceedings of spatial accuracy assessment in natural resources and environmental sciences.* Fort Collins, Colo.: USDA.

Griffiths, G. H., J. Lee, and B. C. Eversham. 2000. Landscape pattern and species richness: Regional scale analysis form remote sensing. *International Journal of Remote Sensing* 21(13/14): 2685–704.

Gustafson, E. J. 1998. Quantifying landscape spatial pattern: What is the state of the art? *Ecosystems* 1: 143–56.

Hajek, B. 1988. Cooling schedules for optimal annealing. *Mathematics of Operations Research* 13: 311–29.

Harcourt, A. H., S. A. Parks, and R. Woodroffe. 2001. Human density as an influence on species/area relationship: Double jeopardy for small African reserves? *Biodiversity and Conservation* 10: 1011–26.

Harris, B. 1998. Optimization and design. *Environment and Planning B: Planning and Design,* 25th Anniversary Issue: 23–28.

Henein, K., and G. Merriam. 1990. The elements of connectivity where corridor quality is variable. *Landscape Ecology* 4: 157–70.

Ingber, L. 1993. Simulated annealing: Practice and theory. *Mathematical and Computer Modelling* 18(11): 29–57.

Kirkpatrick, S., C. D. Gelatt, and M. P. Vecchi. 1983. Optimization by simulated annealing. *Science* 37: 671–80.

Lamberson, R. H., B. Noon, C. Voss, and K. McKelvey. 1994. Reserve design for territorial species: The effects of patch size and spacing on the viability of the Northern Spotted Owl. *Conservation Biology* 8: 185–95.

Lindenmayer, D. B., I. Ball, H. P. Possingham, M. A. McCarthy, and M. L. Pope. 2001. A landscape-scale test of the predictive ability of a spatially explicit model for population viability analysis. *Journal of Applied Ecology* 38: 36–48.

Liu, Y. B., S. Nishiyama, and T. Kusaka. 2003. Examining landscape dynamics at a watershed scale using landsat TM imagery for detection of wintering hooded crane decline in Yashiro, Japan. *Environmental Management* 31: 365–76.

Loehle, C. 2000. Optimal control of spatially distributed process models. *Ecological Modelling* 131: 79–95.

Löfvenhaft, K., C. Björn, and M. Ihse. 2002. Biotope patterns in urban areas: A conceptual model integrating biodiversity issues in spatial planning. *Landscape and Urban Planning* 58: 223–40.

McAlpine, C. A ., and T. J. Eyre. 2002. Testing landscape metrics as indicators of habitat loss and fragmentation in continuous eucalypt forests (Queensland, Australia). *Landscape Ecology* 17: 711–28.

McGarigal, K., and B. J. Marks. 1995. FRAGSTATS: Spatial pattern analysis program for quantifying landscape structure. General Technical Report PNW-GTR-351, USDA Forest Service. Pacific Northwest Research Station, Portland, Ore.

McHarg, I. L. 1969. *Design with nature.* Garden City, N.Y.: Natural History Press.

McIntyre, N. E., and J. A.Wiens. 1999. How does habitat patch size affect animal movement? An experiment with darkling beetles. *Ecology* 80: 2261–70.

————. 2000. A novel use of the lacunarity index to discern landscape function. *Landscape Ecology* 15: 313–21.

Metropolis, N., A. Rosenbluth, M. Rosenbluth, A. Teller, and E. Teller. 1953. Equation of state calculations by fast computing machines. *Journal of Chemical Physics* 21: 1087–92.

Nassauer, J. I. 2002. Ecological science and landscape design: A necessary relationship in changing landscapes. In *Ecology and design,* ed. B. R. Johnson, and K. Hill. Washington, D. C.: Island Press.

Nassauer, J. I., and A. Caddock. 1996. Project Report: MES Growth Management Project. Hubert H. Humphrey Institute, University of Minnesota.

Nicklow, J. W., and M. K. Muleta. 2001. Watershed management technique to control sediment yield in agriculturally dominated areas. *Water International* 26: 435–43.

O'Neill, R. V., R. H.Gardner, M. G. Turner, and W. H. Romme. 1992. Epidemiology theory and disturbance spread on landscapes. *Landscape Ecology* 7: 19–26.

O'Neill, R. V., A. R. Johnson, and A. W. King. 1989. A hierarchical framework for the analysis of scale. *Landscape Ecology* 3(3/4): 193–205.

Opdam, P., R. Foppen, and C. Vos. 2002. Bridging the gap between ecology and spatial planning in landscape ecology. *Landscape Ecology* 16: 767–79.

Otto, R. D. 1996. An evaluation of forest landscape spatial pattern and wildlife community structure. *Forest Ecology and Management* 89: 139–47.

Pressey, R. L., S. Ferrier, C. D. Hutchinson, D. P. Sivertsen, and G. Manion. 1995. Planning for negotiation: Using an interactive geographic information system to explore alternative protected area networks. In *Nature conservation 4: The role of networks,* ed. D. A. Saunders, J. L. Craig, and E. M. Mattiska, 23–33. Sydney: Surrey Beatty.

Pressey, R. L., H. P. Possingham, and C. R. Margules. 1996. Optimality in reserve selection algorithms: When does it matter and how much? *Biological Conservation* 76: 259–67.

Revees, C. R. 1993. *Modern heuristic techniques for combinatorial problems.* New York: John Wiley and Sons.

Riitters, K., J. Wickham, R. O'Neill, B. Jones, and E. Smith. 2000. Global-scale patterns of forest fragmentation. *Conservation Ecology* 4(2): 3.

Ripley, B.D. 1978. Spectral analysis and the analysis of pattern in plant communities. *Journal of Ecology* 66: 965–81.

Ritchie, M. W. 1999. A Compendium of Forest Growth and Yield Simulators for the Pacific Coast States. General Technical Report PSW-GTR-174. USDA Forest Service. Pacific Southwest Research Station, Albany, Calif..

Rosing, K. E., C. ReVelle, and H. Rosing-Vogelaar. 1979. The p-median model and its linear programming relaxation: An approach to large problems. *Journal of Operational Research Society* 30: 815–23.

Saura, S., and J. Martínez-Millán. 2000. Landscape patterns simulation with a modified random clusters method. *Landscape Ecology* 15: 661–78.

Schmid-Holmes, S., and L. C. Drickamer. 2001. Impact of forest patch characteristics on small mammal communities: A multivariate approach. *Biological Conservation* 99: 293–305.

Schumaker, N. 1996. Using landscape indices to predict habitat connectivity. *Ecology* 77: 1210–25.

Seppelt, R., and A. Voinov. 2002. Optimization methodology for land use patterns using spatially explicit landscape models. *Ecological Modelling* 151: 125–42.

Sorensen, P. A., and R. L. Church,.1996. A comparison of strategies for data storage reduction in location–allocation problems. *Geographical Systems* 3: 221–42.

Stewart, T. J., R. Janssen, and M. van Herwijnen. 2004. A genetic algorithm approach to multiobjective land use planning. *Computers and Operations Research* 31: 2293–313.

Stoms, D. M. 2001. Integrating biodiversity into land-use planning. Proceedings of American Planning Association 2001 National Planning Conference, New Orleans, L.A.

Tomlin, C. D. 1990. *Geographic information systems and cartographic modelling.* Englewood Cliffs, N.J.: Prentice Hall.

Trap, P. and F. Helles. 1997. Spatial optimization by simulated annealing and linear programming. *Scandinavian Journal of Forest Research* 12: 390–402.

Turner, M. G., W. H. Romme, R. H. Gardner, R. V. O'Neill, and T. K. Kratz. 1993. A revised concept of landscape equilibrium: Disturbance and stability on scaled landscapes. *Landscape Ecology* 8: 213–27.

Urban, D. L. 1993. Landscape ecology and ecosystem management. In *Sustainable ecological systems: Implementing an ecological approach to land management,* ed. W. W. Covington and L. F. DeBano. USDA Forest Service General Technical Report RM-247. Fort Collins, Colo.: Rocky Mountain Forest and Range Experiment Station, USDA.

Van Laarhoven, P. J. M. 1987. Theoretical and computational aspects of simulated annealing. PhD thesis, Erasmus University, Rotterdam.

Vos, C. C., J. Verboom, P. F. M. Opdam, and C. J. F. Ter Braak. 2001. Towards ecologically scaled landscape indices. *American Naturalist* 157: 24–51.

Wegener, M. 1998. GIS and spatial planning. *Environment and Planning B: Planning and Design,* 25th Anniversary Issue: 48–52.

Xiao, N., Bennett, D.A., and Armstrong, M.P. 2002. Using evolutionary algorithms to generate alternatives for multiobjective site-search problems. *Environment and Planning A* 34: 639–56.

Young, W. and Bowyer, D. 1996. Modelling the environmental impact of changes in urban structure. *Computers, Environment and Urban Systems* 20(4–5): 313–26.

Chapter 21

GIS, Spatial Analysis and Modeling: Current Status and Future Prospects

DAVID J. MAGUIRE

DIRECTOR OF PRODUCTS

ESRI

REDLANDS, CALIFORNIA

MICHAEL BATTY

CENTRE FOR ADVANCED SPATIAL ANALYSIS

UNIVERSITY COLLEGE LONDON

LONDON, UNITED KINGDOM

MICHAEL F. GOODCHILD

NATIONAL CENTER FOR GEOGRAPHIC INFORMATION AND ANALYSIS

UNIVERSITY OF CALIFORNIA

SANTA BARBARA, CALIFORNIA

ABSTRACT

THIS FINAL CHAPTER summarizes the main themes presented in the book and reflects on the state of the art in spatial analysis and modeling in GIS. We identify some of the major gaps in our knowledge and toolset. Finally, we highlight some of the promising avenues for future research.

It is clear that spatial analysis and modeling in a GIS context has come a long way in the past four decades. There have been major achievements in methodology, techniques, data management, software, and applications. GIS has been critical to much of this because of the capabilities it provides for data management, transformation, visualization, and dissemination. More than this, GIS software systems have become a platform technology in their own right for developing and executing spatial analysis and modeling. In spite of the enormous progress, this is still a rapidly advancing field and much remains to be done. We are especially aware of the need for work in dealing with error and uncertainty and in extending our reach into dynamic modeling of multidimensional data.

Over the past four decades, GIS has evolved to become a major technology and an applied problem-solving methodology. In the early days, the emphasis was very much on data collection and maintenance, with massive effort and expenditure on building inventories of the natural and built environment, as well as population counts and other socioeconomic indicators. From the beginning to the present day, such inventories have been used for making measurements (e.g., acreage under wheat, length of roads, and number of customers in a store catchment area). Then, maps and later visualizations of many types became increasingly important as ways to communicate and summarize geographic information. More recently a third tradition, implicit in the early origins of the field, based on spatial analysis and modeling, has reasserted itself, and this has become the most advanced and potentially most useful application of GIS. These three aspects of GIS are not, of course, mutually independent or exclusive. Indeed, two of the major reasons for undertaking spatial analysis and modeling in a GIS context lie in the ability for GIS software to manage data and to make maps and other visualizations.

GIS-based spatial analysis and modeling is critical in helping us describe, explain, and predict patterns and processes on the surface of the earth. Data models allow us to represent aspects of the complexity of the real world in a digital geographic database. A data model is a well-defined set of rules about what objects to represent and how to represent them. We can populate geographic databases with information describing the state of the world using geographic data models as templates. From these databases we can summarize the characteristics of regions and develop general inductive rules concerning spatial variations and patterns. In recent years, a considerable amount of effort has been put into building specific and general-purpose geographic data models. This approach is encapsulated in this book in the work of Hopkins et al. in chapter 9 and to a lesser extent that of Maidment et al. in chapter 15. Other pertinent reviews are provided by Arctur and Zeiler (2004) and Longley et al. (2005).

Data models are very useful inventions and often reveal new insights about the world. However, their uses are restricted to inductive reasoning about current objects and the relationships between them. In order to understand the processes that shape the world and to predict how things evolve over time, we need to build mathematical models and encode them in computer software so that we can execute them at our own convenience. There are many different approaches to geographic modeling and many types of models as Goodchild in chapter 1 and Batty in chapter 3 point out. Deterministic models are useful for explaining and predicting well-defined static systems, but are less well suited to problems that require dynamic simulation of complex systems. It is this last area which is perhaps the most challenging, but potentially the most rewarding area of future work.

Today there are very many well-developed applications of GIS-based spatial analysis and modeling. The examples in this book cover the full spectrum of spatial analysis and modeling applications: dispersion of infectious diseases, ecological dynamics of watersheds, flood management and erosion control, habitat suitability prediction, hydrological analysis, land cover change, landscape simulation, land-use and transportation simulation, large-scale sedimentology, retail and service planning (e.g., store location and performance), urban growth, and volcanic erosion and sedimentation.

GIS, SPATIAL ANALYSIS, AND MODELING SOFTWARE

Clearly, enormous progress has been made in recent years in the mathematics, science and technology of spatial analysis and modeling. As far as software is concerned, there are at least three centers of gravity: GIS, modeling, and statistical. In chapter 2, Maguire outlined the progress in the GIS field, and Anselin did the same for statistical modeling in chapter 5. To understand the motivations and progress of the modeling fraternity, readers will need to examine the chapters by Maxwell and Voinov (chapter 7) and Miller et al. (chapter 6) for examples of the genre. The systems built by the groups led by Burrough in chapter 16 and Eastman in chapter 17 are very interesting because they are combined GIS and modeling systems—this surely is the way forward for the spatial analysis and modeling community. In chapters 4, 13, and 15 respectively, Krivoruchko and Gotway Crawford, Israelson and Frederiksen, and Maidment et al. discuss some very promising work that is moving ArcGIS, the most widely used commercial GIS, into the same GIS—spatial analysis—modeling space.

All the six systems discussed in the previous paragraph are commercial off-the-shelf packages. There is a strong parallel tradition in the analysis and modeling communities of developing and using public domain and open-source software. Maguire (chapter 2) and Parker (chapter 19) discussed the open-source SWARM and RePast agent-based modeling and cellular automata libraries that represent an important source of modeling ideas and functions. A number of workers have used these systems to model geographic systems (e.g., Brown et al. 2004, Dibble and Feldman 2004). Several projects are attempting to link these to commercial GIS. For example, ESRI and Argonne National Labs are linking ArcGIS and RePast via a common Java API as we show in figure 1. Here the RePast functions are exposed as dialogs with the ArcGIS user interface. ArcGIS is used to manage data and visualize results.

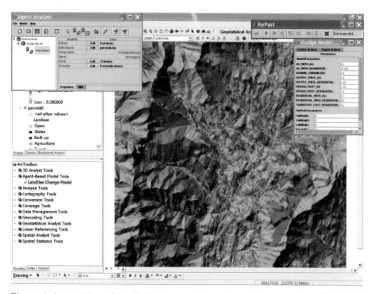

Figure 1: Integration of the RePast agent-based modeling system with ArcGIS.

There is also a long standing tradition in the geographic community of linking GIS with spatial analysis and modeling systems. For example, in chapter 8, Batty and Xie write about linking ArcView and DUEM (Dynamic Evolutionary Urban Modeling); in chapter 11, Birkin describes how the spatial interaction package NIMS (National Information and Modeling System) is linked to MapInfo; in chapter 14, Yeh links a case-based reasoning (CBR) shell called ESTEEM to ArcView; and in chapter 15, Maidment et al. examine ArcGIS linked to hydrological modeling tools. Modern approaches to software engineering offer many options for linking systems together using a range of options from simple file interchange to component integration.

Much of the material covered in the book models the world at an aggregate level (pedestrian flows, land-use change, transportation, etc.). In contrast, Ahern and Smith (chapter 18) illustrate the value of individual models. In their case, they model human–tiger interactions in forests. Parker (chapter 19) also provides some examples of agent-based models of individuals.

The motivations for using GIS software in spatial analysis and modeling are discussed in chapter 2 by Maguire, and it is worth summarizing the main points again here. In essence, GIS software systems offer a useful set of capabilities for data management, data integration/transformation, visualization/ mapping, spatial analysis and modeling, model specification and execution, customization/scripting/interfacing, and knowledge dissemination

All of the debate about which type of software is best or most appropriate begs the question: *who are the GIS, spatial analysis, and modeling users and what are their requirements?* At the risk of overgeneralizing, we can identify at least three interest groups: advanced researchers, professional analysts, and end users. Parker (chapter 19) provides examples of the first and third type. Advanced researchers typically operate in academic, government, and to a lesser extent, private organizations. They often have strong skills in computer programming, geography, modeling, and statistics. Workers in this group are able to create new methods and techniques, as well as author software, from first principles or based on existing component libraries. Professional analysts and modelers are often strong in one or more application domains, but do not always have the same mathematical or software engineering backgrounds. Nevertheless, they are usually able to author new models and apply methods and techniques into new areas using scripting (e.g., Python, PERL, JScript or VBScript). They are quite comfortable working with a toolbox of built-in functions, menus, and software wizards. End users are the least technically competent (or perhaps can afford less time to author models and new techniques). Workers in this group are interested in consuming prebuilt models and/or analytical processes. They have limited capacity for creating new tools or techniques. Clearly, the user base of GIS, spatial analysis, and modeling is more complex than this, but this threefold classification serves to highlight some of the key user types and the broad base of potential users. It also partly explains why there is a plurality of software types and approaches to spatial analysis and modeling.

PROSPECTS FOR THE FUTURE

There is no doubt that current systems are limited in various ways as many of the authors writing here have been at pains to point out. Several models remain only loosely coupled with GIS, where GIS is being largely used for visualization and map analysis or even as storage medium for spatial data. However, the fact that many models are not embedded deeply within GIS is as much due to the unfamiliarity of the embedding procedures by the authors who are responsible for their programming as by any intrinsic mathematical difficulties that characterize the models in question. Only when it comes to temporal dynamics and explicit sequential processes where time is characterized in convoluted ways do difficulties of embedding become severe. For example, many of the static models of urban activities, such as those described by Wegener, Birkin, Israelsen and Frederiksen, and Duh and Brown in chapters 10, 11, 13 and 20, respectively, can easily be written within the contemporary scripting languages that are now basic to state-of-the-art commercial GIS or indeed as stand-alone programs that can be seamlessly linked to GIS. In fact, Israelsen and Frederiksen show that this is eminently possible with respect to the four stage transportation modeling process using current modeling and map algebra tools that exist within ArcGIS.

Software technologies too are still rapidly advancing, and new kinds of authoring systems are making it ever easier for programmers to combine what at first sight appear to be quite dissimilar systems. New modeling languages are noted by Maguire in chapter 2, and the veritable explosion of styles that now pervades the field is likely to enable many new and innovative applications of GIS based models in the near future. Combined with new extensions which make it easier for both end users and programmers to interface different system together and dramatic increases in computing power which enable users to generate spatial models using brute force if necessary (for many locations and over many time intervals for example), modeling and spatial analysis possibilities that hitherto were simply judged impossible now appear feasible. This is due to a combination of new modeling languages that make interfacing much simpler (as in Python, for example), new ways of treating time, and new ways of developing spatial representations, particularly in extensions to the third dimension. A good example of such developments is in the open source package NetLogo (ccl. northwestern.edu/netlogo) which is a dynamic agent-based modeling package targeted at educational users but which has recently been extended not only to Web-based access but also to the third dimension. How long before such packages can be interfaced easily and coherently with commercial GIS? Moreover, many packages designed for one market or audience often get extended and upgraded as the software and hardware technologies develop. NetLogo, for example, is designed for education, but as functionality has been added, it has been used quite successfully for fully fledged professional usage. The same is also true for much longer for packages such as MATLAB (as demonstrated by Bian and Liebner in chapter 12), Mathematica®, and AutoCAD® which all began life as much more basic and rudimentary systems.

Extending GIS from 2.5D to true 3D and 4D (x,y,z and t [time]) remains a challenge as Batty describes in chapter 3 and as Burrough et al. seek to resolve in chapter 16. This is especially the case for those interested in modeling the lithosphere (e.g., mining geology), hydrosphere (e.g., ocean ecosystems), and atmosphere (e.g. global circulation). There are some promising areas of work that are extending the current frontiers, but much more remains to be done. For example, ArcGIS Tracking Analyst can handle temporal data, and Maidment, Robayo, and Merwade (chapter 15) show how to work with hydrological time-series data in ArcGIS. Some of the developments in cellular automata models sketched by Batty and Xie in chapter 8 are now being linked to generic agent-based software such as RePast (Barros 2005), and we show such as an interface in figure 2 below.

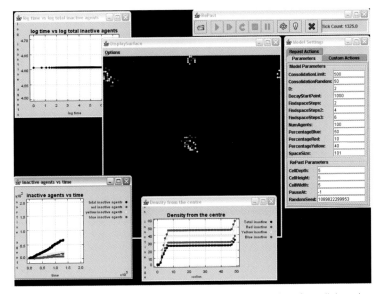

Figure 2: Various windows showing the dynamic trajectories of a cellular urban growth model with the software RePast (from Barros 2005).

Compare figure 1 and figure 2. The same agent-based framework is linked to ArcGIS (fig. 1) and to a purpose-built cellular automata model of urban growth in Latin American cities (fig. 2). How long before all these links are put together? This then is the prospect, and a rich one it is. What, in fact, is going to be required is not one way of putting together different software and models and GIS representations but a generic framework for GIS, spatial analysis, and modeling which users can adapt to the many kinds of problems and applications discussed in this book, and in the next decade this is sure to be forthcoming.

GIS users have known for a long time that no database can be a perfect representation of the real world and that any database must therefore leave the user uncertain to some degree about the real phenomena that it purports to represent. Measurements of aspects of the real world, such as elevation, are never exact and instead include various degrees of inaccuracy or error that constitute one form of uncertainty. Definitions of geographic terms, such as the types of soil or land use that form the basis for many GIS layers, are themselves somewhat vague, creating another form of uncertainty. Data documentation may be incomplete or wrong, again leading to uncertainty about the real world.

Research on uncertainty in geographic information began in earnest in 1988, when the National Center for Geographic Information and Analysis began a research initiative on the topic (Goodchild and Gopal 1989). In essence, it seeks answers to the following questions:

- What forms of uncertainty exist, and what are their sources?
- How can uncertainty be modeled?

- How can uncertainty be visualized in maps and on-screen displays of geographic information?
- How does uncertainty in input data impact the results of analysis and modeling through processes of error propagation?

Today an extensive literature exists on these topics. Zhang and Goodchild (2002) provide a mathematical treatment of models, while Heuvelink (1998) has assembled an excellent text on what is known about error propagation. But by and large, the user community has not adopted these methods to date. In part, we suspect this is due to the essentially negative picture presented by much of the research: users simply do not want to know, preferring to assume that the data input to GIS, and the results produced by GIS, are as accurate as the precision of computers would lead them to believe. This position is of course, untenable, especially when one considers its implications for litigation and legal liability.

However, there are reasons to believe that interest in uncertainty will increase in the near future. The move to analysis and modeling, as reflected in this book, will inevitably bring questions of uncertainty to the fore. How does one know that the predictions of a model are correct? What are the appropriate confidence limits on a particular forecast? Why would one trust the results of one model over another? The work of Krivoruchko and Gotway Crawford in chapter 4 and Anselin in chapter 5 and the survey publications cited earlier demonstrate that solutions to this problem are tractable and that they can be readily implemented in extensions to existing software.

In terms of future representations, we have noted that dynamics is increasingly important in building models of an uncertain and increasingly unpredictable world. Today's GIS are very much a product of their roots in static map-based analysis and their considerable success at managing natural and physical resources as assets. The real world, however, is fuzzy, uncertain, and dynamic, and to be successful at characterizing and simulating real world processes, GIS must be able to incorporate multidimensional space–time modeling. The absence of these subjects is all the more surprising given the richness of implementations in nongeographic modeling and simulation software systems, for example, GoldSim which Miller et al. discuss in chapter 6 and STELLA as developed by Maxwell and Voinov in chapter 7. There are some encouraging signs that ArcGIS, Idrisi and PCRaster now support some dynamic simulation capabilities through scripting.

It is now well understood that much of classical statistics is inappropriate for exploring, describing, and testing hypotheses on geographic data (Bailey and Gatrell 1995, O'Sullivan and Unwin 2003). There is a real need for GIS to support advanced spatial analysis and statistical functions, directly or indirectly, through an interface to external systems. At the most basic level, the requirement is for descriptive and exploratory spatial data analysis tools of the sort described by Anselin in chapter 5. The need also extends to improved geostatistical estimation procedures as discussed by Krivoruchko and Gotway

Crawford in chapter 4 as well as confirmatory spatial statistical procedures. Significant progress has been made on adding spatial interaction, location-allocation and operational research optimization techniques to GIS software (e.g. ArcGIS 9.1), but much more remains to be done before commercial GIS can be effective in these domains.

CONCLUDING REMARKS

Much has been written about linking GIS with spatial analysis and modeling systems. In fact, we think rather too much has been written and not enough has been done. With today's software architectures, it is relatively simple to build spatial analysis and modeling into a commercial GIS (and vice versa), and there are several examples of success discussed in this book. Similarly, it is a comparatively straightforward software engineering task to link today's open GIS and spatial analysis and modeling systems together. Certainly it is no more challenging than building a model using one of the commercial or public domain toolkits that we have spoken about earlier.

Why then has spatial analysis and modeling not been more widely deployed in a GIS context? Several factors account for the current situation. Only relatively recently have GIS platforms been open and easily extensible. The GIS and modeling systems that are in the marketplace today are quite complex and take weeks, if not months, to master, and many use advanced mathematical constructs. Linking them together will require at least basic skills in a third generation scripting language. Although spatial analysis and modeling are undoubtedly very powerful and essential for the investigation of many of the most pressing geographic problems that we face, there are many areas and applications in which they are not required (creating asset inventories, mapping, monitoring change, etc.). If we were to take a purely market-driven perspective, we could say that when the market is big enough, then spatial analysis and modeling capabilities will show up in commercial GIS products.

In the final analysis, what exactly does this new emphasis in GIS achieve? From this perspective, the methods discussed in this book fall into several distinct categories. Some are concerned with calculating indicators of vulnerability or sustainability or other useful properties that can be used as a basis for planning and for improved decision making. Others are concerned with finding patterns and anomalies in geographic data that may in turn lead to new hypotheses or new discoveries about the processes that operate on the landscape. Others again are concerned with prediction, taking knowledge about processes and forecasting future states of geographic systems. Some of these objectives fall under the heading of science—they seek to advance our understanding of the world around us, through means that are objective, widely understood, and replicable. Others fall under the heading of problem solving—they seek better ways to plan or manage aspects of the geographic world. Such efforts have often been termed *applied* to distinguish them from the pure or curiosity-driven objectives of science, and the distinction between science and engineering is often drawn along similar lines.

In the world of GIS, however, these distinctions are less and less important. A model that is used to manage and forecast must still be based on processes that have been discovered through science, and the researcher who makes significant new scientific discoveries may be the same person who tomorrow applies those to a problem in management, using GIS. In this sense, GIS is an invaluable tool because of its ability to bridge science and problem solving. Science is about discovering general principles in the complex, messy world of geographic reality—of abstracting knowledge from space and time—while management and problem solving are about applying those general principles in specific space–time contexts. GIS serves both purposes: its database contains the details of real geographic phenomena, while its programs, data models, and procedures represent general scientific knowledge. Laudan (1996), a philosopher of science, and Hills (1999), speaking about the future of universities in Britain, have argued that there is no longer an effective distinction between science and problem solving. We tend to agree and argue that GIS provides the tools to build an effective and practical bridge between the two.

REFERENCES

Arctur, D., and M. Zeiler. 2004. *Designing geodatabases: Case studies in GIS data modeling.* Redlands, Calif: ESRI Press.

Bailey, T. C., and A. C. Gatrell. 1995. *Interactive spatial data analysis.* Harlow: Longman Scientific and Technical.

Barros, J. Forthcoming. Urban dynamics in Latin American cities: An agent-based simulation approach. *Environment and Planning B.*

Brown, D., R. Riolo, D. Robinson, W. Rand, M. North, and K. Johnston. 2004. Toward integration of spatial data models and agent-based process models. Paper presented at GIScience 2004: Third International Conference on Geographic Information Science, University of Maryland.

Dibble, C., and P. G. Feldman. 2004. The GeoGraph 3D computational laboratory: Network and terrain landscapes for RePast. *Journal of Artificial Societies and Social Simulation* 7 (1). jasss.soc.surrey.ac.uk/7/1/7.html.

Goodchild, M. F., and S. Gopal. 1989. *Accuracy of spatial databases.* Basingstoke, UK: Taylor & Francis.

Heuvelink, G. B. M. 1998. *Error propagation in environmental modelling with GIS.* New York: Taylor & Francis.

Hills, G. 1999. The University of the future. In *Foresight: Universities in the future London,* ed. M. Thornes, 213–32. Department of Trade and Industry.

Laudan, L. 1996. *Beyond positivism and relativism: Theory, method, and evidence.* Boulder, Colo.: Westview Press.

Longley, P. A., M. F. Goodchild, D. J. Maguire, and D. W. Rhind. 2005. *Geographic information systems and science.* Hoboken, N.J.: John Wiley and Sons.

O'Sullivan, D., and D. J. Unwin. 2003. *Geographic information analysis.* Hoboken, N.J.: John Wiley and Sons.

Zhang. J. X., and M. F. Goodchild. 2002. *Uncertainty in geographical information.* New York: Taylor & Francis.

Acronyms

AAD	average absolute difference
ABM	agent-based models (or modeling)
AI	artificial intelligence
API	application programming interface
BHPS	British Household Panel Survey
BMP	Best Management Practices
BPN	back propagation neural network
CA	cellular automata
CAD	computer aided design
CASA	Center for Advanced Spatial Analysis
CATS	Consequences Assessment Tool Set
CBR	case-based reasoning
CBS	case-based system
cdv	cartographic data visualizer
CG	Code Generator
COM	Component Object Model
COSP	change of support problem
COTS	commercial-off-the-shelf
CRAN	Comprehensive R Archive Network
CRWR	Center for Research in Water Resources
CS	cell space
CSISS	Center for Spatially Integrated Social Science
DBMS	Database Management System
DEM	digital elevation model
DEVS	Discrete Event System Specification
DRASTIC	Depth to water table, Recharge, Aquifer media, Soil media, Topography (slope), Impact of Vadose Zone media, and hydraulic Conductivity

DSS	decision support systems; also data storage system
DUEM	Dynamic Urban Evolutionary Model
EAI	enterprise application integration
ELM	Everglades Landscape Model
EPA	Environmental Protection Agency
ES	expert systems
ESDA	exploratory spatial data analysis
GA	genetic algorithms
GAS	geographic automata system
GIS	geographic information system(s)
GML	Geography Markup Language
GUI	graphical user interface
HEC	Hydrologic Engineering Center
HMM	Hidden Markov Model
HMS	hydrologic modeling system
IBMM	individual-based movement models
Inf	actual infiltration
InfCum	cumulative infiltration
ISTEA	Intermodal Surface Transportation Efficiency Act
ITU	integrated terrain unit
IWST	Integrative Water Quality Simulation Toolset
KBS	knowledge-based systems
KISA	knowledge-informed simulated annealing
Ldd	local drain direction
LEAM	Land use Evolution (or Evaluation) and impact Assessment Model
LISA	local indicators of spatial association
LUC	land-use change
LUCC	land-use and land-cover change
MAUP	Modifiable Areal Unit Problem
MCE	multicriteria evaluation
MCMC	Markov Chain Monte Carlo
MIS	management information systems
ML	maximum likelihood

MPI	message passing interface
MPRG	multipatch parameterized region growing (algorithm)
MSF	module specification formalism
NIH	National Institutes of Health
NIJ	National Institute of Justice
NIMS	National Information and Modeling System
NSF	National Science Foundation
OBEUS	object-based environment for urban systems
OFV	objective function values
OLS	ordinary least squares
OO	object oriented
OZP	outline zoning plans
PDEs	partial differential equations
PDM	Planning Data Model
PGL	PointGrid Library
PLM	Patuxent Landscape Model
PO	Point Objects
PSS	planning support systems; also Pierce skill score
RePast	Recursive Porous Agent Simulation Toolkit
RAS	river analysis system
RBSIM	Recreation Behavior Simulator
RIS	recursive importance sampler
ROC	relative operating characteristic
SA	simulated annealing
SARA	San Antonio River Authority
SDSS	spatial decision support systems
SIM	spatial interaction model
SIR	susceptible, infective, recoverable
SME	Spatial Modeling Environment
SMML	Simulation Module Markup Language
Spatial SUR	spatially seemingly unrelated regressions
SPOP	spatial pattern optimization problem
STARS	space–time analysis of regional systems
SWARM	Secure Wide-Area Response Management

TEA-21	Transportation Equity Act for the 21st Century
TIN	Triangular Irregular Network
TS	Tabu search
TSUNAMI	Tactical Sensor and Ubiquitous Network Agent-Modeling Initiative
UGB	Urban Growth Boundary
UML	Universal Modeling Language; also Unified Modeling Language
USACE	U.S. Army Corps of Engineers
USLE	Universal Soil Loss Equation
WASMOD	Water And Snow balance Modeling system
WIMP	Windows, Icon, Mouse, Pointer
WIPP	Waste Isolation Pilot Plant
WPI	weighted performance index
WWW	World Wide Web

Index

Books from ESRI Press

Advanced Spatial Analysis: The CASA Book of GIS *1-58948-073-2*
ArcGIS and the Digital City: A Hands-on Approach for Local Government *1-58948-074-0*
ArcView GIS Means Business *1-879102-51-X*
A System for Survival: GIS and Sustainable Development *1-58948-052-X*
Beyond Maps: GIS and Decision Making in Local Government *1-879102-79-X*
Cartographica Extraordinaire: The Historical Map Transformed *1-58948-044-9*
Cartographies of Disease: Maps, Mapping, and Medicine *1-58948-120-8*
Children Map the World: Selections from the Barbara Petchenik Children's World Map Competition *1-58948-125-9*
Community Geography: GIS in Action *1-58948-023-6*
Community Geography: GIS in Action Teacher's Guide *1-58948-051-1*
Confronting Catastrophe: A GIS Handbook *1-58948-040-6*
Connecting Our World: GIS Web Services *1-58948-075-9*
Conservation Geography: Case Studies in GIS, Computer Mapping, and Activism *1-58948-024-4*
Designing Better Maps: A Guide for GIS Users *1-58948-089-9*
Designing Geodatabases: Case Studies in GIS Data Modeling *1-58948-021-X*
Disaster Response: GIS for Public Safety *1-879102-88-9*
Enterprise GIS for Energy Companies *1-879102-48-X*
Extending ArcView GIS (version 3.x edition) *1-879102-05-6*
Fun with GPS *1-58948-087-2*
Getting to Know ArcGIS Desktop, Second Edition Updated for ArcGIS 9 *1-58948-083-X*
Getting to Know ArcObjects: Programming ArcGIS with VBA *1-58948-018-X*
Getting to Know ArcView GIS (version 3.x edition) *1-879102-46-3*
GIS and Land Records: The ArcGIS Parcel Data Model *1-58948-077-5*
GIS for Everyone, Third Edition *1-58948-056-2*
GIS for Health Organizations *1-879102-65-X*
GIS for Landscape Architects *1-879102-64-1*
GIS for the Urban Environment *1-58948-082-1*
GIS for Water Management in Europe *1-58948-076-7*
GIS in Public Policy: Using Geographic Information for More Effective Government *1-879102-66-8*
GIS in Schools *1-879102-85-4*
GIS in Telecommunications *1-879102-86-2*
GIS Means Business, Volume II *1-58948-033-3*
GIS Tutorial: Workbook for ArcView 9 *1-58948-127-5*
GIS, Spatial Analysis, and Modeling *1-58948-130-5*
GIS Worlds: Creating Spatial Data Infrastructures *1-58948-122-4*
Hydrologic and Hydraulic Modeling Support with Geographic Information Systems *1-879102-80-3*
Integrating GIS and the Global Positioning System *1-879102-81-1*
Making Community Connections: The Orton Family Foundation Community Mapping Program *1-58948-071-6*
Managing Natural Resources with GIS *1-879102-53-6*
Mapping Census 2000: The Geography of U.S. Diversity *1-58948-014-7*
Mapping Our World: GIS Lessons for Educators, ArcView GIS 3.x Edition *1-58948-022-8*
Mapping Our World: GIS Lessons for Educators, ArcGIS Desktop Edition *1-58948-121-6*
Mapping the Future of America's National Parks: Stewardship through Geographic Information Systems *1-58948-080-5*
Mapping the News: Case Studies in GIS and Journalism *1-58948-072-4*
Marine Geography: GIS for the Oceans and Seas *1-58948-045-7*
Measuring Up: The Business Case for GIS *1-58948-088-0*
Modeling Our World: The ESRI Guide to Geodatabase Design *1-879102-62-5*
Past Time, Past Place: GIS for History *1-58948-032-5*

Continued on next page

When ordering, please mention book title and ISBN (number that follows each title)

Books from ESRI Press (continued)

Planning Support Systems: Integrating Geographic Information Systems, Models, and Visualization Tools *1-58948-011-2*
Remote Sensing for GIS Managers *1-58948-081-3*
Salton Sea Atlas *1-58948-043-0*
Spatial Portals: Gateways to Geographic Information *1-58948-131-3*
The ESRI Guide to GIS Analysis, Volume 1: Geographic Patterns and Relationships *1-879102-06-4*
The ESRI Guide to GIS Analysis, Volume 2: Spatial Measurements and Statistics *1-58948-116-X*
Think Globally, Act Regionally: GIS and Data Visualization for Social Science and Public Policy Research *1-58948-124-0*
Thinking About GIS: Geographic Information System Planning for Managers (paperback edition) *1-58948-119-4*
Transportation GIS *1-879102-47-1*
Undersea with GIS *1-58948-016-3*
Unlocking the Census with GIS *1-58948-113-5*
Zeroing In: Geographic Information Systems at Work in the Community *1-879102-50-1*

Forthcoming titles from ESRI Press

Arc Hydro: GIS for Water Resources, Second Edition *1-58948-126-7*
A to Z GIS: An Illustrated Dictionary of Geographic Information Systems *1-58948-140-2*
Charting the Unknown: How Computer Mapping at Harvard Became GIS *1-58948-118-6*
Finding Your Customers: GIS for Retail Management *1-58948-123-2*
GIS for Environmental Management *1-58948-142-9*
GIS for the Urban Environment *1-58948-082-1*
GIS Methods for Urban Analysis *1-58948-143-7*
The GIS Guide for Local Government Officials *1-58948-141-0*

Ask for ESRI Press titles at your local bookstore or order by calling 1-800-447-9778. You can also shop online at www.esri.com/esripress. Outside the United States, contact your local ESRI distributor.

ESRI Press titles are distributed to the trade by the following:

In North America, South America, Asia, and Australia:
Independent Publishers Group (IPG)
Telephone (United States): 1-800-888-4741 • Telephone (international): 312-337-0747
E-mail: frontdesk@ipgbook.com

In the United Kingdom, Europe, and the Middle East:
Transatlantic Publishers Group Ltd.
Telephone: 44 20 8849 8013 • Fax: 44 20 8849 5556 • E-mail: transatlantic.publishers@regusnet.com

ESRI Press • 380 New York Street • Redlands, California 92373-8100 • www.esri.com/esripress